Toward a
New Public Administration

The Minnowbrook Perspective

Chandler Publications in
POLITICAL SCIENCE
VICTOR JONES, *Editor*

Toward a New
Public Administration

The Minnowbrook Perspective

Edited by

Frank Marini

The Maxwell School of Citizenship and Public Affairs
Syracuse University

CHANDLER PUBLISHING COMPANY

To Dwight Waldo
Teacher, Colleague, Friend

Contents

Foreword

All but the last three essays in this volume were presented to the participants of a conference of "young Public Administrationists" held in September 1968 at the Minnowbrook conference site of Syracuse University. While I was not a participant in the conference, I was involved as sponsor and was present as observer part of the time. Accordingly I have been invited to speak to the origins and purposes of the conference and, if I wish, to offer some observations on the conference and its results.

My interest in sponsoring the conference was, to be sure, a reflection of a career-long interest in the study and practice of Public Administration,* but the grave happenings and urgent problems of the times were my reasons for becoming involved, and some particular circumstances and events were the "causes."

With regard to the former only two things need be said. One is that I had reached the conclusion that neither the study nor the practice of Public Administration was responding in appropriate measure to mounting turbulence and critical problems. My thoughts on this problem had been expressed in a piece titled "Public Administration in a Time of Revolutions,"[1] which was included among the background materials sent to the conferees by the organizing committee. The other matter concerned the enduring but nowadays accentuated problem of the relationship of youth and age. While all professions and disciplines worry about whether they are getting an adequate portion of the ablest new talent, I thought there was special reason to be concerned about recruitment into Public Adminis-

*Throughout this book a distinction is made between "public administration" and "Public Administration." The former refers to the activities having to do with the administration of public organizations and public policies. The latter is used to denote the study of behavior in public organizations, that is, the field as academic subject matter. The capitalized form is also used when reference is made simultaneously to the study and practice of Public Administration.—Ed.

[1]*Public Administration Review* (July/Aug., 1968), pp. 362–368.

tration. What was the import for us of the "generation gap" and the "revolt of youth"? To what extent were the "generations" in Public Administration in communication with each other? What could be done to encourage new thinking, enlist new energies, and attract more and better talent to the task of dealing with public problems?

Given this mood of concern and questioning, two events proved critical in moving me toward such remedial action as might be within my own control. The first was the Conference on the Theory and Practice of Public Administration, sponsored by the American Academy of Political and Social Science and held in December of 1967. I was invited to the conference and judged it successful in achieving its objective of a high-level, critical assessment of the status and problems of Public Administration.[2] But I found myself troubled by the fact that probably not one of the conferees was under thirty-five and most were in their fifties and sixties. Where was the *future* of Public Administration? The second event was a conversation I had some two months later with a young teacher of Public Administration. The subject of the conversation was the special issue of *Public Administration Review*, published in November 1967, featuring Higher Education for the Public Service. I thought—and still think—the special report and commentaries in this issue of high quality. But not my young friend: The issue (for which as Editor-in-Chief I had a responsibility) was "shameful." I was startled: Why? Because it presented old men talking to old men about irrelevancies, old men out of touch with the real problems of a chaotic and dangerous world and the youth who would have to deal with them.

Within a few days of this encounter there was born the idea of a "youth" conference, a conference organized and attended by younger persons in Public Administration to discuss whatever seemed important *to them*. Fortunately, the very generous funding of my Chair enabled me to give substance to the idea.

Three of my junior colleagues at the Maxwell School— H. George Frederickson, W. Henry Lambright, and Frank Marini—were named as a committee to arrange a conference.

[2]The product of the conference was published as *Theory and Practice of Public Administration*, Monograph No. 8 of the American Academy of Political Science, Philadelphia (October, 1968).

My specific requests to the committee concerned only such matters as geographical inclusiveness, a reasonable balance between academics and practitioners, and a systematic search for younger persons of achievement and promise.[3] Agenda, topics, emphases, format—these, I specified, were the committee's business; at least they were not *mine*.

So much for the genesis of the conference from my point of view. Frank Marini, as informal chairman of the organizing committee and editor of this volume, will further address himself to the subject, as well as comment on the procedures and dynamics of the conference itself. But I shall proceed to some reflections on the enterprise as a whole and some comments on its product.

1. The extent to which the conference reflected and helped to catalyze a "new" Public Administration is a complicated question. Present opinions may legitimately differ, and only time will give an unequivocal answer. Though only a part-time observer, as a seasoned attender of conferences I can testify that this conference was remarkable in the intensity of personal interaction, in its feeling of importance for the subject, and in its sense of urgency. Despite the heterogeneity of the group, despite doubters and dissenters, something emerged as a predominate cluster of sentiments and beliefs.[4] In their emphases, and in the ensemble,

[3] Some further words on the composition of the conference are in order. The committee wrote letters to more than two score "leading figures" in Public Administration, both academics and practitioners, asking them to designate young men of outstanding ability. Responses to these letters yielded about one hundred and fifty names. The recruiting of responses was followed by winnowing and balancing, reducing the list to about fifty names regarded as "first choices." Some invitees were uninterested; some were interested but for one reason or another unable to accept; some accepted but later found themselves unable to attend. Thirty-four conferees—practitioners, teachers, and graduate students—eventually presented themselves.

Two points deserve emphasis: (1) While a serious effort was made to assemble "promising" young Public Administrationists, neither I nor the organizing committee would assert that the conferees were "the elite" of the most promising of their generation. Of this we will know more in a decade or so. (2) No attempt was made to assemble a group which had in common any particular skill, opinion, or inclination. On the contrary, there was some effort to bring together a group with differing skills, opinions, and inclinations.

[4] Divergence in the conference and diversity in the product obviously create problems of accuracy and fairness for anyone attempting, as I am now, to comment briefly. I will speak for the most part to what seem to me main emphases, to what came to be called by many of the conferees "the Minnowbrook perspective." I regret and offer apologies for any resulting distortion or inequity.

the essays in this volume unquestionably represent something new in Public Administration.

2. While the essays represent something new in Public Administration they also, in one way or another, present much from the past. Listening to the conference discussion or reading the essays I often thought (for example): "This is much like Mary Parker Follett's idea of 'power with, not power over,'" or "Essentially this is an updated version of Taylor's 'functional foremanship.'" In general, I should say, the critique of the "orthodox" Public Administration made by my generation was accepted by the conferees as valid. There is no return to the past in that sense. Rather, there is a tacit or overt rejection (or at least qualification) of some recent "new directions" and a significant probing of questions posed by my generation's critique of the old Public Administration—but on the whole not seriously addressed by us.

3. What is the essence of the "new"? At the close of the conference I stated my impression that what seemed to characterize the event was "some sort of movement in the direction of normative theory, philosophy, social concern, activism." This impression still stands. But much the same thing can be put in other words, and certainly these words do not express *all*. Negatively, there was a turning away from positivism and scientism (but not from *science*, most of the conferees would argue). With regard to techniques: ambivalence. There was a disinterest in if not a turning away from certain techniques; there was a notable lack of interest in, say, planning, budgeting, and operations research. On the other hand, techniques associated with personal growth, interpersonal relations, and group dynamics were close to the center of interest. Positively, there was an interest in philosophy (explicitly in existentialism and phenomenology), a concern for finding and realizing the proper "values," even overt interest in personal-organizational "morality." Certain key words and expressions, such as "relevance," "social equity," "adaptation," and "client-focus," suggest the emotional tone and indicate specific interests. (Efficiency and economy? If these were mentioned it was only in passing.)

4. The "new" Public Administration, of course, exists in a particular historical context, to which it is a response and which it more or less reflects. This is not the place to try to recount the

events and characterize the movements of recent years; these must be assumed as given, known. Suffice it then to say that the Minnowbrook proceedings and this book are related to political currents engendered by the war in Vietnam, to the movement toward equal treatment of minorities, to the "war against poverty." They reflect, albeit at some remove, movements of protest and concern on the campus. They reflect the widespread worry about the "urban problem," growing alarm over a runaway technology, and increasing preoccupation with problems of violence. And, I daresay, at some level they reflect what has come to be called neoisolationism (in their turning inward to *our* problems) and even—somewhat paradoxically—the wave of sentiment against "government solutions," "centralized government" and "bureaucracy" (in the concern for personal wholeness, organizational fluidity, adaptability, and "love").

5. The conference and its product strikingly demonstrate the close relationship of the enterprises of Public Administration and political theory, and the deep involvement and great importance of Public Administration in the making of policy. This relationship was implied in my statement above that there is now serious attention given to problems posed by the critique of the old Public Administration by my generation. If a rigid division between politics and administration will not hold, what then follows? If administrators make policy, what does this imply or dictate? What is the import of democracy, freedom, equality—our national "holy words"—in and for administration in the name of the public?

While I must commend the conferees on their energy, boldness, ingenuity, and obvious good will in addressing problems too long neglected, I must also say that in my opinion the results are more an indication to me of the complexity and intractability of the problems than acceptable and workable solutions.[5] This conclusion, however, may reflect a scarcity of generosity, flexibility, and insight on my part. Each must assess for himself, and the proof of the pudding will be in the eating. In any event we should be grateful for fresh and vigorous thinking about items on a neglected agendum.

[5]It would have to be conceded, at least, that there are serious divergences between some of the proposals and "solutions" and the main bent of our constitution-institutional evolution.

6. At the risk of distortion and unfairness, but to make a point: what is proposed by the "new" Public Administration is not so much programmatic as procedural.[6] That is, if one takes the range of conventionally defined problems, from destruction of the biosphere to juvenile delinquency, from nuclear holocaust to control of drug abuse, from world overpopulation to provision of housing, very little is proposed or suggested in the way of solution. There is a great deal of concern with "problem solving," but mostly on a small scale, so to speak. There is much concern for individual morality, authenticity, effectiveness—almost for individual "salvation."

The conferees, to be sure, could present reasonable responses to this generalization. They might argue that "tactics" or even "strategies" are better designations than "procedures." They might argue that collectively a set of procedures (tactics, technologies, or whatever) appropriate to Public Administration constitute *a program for Public Administration* and that a reconstructed program for Public Administration is necessary before it can fulfill its role in the creation and implementation of "program" in the substantive sense. In any event, they might protest, the critical center of the present turbulence is in the individual and his immediate social-organizational relationships, and unless we can deal promptly and effectively with personal and organizational stress, confrontation, and potential violence, it is futile to talk of "programs."

A discussion of my impressions and reservations could be indefinitely expanded. Is history well served when indeed it is recognized? In the concern for the individual bureaucrat, for disadvantaged minorities, for seeking solutions at the individual and small-group level, is the "power to govern" neglected and imperiled? (Would only an oldster ask such questions?) For all the concern, are *representation* and *responsibility* given more than a glancing blow? How are some of the proposed "reforms" to be reconciled with received political-constitutional arrangements? But perhaps enough has been said to sensitize the reader to some of the main issues.

[6]To the extent this interpretation is true, there may be more essential continuity with "old" Public Administration than presumed.

I close on the affirmative: What Minnowbrook helped to inaugurate was a greatly needed and highly significant discussion. Here was fresh and original thinking on the role of Public Administration in the "time of revolutions" in which we find ourselves. I feel privileged to have been auxiliary and spectator, and I hope to be participant as well as the discussion continues.

DWIGHT WALDO
Albert Schweitzer Professor in the Humanities
Syracuse University
January 1970

Acknowledgments

It is a great pleasure to thank those who have helped in the production of this volume. Dwight Waldo, Albert Schweitzer Professor in the Humanities at Syracuse University, initiated the idea of a conference of young people in Public Administration, funded the conference, and has provided friendly advice at every stage of the arranging of the conference and the production of this book. The authors of the essays herein have been patient and cooperative beyond the call of their original agreements. Other conference participants have improved the volume by offering criticism and advice to the authors and editor. Victor Jones offered friendly encouragement when it was most important. Mrs. Mary Braundel and Mrs. Alondra Mariani have retyped the entire manuscript several times and have cheerfully performed the many, many other chores connected with manuscript production. Sincere thanks are here extended to all of these friends, without whom this volume would not have been possible; and the deepest thanks of all are here delivered to my wife, Madeline, without whom nothing is possible.

Notes on the Contributors

Robert P. Biller is Assistant Professor in the School of Public Affairs, University of California at Berkeley. Professor Biller received his Ph.D. from the University of Southern California. He is the author of *Science, Technology and Political Development*. His current research interests include work on science and technology transfer strategies as related to political-development strategies, city services and city politics as developmental problems, and urban redesign as related to the perspectives of organizational research.

Matthew A. Crenson is Assistant Professor of Political Science at Johns Hopkins University. Professor Crenson received his Ph.D. from the University of Chicago. He was formerly Assistant Professor of Political Science at the Massachusetts Institute of Technology. His interests include metropolitan and urban government and politics, administration, and political theory.

George Frederickson is Assistant Professor of Political Science and Associate Director of the Metropolitan Studies Program at the Maxwell School, Syracuse University. He is on the Board of Editors of the *Public Administration Review*, and his writings have appeared in *Administrative Science Quarterly, International Review of Administrative Sciences, Public Administration Review*, and *Urban Affairs Quarterly*. He holds a Ph.D. in Public Administration from the University of Southern California.

Edward Friedland is Assistant Professor of Political Science, State University of New York, Stony Brook, and consultant at the United States Atomic Energy Commission. Professor Friedland received his Ph.D. from the University of California at Los Angeles. He is the author of *The Study of Decisions* and several publications on the subject of systems analysis. Previously he served as systems analyst with a number of nonprofit defense advisory corporations.

Michael M. Harmon is Assistant Professor of Public Administration at George Washington University. He holds a Ph.D. from the University of Southern California. Previously he was Assistant Professor at the Federal Executive Institute and an instructor at the School of Public Administration at the University of Southern California. He is the author of "Administrative Policy Formulation and the Public Interest," *Public Administration Review* (September/October, 1969). His interests include organizational development, executive training and development, sensitivity training, and administrative style in policy formulation.

Keith M. Henderson is Professor and Chairman, Department of Political Science, State University College at Buffalo. Professor Henderson received his D.P.A. from the University of Southern California. He has been employed as a budget analyst, personnel technician, and field deputy to a city councilman. He is the author of *Emerging Synthesis in American Public Administration* and articles in *American Behavioral Scientist, Public Administration Review, International Review of Administrative Sciences, Journal of Comparative Administration*, and other journals.

S. Kenneth Howard is Associate Professor of Political Science, Institute of Government, University of North Carolina at Chapel Hill. Professor Howard received his Ph.D. from Cornell. He has been employed as a government consultant and has also taught at Rutgers and the University of New Hampshire. He is co-author of *State Capital Budgeting, Revenue Estimating by Cities*, and *Perspectives on Local Finance in North Carolina*. His articles have appeared in *Midwest Review of Public Administration, Physical Therapy, Modern Hospital*, and *Popular Government*.

Satrio B. Joedono is Professor of Economics at Fakultas Ekonomi Universitas Indonesia. Professor Joedono received his Ph.D. from the State University of New York at Albany. He is interested in development administration and the philosophy of the social sciences.

Kenneth Jowitt is Assistant Professor of Political Science at the University of California at Berkeley, where he also received his Ph.D. He is interested in comparative Public Administration and particularly in Public Administration in Eastern Europe.

Larry Kirkhart is Assistant Professor of Political Science, The Maxwell School, Syracuse University. Professor Kirkhart received his Ph.D. in Public Administration from the University of Southern California. He was formerly Assistant Professor at the Federal Executive Institute and has taught in the School of Public Administration at the University of Southern California. His current research interests include organizational change and development, the role of ambiguity and stress in temporary groups and in individual development, and leadership behavior.

Philip S. Kronenberg is Assistant Professor of Political Science and Director of the Institute of Public Administration, Indiana University. Professor Kronenberg received his Ph.D. from the University of Pittsburgh. He is the author of "Cooptation by Consultation in Saigon," in Seipp, *et al.*, *Coordination, Planning, and Society*, and co-author of "Toward Theory-Building in Comparative Public Administration: A Functional Approach."

W. Henry Lambright is Assistant Professor of Political Science at The Maxwell School, Syracuse University. Professor Lambright received his Ph.D. from Columbia University. He is the author of *Shooting Down the Nuclear Plane* and *Launching NASA's Sustaining University Program*. His fields of interest include science and public policy.

Todd R. La Porte is Associate Professor of Political Science at the University of California, Berkeley. He has taught in the School of Public Administration, University of Southern California, and at Stanford University. His work has been published in *Administrative Science Quarterly*, *Public Administration Review*, *American Behavioral Scientist*, and *Human Organizations*. Presently he is working on problems arising from intensive social complexity in organizations, the relationship between technology and political forms, and professionals in complex organizations, especially research and development laboratories. He holds a Ph.D. from Stanford University.

Francis P. McGee is Assistant Professor of Political Science and Director of the Institute of Urban and Regional Studies at Ball State University. He is working on his D.P.A. at The Maxwell School, Syracuse University. He was formerly Administrative

Assistant to the City Engineer of Lowell, Massachusetts. Professor McGee is the author of "The New Public Administration: A Commentary" in the *Maxwell Review*, Syracuse University. His research interests include the politics and economics of transportation systems in an urban environment, dimensions of group research behavior in university environments, and the role of Public Administration in higher education.

Frank Marini is Associate Dean of the Maxwell School, Syracuse University. He received his Ph.D. from the University of California at Berkeley. He is currently the managing editor of *Public Administration Review*. His articles have appeared in *Western Political Quarterly* and *Midwest Journal of Political Science*. He is the author of the forthcoming *Images of Classical Democratic Theory*.

Herman Mertins, Jr., is Associate Professor of Political Science and Director of the Public Administration Program, West Virginia University. Professor Mertins received his D.P.A. from The Maxwell School, Syracuse University. He was previously Assistant to the Director of Planning and Development of the Port of New York Authority. He is the coeditor of and a contributor of the 1971 Special Issue of *Public Administration Review*.

David F. Parker, coordinator for the Buffalo-Amherst Corridor project, New York State Office of Planning Coordination, was formerly research consultant with the New York State Division of the Budget. Before joining the Division of the Budget in 1966, he was employed as a state transportation planner in New York, and as a county planner in Michigan. He is the author of several articles and papers on urban planning-programming-budgeting. Mr. Parker is presently a doctoral candidate in Public Administration at the State University of New York at Albany.

John Paynter received his Ph.D. in Political Science from the University of Chicago. He was previously Assistant Professor of Social Science at Lemoyne College, Memphis, Tennessee. Currently Professor Paynter teaches at James Madison College, Michigan State University.

Ira Sharkansky is Associate Professor of Political Science at the University of Wisconsin (Madison). Professor Sharkansky received his Ph.D. from the University of Wisconsin. He has taught at Ball State University, Florida State University, and the University of Georgia. Among his publications are *Spending in the American States, The Politics of Taxing and Spending, Regionalism in American Politics, Public Administration: Policy-Making in Government Agencies, The Routines of Politics*, and he has edited books of readings and published numerous articles in the fields of comparative state politics, Public Administration, public financial administration, public-policy analysis.

Dwight Waldo is Professor of Political Science and Public Administration, and Albert Schweitzer Professor in the Humanities at Syracuse University. He was formerly Professor of Political Science and Director of the Institute of Governmental Studies, University of California, Berkeley. His works include *The Administrative State, Perspectives on Administration,* and *The Study of Public Administration.* Since 1966 he has been Editor in Chief of *Public Administration Review.* He holds a Ph.D. from Yale University.

Orion F. White, Jr., is Associate Professor of Political Science at The Maxwell School, Syracuse University. Professor White received his Ph.D. from Indiana University. He is co-author of *Politics in the Post-Welfare State: A Comparison of the United States and Sweden, Post Apollo Planning in the National Aeronautics and Space Administration,* and *Rush County Indiana: Voting in General Elections 1890–1965.* His articles have appeared in the *Public Administration Review, Public Affairs Comment,* and the *Southwestern Social Science Quarterly.*

Bob Zimring is an institutional research analyst at the University of Pennsylvania and coadjutant instructor at Rutgers State University. He received his M.S. from the University of Wisconsin. He was formerly an Assistant Professor at Pennsylvania State University.

Toward a
New Public Administration

The Minnowbrook Perspective

1

Introduction: A New Public Administration?

Frank Marini

The question mark in the title of this chapter is mine. The faith that there *is* a new Public Administration—as a reading of this volume will make clear—is held in different degrees even by those widely credited with being a part of a new Public Administration. In some circles, the Minnowbrook Conference is considered an important—perhaps formative or critical—chapter in the genesis of a new Public Administration. For the time being, I prefer to put "newness" forth as a question rather than an assertion or a celebration.

If the Minnowbrook Conference were a glimpse of a wave cresting, and if the output of the conference were completely reflected in the papers presented at Minnowbrook, the reader could at this point simply be told that the answer to the question which the title raises is to be found in Chapters 2 through 10 of this volume. I believe that the conference was more of the order of beginning ripples than cresting waves, and that it meant more to the participants than simply the formal papers. Because of these two beliefs, I have added to the original papers and commentary some interpretive material: Dwight Waldo's foreword, the three concluding chapters, editorial notes at the end of some chapters, and this Introduction.

The function of the present chapter is to convey some of the content and procedures of the Minnowbrook meetings not reflected in the conference papers. This information is broken down under four rubrics: the dialectical agenda, the small-group sessions, the wider context, and the Minnowbrook papers.

The Dialectical Agenda

When the planning committee of the conference had finished its negotiations and renegotiations regarding authors, topics, and commentators, nine panels had been designed. For each panel, a paper and commentary had been commissioned.

Plans were to circulate copies of the principal papers to each participant prior to the conference. Schedules being what they are, the papers were not circulated in many cases as far in advance as had been planned. In addition to the papers written by participants, any participant who had ideas which he wanted to write out for circulation to all others was encouraged to do so. No participants accepted this offer. Material in addition to the major papers was also circulated to participants in advance. Our experience had indicated that the so-called "Honey Report" was a topic of some controversy and conversation in Public Administration circles, and so a copy of the Report was sent to each participant. Also, in the hope that it would stimulate reactions or comments, a copy of Dwight Waldo's short paper, "Public Administration in a Time of Turbulence" was circulated to all participants. And an exchange of letters between Professors John C. Honey and Peter Savage (the latter was a participant in the conference) about the implications of the Honey Report and the present state and necessary future of Public Administration was also circulated to each participant.[1] These materials were sent—and much time was left "open" on the conference agenda—in the hope that discussions and interactions would take place beyond the formal words of the panel presentations.

Minnowbrook conferees first met as a group on the Syracuse University campus. The list of participants with their institutional affiliation at the time of the conference follows:

Robert P. Biller, University of California (Berkeley)
Edward S. (Brack) Brown, Syracuse University
Matthew Crenson, Massachusetts Institute of Technology
George Frederickson, Syracuse University

[1] The materials here referred to have all been published in the *Public Administration Review:* The November, 1967 issue was devoted to the "Honey Report" ("A Report: Higher Education for Public Service") and various comments on it; Dwight Waldo's article and the letters between Savage and Honey appeared in the July/August, 1968 issue.

Edward Friedland, State University of New York (Stony Brook)

Louis C. Gawthrop, State University of New York (Binghamton)

Michael M. Harmon, Federal Executive Institute

Keith M. Henderson, New York University

S. Kenneth Howard, University of North Carolina

S. B. Joedono, State University of New York (Albany)

Kenneth Jowitt, University of California (Berkeley)

Larry Kirkhart, University of Southern California

Philip S. Kronenberg, Indiana University

W. Henry Lambright, Syracuse University

Wilber F. LaPage, Syracuse University

Todd R. La Porte, University of California (Berkeley)

Frank McGee, Syracuse University

Frank Marini, Syracuse University

Michael Meriwether, Public Administration Service

Herman Mertins, Syracuse University

Albert F. Moncure, Department of Social Services, City of New York

Richard S. Page, University of Washington

David F. Parker, Division of the Budget, State of New York

John Paynter, University of Chicago

Ray D. Pethtel, American Society for Public Administration

David Porter, Syracuse University

Peter Rumsey, U.S. Bureau of the Budget

Peter Savage, University of New Hampshire

Joseph W. Scott, University of Toledo

Moshe Shani, Cornell University

Ira Sharkansky, University of Wisconsin (Madison)

Orion F. White, Jr., University of Texas (Austin)

Bob Zimring, University of Pennsylvania

The conferees proceeded by chartered bus from Syracuse to the conference site in the Adirondacks. In retrospect, this choice of transportation may have been more important than it seemed. We had earlier thought that there were many advantages to retreating to the woods because this move would isolate the group and to a certain extent induce more sustained and more intense interaction than would be possible in more distracting environs. If the conference site had this effect, certainly the isolation of a four-hour trip on a bus achieved it with an even greater intensity. In a way, the conference was kicked off in the small confines of the bus and, looking back upon it, many of the features that were to become characteristics of Minnowbrook emerged on this trip. There was much talk of what should be done at Minnowbrook, what sorts of importance the gathering could take, what was important about it in itself; and much conversation and many questions were directed at the planning committee on the nature of our "real" purposes and the like, as well as some suggestions which had not occurred to us (such as, whether this was going to be a T-group exercise of some kind, and so on).

There were no formal panels or arrangements for the first evening, but talk and discussions grew in the informal discussions. Perhaps informal puts the wrong color on the first evening. A discussion involving almost all participants took place in the main lodge of the conference site. The principal theme of a wide-rambling discussion was the structuring (or, since the conference was supposedly already structured, I suppose the restructuring) of the conference, with special reference to the presentation of formal papers and the meeting as a single group for all formal meetings.

The discussion of the function and importance of the formal papers was to be a recurrent one and the dynamics of the discussion became familiar to all: Why did we have to have formal papers? If we were really the young and the new, why were we so bound by the traditional in our conference arrangements? Who chose the topics? Weren't there more important topics? Shouldn't we break down into small groups? Weren't people invited here because of what *they* might be thinking and could they really make the contributions that implied within the constraints of structured discussion around formal papers? All of these arguments and sentiments were to be heard again, but for the time being the group decided—late at night and after hours of intense discussion—to proceed according to the set agenda for the next day and reconsider such matters the next evening.

In the morning of the next day there were two consecutive meetings, the first of which considered Orion White's paper and

Matthew Crenson's comments, and the second of which considered Philip Kronenberg's paper and Bob Zimring's comments. These sessions were lively and provocative, and my personal assessment—I think fairly widely shared—was that the morning was very successful and had opened themes which were bound to relate to other papers and which bode well for the conference. In the afternoon there was a scheduled but previously unpublicized presentation. Steven Brams, a colleague from Syracuse University, presented a brief talk on the utility of mathematical modeling. To a striking extent this was a change of pace from the morning sessions and quite different from any other presentation at the conference. The purpose behind our invitation to Brams was to give the participants an opportunity to hear a strong case for one of the new trends in political science as made by an extremely competent proponent of the approach. It was our hope that, drawing upon his own experience with administrators in federal government, Professor Brams could indicate challenging opportunities and new vistas for Public Administrators via the route of mathematical modeling. For a variety of reasons the presentation did not have this effect. As Brams was well aware, his discussion did not seem to dovetail well with the interest of the participants. The extension of mathematical modeling to Public Administration never developed in the discussion as he hoped it would. The total effect was that the conference participants listened politely to a talk which did not seem to them to be clearly relevant to their interests and problems.

When we returned to our "rediscussion" of the planned agenda at the informal evening gathering, a revolt of considerable proportions against the agenda was obvious. Quite "confrontational" discussion went on for hours, and set the major themes, major roles of certain participants, much of the style of future discussions: we were all to come to feel that the discussion of this evening would recur again and again and again. In forceful statements we were reminded of relevance, social problems, personal morality, innovation, clients, the evils of hierarchy and bureaucracy, the academic-practitioner split, and the fact that we had neglected the practitioners.[2] The most persistent demand was

[2]This last item, though originally put in strong terms (one self-identified practitioner said that if we broke into groups, finding the room for the practitioner group

that we somehow do away with the panels and formal meetings
and break into small groups to probe whatever pressing problems
concerned members of that group without necessary reference to
any of the formal papers. The revolt against the conference structure, though, got its impetus from substantive complaints which
reflected aspects of the contemporary social and political scene
with which many of us were familiar. The manner and language
with which we reminded one another of these "real problems"
and the frequent insistence that Public Administrators, for all of
their highly developed skill and professionalism, were not doing
much to help the starving and the repressed of our society were
probably what caused some members of the conference to characterize it as a New Left caucus in action.

After a long evening of very active argument we finally dealt
with the agenda question. The next day, it was agreed, we could
accelerate the panels so as to "finish" all papers by the end of the
day. Our third full day could then be devoted to small-group sessions. The remainder of the papers were all discussed the next
day. This busy schedule was capped by an evening session which
attempted to arrive at a general statement of the "relevant" questions and issues to which the small-group sessions might devote
themselves.

Several agenda were proposed, but the one which Peter Savage
offered was adopted because it seemed to encompass the main
points of the other proposals and of the concerns which had
emerged from our discussions. The Savage statement went as
follows:

> The ends of the conference are appropriately ambitious: basical-
> ly we would like to identify and consider important and interesting
> problems and issues that have emerged or ought to emerge
> within the terrain of Public Administration, and to lay out prom-
> ising plans of future inquiry into these matters. It would be good if

---

to meet in would be no problem because they could meet in the phone booth), was
largely abandoned as we came to know one another's concerns better, I believe. It
became obvious after a while that even those who felt most strongly about their
own identification with one half of the practitioner-academic dichotomy could not
agree even on which other participants were in their category, let alone on much else
The questions and problems that were to separate us and lead to debate were
simply not very relevant to this dichotomy.

we could, through the demonstration of a compelling manifest expertise, assert an authority of legitimacy and thereby influence the course of future inquiry and endeavor in Public Administration. To do this, we must contrive to stir some people with statements of manifest relevance about certain aspects of the state of our art and particularly with statements about or focused upon manageable substantive topics that would lead to further questions. Here, then, is a modest beginning of a prospective list of topics about which systematic statements could usefully be made by this conference:

1. What is the proper terrain of Public Administration? We need to separate the generally common areas of interest and concern from the peripheral areas, and to reach some agreement on the common referents of the term "Public Administration."

2. What are the logics of inquiry appropriate to the terrain? Different sorts of theories tend to accompany different sorts of definitions of the terrain. Thus, answers to the first question carry with them some answers to the appropriate logics of inquiry for description and analysis within the terrain.

3. Given some measure of agreement or consensus on this, what is the social relevance of knowledge in Public Administration? The creation and application of knowledge in Public Administration is not a socially neutral act, and this fact has consequences for our logics of inquiry. I have argued elsewhere that our concerns should be with: (a) What standards of decision do we use to select which questions ought to be studied and how we study them? (b) Who defines our questions and priorities for us? (c) To what extent are we aware of the social and moral implications of knowledge in Public Administration? (d) What are the uses of Public Administration as a social and political science? (e) Does Public Administration presently yield knowledge useful to certain institutions in society (usually the dominant ones) and not to others? (f) To whose advantage does Public Administration work (to the dominant institutions of society or to those without power, like the Blacks)? and (g) What are the assumptions and consequences of teaching and research in Public Administration?

4. What is the normative and/or ethical substance of the terrain? I realize that I have already spilled over into the question of normative and ethical substance: where the conditions within our terrain raise normative and ethical issues. Generally, we have ignored the ethical and normative problems inevitably involved in our concern with the purpose of administrative action. Indeed, whether we should or should not be concerned with normative aspects is a part of this question.

It was decided that this statement would serve as the general framework for small-group sessions to which a committee of three would arbitrarily assign participants.

Small-Group Sessions

Reporting about the small-group sessions, or even attempting to supply something of their flavor, is a difficult task. No one was present at all of them, and our otherwise ubiquitous tape recorder was at none of them. Yet many participants felt they were the most important part of the conference. The small-group sessions will be characterized here by reproducing the reports of some of their spokesmen to the plenary session of the last evening. Such treatment is radically defective in some respects, of course: it incorporates almost nothing of the process and dialogue of the sessions and only skeletal information as to the substance considered. Yet aside from the fact that it is the only information available at this stage, the method has some merits: it does incorporate those aspects which the spokesmen felt characteristic and important enough to stand before the plenary session as an informal report of their sessions. Thus one group[3] reported, through its chosen spokesman, as follows:

We dealt with three major issues: questions of *value*, much in the way we have been discussing them in the general sessions up to this point; questions of *organizational arrangement*; and questions of certain kinds of *procedures*. And a fourth issue was composed of certain kinds of *educational* questions. We talked about a *lack of policy* commitment which certain people thought was now characteristic of our system, and we moved through PPB. In that discussion, *PPB* [planning-programming-budgeting system] *was emphasized as a potential instrument of subtle political revolutionary force.* We then moved into a discussion defining the *terrain* of Public Administration, and I think we identified some coordinates of what that terrain might look like. We discussed things that now seem not as good as they ought to be, and *possibilities* for improvement.

There was considerable discussion focusing on the various *devolutionary* strategies: looking at functions like police, planning, education, public health, and social welfare systems in terms of how things might be devolved. There was considerable discussion about a more *clientele-responsive organization*, with many disadvantages and advantages and a *variety of procedures* discussed. We felt that Public Administration ought to require some competence in focusing upon *interface problems* rather than just functional problems of the interservice areas. We discussed the *catalytic role* which people trained in *Public Administration* ought to be able to play in relation to *public policy* and *organizational development* issues. At one point we considered the possibility that

[3]It does not seem necessary or desirable to attempt to identify small-group composition or spokesmen. The reports have been slightly edited.

Public Administration as a field ought simply to cease seeking to train people for administrative careers. We ended up rejecting that possibility, but thought that the *educational process* ought to be much more characterized by training for catalytic organizational stability and interface support for other professional fields which often work in policy and change.

A good deal of discussion focused on *value* issues, the extent to which political science and Public Administration seemed to be moving into a vacuum area here, and many feel uncomfortable about the things that need to be done. We talked about the strategies by which organizations could move toward the kind of *confrontation* and *consociated model* which Larry Kirkhart talked about yesterday. We speculated as to the kinds of governmental functions which could more usefully be designed on a temporary rather than permanent basis.

We talked about the extent to which *Public Administration education* ought to take as part of its terrain the strategies by which public organizations would develop confrontational and development units within themselves which would have a combination of scanning and facilitation for those organizations. Those catalytic units ought themselves, probably, to be temporary, and their members would be expected to go on elsewhere. We talked about problems of Public Administration as an *academic discipline*. How could it develop the kinds of people these catalytic units would need?

We concluded that labor management issues in the public sector ought to be moved as quickly as possible to a confrontational model, in which the fullest array of issues possible—including pay and other incentive systems—ought to be put into the confrontational arena rather than circumscribed as they are now. What kinds of changes in incentive systems would be appropriately required by an organization operating in the consociated model? We then launched into a variety of things, ranging from classification and accounting and the sorts of procedures which are now designed on the assumption different from those required for client openness, to achievement of values as we saw them, or effectiveness of value accomplishment.

Another group's spokesman said:

In trying to discuss some of the distinctions and some of the concerns of several of the papers, we looked at certain points raised in the papers by White, Kirkhart, Biller, and La Porte. We discussed relationships between the papers. And that led us rather rapidly to the question of whether these points we were trying to look at have some relevance for a distinction between an old and a new Public Administration. We went from there into a discussion of how environment impinges upon Public Administration. An early distinction was that what we were labelling the old Public Administration was relatively unaffected by an external environment and that what had happened, in a way, was that an environment had developed which could no longer be ignored or which had forced itself or impinged upon current practitioners and academics in our area.

We did not pursue, in any real way, where that would lead us. Instead, we got into a discussion of the questions of how we look at the environment, how we ought to look at the environment, what it is that we need to know or must know about the environment that would help us to order our concerns. We discussed some factors which we thought were of most consequence in the environment. These were obvious things like technology, the rapidity of change, size of organizations, number of organizations, number of people in organizations, and so on. We covered these rather quickly and we got to Biller's distinction between placidity and turbulence in the environment, and we tried to take a look at this and to pursue, as we understood it, some of the implications that it might have for the context in which Public Administration is pursued. We didn't get to any solid conclusion, but we explored some of the questions that it raised. We went from there on to the question of the validity of the private-public distinction of the past, and then to the question of whether we need a new kind of distinction which would point up the organizations which shared certain characteristics.

Then we turned to a set of overlapping questions which centered on what academicians need to know or to be concerned with about the environment. And this suggested some things that might go into a new education for Public Administrators. We turned first to the concepts of the field: What sorts of concepts do we have? This assumes, I think, that we perceived some inadequacies in the old concepts when we start talking about new ones, as we did in the papers and in the questions about environment.

We took up the question of modes of inquiry, and how we ought to focus on the education of people who are concerned with Public Administration. Should we try to give them a range of modes of inquiry which they will be able to utilize in their pursuit of the field? How are they going to be able to have a cast of mind that will allow them to continually ask questions, and questions of the right kind? I think we were all agreed that there was a need for this question-asking characteristic of individuals, not only in schools of Public Administration but also in public organizations.

We got into matters such as the obligations associated with what one of us called "the rising levels of ignorance." Our situation is getting much more complex and there are so many more variables that those who have to cope with ongoing operations can't expect to be very knowledgeable about all the intricacies. We also tried to state this conversely, and tried to identify the obligations that were involved in the rapid concentration of knowledge. In other words, perhaps people who are concerned with the day-to-day operations can't grasp the field because to the extent that knowledge exists it is becoming concentrated in the hands of a relative few. This led to a whole range of questions about the implications of that kind of thing. Assuming that there is a concentration of knowledge, what sorts of obligations does that place upon the person who holds the knowledge? How can he dispense this knowledge? What sorts of risks are involved in dispensing knowledge? These are the kinds of questions which we think we ought to try to resolve. We didn't resolve them, but we moved around a little bit.

I think I can close by mentioning a couple of questions about these problems which seemed important to us: How can we take advantage of our knowledge in a credible way, in a way commensurate with the magnitude of the problems we face? This in turn raises questions of anticipating problems and, further, coping with the existing backlog of dilemmas. One of the things we got into was the question of risk-taking. That is, we may possess knowledge that has implications for the real world, but we get into difficulty defining where our strengths lie. And the proposition that people in our position—many of us academics—have to rely on credibility as a going concern was set out. We dare not weaken our credibility by propaganda or other kinds of efforts. We dare not destroy our credibility in order to really be effective or make some contribution. So the question becomes: How do you maintain credibility without losing significance or relevance?

A member of another group stated:

One of the points brought up in our group was: How does an administrator justify organizationally destructive forms of activity, or at what points is it justifiable for an administrator or anybody in an organization to justify destructive kinds of behavior? But the question can very appropriately be reversed: At what point does an organization justify not letting an individual destroy his organization? The burden is really on the organization. The assumption behind the idea that an individual must justify his sabotage is that organizational permanence is a legitimate value. I don't think it is.

A member of the same group appended:

And this position can be taken without using words like "sabotage." You can simply ask at what point an administrator should stop making an investment of energy in trying to maintain the organization. For a welfare administrator to immediately devolve authority to multiple neighborhood "little city halls" at this point might be mad because those little city halls would quickly get chewed up. But if such neighborhoods or subcities compellingly demonstrate their political capacity to elicit and control subunit organizations on their terms, at what point does it become unjustifiable to exert effort to try to maintain a monolithic organization? At what point does it become reasonable to let it collapse rather than try to preserve it?

Even these brief snatches from the reports of some small groups indicate that the groups behaved differently, covered variegated ground, and, I think, for the most part were not as unrelated to the papers as some might have expected. Probably no further benefit could be obtained by reproducing comments from the small-group reports. Matthew Crenson—who presided over the plenary session at which most of these reports were offered —was credited by most with a superb job of summarizing the essence of the reports. Perhaps his summary can serve here as well as it did there:

Well, it might be useful to try to sum this up, and under two general headings. First, are there any common themes under all this smoke of discussion as reported to us; and second, are they new?

First, I think there are common themes: Almost every group arrived at the conclusion that there ought to be greater emphasis upon normative concerns in Public Administration. That leads to the question about the role of the administrator, whether he should be value neutral or somehow committed to policies or to value neutrality. That leads to the next question: If administrators are committed to certain values, what do they do? And the answer to that on the part of some people seems to be that Public Administrators should act as agents of change, which leads to the next question: What sorts of organizations must there be in order for change to be facilitated. Which leads to: What things should organizations respond to in changing, namely, the environment? Others seem to put greater emphasis upon environmental factors, consequences for the environment of things in the organization administration. The question is, of course, whether there is agreement on all these things, and if there is, whether that's "new."

The Wider Context

There are a number of themes which constitute the context of the Minnowbrook meetings and which I believe help one to understand something of what transpired. The correspondence with participants had suggested that they had been identified as the leaders of the future, if not the present, and that their opinions were important. Yet the discussions and the conference had been structured in ways that appeared to them not conducive to their unique contributions (that is, the planning and administration of the conference did not have a large enough "participatory" aspect to it). Also, as became obvious in discussions at the conference, many of the participants were greatly disturbed by social and political problems: Their concern had been exacerbated by the debate and turmoil of the presidential campaign, the McCarthy movement, the assassination of Robert Kennedy, and just a short time prior to their gathering at Minnowbrook, by the televised encounter with the events of the Chicago Democratic Presidential Nominating Convention. The Chicago Convention, moreover, had been a focal point for many impassioned arguments at the American Political Science Association meeting, directly from which many of these participants came to Minnowbrook. The Political Science meeting had also witnessed revolts against formality and structure. Perhaps the Minnowbrook gathering inherited the effects of lost battles at the Political Science meeting. Then, too, there were rumblings in all the social sciences that one could identify more or less loosely with the "new generation." Economists, sociologists, and others also had their revolts at professional meetings. One could identify "new sociology," "new history." Sometimes one could even see attempts to institutionalize, to set up counterinstitutions in professional associations (perhaps the "caucus for a new political science," which had been so active at the Washington American Political Science Association, might be so characterized). In academic circles it was not unusual to ponder the relationship between the young intellectual revolts against the disciplines and university structures and the aspects of confrontational politics on university campuses and in the wider society which are sometimes characterized as "the New Politics." Minnowbrook was not alone in the impact of turbulent times; perhaps the planning committee had been naive in not foreseeing the consequences of gathering together young men who were concerned about Public Administration at a time when it was becoming clear that "Public Administration in a time of turbulence" had profound and critical aspects. Perhaps we had even exaggerated the situation by circulating Dwight Waldo's essay on that theme to participants prior to our gathering.

The mix of these elements—a dissatisfaction with current aspects of social science (perhaps exacerbated by our mathematical modeling session); a revolt against formality (perhaps exacerbated by rulings from the Chair at the Chicago Nominating Convention and the Washington Political Science Convention); intense awareness of the problems of our society, social and economic injustice, and the role of administrators in societal in-

justice (which had in recent months been topics of public debate)—were part of the wider intellectual context of the Minnowbrook Conference. I do not mean to give the impression
that all of the conference participants were in agreement, were
New Left politicos sublimating their revolutionary fervor. Few
things so characterized the Minnowbrook Conference as did
disagreement. If one of the conference participants publicly characterized the conference in terms that some might read
as giving support to notions of New Left consensus, he did so
for the explicit purpose of disassociating himself from what he
perceived to be the majority position at Minnowbrook.[4]

Dissent, argument, factions—all these we had. Yet there was a
predominant sentiment emerging from the conference and there
was something that could be called the Minnowbrook perspective. As one participant wrote in his brief report of the conference
in the *Public Administration Review:*

> Clearly, there was disagreement among the participants, both as to
> the present state of the discipline and probably as to the value of the
> Minnowbrook meeting. A majority of participants, however, now find
> the present field of public administration wanting, not only a re-
> liable set of concepts and techniques to guide the contemporary pub-
> lic administrator, but equally a set of concepts and ideas to explain the
> modern world of administration.[5]

The Minnowbrook Papers

Although the point was sometime in debate at Minnowbrook,
I believe the final judgment was that the papers and comments
written for the conference did in fact address the important concerns of most of the participants. I would go beyond this: It seems
to me that many of the arguments for setting the formal papers
aside so as to get down to the real, important, pressing questions
did a great disservice to the extent to which such questions *were*
addressed by the papers. The question of what precisely were the
"real, important, pressing questions" identified at Minnowbrook
is itself open to serious debate and has been actively argued by
Minnowbrook participants on a number of occasions subsequent

---

[4]See Keith M. Henderson's letter to the *Public Administration Review* (January-
February, 1969), pp. 108–109.

[5]Richard S. Page, "A New Public Administration?" *Public Administration
Review* (May-June, 1969), pp. 303–304.

to the conference. I was moved to consider this question shortly after returning from the Minnowbrook Conference when I met with some candidates for the doctorate in Public Administration at the Maxwell School for the purpose of describing new currents in Public Administration. I attempted to summarize the principal themes of the Minnowbrook Conference under the following heads: relevance, antipositivism, personal morality, innovation, concern for clients, antibureaucratic philosophy. Six months later, when I turned with my colleague and coorganizer of the conference, George Frederickson, to the formulation of a similar characterization, we utilized the following subtopics: dissatisfaction with the state of the disciplines; morals, ethics, and values; social equity; client-focus; and repression.

There are other topics, perhaps more basic, and other characterizations of the Minnowbrook themes are also possible. When one of the conference participants described the conference in the *Public Administration Review*, he identified the following as important characteristics: a debate over "whether there was a 'new' public administration and if [there was] ... what were its key elements"; a concern for "seeking ways for public organizations to become more representative of constituent desires, emphasizing the study of external results and outcomes of administrative actions, and understanding interorganizational relationships and behavior in addition to intraorganizational techniques and mores"; an assessment of a need for public organizations to find new supporters and resources and for a bridge between analysts and actors in public administration; and a feeling that the normative aridity of public administration can be partly dealt with by recognizing that students and practitioners "carry a responsibility to think out, articulate as explicitly as possible, and act upon their values, and . . . may have the clearest insight into the normative shortcomings of public organizations, administrators, and policies."[6]

Since the authors of the concluding chapters in this volume take upon themselves the task of thematic interpretation (that is, they attempt to identify principal themes of the Minnowbrook papers as they interrelate), I will eschew further discussion of the themes of the papers here. A word on the order in

[6]*Ibid.*

which they appear in this book: The papers do not appear
here precisely in the order in which they were discussed at the
conference; rather, they have been rearranged in the order which
seemed to me suggested by the papers themselves. That order
is roughly a progression from discussions of the relevance of Public Administration to changes in our society, through methodological and philosophical concerns, to some specific problem
areas in contemporary Public Administration literature and practice. After the original Minnowbrook papers were rearranged
(to the extent that it was possible) in an order with this sort of
progression in mind, three concluding chapters written specifically for this volume were appended.

2

Relevance

"Relevance" was an extremely popular word at Minnowbrook and can be identified as one of the three or four major rubrics under which the themes making up the "Minnowbrook perspective" can be grouped. In this chapter, Todd La Porte discusses "The Recovery of Relevance in the Study of Public Organizations" and Edward Friedland comments on "The Pursuit of Relevance." La Porte argues that our discipline and profession, our values, our literature—in short, the components of our public presence—are out of keeping with the problems we face. And he tries to show us the way to bridge this chasm, the way to "recover relevance."

The Recovery of Relevance in the Study of Public Organization

Todd R. La Porte

Contemporary Public Administration is subject to great conceptual confusion.[1] As an intellectual enterprise it encompasses

[1]The temper of this paper was nurtured by the frustration of teaching Organization Theory and Public Organizations to political-science students who often come to the course principally interested in any aspect of politics other than Public Administration. Much of its substance is informed by a growing effort to relate theory and research to action and bring some meaning to the obvious effects of complex technologies upon public organizations and politics. My thanks to Professors L. Vaughn Blankenship, SUNY (Buffalo), and Robert Biller, a colleague at Berkeley, for the many occasions they have afforded to talk out sections

basic underlying ambiguity in many implicit models mixing
various normative and substantive concerns, analytical assumptions, and preferred methodologies. A cursory review of its major
literature reveals little attention to the resulting diffuse focus or
potential analytical and normative tensions. There is almost no
examination of the relevance of concepts to social or organizational reality.[2]

The major elements in the confused mix are familiar. We
alternatively or simultaneously view public administration and
organizations as conducting the business of government; serving
the public interest at home; carrying on political development
the world over; a primary arena of politics (interest aggregation,
articulation, choice, and action); or a system of social interaction
seeking to adapt, survive, and function. Implicit within each of
these perspectives are premises about salient relationships and
normative significance. Each incorporates necessarily partial
views of reality and standards of a "good" state or public organization.[3] In the interests of intellectual economy each approach
seeks to suggest what is most important to understand and to aid
in defining the "proper" focus of normative concern. Caricatures
of some focal points are efficiency in the business of government,
the public interest in service to the polity, the desideratum of
representativeness, or functionality in the name of survival. Efficiency, public interest, representativeness, or survival *for what*
is scantily emphasized.

Each perspective also carries a baggage of conceptual imperatives and methods of knowing. Each implicitly calls for its own
acceptance as a means of understanding and interpreting infor-

---

of this paper. Let me absolve both of them from any errors of fact or judgment that
may remain. I gratefully acknowledge the support of the Institute of Governmental Studies, University of California (Berkeley), which enabled me to devote
concentrated effort to this paper.

[2]An important exception is Dwight Waldo, "Organization Theory: An Ele-
phantine Problem," *Public Administration Review* (Autumn, 1961), pp. 210–225.
See also Alvin E. Gouldner, "Metaphysical Pathos and the Theory of Bureau-
cracy," *American Political Science Review* (June, 1955), pp. 496–507; and
Sheldon Wolin, *Politics and Vision* (Boston: Little, Brown, 1960), Chap. 10, "The
Age of Organization and the Sublimation of Politics."

[3]James D. Thompson characterizes these implicit assumptions about reality
as "cause/effect beliefs" in his interesting discussion of the consequences for organizational behavior of differences in these beliefs. *Organizations in Action* (New
York: McGraw-Hill, 1967).

mation about the substance and processes of public affairs. Very often a muted call to action is issued, though sometimes cloaked in the neutral language of the social sciences. Such policy recommendations, however, require close scrutiny, for the analysis upon which they rest is frequently based on the assumption that the underlying cause/effect beliefs about social reality have a high correspondence to that reality, and that the philosophical inertias embedded within a statement of "fact" are complementary (or at least not erosive) to the values which ought to be the focus of public effort. Donning the trappings of one or several of these models without examining its conceptual underwear leads to misshapen analysis and ill-fitting, itching recommendations.

It is my impression that the literature in Public Administration has contributed almost nothing to major advances in either the analysis or the normative understanding of complex public organizations.[4] We have rushed to borrow the analytical models proffered from a range of other disciplines without first (or second) examining the larger implication of the limits of this or that model in understanding large, complex public organizations. Thus we have brought in the back door a number of emphases we might have wished to clean up, wash down, or otherwise make appropriate if we had sought to introduce them in the front door.

Several years ago, in what is almost the only recent analysis of concepts of organization theory as data for political-philosophical analysis, Sheldon Wolin asserted that politics is being sublimated in organization; after an extensive attempt in demonstration, the final evaluation was one of tragedy for the life of the polity.[5] Let me assert that this sublimation seems to be increasingly the case, and for a number of theoretical reasons can be expected to increase. It seems to some of us that complex public organizations *are* becoming the major arena of political

---

[4]Don K. Price, *The Scientific Estate* (Boston: Harvard University Press, 1965) is perhaps the sole exception. It is a fruitful effort, combining elements of political philosophy and the less analytical perspectives of Public Administration, in addressing the consequences for both of a highly technicalized government. Another quite different contribution comes from Aaron Wildavsky in his work laying open the normative content of budgetary reform and PPB signaled by *The Politics of the Budgetary Process* (Boston: Little, Brown, 1964).

[5]Wolin, *op. cit.* For an earlier effort attending to concepts of administration within a political-philosophic context, see Dwight Waldo, *The Administrative State* (New York: Ronald Press, 1948).

action, increasingly taking the place of legislative bodies as the source of creative political solutions and the definition of important political problems. Rather than deplore this apparent trend (though some may deplore it), let us take it as given for a moment and reflect on its implication for the study of public organizations.

To the extent that it exists, the increasing inclusion of the political into complex organizations represents a significant challenge to us all. It suggests that the vacuum of political philosophical analysis within which we study Public Administration is a serious, perhaps disastrous, situation. The decline of philosophical consciousness in the study of public organizations to a low ebb comes at a time when many of the traditional underlying presuppositions of democratic politics and administration are eroding in the face of vastly changing conditions in the society, economy, polity, and in complex organizations themselves. Our current levels of analytical understanding and normative resolve are plainly inadequate for understanding or responding to conditions more complex, ethically murky, and politically disorienting than at any time in recent history. Add to this inadequacy the suspicion that past experience is only marginally useful in providing guides to understanding or action as public organizations become the major representative institutions of the culture and we are indeed subject to confusion.

Political and social values which firmly anchored Public Administration in its role as keeper of social order no longer have their traditional currency.[6] At a time requiring great moral, ethical, and philosophical vision we fall back upon analysis sprung from weakened, atrophied philosophical roots and premises. An increasing crisis in meaning seems to underlie much in the study and actions of public organizations: a loss of confidence in traditional, stabilizing values; a loss of conceptual direction; foreshortened vision and a failure of nerve in exploring the consequences for public organization and politics occasioned by new conditions, new aspirations, and new anger with the underfulfilled promises of abundance.[7] We are subject

[6]See Frederick C. Mosher, *Democracy and the Public Service* (New York: Oxford University Press, 1968), especially pp. 209–216, for a similar view directed principally toward values connected with the present civil-service system.

[7]See the more extensive analysis by Orion F. White, Jr., "Social Change and Administrative Adaptation," Chap. 3 below.

to a kind of intellectual puniness in the face of enormous philosophical and analytical demands. Demands for relevance come shrieking at us from outside the discipline and more muted from our compulsive interiors. The young, the men on the job, and, I suspect, we too seek a reaffirmation of worthiness—a sense of significance, and a promise that what we study and teach is worth the effort—born of something more than a simple "leap of timid faith" to the belief that public organizations are important because they are public.

The major problem of Public Administration as an intellectual enterprise is this: Contemporary Public Administration exists in a state of antique or maladapted analytical models and normative aridity. There is almost no basis for rejecting or accepting either substantive problems or analytical models save political-administrative crises or academic fashion. Teaching and research tend to be based on past problems or instant response to present "establishment" problem definitions. Both bases have limited utility in developing administrative vision, political leadership, or intellectual vitality of lasting quality. The result has been a deadening of intellectual vigor and a kind of wandering relevance to students, practitioners, and the future.

Younger students, men in public affairs at various levels, and many among us complain that we are not relevant, that the intellectual stuff of Public Administration has restricted meaning and limited significance to their experience, that it misses the drama of social change ... that it misses the point! Most of our efforts *do* come perilously close to missing the point; they fall between the stools of searching normative interpretations and detailed practical solutions to specific problems faced by administrators. Most are neither normatively nor practically relevant.

Theories of Administered Organization:
The "Babble" of the Literature

Let us take the place for a moment of a student intent upon discovering the delights of Public Administration. Fired by the obvious importance of public organizational action upon the quality of national life, he turns to the "field" to share with us our understanding. He starts a journey hoping to find that combination of substantive and analytical thought which has political and personal meaning in understanding and assessing complex public organization. Beginning students in any unfamiliar area soon discover the problem of basic definition and primary terms. I shall not recount here the past or recent troubled discussions among students of Public Administration about whether we have a "field," what organizations are, what administration is, or what is public. Rather let me quickly set some personal boundaries on this discussion by introducing several distinctions I find helpful in sorting things out.

First, there is the distinction made by Rapoport and Horvath between organization theories and theories of organization.[8] This distinction is between the general and abstract principles related to *all* systems exhibiting organized complexity and those collectivities of *human beings* engaged in cooperative action. Let us set aside "organization theories," for these are the extensions of mathematical physics such as cybernetics, relational mathematics, and some forms of decision theory which at some future time may be applied to human organization. These logically constructed models and theories require a good deal more refinement enabling a less forced coupling to social theory and research before successful transplant is likely. Theories of organization encompass the concepts and models of social systems with human beings as the primary focus of attention, and draw on sociology and political science as well as fragments of social psychology and economics. All of social organization beckons in too many directions, however, so let me advance a *second* distinction, made by J. D. Thompson and his associates in specifying *administered organization* as an object of study.[9] This type of social organization is characterized by sustained collective activity, integration within a larger social system, specialized and delimited goals, and dependence upon exchanges with elements in its surrounding social enviroment.

[8]A. Rapoport and W. J. Horvath, "Thoughts on Organization Theory and a Review of Two Conferences," in Ludwig Von Bertalanffy and A. Rapoport (eds.), *General Systems Yearbook*, Vol. IV (Society for General Systems Research, 1960), Part II, p. 90. Quoted in Waldo, "Organization Theory: An Elephantine Problem," *op. cit.*, p. 222.

[9]James D. Thompson, *et. al.*, "On the Study of Administration," in James D. Thomspon, *et. al* (eds.), *Comparative Studies in Administration* (Pittsburgh: University of Pittsburgh Press, 1959), p. 5ff.

A *further* internal boundary will increase intellectual economy and normative salience: the object of study is the *public-administered organization.* Such organizations are loosely denoted by predominant support from resources of the polity (mainly taxes and political legitimacy) mediated through the institutions of the state.

Finally, can we specify the processes and interaction which have conceptual primacy in understanding public-administered organizations? In a most interesting and useful review of definitional problems in Public Administration, Martin Landau asserts that, when all is said and done, the major and perhaps only point of general agreement among us is that the process of *cooperative rational action* is the conceptual "tie that binds."[10]

Assuming that our student—with relief and possibly resolve—accepts these boundaries, he may search for those who have attempted to add greater meaning and detail to them. Searching the literature of Public Administration since about 1960 reveals a twin emphasis: the familiar policy-problem perspective generally dealing with the politics of bureaucracy and democratic policy making, and the attempts at integrating analytical concepts.[11]

In the public-policy literature, analytical concepts of public-administered organization are scant, normally just enough so that the author can get on to his evaluation of modern public policy or bureaucracy. These works generally are within the framework of "process democracy" largely devoid of substantive content, and there are few efforts to summarize or integrate analytical concepts and theory relevant to public organization.

Scanning the analytical summary work in textbook form, one is confronted with an astonishing variety in concepts, theories,

[10]Martin Landau, "The Concept of Decision-Making in the Field of Public Administration," in Sidney Mailick and Edward H. VanNess (eds.), *Issues in Administrative Behavior* (Englewood Cliffs, N.J.: Prentice-Hall, 1962), p. 27ff.

[11]See for example, Charles E. Jacob, *Policy and Bureaucracy* (Princeton: Van Nostrand, 1966); John D. Millett, *Organization for the Public Service* (Princeton: Van Nostrand, 1966); Marshall E. Dimock and Gladys O. Dimock, *Public Administration*, 3rd ed. (New York: Holt, Rinehart and Winston, 1964); William W. Boyer, *Bureaucracy on Trial* (New York: Bobbs-Merrill, 1964); Peter Woll, *American Bureaucracy* (New York: W. W. Norton, 1963); and the readers by Francis E. Rourke (ed.), *Bureaucratic Power in National Politics* (Boston: Little, Brown, 1964) and Alan A. Altshuler (ed.), *The Politics of the Federal Bureaucracy* (New York: Dodd, Mead, 1968).

and unconnected propositions. Perhaps the best examples of survey attempts are the fifth edition of *Public Administration,* by Pfiffner and Presthus, and *Administrative Organization,* by Pfiffner and Sherwood.[12] Both these books give a kind of college try in presenting the new and the old concepts about public organization. Typifying the tension within the area, they both swing back and forth between behavioral surveys and a kind of neostructuralism. One after the other come chapters of this or that collection of concepts, then whole sections cast in the familiar language of Public Administration before World War II. Neither book shows more than a passing effort at the integration of the dozen or so separate concepts borrowed from a range of disciplines. The only potentially interesting try is the "overlay" notion in *Administration Organization,* where pattern after pattern is piled one upon the other. Each book is a good sample of the array of concepts and illustrates the difficulty of sorting out one from the other or providing some set of ordering principles and assessment of the appropriateness of one or the other for public organization today. It's all there . . . all of it . . . in linear form!

Several attempts—notably those of Victor A. Thompson, Robert Presthus, and Wiliam Gore[13]—have been made to deal in a more

[12]James M. Pfiffner and Robert Presthus, *Public Administration,* 5th ed. (New York: Ronald Press, 1967); and James M. Pfiffner and Frank Sherwood, *Administrative Organization* (Englewood Cliffs, N.J.: Prentice-Hall, 1960).

[13]Victor A. Thompson, *Modern Organization* (New York: Knopf, 1961); Robert Presthus, *The Organizational Society* (New York: Knopf, 1962); William J. Gore, *Administrative Decision-Making: A Heuristic Model* (New York, Wiley, 1964). Two men who have contributed very significantly to the general understanding of organizations have come to their present positions from initial studies in political science. I think it regrettably unfair, however, to include either Herbert A. Simon or James G. March in the company of Public Administration. Their respective departures to the social sciences more generally and the social psychology of decision making in particular may be testimony to the constricting confines of Public Administration as they found it. See Herbert A. Simon, *Administrative Behavior,* 2nd ed. (New York: Macmillan, 1957); James G. March and Herbert A. Simon, *Organizations* (New York: Wiley, 1958); Richard M. Cyert and James G. March, *The Behavioral Theory of the Firm* (Englewood Cliffs, N.J.: Prentice-Hall, 1963); and James G. March, "The Power of Power," in David Easton (ed.), *Varieties of Political Theory* (Englewood Cliffs, N.J.: Prentice-Hall, 1966). For Simon's latest contribution to Public Administration, largely affirming his stance taken a decade earlier, see "The Changing Theory and Changing Practices of Public Administration," in Ithiel de Sola Pool (ed.), *Contemporary Political Science: Toward Empirical Theory* (New York: McGraw-Hill, 1967), Chap. 4.

integrated fashion with theories of organization. Both Thompson and Presthus ultimately worry about the effect of organization upon the personalities of its participants. Proceeding from within a broadly Weberian perspective, they echo Merton's concerns for individual responses to structures of hierarchical authority. Their emphasis is upon the results of organizationally generated anxiety for the psychic behavior of bureaucrats. Presthus describes the results in terms of three major types of personality accommodation to this situation: upward-mobiles, indifferents, and ambivalents. In his turn, Thompson fastens on the phenomenon of "dramaturgy" and "bureaupathic behavior" in attempts to reduce personal insecurity engendered by complex and technically infused organizational structures. In neither case do the formulations include research designed to test the theory; rather they organize supporting studies to give plausibility to their conceptual schemes. While their range of conceptual language is rather different, their concerns and to a certain extent their conclusions are similar. Gore, on the other hand, in his latest offering, based on a long-term interest in organizational decision making, presents an elaborate scheme and terminology for describing the processes of organizational decision making quite analogous to the social-psychological processes of group-decision studies combined with the models of choice noted, for example, in March and Simon, *Organizations*.[14] Comparing Presthus and Thompson with Gore shows a startling difference in symbol, language, and concept with very little apparent connection between them.

One other political scientist deserves mention here. Bertram Gross' voluminous effort in *The Managing of Organizations* is an attempt to bring the wide-ranging literature relevant to public organization into some coherent form.[15] This work reflects the difficulty of combining theoretical integration, historical overview, and, ultimately, concern for the teaching of public officials. Mixing behavioral categories with more traditional language, he

[14]William J. Gore, *op. cit.* See also "Administrative Decision-Making in Federal Field Offices," *Public Administration Review* (Autumn, 1956), pp. 281–291; and William J. Gore and F. S. Silander, "A Bibliographical Essay on Decision Making," *Administrative Science Quarterly* (June, 1959), pp. 97–121.

[15]Bertram Gross, *The Managing of Organizations* (New York: Free Press, 1964).

has tirelessly summed up the variety of language, submitted a seemingly endless list of implicit and explicit propositions cast in a vague systems-like structure. Asserting that he has introduced only three new terms—commergence, purpose surrogate, and teletics—Gross has incorporated all technical languages into a "cinerama" of administrative semantics. Covering almost all the traditional concerns of the responsibility and democracy school, as well as many of the "scientific" issues of generalization level and language of conceptualization, he has produced two volumes that overwhelm and dismay. The "integration" is linear—often through time—with little use of the tools of conceptual reduction linking one set of concepts to another through specification of theoretic common denominators. When this work is coupled with the summary texts noted above, the student in search of a coherent field is tempted to flee from the endless vistas of semantic variation and seeming infinity of concepts.

Since the summary and "integrative" work available in the field encompasses so much, one could assume that time and space did not permit writers the luxury of detailed analysis of sufficient clarity to explicate these notions in a coherent way. Perhaps the sense of confuson would be relieved if we retreated back to the "originals," seeking the possibility of integration there. Another set of summary works, drawing together more general efforts to develop theories of administered organizations, provide a point of departure. A brief review of some of these works does little to encourage our entering student of public organization.[16]

In 1959 Mason Haire's introduction to *Modern Organization*

---

[16]Mason Haire (ed.), *Modern Organization Theory* (New York: Wiley, 1959); Amitai Etzioni (ed.), *Complex Organizations: A Sociological Reader* (New York: Holt, Rinehart and Winston, 1962); Peter Blau and W. Richard Scott, *Formal Organizations* (Scranton: Chandler, 1962); and Albert H. Rubenstein and Chadwick J. Haberstroh (eds.), rev. ed., *Some Theories of Organization* (Homewood, Ill.: Dorsey Press, 1966). For material illustrating the linkages between theory, organizational action and design see William W. Cooper, H. J. Leavit, and M. W. Shelly III (eds.), *New Perspectives in Organization Research* (New York: Wiley, 1964); James D. Thompson (ed.), *Approaches to Organizational Design* (Pittsburgh: University of Pittsburgh Press, 1966) [especially the incredible summary article by R. M. Stogdill, "Dimensions of Organization Theory"], Victor H. Vroom (ed.), *Methods of Organizational Research* (Pittsburgh: University of Pittsburgh Press, 1967); and finally, the book that is the best effort in cogent summary, James G. March (ed.), *Handbook of Organization* (Chicago: Rand McNally, 1965). A number of summary journal articles are omitted here in the interests of economy.

Theory summarized the "Recurrent Themes and General Issues in Organization Theory" as the conflict between personality and organization, after the fashion of Chris Argyris and others; the structure of organization in terms of linkages, levels, and bonds between elements; decision process as affected by organizational factors and as an independent variable in the behavior of organizations; the ecology of organization in terms of those environmental variables which shape organizational behavior; and problems of organizational stability and survival in the face of threatening conditions. Add to this list a concern for the nature of theory and an emphasis upon research, and one can roughly comprehend most of what has been done in conceptualizing and studying organization. Reviewing other summaries, one finds, however, that within each general category a number of dialects have, in turn, developed to explicate factors of ecological influence, organizational structure, and the organizational impact upon members. A comparison of the Rubenstein and Haberstroh reader and the Etzioni reader reflects this internal variation of conceptual language, even though some of their major categories are similar. Rubenstein, for example, has whole sections on matters of leadership and morale, communication, control and evaluation, and decision making which are ignored by Etzioni.

Blau and Scott provide a commendable survey of the sociological perspective which, when used comparatively, highlights the differences between sociological, psychological, and economic approaches. The volume edited by Cooper and his associates adds another dimension to the expanding landscape. His survey includes the mathematically based management-science perspective and an enthusiasm for information and decision theory coupled with systems and analysis. This book, in addition to the others reviewing research and design, increases the conceptual variation by including a growing number of research "technologies" with languages prompting problem solution in their own terms often quite apart from the conceptual elements of sociologically based theories of organization.

Finally, the best example of helpful summary and theoretic contribution is found in March's *Handbook of Organization.* This book presents, in one place, the entire range of languages, issues, and perspectives currently extant. A careful reading of the book is likely to result in a clear perception of the variety in the field and a sense of its diffuseness. It is less likely to provide guides to integrating the rich variation presented. Worth noting here is that while seven of the chapters in the last parts of the book cover organizational types included in our definition of public-administered organization, only one chapter is explicitly devoted to public bureaucracy.[17]

The sweep of organization theory, theories of organization, administrative theories, and theories of cooperative action and the number of different concepts, models, propositions, and hypotheses have become depressingly disparate. One suspects that the appearance of cumulation is deceptive, that conceptual differences are more semantically apparent than operationally real. It is increasingly irritating to read the newest dialect presented as if it were describing unique aspects of organizational activities when it is largely a translation of previous language into another set of symbols. One feels a growing impatience and imperative to search for points of conceptual parallel and overlap between theories; ways of seeing the relationship of one theory to another and of determining the actual addition of one to another. The literature has become a huge supermarket of possible theoretical edibles. Such a wide range of choices provides an optimum situation—*if* we have a menu in mind. But I suspect we have only a glimmering of what we want to serve our guests.

The Need for Conceptual Convergence

By now our student, weary and subject to battle fatigue, has either left the field or senses that there is more variation than is necessary. He will know that the array of language, concepts, theories, models, and empirical studies discussed above is a result of the greatly increased attention given organizational phenomenon since World War II. At the time of the war the level of conceptual and empirical understanding about complex administrative organizations was most modest. The growth of activities from that time to the present has been received with enthusiasm and welcomed as necessary for increased intellectual understanding and potentially more effective administrative action.

There comes a time, however, when the process of generating new languages or variations on existing ones needs to be complemented by efforts to reduce the welter of terms and variations in

---

[17]See Robert L. Peabody and Francis E. Rourke, "Public Bureaucracy," in March, *Handbook, op. cit.*

apparently different conceptual formulations. Theoretical language and concepts must be sorted out at the level of operational meaning, and statements should be made in propositional form so that if they are false we can come to know them to be so. Appearances of cumulative advance, often accompanying new formulations, should be put to the test. Furthermore, greater attention should be paid to the cluster of concepts, propositions, and theory most appropriate to public organizations in a swiftly changing, technologically based political system.

Convergence of theoretical language and ordering of propositions about *all* organizations on a highly abstract scale is not enough. There is probably a fairly good number of general propositions within a "grand theory" of complex organization after the General Systems mode, though this set of propositions is still quite a distance from analytical clarity and empirical verification. However, the level of generality necessary for a "grand theory" often masks the intermediate range of propositions and theory related more concretely to types of organizations. Students of Public Administration are most interested in the particular variable values which occur within and among *public* organizations. Do theoretical formulations vary in their appropriateness for the world of public organizations? How would we know if we stumble on theoretical relevance?

In efforts to begin modest convergence of theories of organization, sorting out that portion of each that may have the greater currency for public organization, one is straightaway confronted with a quandary of choice. Where to go first—decision theory, systems analysis, functional analysis, role theory, communications, information theory . . . ? Each of these and others now has its own growing subset of theoretical variation—dialects within languages. In the midst of this variation, upon what basis ought one to choose this or that theoretical fragment? On what basis does one reject, modify, or clutch to his analytical bosom one theoretical formulation or another?[18]

[18]In an interesting theoretical fragment, Simon draws attention to "attention" as a major element in the political control of values. That is, to what extent do political bodies determine what decisions, information, and issues are noticed and attended to by bureaucratic decision makers? Our problem is similar: Upon what basis do we *notice* elements in the landscape of theories of organization? We cannot attend to all equally and what draws our attention is critical to the development of theories of public-administered organization. Simon, "The Changing Theory . . . ," *op. cit.*, p. 99ff.

Analytical Concepts and Normative Presuppositions

It is clear that theoretical development does not spring, even in infancy, from itself. Analytical concepts are most often derived from the major conceptual questions asked about the phenomenon. These concepts in turn are rooted in underlying normative presuppositions held by the theorist (often implicitly) to be important reasons for asking his set of questions.[19] Therefore, a beginning step in sorting out theories and concepts is coming to an understanding of the underlying presuppositions implied by the analytical questions posed and the answers offered. Without a reasonable understanding of these elements, the implications of one theoretical notion or another are difficult to assess fully.

When students of public organization attempt to reduce or sort out useful theory they need to have this linkage between model, analytical question, and normative presupposition clearly in mind. Adoption of models and concepts without this awareness makes probable the implicit adoption of the underlying presuppositions of the model's originator. Enthusiastic acceptance of decision models, systems analysis, or conflict models stressing efficient productivity leads the adopter along a path of analysis which is often much too confining for an adequate understanding of public organization. Sociological formulations of cooperative systems in equilibrium, for example, may need modification if the range of questions relevant to contemporary public organizations are to be asked and answered cogently. Systems maintenance and adaptation are important ways of dealing with complex organization; however, to the degree these formulations make it difficult to address the problem of intended organizational change they are also too confining.

Whether the perspectives used here as illustrations do in fact lead to theoretical confinement is open to question, and in a way is beside my point. I am arguing that more thoughtful examination of the models we borrow, modify, and build is needed. Most of the concepts and models we use have their origins in the study of complex industrial organizations either from the economic-

---

[19]See the discussion of this problem in Ralf Dahrendorf, *Essays in the Theory of Society* (Palo Alto, California: Stanford University Press, 1968), Chap. 1, "Values and Social Science," pp. 1–18.

business administration or the sociological perspective. Other more recent attempts have emanated from the social psychology of groups lately colored by the fervor of "encounter-group" advocates. In each case, serious normative limitations exist which narrow the range of questions deemed worthy of attention.

Consideration of the normative presuppositions and premises of organizational theories and the appropriateness of these theories for public-administered organizations has two aspects. Clearly it is difficult to assess these models without some idea of the underlying directions implicit in them. It is, however, equally difficult to complete the assessment if there is significant and unrecognized ambiguity in the assessor's values, that is, in the clarity of his own normative understanding of public organization. It is this latter requirement that makes the convergence of theories to personal understanding salient, and to which I now turn.

Normative Bases for Conceptual Choice

The area to be ventured into is so scantily attended in Public Administration that I am ill-prepared and almost embarrassed to continue. The mode of objective social science applied to complex organizations has for the most part resulted in either avoidance of the question of what conditions are preferable, or policy-neutral attention to the process of decision making. Most contemporary theories of organization seem simply to assume that productivity is good if it is efficient, that rational decision making will somehow return good decisions in terms of the social conditions associated with them, and that organizational control systems and structure which promote efficiency and rational decision making are desirable social arrangements for individuals. Recently, some social-psychologically derived theories widened the scope a little, raising questions about the potentiality of personal development, "self-actualization," the quality of encounter maintained within organizations, and the possibility of greater individual as well as collective productivity.

These norms are relevant and pertinent to organizational life. However, the role of public organizations in the polity must be seen in wider perspective than either output or internal maintenance as prime virtues allow. Since public organizations are becoming the major vehicles for social change, the direction of change is increasingly important. More attention to the impact of public organizations on surrounding social conditions is required in evaluating either analytical questions or emerging theories of organization. Incremental advance toward the "public interest" is not enough, though it may be one way to proceed. But incrementalism begs the question: Which increment, for how long? Clearly, organizational action can make some increments more possible than others.

As a beginning to an answer, I would argue that our primary normative premise should be that *the purpose of public organization is the reduction of economic, social, and psychic suffering and the enhancement of life opportunities for those inside and outside the organization.*[20] Translated into more detailed sentiments, this statement means that public organizations should be assessed in terms of their effect on the production and distribution of material abundance in efforts to free all people from economic deprivation and want. Furthermore, it means that public organizations have a responsibility to enhance social justice by freeing their participants and the citizenry to decide their own way and by increasing the probability of shared political and social privilege. Finally, it means that the quality of personal encounter and increasing possibilities of personal growth should be elevated to major criteria of organizational assessment.

When these values are used as a basis for assessment, the consequent conceptual and informational imperatives require attention to (a) the impact of public organizations upon the underlying economic, social, and political conditions associated with economic abundance and political privilege—that is, what are the consequences of cooperative rational action for those acted upon? and (b) the organizational and group conditions which increase the probability of creative challenge and personal encounter within organization—in other words, What are the consequences of executive action and organizational design for the persons living significant portions of their lives within organizations?

[20]I take the spirit of eliminating barriers embedded in this statement to be in keeping with Robert Biller's concept of freedom noted below in "Some Implications of Adaptive Capacity for Organizational and Political Development," Chap. 4.

To the degree these emphases are missing from theories of public organization, the theories are wanting.

Normative bases for evaluating either organizational theory or action bring one squarely into the province of political philosophy. Unfortunately, students of public organization cannot turn readily to literature which treats political thought in ways that clarify the questions that should be addressed in the context of complex organization. What attention has been given by political philosophers appears to be mostly in the mode of peevish criticism or wholesale rejection of complex organizations as a legitimate form of human association. Such a stance does not aid in the clarification of values as a basis for assessment. There is little attempt to specify, from a philosophic vantage which recognizes the empirical or theoretical work already done, what the best or possible social organizational arrangements might be.[21] Finally, to my knowledge there has been little creative political philosophy lending insight or inspiration to development of future organization. Most students of political philosophy and theory have not responded to the challenge—perhaps the obligation—of understanding a major medium of social life in ways that contribute to action or assessment. In a sense they have been loath to meet their obligation to provide alternative normative guides to the less philosophically literate, though at least equally concerned, students of administration. Perhaps this failure is a major one of contemporary political philosophy: It has left us trackless to venture largely unaided into a philosophically barren landscape.

Analytical Bases for Convergence

The normative premises discussed above may be used as grounding for questions which could guide us in efforts to select and integrate theories applicable to public organizations. In combination they suggest a range of questions concerning who decides matters of resource allocation, the bases and character of the authority systems within administered organizations, and the consequences of administrative action for the economic and social conditions of the society. Analytical questions related to

[21]See M. Shubik, "Information, Rationality, and Free Choice," in *Toward the Year 2000: Work in Progress, Daedalus*, (Summer, 1967), pp. 771–778.

these kinds of issues should be the basis for assessing the utility of theory in Public Administration.

Stated in summary form, five such questions follow: What factors account for (1) variations in the *power of public organizations* relative to agencies of political regimes? (2) variations in the administrative *productivity of public organizations*? (3) variations in the internal *authority structures of public organizations*? (4) variations in *role behavior of public executives* and other organizational members? And finally, perhaps the most important question, (5) What are the reciprocal *consequences of administrative actions* for the political, social, and economic conditions of the polity?

These questions are formulated as a series of dependent variables to be related to antecedent conditions. Each can also be used as an independent variable for the other dependent variables (see Figure 1). If the details of this matrix of variables are worked out, a long stride will have been taken toward understanding the empirical conditions necessary to assess the public organization's performance in fulfilling its purposes in a democratic polity.[22]

FIGURE 1. MAJOR VARIABLES IN THE STUDY OF PUBLIC ORGANIZATION

As Dependent Variables

	Environment	Exchange		Internal	
	Social/Economic Conditions	Organizational Power	Organizational Productivity	Authority Structure	Role Behavior
Social/Economic Conditions	X				
Organizational Power		X			
Organizational Productivity			X		
Authority Structure				X	
Role Behavior					X

(As Independent Variables)

[22]For an attempt to specify and relate these variables to each other, see Warren F. Ilchman and Todd R. La Porte, *Comparative Public Organization: Analysis and Synthesis* (Boston: Little, Brown, forthcoming).

These questions assume that public organizations are "open and partial systems": "open" in the sense that they are related to the social structure surrounding them in various degrees of interdependence; "partial" in that, unlike organic structure, in which the elements of the system are joined continuously together, members of organizations are only partially integrated into the social network, entering and leaving the organization through the course of each day.[23] It is also assumed that social interaction is essentially based on an exchange relationship between individuals and groups in society and organizations; that individuals are related to one another through exchanges of resources based on the needs for sustenance, affection, security, and "space for growth."[24] When translated into organizational terms, these resources are economic goods and services, information, social status and legitimacy, and often tools of coercion.[25] Using these conceptual assumptions as a kind of analytical floor, the variables in question require brief explanation, for each of them is subject to the semantic confusion discussed earlier.

The Power of Public Organizations

Our concern is with the variations in relative "influence" evident among legislatures, kings, councils, executive offices, bureaus, military or educational organizations, and other public organizations in determining the course of civic action, political domination, and the quality of national life. Public-administered organizations are compared with agencies of political regimes, such as heads of state, politically appointed officials, and legislatures. One avenue in developing a concept of organizational power is to begin with our assumption that organizations are not self-sufficient, but depend upon resources from other organizations in their environment. The degree to which an organization is dependent on some other organization is related to the importance of the resources other organizations can provide and the number of other organizations able to meet and fulfill those needs.

[23]Daniel Katz and Robert L. Kahn, *The Social Psychology of Organization* (New York: Wiley, 1966), Chap. 1.

[24]See Peter Blau, *Exchange and Power in Social Life* (New York: Wiley, 1964).

[25]For a similar specification of resources and a concerted discussion of each see Warren F. Ilchman and N. F. Uphoff, *The Political Economy of Change* (Berkeley: University of California Press, 1969), Chap. 3.

The notion of organizational power can be considered the inverse of organizational dependence, that is, an organization's power is relative to the needs others have for resources it can command. Organizational power varies to the degree that organizations have resources others want and it is the only source of satisfying those needs. Seeking to satisfy organizational, group, or individual needs can be thought of as pressing claims upon organizations able to provide satisfaction. Using this modification, then, we can define relative organizational power as the degree to which one organization has the capacity to fulfill or reject claims made upon it by other organizations, groups, or persons in its environment compared to other organizations in the same environment.[26]

We are interested in the relative power or claim-settling activity carried on by public organizations and political organizations between one another and other groups in the polity. Many of the exchanges that take place in politics are between groups and persons pressing claims upon either public or political organizations. Other power relationships—some of the most interesting—involve claims from one organization (say a political pressure group) upon another (the legislature) to direct a third (the bureaucracy) to allocate resources to a fourth (a private interest). Networks of these indirect lines of power are numerous and probably make up a good share of the activities in complex situations.

Thus, a variable of relative power can be developed indicating the proportional share of claim settling carried on by public organizations compared to political agencies. This proportion can range from complete administrative domination in which political agencies settle no claims, to situations in which political agencies settle them all. In this way of viewing the power of public-administered organizations, there are several things that can vary with regard to *each* particular kind of resource sought: (1) the degree to which each potential claim settler is assured a supply of the resource, (2) the perceived intensity of need prompting the claimant to seek the resource, (3) the perceived number of potential suppliers of that resource, and (4) the magnitude of the

[26]This perspective of power is discussed more fully in Blau, *op. cit.,* Chap. 4; and Thompson, *Organizations in Action, op. cit.,* Chap. 3. See also R. M. Emerson, "Power-Dependence Relations," *American Sociological Review* (February, 1962), pp. 31–40.

"cost" or condition of settlement to the claimant for settlement of his claim.[27] The over-all power of any public organization, then, is the net total of dependence others have upon it for the resources it can dispense, compared to other public or political organizations.

These aspects of the power variable, all too briefly outlined, can be a basis upon which to evaluate organizational concepts. Which ones lend insight regarding the factors affecting any one of the subvariables? Under what conditions do these aspects change and how much? Again, as these change, what then for changes in productivity, the behavior of executives, or organizational structure? Those theories which aid in specifying fruitful relationships and are phrased so that verification research can be done are candidates for inclusion; those that do not can be laid to one side. Clearly this process can be duplicated with regard to the other variables as well.

The Productivity of Public Organizations

Productivity is the major output or exchange variable in this formulation. It refers to the quantity of things, services, or activities provided for consumption by the various claimants on the resources of the organization, and denotes increases or decreases in the "product" provided for exchange. Change in productivity is one of the thorniest problems in the assessment of public organizations, and is often critical to the quality of life in the polity. Whether production is a distributive, regulative, extractive, or integrative activity, public organizations' products, and the organizations' capacity to increase production or keep it constant with fewer resources is clearly related to a number of

[27]Symbolically this relationship might be summarized as follows. The ratio of the power of political organizations (P) to public-administered organizations (A) relative to resource (R) is:

$$\frac{P_r}{A_r} = \frac{\dfrac{R_p}{S}(N_r - C_p)}{\dfrac{R_a}{S}(N_r - C_a)}$$

when R_p and R_a is the probability of available resources R to P and A; S is the total number of perceived sources for R; N_r is the intensity of perceived need for R by the claimant; and C_p and C_a is the cost to the claimant incurred by P or A for settling claims for R.

other variables. For present purposes, productivity is understood in two related ways. The first, closely related to goal attainment insofar as the goals are made explicit, is in terms of productive effectiveness or increases in output with secondary regard for amounts of inputs. The second aspect is the familiar input-output ratio or variations in the efficient use of the resources available for production. In a sense, effectiveness deals with external exchanges, and efficiency with the internal organizational exchanges of resources which convert them into "public products." The most important aspect in assessing organizational productivity is in establishing the goal or "product." Attempting this definition has troubled students of public organization because the "public product" is not always easily discernible in the confusion of the conditions presumably satisfying the distribution of economic abundance, the common defense, and so on. In Thompson's language, there is often no clear agreement about cause/effect relationships in the pursuit of public-organization goals.[28]

In this tentative formulation there are two major subvariables, each undeveloped here: the mix of available resources and the character of the organizational "technostructure." Productivity will vary in relation to the adequacy of available resources in meeting the demands of the "product" technology. It also varies as a function of the proportion of resources consumed in direct output production to those consumed for internal maintenance or adaptive activities. The more resources available for conversion into organizational output after consuming those necessary for internal coordination, adjudication, and maintenance, the more output is available for exchange with elements in its environment or the more productive the organization. These internal processes include the coordination of both skill technologies and physical technologies associated with the types of output central to the organization. Quite probably, as the technologies necessary for goal attainment become more complex, more resources are required to maintain the administrative and technical social structure of skill and coordination relationships.

Authority Structures of Public Organizations

Masked behind the facade of formal organization are the relationships of personal interaction, decision, and choice which

[28]Thompson, *Organizations in Action, op. cit.*, Chap. 7.

give motion to internal organizational life. Outsiders seldom see the struggles for position and status associated with the activities of decision making or the instances in which personal advantage is set aside in the face of severe organizational test or challenge. The network of relations between men of like or different organizational status and dependence is the arena where orders are given and sometimes refused, persuasion is attempted and often succeeds, battles over decisions and mission are fought, and groups cohere in sometimes superb instruments of action and accomplishment. Our interest here is upon the structure of authority relations: the arrangements of the "parts" of the organization in varieties of decision concentration.

Similar to the basic premises used in the discussion of power, interactions between people and groups within organizations can be thought of as a series of dependent relationships. In large organizations some groups are called upon to furnish skills and information in the technical aspects of mission accomplishment. Other groups are called upon to settle demands for relating the skills and information of one group to those of another so that in combination they are able to do things neither can do alone. Groups are also called upon to allocate resources to others so that the job of relating group activities can go on. Finally, some groups are called upon to make choices between conflicting claims from competing groups. In effect, groups and persons press claims upon others for resources, coordination of activities, or adjudication of disputes. In return these claims stimulate direction, authorization, and commands in a process of choice and action reflecting various arrangements of reciprocal dependence, asymmetry, or autonomy between identifiable units.[29]

These processes involve decisions about whether and under what conditions to make claims or answer demands. An organizational network can be thought of as a series of related groups or positions having different degrees of decision capacity in ref-

[29] This is similar to our interests in organizational power, but complicated in detailed conception by several quantitatively different conditions in the interaction *between* organizations compared to those *within* them: (1) Administrative organizations have a higher degree of continuous interaction between persons and groups making it up than between organizations in the polity; (2) there is a higher degree of orientation toward collective, relatively delimited goals recognized by the participants within organizations; and (3) coercion as a resource of last resort is much less explicitly available for use upon members of administrative organizations.

erence to claims pressed upon them. One can ask how these decision loci are related to each other, how much autonomy each has in making final decisions or definitively settling claims, and what scope or kinds of decision each makes. Position or group authority increases (that is, others are increasingly dependent upon them) as the range of the decisions it makes and the types of claims it can settle without necessary approval or potential veto increases.

This variable can be seen as two proportions: the proportion of decisions made by the group (or person) relative to all types of decisions made in the organization, and the proportion of decisions it (he) settles *definitively* to those it (he) settles. The higher these proportions, the greater its *concentration of authority*. A third aspect is the variation of authority concentration between status levels in the organization. The positions at each status level may vary in degrees of authority concentration. An average of this concentration, if plotted for each level, would give an indication of the over-all pattern of authority in the organization. For example, the Weberian "ideal type" bureaucracy locates, by definition, the only autonomous position at the apex of the hierarchy. All other positions must defer to the next highest level for potential approval or appeal. This organization's *curve of authority concentration* would be a gently rising curve from lowest to second highest status level and then a sharply rising curve to the apex. More realistic curves can be established for less "pure" structures.[30] When this curve is made, a summary variable

[30] In symbolic form a position's authority (A) is

$$A_p = \frac{D_p}{D_o} + \frac{D_d}{D_p},$$

when D_p is the range or types of decisions made by a particular position; D_o is the range or types of decisions made in the whole organization; and D_d are those types of decisions a position makes definitely, that is, without potential approval or veto. My thanks to Michael Leiserson for his assistance in developing this way of symbolizing concentrations of authority.

The summary figure for the concentration of authority for any status level (L_i) is

$$A L_i = \frac{\sum\limits_{p \epsilon L_i} A_p}{\text{No. of } p \epsilon L_i}$$

of the mean authority for that level. An indication of the dispersion of authority within a status level L_i can be developed using the standard deviation formula.

ranges from organizations of very concentrated authority approximating the Weberian bureaucracy, to more diffuse organizations such as research laboratories, academic institutions, and collegial bodies.

The final aspect of organizational-authority structure is the variation in resources used to increase the probability of consistent decision or claim-settling behavior among positions and groups. Assuming that all organizational members seek a relatively stable social environment, and that upper-status members have access to resources enabling them to reinforce behavior consistent with their definition of "proper" concentrations of authority, what are the types of resources used to secure compliance from organizational members? Are there characteristic compliance means for different patterns of authority relations? This aspect is closely related to those of role expectations and behavior discussed in the next section.

Etzioni's array of compliance means—from coercive through utilitarian to normative (or identitive)—is suggestive. These means are symbolic ways of summarizing certain types of resources available in variable quantities to upper-status figures in the organization to "elicit the performances [they] need and to check whether the quantities and qualities of such performances are in accord with organizational specifications."[31] Coercive means are the threats or applications of physical means for purposes of control. The use of material rewards—direct goods and services or the allocation of symbols which can be exchanged for goods and services—are utilitarian means. Finally, normative-compliance means are the allocations of rewarding symbols of prestige and esteem, such as status positions and access to decision structure. Normative-compliance means include the pressure of peers—often in other organizations, for example peer control of professional activities—to increase the consistency of behavior in the person's organization. In general, as upper-status members move from coercive toward normative means, more organizational commitment is generated. And it is quite probable that as the task and decision structure of the organization requires

---

[31] Etzioni, "Organizational Control Structure," in March, *Handbook, op. cit.*, Chap. 15, p. 651. See also Etzioni, *The Comparative Analysis of Complex Organizations* (New York: Free Press, 1961), in which these categories are first used. In the later work he substitutes identitive for normative power means.

increased positive contribution from lower-status members, the more normative compliance means will predominate. This trend suggests that the greater the diffusion of authority concentration, the more likely it is that normative compliance means will characterize the organization.[32]

Role Behavior of Public-Organization Members

A public organization can also be conceived as a multitude of formal positions designed and arranged by the upper-status members (called the dominant coalition by J. D. Thompson[33]) in accord with their image of what is necessary to fulfill the technical and control aspects of mission accomplishment. These positions become the major ground of organizational being for persons in the organization. They define the minimal set of behaviors expected of persons in related positions and provide cues for executive action. An organizational role and the cluster of expectations surrounding it encompass the occupant's social environment while he is in the partial system of organization.[34] The role is a source of psychic satisfaction or pain, often a mark of social status, and sometimes the measure of a person's sense of significance. In a sense, a person's role is largely derived from the structures defined by the organization's power, its productive capacity, and pattern of authority concentration. In this interpretation, a person's role includes all *organizational* behavior and is as difficult to encompass parsimoniously as any of the other variables.

There are at least three salient aspects of variable role behavior of concern here: first, the variation of modal social expectations placed upon organizational roles extant in the culture at

[32]This case refers to the social type of normative power. There are instances in which "pure normative power means" are used, especially in ideological and religious organizations; however, these are rarely included in public-administered organizations.

[33]Thompson, *Organization in Action, op. cit.,* p. 128.

[34]For discussion of role theory see Katz and Kahn, *Social Psychology of Organizations, op. cit.,* Chap. 3; Robert Kahn, *et. al., Organizational Stress: Studies in Role Conflict and Ambiguity* (New York: Wiley, 1964), especially Chap. 2; Bruce J. Biddle and Edwin J. Thomas (eds.), *Role Theory: Concepts and Research* (New York: Wiley, 1966); and Neal Gross, *et. al., Explorations in Role Analysis* (New York: Wiley, 1958), especially Chap. 2–5. See also Dahrendorf, *op. cit.,* Chap. 2, "Homo Sociologicus," pp. 19–87.

large; second, the condition prompting discretionary action associated with executive roles; and finally, the degree of role conflict, ambiguity, and consensus within the organization. In the first instance, it is clear that the kind of activities expected to be associated with organizational behavior vary among cultures and communities. These expectations have several dimensions, each related to the degree of commitment to organizational activities: the public-serving or self-serving orientation of members, the degree to which ascriptive or achieved attributes are expected as a major performance criteria, and orientations toward particularistic or universalistic treatment of members and clients. Similarly, the degree of potential and actual discretion characteristic of executive roles in public organizations varies from role to role.[35] As a position's autonomy increases, so do opportunities for the exercise of discretion in claim settling and initiation. Occupants may choose to exercise discretion fully, attempt to expand their range of discretion, or avoid its use. Thus, the proportion of actual to potential exercise of discretionary opportunities summarizes an important aspect of both organizational adaptiveness and personal growth.[36] Finally, the degree to which persons occupying significant roles related to a particular role occupant agree among themselves and with the occupant about what he should do and how he should behave is a significant element in the social and psychological parameters of his organizational life. Ranging from high consensus among significant others, through ambiguity, to conflict about the legitimate expectations associated with role behavior, this variable summarizes the over-all pattern of relative agreement about organizational behavior within the organization.

Role concepts provide a way of understanding the social experience of executives and other members, in terms of the values they bring into the organization, the consequences and causes of role conflict, and the parameters of discretionary activity. Theories and concepts which provide refinements in explicating the variable and suggesting the factors affecting discretion and role conflict can be of signal use in understanding public organizations.

[35]See Thompson, *Organizations in Action, op. cit.,* Chap. 9 and 10.
[36]See particularly Argyris, *op. cit.*

Consequences of Organizational Actions

The variables discussed above are, in a sense, questions of continuing concern in the understanding of public organizations within various political contexts. As questions they are not bound in time or rooted in a particular era. Their answers, however, *are* rooted in particular time frames and will differ depending upon the conditions of the time and the experiences of the seeker. It is in this connection that our last question, or variable, is included.

The social and economic conditions of a polity are affected by the actions of public organizations. Similarly, the social and economic contexts deeply affect internal structure, role relationships, and power positions of complex organizations. Several contemporary conditions especially seem to be of major importance in understanding the developments in public-administered organization today. These are conditions which characterize a time of socio-economic upheaval within a massive technologically based culture and necessarily shape answers to the other questions.

The most salient environmental feature for public organizations in most of the modern world is a social fabric which is highly *differentiated* into a multitude of institutions and organizations of greatly varied size bound together with increasing *interdependence*. While social interdependence has always been considerable in a kind of unconscious, organic sense, we now experience the interdependent consequences of *intended* relationships. Our organizational systems are more consciously linked to one another and are often designed to increase interdependence. Both the differentiation of social and political elements and their interdependence are largely consequences of economic institutions based upon very sophisticated technological developments. Through these developments, our capacity to shape our physical environment, attempt past impossibilities, and literally "invent the future" has become a reality.

Faced with these conditions, public organizations are confronted with the necessity to respond to increasingly widespread *environmental uncertainty* and *technological complexity.*[37] As

[37]These paragraphs echo a theme basic to both the Biller and White chapters below and to those by Larry Kirkhart, "Public Administration and Selected Developments in Social Science" (Chap. 5), and Michael Harmon, "Normative Theory and Public Administration" (Chap. 6).

the movement in environmental conditions accelerates, technological complexity is compounded, and many familiar patterns of administrative structure, power relationships, and behavior styles fashioned during periods of relatively stable organizational experience undergo a kind of administrative devaluation. Therefore, in efforts to recover theoretical relevance in public-organizational studies, the conditions of interdependence and uncertainty should hold a high place.

Verification in the Study of Public Organization

Thus far we have discussed two major requirements for theoretical convergence and integration: awareness of the normative directions of the theorist and clarity of the integrator's own normative presuppositions; and a set of derived analytical questions to be used as a conceptual screen for sorting out useful from inappropriate concepts, models, and theories. If our student, now well into a state of depression, hardened and fatigued, fashions a fragment of integrated theory, he is at the halfway house on the road to relevant theory. Many of us have come to rest a bit, sometimes remain, in the reflective halfway house of theory. Ultimately, however, more distance is to be traveled before the obligations of this field are fulfilled.

As fragments of integrated theory are developed and joined, they become explicit descriptions of the structure, processes, and behavior of public-administered organizations and implicit prescriptions for thought and action. Every theoretical statement is a persuasive document implicitly suggesting that we should put credence in the cause/effect beliefs of the theorist. Theoretical fragments or reformulations call for seeing the world through different or clearer lenses, and then acting in relation to the view in the new frame. From the decision-maker's vantage, it is a call to act differently, to make possibly different kinds of decisions. It is to say, "Believe the way I believe, act the way that is implied by those beliefs and the world will be better, or at least you will have firmer grounds for despair."

To the implicit conceptual and action imperatives of theories of organization, the student or administrator quite properly should respond, "Why should I believe your theory? If I am to act in significantly different ways because of it, I want to know upon what grounds it is believable." This is another way of saying that the theorist has an obligation to specify the evidence, the verifying experiments, and the propositions which *if proved false* would seriously erode or demolish his theory.

Jacob Bronowski, in his very literate paean to science, lays down the "social axiom" of science: *"We OUGHT to act in such a way that what IS true can be verified to be so."*[38] Let me modify it slightly to assert the axiom of social-science theory: *We ought to write theory in such a way that if it is false it can be verified to be so!* Theoretical credibility through attempted disproof is so seldom an emphasis in theories of organization as to be almost nonexistent. It is virtually unheard of for a theorist to specify the two, three, or four experiments or research projects which could disprove his theory. Yet without greater emphasis upon this matter, conceptual convergence will remain only that and its substantive relevance will occur only incidentally.[39]

Devising alternative hypotheses concerning phenomena of theoretical importance in public organizations, specifying the single or several crucial researches with their alternative outcomes, each excluding one or more hypotheses, and then carrying out the research is a cycle of activity seldom attempted in our field.[40] We see almost no examples of the specification of alternative hypotheses concerning the same phenomenon. The field is afflicted by the single theory-hypothesis syndrome of the "All Encompassing Theory Which Can Never Be Falsified."[41]

It is the task of students of public organizations to devote their intellectual labor to linking analytical questions derived from

[38]Jacob Bronowski, *Science and Human Values* (New York: Harper Torchbook, 1959), p. 74; the emphasis is his.

[39]See H. L. Zetterberg, *On Theory and Verification in Sociology*, 3rd enlarged ed. (Totowa, N.J.: Bedminster Press, 1965) for an excellent discussion of verification in the social sciences, particularly appropriate to theories of public organization. Theory verification is, of course, verification in the probabilistic sense.

[40]The best example of this process devoted to material of interest to the study of public organization is P. Sperlich, *Voters in Conflict* (working title), (New York: Rand McNally, 1970). It is a most effective attack on simplistic notions of congruence or conflict-avoidance assumptions in social science.

[41]See John R. Platt, "Strong Inference," *Science* (October 16, 1964), pp. 347–353, reprinted in John R. Platt, *The Step to Man* (New York: Wiley, 1966), pp. 19–36, for a cogent discussion of this process in the natural sciences.

explicit normative directions with theoretical formulations stated in ways so that their assertion of cause/effect beliefs about public organizations may be shown false if they are so. It is our task to find the *juncture of optimum disproof*—framing the problem in ways which enable the rejection of one explanation and the acceptance of another. Without much greater attention to this, the credibility of theory will not improve and its relevance to the issues of major concern in the polity will be left obscure. Empirical research without theory is barren; theory without normative awareness is pernicious; normative awareness without conceptual analysis and research is a denial of intellectual responsibility.

Conclusion

This discussion is about the future. I agreed at the outset that the organizational sublimation of politics is upon us; it has gone some distance already and I think will continue at an accelerating pace. As the spread of technological systems grows, more and more of the organizational capacities of a polity are required to realize technological potential. This requirement leads to organizations of increasing size and drives up their internal and external interdependence and complexity. I submit that this growth will continue as long as the western world defines progress in terms of increasing economic and organizational capacity. As the fabric of a society takes on a quite complex texture, all organizations of large scale take on the character of public institutions regardless of their original legal character. Using the term *complex society* is another way of summarizing the pervasiveness of complex organizations, and asserting the crucial character of these organizations as a source of change and as a major definer of social, economic, and political reality. This function has prompted a situation in which public organizations are becoming qualitatively different from their predecessors; in many ways history is a spurious, uncertain teacher and traditional categories are no longer sure guides to either thought or action.

To the degree the analysis presented here is sound, there are several implications for how the young and near-young students of public organizations approach the future of this field. It is, after all, their future, for they will make it. The implications for our intellectual labors have been outlined above. At minimum it suggests a hardy sprinkling of normative introspection and discourse, and theory integration and verification. Implications for teaching are implicit: We must engage our students in this enterprise as well, though that will require students to be a good deal more capable than has seemed necessary in the past. It also means that in the final analysis we must begin to conduct policy research based upon clear normative awareness and the analytical questions implied by that awareness and conducted with a degree of rigor seldom encountered in current literature.

In a sense, the analysis of public policy and the operation of public-administered organizations are much too important to be left predominantly to the policy-maker and the administrator. Shaping public policy and the conduct of public affairs require a relatively high sense of certitude regarding the cause/effect beliefs about the political-organizational world. Before decisions can be reached and acted upon with confidence, we should be assured that the descriptive notions upon which they are based have some correspondence to reality. I do not think that can be assumed at present. The study of public organization should add to that assurance. We are under an urgent requirement to recover substantive and analytical relevance so that our intellectual efforts afford insights and understanding about the major changes of our culture and clarify our vision of what *can* be the future as well as what *is* present and past. Unless much more vigorous attention is paid to this recovery, we shall preside over the continued decline and withering of Public Administration as an intellectual enterprise.

Comment: The Pursuit of Relevance

Edward Friedland

If one wanted to characterize the predominant flavor of our intellectual business at the Minnowbrook Conference, he would surely note the attention devoted to discussions of values. And nowhere is the shift of concern on the part of students of Public

Administration away from improvements in technique and toward the examination of purpose illustrated more clearly than in Professor La Porte's discussion. Citing the inadequate, indeed the virtually nonexistent, state of normative analysis within the field, he rightly argues the need for systematic inquiry into the evaluative suppositions inherent in the conceptual structure of organization theories, the values which inform administrative choice, and the values that shape our own choices as scientists engaged in the construction of theories about complex public organizations.

It does no injustice to Professor La Porte to suggest that his perception of the need for such normative analysis is an important contribution to our understanding of the basic problem of Public Administration not because of its originality—for the need for such inquiry has long been noted—but because of the obvious intensity of his feeling about the need for it. He is most eloquent in depicting the stakes of the intellectual enterprise which he calls for.

The Search for an Integrated Theory

La Porte's aspiration toward an integrated theory of complex public organizations encompasses far more than have similar appeals made in the past. For plainly there is a psychic dimension in his discussion which one would not encounter in less recent reflections on the state of the discipline. His contention is not merely that the creation of such theory is a scientific necessity in order to achieve a body of descriptive propositions whose verifiable accuracy will permit us to accurately predict and ultimately to enlarge and refine our power to control the behavior of public organizations. Even if we were to be delivered from our scientific frustrations by some as yet unknown Isaac Newton of Public Administration and could create this kind of theory, we would be in an intellectual condition which is necessary but not sufficient to satisfy the author. For he is engaged in a quest that transcends the more usual requirements which social scientists impose on their theoretical labors. By his own description, his is a search for meaning, for a personal "normative understanding" of the basic social issues and their significance for the goals and design of public organization. Briefly, what he is after is a combined general theory of public organization and guide to the perplexed.

Elsewhere I have argued that rejection of the "decision-making" approach as the organizing conception of a truly integrated theory of Public Administration has been premature.[1] I believe that a careful examination of La Porte's concerns will bear out my claim even though he explicitly denies the possibility. I do not disagree with his conclusion that the vast majority of studies focused on the process of decision making have paid inadequate attention to the substance or content of decisions. Nor is it possible to overlook what has been the almost exclusively behavioral preoccupation of its advocates. But, and this is the crucial "but," the study of decisions, properly envisioned, is able to restore relevance to the study of complex organizations. It does this by restoring philosophical emphasis upon the questions that La Porte and most people care most about, namely, how and what to choose.

Indeed, the fundamental truth which students of decision making must realize is that all decisions depend upon normative suppositions. Whether the problem at hand involves the determination of public policy, the reshaping of organizational structures, or the selection of concepts upon which to build a more satisfactory theory of Public Administration, evaluative standards are a prerequisite to choice. La Porte's discussion testifies to the growing recognition that our responsibility as social scientists requires us to examine explicitly the normative perspectives that are inherent in our formal analytic models and in the way we conceive of social reality. It is precisely this kind of awareness to which students of Public Administration can be directed by the decision-making approach.

While the task of calibrating the intellectual tools of our discipline with regard to the standards of evaluation implicit therein is as necessary as it is difficult, it still can solve only part of the problem La Porte portrays. For his problem requires more than analysis. As a theorist and a concerned citizen he must *choose*. Thus, no matter how much skill we are collectively able to summon for the unmasking of normative standards incorporated in our models and modes of reasoning, the ultimate

[1]*The Study of Decisions* (New York: Appleton-Century Crofts).

responsibility for the values upon which his choices are based rests with him. A strong point of this discussion, in my view, is the author's willingness to accept that burden and to indicate, explicitly, his own normative predisposition: *"The purpose of public organization is the reduction of economic, social, and psychic suffering and the enhancement of life opportunities for those inside and outside the organization."*

It is easy, and therefore occasionally tempting, to criticize general value statements on grounds that they are difficult to operationalize. I shall refrain from doing so, however, partly in recognition of the fact that to produce a suitably operational set of prescriptions along the lines suggested by the above quotation would require more than one paper, and perhaps more than one lifetime; and partly because it is more instructive to examine some of the logical implications of the statement in its present form.

It seems clear that the author's concern with the consequences of organizational action is ultimately psychological. And, given his primary emphasis on the reduction of suffering, I believe that his normative premise can be best described as Buddhist in its ethical perspective. But regardless of its philosophical origin, the formulation as presented poses certain logical problems; specifically those raised by the existence of situations in which trade-off opportunities among the criteria are possible. For example, what guidance does the statement provide if we are considering a proposal that we believe will cause suffering to those within the organization in order to "enhance the life opportunities" of its clients? Or, to select a conceptually more simple but socially no less vexing problem, what is to be done where a reduction in economic suffering can be procured at the cost of some additional psychic suffering?

While these sorts of examples can be easily multiplied and fleshed out with reference to an enormous variety of actual proposals to improve the operation of complex public organizations, the fact of their existence could scarcely have gone unnoticed by the author. But he is not engaged in the writing of normative formulae. His main point is analytical: Our conceptions of value determine the kinds of phenomena we theorize about. And thus, rather than refine his own view of the proper goal of public organization, he establishes the implication of his normative premise for the task of creating an integrated theory of public organizations. In effect he argues that such a theory cannot be built on a purely behavioral basis, but instead must be founded upon a conception of "the valuable," the dimensions of which identify the kinds of phenomena to be investigated.

If I understand correctly, his view of "the valuable" coincides closely with what I have suggested is the central feature of the decisionist approach to social science: attention to the distribution of choice in society. As I see it, the range of his requirement for an integrated theory of public organization extends beyond the familiar concern with determining who gets what, when, and how, to include inquiry into the nature of public organizations insofar as their actions influence both who decides who *gets* what, when, and how, and perhaps of still greater importance, who decides who *does* what, when, and how. Where he speaks of social justice and the opportunity of those within organizations to face creative challenge and engage in "personal encounter," he is most surely and directly recommending that our theories permit us to assess the kinds and extent of choice that the activity of public organizations present to members of society.

Some Issues of Scientific Theory

A number of additional comments pertaining to La Porte's view of the theoretical tasks ahead are in order.

First, and most important, his paper demonstrates a basic understanding of the significance of scientific theory rarely encountered in the work of social scientists. His stress on the fact that scientific inquiry has an indispensible role to play in both our ability to "tell it like it is" and our ability to "tell it like it can be" is most apt. Although we are enjoined to recover "a sense of normative salience" and "substantive and analytic relevance," the author does not let it go at that. His argument does not degenerate to the point of simply cursing the darkness of our present theories of Public Administration. Nor does he resort to that last and fashionable refuge which he poetically describes as "peevish criticism or the wholesale rejection of

complex organizations as a legitimate form of human association." Instead, he announces what I consider to be our continuing
scientific obligation by asserting that "normative awareness without conceptual analysis and research is a denial of intellectual
responsibility."

Second, it is important to note that while the methodological
demand that our theoretical propositions be cast in a form consistent with the possibility of empirical falsification seems reasonable, it carries with it two implications that I am unprepared to
accept. The first of these relates to a logical difficulty. Specifically, the fact is that as long as our theories about public organization are essentially stochastic—that is, statements of probability
or general tendency—they will not be "falsifiable" in the strict
sense of the term. Only deterministic theories can be disproved
by any set of empirical circumstances. As theorists, therefore,
we face the choice of limiting ourselves to an obsolescent mode of
theorizing or settling for probabilistic standards of truth and
falsity which no amount of empirical testing can convert to the
absolute notions of truth and falsity with which we are all more
comfortable. The second unacceptable implication is that our
theories of Public Administration will rest on straightforward
empirical evidence. If the psychic consequences of actions taken
by public organizations ought to be of vital concern to the
theorist, given the inadequate state of psychology as a scientific
discipline it follows that our own personal comprehension of
social reality must be based more upon *verstehen* than the kind
of evidence which could be used to "falsify" a prospective theory.
If our theories of Public Administration are to be relevant—at
least in that they explicitly account for the "meaning" individuals
derive from their activities inside and outside of public organizations—then for the foreseeable future we shall have to rely upon
fundamentally subjectivist techniques of "knowing." I am not
sure it is an overstatement to assert that eventually we shall
have to sacrifice either our present epistemological conceptions
or our notions of relevance.

As a final comment on the scientific issues raised, I am afraid
that the author has seriously misunderstood the enterprise of
theory building. His impatience with the lack of a unified theory
of public organizations is a natural one, and one with which each

of us will have little trouble sympathizing. But the diversity of conceptual schemes that may appear to be "babble" or merely additional "overlays" describing the same set of organizational phenomena appear so only in hindsight. Unified theory is not developed by exhortation. Nor is it likely to proceed along a linear course originating from a single well-defined notion of relevance and culminating without misstep in the unified theory of public organizations toward which La Porte aspires. A more reasonable expectation is that if such a theory is to emerge, it will do so in a manner analogous to formation of a wake as the result of a ship's motion. It will not come into being because we need it to, nor because of our unanimity in perceiving the problems to be solved or methods to be employed, but rather, because our theoretical findings prove intellectually useful to one another.

Observations on the Minnowbrook Perspective

I should like to conclude by setting forth a number of personal impressions regarding the general trend of discussions at Minnowbrook.

Despite the widely expressed concern with the turbulence of American society, a fundamentally optimistic tone permeated the sessions. Particularly in the presentations by Kirkhart, Biller, and La Porte there is an apparent confidence that the quality of life in our society can be enhanced by restructuring the social bases of organizational life. There seems to be a faith that the redesign of public organizations in accordance with a "consociational" model and the provision of extensive opportunities for client participation in their operation will bring into being a better, more meaningful life for all members of our society.

Unquestionably a part of our responsibility as students of Public Administration is to appraise (and when possible to invent) alternative institutional arrangements for the conduct of public business. But in doing so we must not become prisoners of our own optimism. Our job is not only to point the way to the solutions we desire, but also to illuminate the darker corners of choice that may actually face future administrators and those they serve. Perhaps more of our attention should be devoted to exploring the options available in a society bent on repression.

Although we do not wish it, it may be that the most significant opportunities for choice that will face future administrators and their "clients" are those which relate to the possibilities of resistance, sabotage, and rebellion.

Historically, it is hardly surprising that within the field of Public Administration there exists no body of literature which could serve as a guide to those wishing to oppose governmental authority. Indeed, the idea is likely to strike many as a curious one. However, it seems no less strange to me that, while we acknowledge the expanded and still growing role of administrative organizations in our political life, we apparently remain content to leave the examination of these problems solely to political philosophers. The latter, despite their theoretical expertise with the basic issue of resistance, are often the least knowledgeable about the realities of organization and are therefore peculiarly inclined toward the "peevishness" La Porte decries.

On a different but related point, I believe that a word of caution is in order before we embark on a program to maximize opportunities for "self-actualization." Let us remember that in this century the regimes of Hitler and Stalin give evidence of some of the ways in which man's potential can be made manifest. Consequently, our interest in seeing that each individual has the opportunity to become *all* that he is capable of being ought to be qualified appropriately. I am certain that the perennial political dilemma of the rights of individuals versus those of the community cannot be transformed into a purely psychological issue. Nor can this dilemma be solved simply by believing that it will evaporate if only men are granted freedom without restraint. Our generation of scholars—so admirably tough minded in rejecting the vague and often defective work of their predecessors—seems strangely uncritical in its apparent acceptance of a purely individualistic and essentially psychotherapeutic criterion of social value.

I would like to emphasize the need to remedy the inadequate state of our knowledge regarding client participation in the operation of public organizations. La Porte's advice that we concern ourselves with the substance as well as the processes of social decision making must hold true for our investigations of participation. In studies of decentralization and the dispersion of choice, our gaze must fall not only on who makes decisions but what they choose and what the consequences of those choices are. However meaningful the act of deciding may be and whatever the psychic benefits the knowledge that one possesses the power to influence administrative action may confer, they are not all-important. As long as others are affected by those choices, their public and political character ought to be recognized and the likely consequences of proposed schemes appraised from a society-wide as well as a particularistic standpoint.

Among the numerous arguments that have been made for and against the desirability of expanded participation, I will point out two—both illustrative of dangers against which we must guard—that I believe are sufficiently serious to warrant more careful analysis than they have yet received. The first is typified by New York City's attempt at school decentralization. Whatever one's view of the exceedingly complex cluster of issues entailed in New York's school dispute, it is clear that efforts to achieve greater community participation in several predominantly Negro areas have thus far failed. The attempt has disrupted education and amplified (or precipitated, if you prefer) racial and religious hostility to a point which can be satisfying only to the most extreme.

On the whole, I believe that much of the difficulty can be traced to the decision to proceed without reasonably clear specification of the authority to be delegated to the local governing boards as well as to the grotesque behavior displayed by key governmental officials. These features are correctable in future experiments. But participatory schemes can fail even when they operate "successfully." For example, token attempts may create the illusion of community participation without really providing its substance. Worse still, an effectively designed program of community participation may enable a government to administer repressive policies too politically or financially "expensive" to be effected by military means (for example the functioning of "Jewish Councils" under the Nazis). By their success such programs may temporarily mask the existence of underlying and irreconcilable conflicts, thereby delaying organization for resistance or revolutionary action.

Editorial Note

The general discussion in these essays tended not only to provide the setting for other discussion, but also to open up topics of debate which were related to other Minnowbrook papers and which became familiar landmarks along the rambling journey traced out by the informal Minnowbrook discussions. Some of the tone of *part* of the discussion may be suggested.

One of the conference participants attempted to tie La Porte's comments about the reduction of human suffering and enrichment of life opportunities to Maslow's notions of synergy, "healthiness," and self-actualizing which were incorporated in the essays by Kirkhart and Harmon. Another participant responded:

> But maybe the "new politics" people are right that there really is conflict in the society and all the mental health, all this "synergy" business, cannot cover up the fact that basically there aren't enough things to go around. Some people want things one way, other people want things another way, and in fact Public Administrators find themselves very shortly concerned not with how would they get to where La Porte would like us to get, but rather, considering what others have been talking about here, what the right way is to handle problems of repression.

One participant provocatively posed this question: "There is a great deal of analysis of that segment of American society that falls within our terrain which is not being done by students of Public Administration; I must confess that Stokely Carmichael and Mario Savio have done a damn sight more for my understanding of the behavior of this insane society of ours of bureaucracy than any six given scholars in the field . . .Why?" The question led to the following interaction:*

> A: The implications of this kind of a question are several: How are you going to set up your structures—say you were heading an academic department—so that the guys who want to do "different" things don't

*This exchange is quoted from the tape recordings of the conference. The process of editing tape recordings of group discussions as well as the informal nature of most of the discussions and selective nature of quotation seem to me to make it inadvisable to attempt to identify speakers. In this quotation, as in similar ones throughout this volume, I have therefore used letters to show changes in speakers.

become penalized for doing so? We know that in bureaucracy we penalize innovation. There is systematic penalizing of guys who try to be innovative, and I think in universities we systematically provide an environment that looks like it will penalize individuals who study certain kinds of things.

B: I am fed up with hearing of this unnamed establishment which represses bright young minds from studying socially relevant issues. I see colleagues all the time engaged in, and rewarded for, studying a number of the socially pressing issues, in a variety of institutions, ... If you are going to indict an establishment, for heaven's sake, say who it is and what it has done, and who has had a project rejected solely because it challenged the establishment. I just don't see this happening.

Another participant seized upon the theme of "relevant public administration" to try—albeit provocatively and somewhat combatively—to leap the "practitioner-academic gap":

A: I want to hear from the practitioners. I want the practitioners to tell me just what is the help they think they need. It has always seemed to me that practitioners are very efficient in drafting people, channeling people, repressing people. You have PPB. Soon you will be able to press a button and annihilate a nation. Now, in doing these sorts of things, what is it you want from academics?

B: What tremendous confidence you have in "practicing public administration"—it's marvelous.

A: I consider some of the "problems" of "practicing public administration" to be of positive value. If General Hershey has budgetary problems, that's great. The more budgetary problems he has, the better I enjoy it. Do you expect *me* to offer some advice—for whatever it's worth—to make channeling of individuals more efficient?

C: I can think of two kinds of things where academics could be of some help. The first is in the area of identifying social needs. I think academic Public Administration can be of help there. The second is an answer to the previous question: Yes, we do look for a little help in "channeling" or getting the job done, because the plain facts are that even after the social needs have been identified, action is desirable and the way the system now operates on different levels makes simply illustrating it almost a nightmare. There is literally almost nothing out there but obstacles—there are people obstacles, there are obstacles of lack of money, there are obstacles of techniques—so when you are talking about Public Administration, it would seem you would have to recognize how difficult it is to expect an administrator to get the job done given the constraints upon him.

D: I think that's really the nub of the whole matter. Every obstacle in the world is out there, and I think that Public Administration as we have known it is becoming essentially irrelevant.

3

Administrative Adaptation in a Changing Society

In this chapter Orion White discusses "Social Change and Administrative Adaptation" and Matthew Crenson comments on "Contract, Love, and Character Building." White analyzes and illustrates some important ways in which our society is changing, indicates how these changes are affecting political and administrative reality, and urges the development of a cluster of adaptations through confrontation instead of our politics of contract and bargain. The "politics of love" and "adaptation by confrontation" which White analyzes as alternatives to "politics by contract" and "adaptation as conflct" are stimulating attempts to begin what La Porte called for in the last chapter: They are attempts to revive some of our theoretical notions and, moreover, they are attempts to develop a technology of adaptation with special reference to the needs of the practicing administrator.

Social Change and Administrative Adaptation

Orion F. White, Jr.

There is some evidence indicating that American society is altering in fundamental ways and at present mechanisms of social homeostasis are not bringing these alterations back into line. It

may happen, of course, that the powerful forces which work toward reequilibration will overcome these currents of change.
However, these trends appear so basic and unprecedented that
it seems useful to assume that both social structure and culture
will be affected, and that one task facing social science is reconceptualization and revision based on long-range extrapolations
depicting the shape of a different future. Moreover, because administrative institutions play such a central role in modern society, this reconceptualization must be set in a framework which
shows the relevance of patterns of change to the future operation
of such institutions. This task is attempted here. The first part of
this essay describes patterns of social change and indicates the
impact these are having on the political system. Then traditional
administrative strategies of adaptation are discussed in order to
highlight the incongruity between these strategies and the
changing environment. Finally, some assertions are made as to
a possible alternative form of adaptation which would be more
compatible with the altering environment, and some suggestions
are offered as to how this alternative might be more fully developed—into a "technology" of adaptation—and transmitted as
a part of the professional training of administrators.

Patterns of Social Change and Impacts on the Political System

Many analysts have concluded that technological development
is the first cause of social evolution, and the transition we appear
to be in now is no exception. It is the fantastic elaboration of
technological capability—that is, the capacity to control outcomes and create opportunities—which is unique about our age.
This uniqueness is the unanswerable refutation to arguments that
current patterns are analogous to former ones.[1]

The potency of technological development as a source of social
change is emphasized in the United States because its impact is

[1]See, for differing examples, *Toward the Year 2000: Work in Progress, Daed-
alus* (Summer, 1967); Jacques Ellul, *The Technological Society* (New York:
Vintage Book, 1964); Clarence Ayres, *The Theory of Economic Progress* (Chapel
Hill: The University of North Carolina Press, 1944), Chap. VIII and IX; Lynn
White, Jr., *Medieval Technology and Social Change* (London: Oxford University
Press, 1962); and Francis A. Allen, *et. al.* (eds.), *Technology and Social Change,*
(New York: Appleton Century Crofts, 1957).

primarily on the socioeconomic middle class. It is in the middle class where the motivation, skills, and position required to realize the potentialities created by technology reside. The middle-class family has the motive and skill to define its problems and ascertain the relevance of the products of technology to them, and it has the resources to obtain and utilize the products. Further, the middle class is not only a user but a producer of modern technology and as such is placed even closer to the social and cultural forces it creates through alterations in the structure of work. Since America as a civilization is primarily a middle-class phenomenon, we can see in technological developments the portents of problems and changes probably much deeper and more serious than those which stem from other sectors, such as the poor or the racial and ethnic minority groups.

Technological development, however, is a prime rather than direct cause of change. Its effects can be analyzed best by examining the intermediate conditions it has created which are directly determining qualitative alterations. There are many such intermediate conditions; the ones selected as relevant for this analysis can be described generally as *youth* in the population, *affluence* in the economy, *decision* as the key element in production, and *process* in communications.

The increasing youthfulness of our population is as obvious and as much remarked upon as the expansion of technology. This youthfulness is evident in at least three aspects. First and most simply, the mean age of the population is dropping at a rate and to an extent that would alone suggest impending changes in social and cultural patterns. Second, in addition to being younger on the average in chronological age, the population is more mature. This maturity has taken a physical form through vastly improved nutrition and the use of modern chemicals; together these measures have eliminated or substantially reduced the prevalence of many childhood diseases and the growth-retarding fevers that often accompany them. In addition, to the extent that maturity entails awareness and understanding of the world, the modern young person is undeniably more mature than his counterpart of even a generation ago—largely as a result of breakthroughs in mass communications and education. Last, the younger generation is more mature (or, more accurately, more "grown up") in its behavioral and moral aspect. Again, probably as a result of the technological developments in the area of contraception, patterns of behavior formerly reserved to adults are becoming widespread among young people. Technology has removed the physical reasons for restraint which in the past gave acute point to the moralistic persuasions of adults.

Unprecedented affluence is an offshoot of modern engineering and managerial technology which is undeniable and unique to the United States. As an economic fact, affluence has mainly meant easy availability of material objects and services for the needs and pleasure of people. As a social and cultural fact it has made clearer the shallowness of material values, and provided the psychological freedom and security to reflect upon and act toward objectives of a nonmaterial and more deeply gratifying nature. Or, failing this, it has provided the experience of frustration over "success" without fulfillment.

Marshall McLuhan has symbolized the most important aspect of the change which has taken place in the area of communications.[2] This change has been described by some as an "information explosion." This term emphasizes the central fact that "data" are being generated and "processed" (that is, analyzed and transferred) at an unprecedented rate. The effect is dazzlement and this in turn has produced the doctrine that the substance of communication is tentative—tied to a specific frame of time and circumstance—and that it is the *process* rather than the ostensible content of communication which really counts. This doctrine appears to be a deeper implication of McLuhan's insight that "the medium is the message." In the critical arena of communication which we call education, this change could have a far-reaching effect. Understanding information in terms of process would mean a shift from the emphasis on "knowledge," or what some call "dogma," as the substance of education to a definition of education as the "process of inquiry."[3] Alterna-

[2]Marshall McLuhan, *Understanding Media* (New York: McGraw-Hill, 1964), and *The Medium is the Message* (New York: Random House, 1967); a related conceptualization can be found in Edward T. Hall, *The Silent Language* (New York: Fawcett World Library, 1959).

[3]As one astute analyst (J.J. Schwab) has put it; see his "The Teaching of Science as Inquiry" (The Inglis Lecture, 1961), in *The Teaching of Science* (Cambridge: Harvard University Press, 1962), Chap. 1.

tively, it would mean a shift from emphasis on the development of "crystallized intelligence" to that of "fluid intelligence."[4] While this is a shift in emphasis rather than objective, it is profound in its implications. If widely adopted as a philosophical framework for communication and education, it would mean a complete alteration in the social structure of the classroom from public shool on up (where much socialization into authority relations takes place) with consequent impacts upon patterns of authority in society generally.

Moreover, the revolution in communications is for the most part responsible for the unmasking of key organizations and institutions in American society which has been taking place over the last few years. Sometimes inadvert, but nearly always merciless, exposures of the workings of our institutions—and the personalities and private manners of their key figures—have become common occurrences in our national life. In the past such instituions enjoyed relative privacy and a good deal of public confidence, deference, or even reverence as a result. But now, as various media have laid to open view the "reality behind the image" of some of these institutions, the patterns of deference of the past might alter. The consequences of this penetration by the public eye could be far-reaching, especially insofar as such revelations have tended to discredit institutional images and lower public confidence in them. And at least one analyst has correlated propensity to violence in societies with the degree of status ambiguity of key institutions.[5]

Another fundamental but subtle change which is being wrought by modern technology is a transformation of work. Whereas traditionally production was seen primarily as activity—the, performance of clearly indicated and concrete acts—it is increasingly becoming a process of decision, even though both aspects obviously continue to be interrelated parts of the production process. The aerospace industry, which is in many important ways the precursor of things to come in the economy, provides an

---

[4]John L. Horn, "Intelligence—Why It Grows, Why It Declines," *Trans-Action* (November, 1967), pp. 23–31.

[5]Arthur Stinchcomb, "Social Structure and Social Organization," in James G. March (ed.), *Handbook of Organizations* (Chicago: Rand McNally, 1965), pp. 142–193

excellent example of this development.[6] This change means that most people, particularly those of the middle class, will not be engaged in the actual production of economic goods, but rather in efforts to contribute to the abstract process preceding actual production which is called very generally "decision rationality." The effect of this change is to make work itself less comprehensible both to the individual performing it and to others. A related and more traditional development—the specialization of the modern job role—reinforces this problem.

What changes are these developments producing which are relevant to the operation of the political system? In very general terms, three changes are discernible: a rising demand for the equalization of power, increasing awareness and sensitivity to the inconsistencies of the ideological framework of American culture—what we call most generally "The American Way of Life"—and what could best be characterized as a breakdown in the "norm of reciprocity."[7] The demand for equalization of power has taken many institutional and ideological forms. At its worst it is "protest without point": a juvenile and purely emotional reaction to established authority which is characteristic of younger generations making a chronological transition. This reaction is its traditional form, however; it is the demand for power equalization in its more sober and sophisticated shape which is the significant new phenomenon. This aspect of the power-equalization demand amounts to an assertion that authority can be exercised legitimately only within functionally defined areas strictly limited by technical boundaries.[8] This demand that authority not be exercised through spheres of power

[6] Robert O. Smith, *Major Factors in Aerospace Planning and Decision-Making,* a George Washington University Program of Policy Studies in Science and Technology Monograph.

[7] See, for a fuller discussion, Gideon Sjoberg, H. Donald Hancock, and Orion F. White, Jr., *Politics in the Post-Welfare State—A Comparison of the United States and Sweden* (Bloomington, Indiana: Carnegie Seminar on Administrative and Political Development, 1967).

[8] Robert T. Golembiewksi has argued persuasively that the problems of line-staff relations in management can be solved through arranging authority along these lines. See Golembiewski, *Organizing Men and Power: Patterns of Behavior and Line Staff Models* (Chicago: Rand McNally, 1967). He relates much the same basic concept to a normative framework in his *Men, Management, and Morality* (New York: McGraw-Hill, 1965).

is in part a contemporary form of the traditional reaction to overextension of expertise,[9] and is a fundmental challenge to the concept of perquisites of rank which reduces all ranks to the plane of functionality. There is obviously a point here. Authority does tend to expand beyond the function which should define its scope; when it does so it becomes dominance and hinders functional "feedback." However, to equalize power by strictly defining authority relationships raises sticky problems. This dilemma can be indicated by imagining the discussion which would follow the statement of the student seeking to equalize his power vis-à-vis a professor: "I will listen to you only so long as you are saying something that is on the point of what I want to learn, and when you get off this point, I may stop you and argue with you about the questions of relevance and importance."

In addition to the demand for redefinition of key authority relations so as to equalize power, an argument is being raised that basic values and aspects of the American life style are inconsistent with human happiness. This lesson, some say, can be learned from the "hippies."[10] This type of critique of American middle-class culture is more than a decade old—going back at least to *The Man in the Grey Flannel Suit* and *The Organization Man.*[11] The difference now is that a large number of the middle-class people are in circumstances of affluence that can support in fact a decision such as the central figure in Wilson's novel took. The fruits of a materialistic society have made the conscious rejection of materialism a palpable alternative to middle-class Americans. In addition, other inconsistencies—placed under such rubrics as "poverty in the midst of plenty," "discrimination in the land of the free," and "injustice under rule of law"—have been made tangible by the advent of true affluence. Probably no other social circumstance is as powerful in promoting such problems into salience as affluence, since it leaves no

[9]Michael Walzer, "Radical Politics in the Post-Welfare State," *Dissent* (January-February, 1968), pp. 26–40.

[10]Fred Davis, "Why All of Us May be Hippies Someday," *Trans-Action* (December, 1967), pp. 10–18.

[11]Sloan Wilson, *The Man in the Gray Flannel Suit* (New York: Simon and Schuster, 1955); and William H. Whyte, *The Organization Man* (New York: Simon and Schuster, 1956).

excuse for their continuation. If necessity promotes invention at the technological level, at the societal level it may be that lack of necessity demands innovation.

One element of social structure—if not the most powerful—which maintains traditional patterns is the ubiquitous norm of reciprocity: "Don't bite the hand that feeds you."[12] The younger generation is still fed to a significant extent by the older—and indeed it is being fed better than ever—but now it is biting harder than it has in the past. Probably all of the intermediate effect of technology described earlier combine to account for this reaction. The institutions and institutional figures of the older generation's establishment have been and are being exposed to a painfully complete extent. There are more people in the younger generation and they are more mature and secure than generations of the past. "They have it too good" is often the retort, but this does little to enforce the patterns of deference and subordination which have worked in the past to maintain the basic outlines of the traditional social structure.[13]

The summary picture of relevant social changes going on in the United States involves these elements: Forces have been set in motion which are resulting in demands for the limitation of authority in a way that reasserts the autonomy of the individual, at a time when some of the basic inconsistencies of our way of life have been starkly exposed, and when one of the critical means by which societal patterns are maintained (the process of reciprocity between generations) is losing its viability.

The Ideological Focal Point in Patterns of Social Change

The pattern outlined above stresses the primary and intermediate aspects of the changes we are experiencing, but in terms more concrete than abstract, so a question remains as to the *philosophical* context of these changes. This context is set by the creed from which we have developed the "way of life" which is undergoing change. More specifically, it is the ambivalence of

[12]See Alvin W. Gouldner, "The Norm of Reciprocity: A Preliminary Statement," *American Sociological Review* (April, 1960), pp. 161–178.

[13]For a suggestive formulation on the dynamic which might be at work in breaking down this norm, see the experiment on lying and cognitive dissonance reported in Leon Festinger, "Cognitive Dissonance," *Scientific American* (July-August, 1964), pp. 677–715.

this creed on the point of how people—or, at the level of organization, collective political entities—are to be *regarded* and, consequently, how they can be expected to *relate* to one another.

There are many ways to illustrate this ambivalence. One can cite, for example, the ambiguities and inconsistencies of the political theory underlying the design of our governmental structure, or examine from a philosophical perspective the range of contemporary public policies. What is highlighted through such analyses is the admixture of *consensual* and *conflictional* elements in our ideological framework.

Consensual elements in our creed derive from its abstract philosophical origins. Here we see man depicted as intrinsically worthy and intellectually sound. He is shown to be basically of good will toward his fellows and even—to the extent that the concept of the public interest entails this—capable of "love" in his political action. It is from this assessment of man that our greatest and most fundamental principles derive. It is on the basis of this set of principles, further, which we as members of a political system putatively share the deep and binding consensus necessary to hold the system together.

In fact, however, as is well acknowledged now, our political theorists (most notably Madison) held some less sanguine notions as to human nature which introduced a highly problematic bifurcation into their theory and consequently into the structure of our governmental system.[14] This view derives primarily from the economic aspect of human existence and it is centered on the idea of self-interest at the individual level and faction at the political level. In this light, man is shown to be lacking in altruism and can only achieve a broadly oriented public policy through a structure which balances narrow interests in a "deal" where all or most parties benefit somewhat.

The dualism of principle and structure in our system has gone further than a simple discrepancy in philosophy and plan; there is a hiatus between plan and practice. This break has come about because the basic value questions which are glossed over in the framework set up by the Constitution have been fought out in the concrete specification and implementation of values and

---

[14]This is analyzed best in Robert Dahl, *Preface to Democratic Theory* (Chicago: University of Chicago Press, 1956).

procedural rules. This struggle has remained implicit because it has been carried out primarily in the economic and only secondarily in the political sector. Hence political practice was subtly shaped after the model of man and organization assumed for the economic sphere.

In sum, our ideals specify a view of man and human relations that argues for a general consensus as the determinant of most of our basic policy questions. Our practice, drawn from economic principles, expects conflict to decide the answer to questions of resource allocation. The result is simply that we have an ambivalent or inconsistent political formula.

It is only now—after our system has developed in the directions outlined above—that this fact is being brought home to the alienated dispossessed who share neither economic nor political power, and the disaffected affluent, who share middle levels of economic position but are politically victims of the concommitant centralization of economic and political power. If we had not said one thing and done another where our principles were concerned, at this point in our history our ideals would not have been so profoundly unrealized.

The present period of disorientation is at least producing a clearer definition of the alternatives for resolving this inconsistency. A sophisticated and growing far-right group is formulating an alternative based on the economic view of man as exclusively self-interested. This position is backed by a libertarian ethical philosophy.[15] Because this alternative conceptualizes human relations purely in terms of negotiations and bargains, it can be said to offer a "politics of contract." The so-called "new left," on the other hand, is actively seeking—though without being able fully and clearly to articulate it—a system which serves transcendental values through a process of consensus where the ethical premises are seen as absolute. Because the term in its broad sense is descriptive, but more

---

[15]See the *New Individualist Review: A Journal of Classical Liberal Thought.* The neoliberal economics is stated most notably by Henry Simons, Friedrich A. Hayek, Frank Knight, Willhelm Ropke, Alexander Rustow, and Milton Friedman. For a representative statement, see Milton Friedman, *Capitalism and Freedom* (Chicago: University of Chicago Press, 1962). Libertarian social philosophy can perhaps be seen most clearly in the works of Ayn Rand, whose "philosophy" has already made a sizable impact in the United States.

because it is a public catch-word of the movement, this alternative can be said to offer a "politics of love."[16]

At bottom what is at issue here is the cultural question described above: How shall man's nature be defined and what assumptions, therefore, are to be made in structuring relations between men? It is only under extraordinary conditions that such a question is raised explicitly in a society. But current conditions in our society are raising the question in a straightforward fashion, so that there seems little or no room for equivocation in the answer.

The Emerging Alternative Reflected in Major Institutions

The emergence of this question and the framework of alternatives apparently arising for its answer are of importance because, while the question is taking one form as a political problem of policy formation and process setting, it also marks a cultural change which could transform the political arena itself. It is possible to see the alternatives of contract versus love in four major institutional areas: the family, the church, the corporation, and higher education.

The Family

Much attention has been devoted recently to the changing nature of the American family, and it has been noted that changing economic status is a key variable. The argument is cogent: Economic independence has led to a redefinition of the balance of power between male and female. In addition, the changing nature of work is reinforcing this effect.[17] Work as creating rational decision is far too abstract even to comprehend fully as an activity, much less to provide the basis for deference to the male work

---

[16]The best method of assessing the new-left position is to follow current magazine and newspaper accounts of their activities. For a basic—and journalistic—background view, see George Thayer, *The Farther Shores of Politics* (New York: Simon and Schuster, 1967), Chap. 15. Also see Paul Jacobs and Saul Landau, *The New Radicals: A Report with Documents* (New York: Vintage Books, 1966).

[17]See Kenneth Keniston, *The Uncommitted: Alienated Youth in American Society* (New York: Harcourt, Brace and World, 1965), especially pp. 277–300; Clifford Kirkpatrick, *The Family* (New York: The Ronald Press, 1963), Chap. 6 and 7; and Warren G. Bennis and Philip G. Slater, *The Temporary Society* (New York: Harper and Row, 1968), Chap. 2 especially.

role. This change in role, plus the increasingly guaranteed security of the middle-class professional, tends to put the male-female family relation on a purely person-to-person, rather than role, basis. On this new basis the relationship must be restructured and the alternatives for this restructuring are, in a very real sense, love or contract. Either a deeply personal relationship where the partners "actualize" themselves through each other results, or an accommodation which mutually satisfies individually defined needs will be implicitly or explicitly negotiated and a contract struck.[18] Or, of course, a mixture of these might occur as the effort to restructure the relationship remains unresolved. The effects of this redefinition will be seen more and more clearly as future generations are socialized under these conditions. A major effect might be to reinforce the movement toward equalization of power relationships.

The Church

Whereas economic developments seem to be the primary cause for shifts in family patterns, all of the conditions created by technology described above appear to be effecting an alteration in religious institutions. The "clientele" of churches in the United States has become liberated from the social, economic, and physical restraints which gave relevance to orthodox religious codes in the past. At the same time a fundamental reorientation in theology has been occurring which can be summarily characterized as a shift from a codified ethic or dogma to a situational ethic which emphasizes a *process* of individual decision.[19] This change itself means that one of the critical ecological supports for traditional bureaucratic organization—religious socialization to codified behavioral rules—is being

[18]An excellent description of these two styles in interpersonal relations can be seen in Herbert Shepard, "Changing Interpersonal Relations in Organizations," in March, *op. cit.*, pp. 1115-1143. The general nature of the concern for new types of interpersonal relationships can be seen easily in the mass media, as apparently "encounter groups" and "sensitivity training" are rapidly and widely diffusing through our culture.

[19]See Edward LeRoy Long, Jr., "The History and Literature of 'The New Morality,' " in Harvey Cox (ed.), *The Situation Ethics Debate* (Philadelphia: The Westminister Press, 1968), pp. 101-116; and Tomas W. Ogletree, "From Anxiety to Responsibility: The Shifting Focus of Theological Reflection," *The Chicago Theological Seminary Registry* (March, 1968), pp. 1-23.

removed, with perhaps deep consequences for the social pattern of organization through bureaucracy. The meaning for the relationship of religious institutions to their members is unclear because the dialogue has not progressed far, but it seems that it is possible to view the change in terms of the love-contract dichotomy. From one point of view, a move to the situational ethic means simply that a deal is being struck whereby churches are trading freedom from strict and specific moral constraints for continued support as an institution. From another perspective, the move seems motivated by a desire to effect—both for churches in their relations to members and for individuals among themselves—the concept of religious love Christians call "agape," which emphasizes the personal and individual nature of moral responsibility. Probably a rationale for the change can be formulated which would make it either a contract or love action, but it seems that this change could be as well conceptualized in one as the other of these terms as it is developing, and it will be another new and powerful socializing force.

The Corporation

The family and church have traditionally been considered—in the terms used here—as love-oriented rather than contract-oriented institutions. In the business world—particularly as it is epitomized in the modern corporation—the reverse has been true. It is not surprising then that in a period of change we should see an apparent movement within corporations toward a greater emphasis on the love orientation. This move is evidenced primarily in a now well-developed business philosophy which sees the modern corporation as operating under a "corporate constitution" constraining it in ways which insure that it will contribute to the "public interest."[20] In addition, however, a potentially more significant movement is the increasing emphasis upon improving interpersonal relations in corporate organizations. The modern techniques employed in this regard are much more personal, therapeutic, and "affective" in nature than the old human-relations movement. Indeed, many participants in

[20]For a critical overview, see Emmette S. Redford, "Business as Government," in Roscoe C. Martin (ed.), *Public Administration and Democracy* (Syracuse: Syracuse University Press, 1965), Chap. 4.

these programs report that the experience makes them capable of truly effective relationships for the first time in their lives. The major purpose of such programs, of course, may be only to improve the efficiency and effectiveness of the corporation's personnel: to better capitalize on the "contract" between the organization and its members. Therefore, as in the case of the family and the church, there is much question as to what form the structure of this institution will take ultimately. It is much less uncertain, however, that the corporation of the future will be different than it is today.

The University

The institution most notably under attack by elements seeking changes in it is the university. The pattern of dissent and the issues over which it has occurred are well known. Students feel that institutions of higher education have become bureaucratic and mainly concerned with increasing funds, prestige, and control. In order to do this, the charge goes, these institutions have compromised the true values of intellectuality in order to fit more securely into the "system" and get along better with the "establishment," even though in the critics' view, the "system" is basically immoral. The course of action students are choosing for coping with this situation is overt, often violent, dissent. As in other institutional areas, the outcome of this period of transition is not obvious. On one hand, there is a definite move to disengage the institution from the affective aspects of its relationship to students which is summarized by the *in loco parentis* doctrine utilized in the past. Such a move, taken alone, seems to indicate a trend toward a purely contractual relationship.[21] When coupled with attempts to involve the institution completely in the students' personal and intellectual development while leaving him free of overt regulation, however, one can see the beginnings of a truly affective relationship. The outcome will probably depend on the practicability of the many "cluster" and "residential" college plans being experimented with at various colleges and universities around the nation. Whatever the outcome, however, it will increase pressures toward change in society generally.

[21]See Burton Clark, "The New University," *American Behavioral Scientist* (May-June, 1968), pp. 1–5.

An overview of these institutions reveals a pattern of transition that is somewhat unclear but deep enough to affect both institutional structure and the elements of culture which underlie it. The inexorable, subtle forces of technological development have brought the hitherto obscured inconsistencies of our "way of life" into the open where they must be confronted and resolved in one direction or the other.

Impacts on the Political System

The political system—as the most immediate context in which public organizations operate—is the arena where the prevailing norms of decision making and negotiation are set and the chief resource inputs and exchanges take place. Hence an analysis of the impact of social changes on administration must interpret these changes for the political arena and show how the impacts of change might be transmitted through it to the administrative system.

One apparent prerequisite to such an analysis is a prediction as to which of the two directions outlined as the "politics of love" and the "politics of contract" the political system will ultimately take. Knowing the answer to this question would be of great value, but the developments described above are far too inchoate to support such a prediction. It is possible, however, to make an assessment of the impacts of these trends because they possess large commonalities. Some major consequences for Public Administration can be discerned at this point *regardless* of which turn the development takes when it reaches an unambiguous fork.

In assessing the possibilities and directions of political change, it is significant to note that political science seems to be beginning the search for a new paradigm through which to view American politics.[22] One reason such searches are initiated is the emergence of anomalies which prevailing schemes cannot comprehend. This may be what is occurring in the political science discipline in the United States. Such changes can be nothing but fundamental—that is, revolutionary—in nature, and

[22]See, for example, Theodore J. Lowi, "American Business, Public Policy, Case Studies, and Political Theory," *World Politics* (July, 1964), pp. 677–715.

they mark both a shift in perspective and in the reality being perceived.[23]

It is in this light that the currently developing critique of the pluralist model of American politics is viewed.[24] It appears, further, that much of what is being said in these critiques reflects the types of social changes described earlier. Generally described, the criticism of pluralist politics is making the point that this model does not fit the true values and objectives sought through the democratic technique of governance.

This general theme normally takes one or both of two aspects. In the first, it is said that the pluralist system of policy formation by "policy clusters" really amounts to elitist rule, in that the great majority of the polity does not participate to any meaningful extent, particularly in the formation of policy alternatives. To the pluralist argument that representation is provided at least through empathy or a sharing of attitudes between the masses and the representatives in the policy cluster, the critiques answer that pluralist subsystems are not plural at all. Rather, it is argued that they are *singular* and represent only a limited number of the possible views in particular policy areas.[25] A second and more important point is that, even assuming that representation by indirect means mirrors the opinion of the electorate accurately, such representation—whereby the represented have no effective power over the representatives—is not true representation.

These arguments reflect, it seems, the types of social development described above as arising from the "intermediate conditions" created by technology. The reaction to elitism and demand for equalization of power, and the breakdown in the norm of reciprocity (in the rejection of representation by empathy) fit

[23]See Thomas Kuhn, *The Structure of Scientific Revolutions* (Chicago: The University of Chicago Press, 1962).

[24]Some examples are Sheldon S. Wolin, *Politics and Vision* (Boston: Little, Brown, 1960), pp. 352–434; Jack L. Walker, "A Critique of the Elitist Theory of Democracy," *The American Political Science Review* (June, 1966), pp. 285–295; Henry Kariel, *The Promise of Politics* (Englewood Cliffs: Prentice-Hall, 1966); John C. Livingston and Robert G. Thompson, *The Consent of the Governed* (New York: Macmillan, 1966). For an older statement see E. E. Schattschneider, *The Semi-Sovereign People* (New York: Holt, Rinehart and Winston, 1960).

[25]A statement of this argument for a particular case is Philip Green, "Science, Government, and the Case of Rand—A Singular Pluralism," *World Politics* (January, 1968), pp. 301–326.

this pattern. The same is true for the impatience with obvious contradictions in policy arising because the system leaves some elements out of the decision arena and relies on an ambiguous consensus qualified and mediated by "overlapping memberships."

The many and various types of social disruptions as well as the implicit unease seen in this emerging critique are recent and obvious and do not need description here. It is interesting, however, to note that these disruptions may possibly be *accompanied* by a "paradigm shift" in the profession supposedly able to account for such events. The social and intellectual events together may indicate that the system is reorienting.

The political system of the future may be different in many ways. The differences of most concern in this analysis are those that relate to the *nature of interactions* between elements in the political system, since it is in this process that the administrative adaptation takes place. In a word, these interactions will become more *militant* as the political style of the system purifies into one or the other of the forms described above. This new militancy will be evidenced in those elements of the political system sensitive to changes in the broader polity: the constituencies of elected representatives, the clienteles of agencies, the Congress, the overhead political executive, and to a lesser extent, the organized interest-group associations.

This militancy may be described by looking at it in terms of the major ideological premises on which both the new left and the new far right appear to agree. Four such premises are apparent:

1. Both agree that there exists a set of fundamental values which are unambiguous and which comprehensively define proper relationships between individuals and hence between institutions and individuals. In short, the notion of tolerance is rejected. For each side, of course, these values are completely different, and can be traced back ultimately to differing views of human nature.

2. Both agree that a basic problem with the current system is the failure of honesty and openness in the operation of institutions. Related to this failure is the assertion that the present system is unable to make large, definite, and lasting commitments to lines of action.

3. Both agree that "institutionalism"—the tendency to iden-

tify the "general good" with the well-being and growth of organizations—is a wrong-headed and destructive concept of the public interest.

4. Both agree that power must be reallocated, primarily by placing within individual and group prerogative a large number of decisions now made by authoritative institutions. The emphasis here is not on content, but on process: that is, on *having* power.

A brief glance at these tenets indicates that movements into a state of purified politics—of contract or love—sufficiently extensive to reorient interactions between elements in the political system around these ideas would mean a deep change in these relationships. The change would be especially notable ministrative adaptation, given the way it has been conceptualized traditionally.

The Traditional Conceptualization of Administrative Adaptation: Adaptation as Conflict

In the "traditional conceptualization" (this term is used advisedly as a summary for a wide array of bits and pieces, some obvious, some obscure) the reverse of the four premises listed above form the set of basic assumptions. It has always been assumed that administrators operate in an environment where basic issues of values or objectives have been settled in the legislative process. No one actually in administration believed this, of course, and it is often pointed out in political-science literature that the real case is that such issues were simply transferred from one arena to another through the legislative process.[26] Nonetheless, the fiction does serve as a myth which administrators can use to gloss over questions of basic policy orientation in their attempt to manage political tensions. Such questions are "answered" by appeals to symbols which call up the outline of a vague assumed consensus, or to the norms of tolerance and compromise.

A combination of the recognizable necessity to cope with difficult problems of setting the basic policy and a firm belief in "institutionalism" leads to the lack of candidness which

---

[26]This is, of course, the way David Truman described Public Administration in his classic formulation, *The Governmental Process* (New York: Alfred A. Knopf, 1962), Chapter XIV.

characterizes administrative adaptation. Given the ideas that basic questions are not at stake and that to protect and build institutions is good, it is understandable that norms of communication allow something less than total honesty. Hence budgets are padded, data are distorted or destroyed, the existence of reports is denied, presentations are exaggerated, and so on. All such occurrences are commonplace in administrative politics. Further, decisions are not made clearly: "hanging back" and "keeping options open" are the more prudent tactics even though the appearance of decisive action is attempted.

This conduct is absolved by the very powerful rationalization of institutionalism—identifying "the good" with the organization—and in the name of the reality of a *power* equilibrium, that is, keeping the allocation of power in society constant. This rationalization is an implicit—but the most binding—assumption under which administrators attempt to implement their programs. It is perhaps this conjunction of the two premises of institutionalism and power equilibrium which accounts for the curious pattern of policy development in the United States. Life has gotten better and better in large part due to the actions of institutions, while patterns of power among classes and groups have changed only incidentally—though sometimes significantly —through the actions of these same institutions.

Hence all the elements of interaction which the new militancy would reject are present in the traditional form of administrative adaptation: avoidance of basic value questions, qualified honesty, institutionalism, and deference to the existing distribution of power. To make the last mentioned point is not to say, however, that administrative institutions avoid struggles for power. Indeed, just the reverse is the case. That such struggles exist is given testimony by the fact that the chief scheme traditionally used for conceptualizing agency-environment relations is "co-optation" (modern organization theory, still scant on interorganizational interactions, has added surprisingly little to this basic notion).[27] Co-optation is an idea centered on the concepts of power balance

[27] A recent article which overviews this work is Shirley Terreberry, "The Evolution of Organizational Environments," *Administrative Science Quarterly* (March, 1968), pp. 590–613; see citations there and in addition Paul R. Lawrence and Jay W. Lorsch, *Organization and Environment: Managing Differentiation and Integration* (Boston: Graduate School of Business Administration, Harvard University, 1967).

and power struggle. Agencies "formally co-opt" (that is, "use external elements to their own ends") when they are smart enough and powerful enough to get away with it and "informally co-opt" (actually share the policy-determination function) when external elements have the upper hand.[28] But the basic objective is getting the upper hand in the struggle for power. This fact is normally kept implicit in instances of administrative politics because such cases are seen most often in terms which emphasize concepts like the "public interest" and the struggles by which it is defined.

The view of such struggles as contests to define the public interest is a euphemism, but it is an honest euphemism. Our system implies—through its reliance on multiple institutional checks—that to struggle for power is to do right and to possess power is to be right. Perhaps the best example on this point is Neustadt's analysis of the presidency, which indicates that the President best protects the national interest by protecting and fostering the interests of his office.[29]

This aspect of our system is fundamental and it derives, it seems, from two cultural foundation stones: our legal system and our economic system. The adversary system of law used in the United States has shaped the political system in a number of ways, and one of the most important is through the premise that truth is inherent in the operation of a process of competition.[30] This assumption says that the process is right and the winners just. There is a critical assumption about the process, however— that the parties involved in the process serve first the goal of justice—that is easily and all too often forgotten. To forget this goal and seek only to win by any means allowed by, or *implied* by, the rules, is to pervert the idea of the process and change it from one of confrontation to one of conflict, that is, from a dialogue in the service of a principle to simply a struggle for victory.

Much the same kind of reliance on process to define right can

[28]The distinction between types of co-optation is not often noted but is clearly set forth in Selznick's work. Philip Selznick, *TVA and the Grass Roots* (Berkeley: University of California Press, 1953).

[29]Richard G. Neustadt, *Presidential Power* (New York: John Wiley and Sons, 1960).

[30]See Herbert Spiro, *Government by Constitution* (New York: Random House, 1959), pp. 211–236, for a discussion of these points.

be seen in our economic principles as they are summarized in the price system: the assumption is that the process, left alone, will create a pattern of winners and losers which amounts to the "right" allocation of resources. Here, too, it is easy to slip from the principle of competition to that of economic conflict, where the large gray areas in the rules are defined on the premise that the sole point is to win.

In politics, too, the point is to win, and the political process is one of conflict. Administrators have played this game as much as other actors in the system, and the publics with which they interact have allowed them to do it. If the type of militancy described above develops, however, it will become increasingly difficult to do this. Not only will the content of the process be different—what it is will depend on whether we move to the right or the left, but in neither case will it be much more ideologically pure—but the militants will demand that the nature of the process itself be changed.

An Alternative Conceptualization: Adaptation as Confrontation

The general ideological framework of the militants suggests their demand will be that *confrontation* be substituted for the traditional *conflict* mode. This new mode would demand that all actors in political institutions—but especially administrators—relate to elements in their environment in a way which stresses that

1. Communication of the whole truth be straightforward and voluntary. Underlying this premise is the empirical assumption that people *can be* completely honest with each other, or indeed, that the most effective type of relationship is one characterized by the absence of defensiveness.

2. All parties to the relationship be placed in equal positions in the sense that power and authority be allocated *functionally* in the manner described earlier.

3. Interactions continually take place within an explicit framework of principles based on a specification of what man is and what his purposes are. The concepts of decision by compromise, reasonableness, tolerance, or balance of interest would become irrelevant for a much wider range of issues than at present.

The purpose of this process—and it assumes that all parties to it operate on this assumption—is not simply to win in the sense of causing defeat for the other party, but rather to achieve consistency in the interpretation of basic ideological principles and in their application to various program areas. Hence, while emphasis would be placed on making the process work, it would be remembered that the overriding purpose is implementation of specific ideological principles.

Toward the Teaching of Administrative Politics as Confrontation

In order to make the change (again, assuming that conditions demand it) from conflict to confrontation, a great deal more emphasis must be placed on the study and teaching of the techniques of administrative adaptation, so that a literature supporting a *technology* of administrative politics can eventually be developed. There has traditionally been a gap in the literature of Public Administration with regard to technology, and changing conditions make the need for filling it all the more obvious and urgent. We can no longer afford to rely on long-term career socialization as the means for transfer of knowledge about these techniques, especially if they are to be the relatively sophisticated and difficult ones of confrontation.

A great deal of analytical and empirical work must be done before the nature of such a technology can be seen clearly, but at this point some major points can be discerned. A technology of administrative politics could be made up of two major parts: a *paradigm* and, to use a purely technical term, a *software* system.

The paradigm, or conceptual system, is needed to handle the ideological aspect of the confrontation-adaptation process. It would specify, if not an ideology itself, at least a process by which ideological (or ethical) discourse can be fruitfully carried out. This specification might mean the development of comprehensive value frameworks so that the structure of such schemes could be made clear, the questions they raise pointed out, and the problems of linking principle to action through interpretation seen. Developing such a conceptual system would be an enterprise in both ethics and "metaethics" (the study of theories about ethical theories), but the metaethical part would be the more important.

The need for such a system argues for a reorientation toward basic philosophical education for administrators, but to be most useful this should be framed in terms of the administrative-political situation. The apparent reemphasis in the discipline on the development of a policy science should help greatly in building this part of the technology, since it is likely that a *methodology* for policy analysis will emerge in the policy-science area.

The software of the technology would be constituted of the procedures and processes to be used for decision making in administrative-political situations. One obvious and important software aspect would be adequate training in interpersonal relations, so that administrators could meet the unusual demands of the confrontation-adaptation technique. Other professionals are prepared in this way, and public administrators need it as much or more than others. "Scanning techniques" would form a second category of software requirements. Many serious political mistakes have been made by administrators through inadequate and inaccurate scanning of their political environment. This deficiency leads to overlooking or misdefining issues and problems and to a consequent inappropriate response. One problem in this regard is the influence of decision stereotypes which grow up in program areas.[31] Processes for accurately scanning and interpreting the environment are badly needed. Techniques for problem solution are also needed and perhaps these can be drawn in part from areas of hard technology. For example, systems-analysis techniques for design of solutions to space-flight problems are being applied in the analysis of the environmental problems of cities. A technique such as this for analysis of political situations would be of tremendous help to administrators in giving coherence (and thereby strength) to their solutions to problems. As a last example, administrators need techniques for revising policy and the rules which implement it so as to keep them internally consistent and, more importantly, congruent with the reality to which they are to be

[31]Aaron Wildavsky, "The Analysis of Issue Contexts in the Study of Decision Making," *Journal of Politics* (November, 1962), pp. 712–732, provides an excellent case example of this problem.

applied. Through such a dialectical process many issues of administrative politics could be avoided.[32] This technique could perhaps be developed out of the organization-theory literature, since it demands primarily an understanding of the subtle processes which impede or aid change inside administrative systems.[33]

These notes are only suggestive and barely begin to picture a technology of administrative politics. Much more would be uncovered as research progressed, and this indicates a last point about both the desirability and feasibility of such a technology. All that is outlined here and more exists already in the minds of some effective administrative politicians who now staff high level government positions. That these people have and use this knowledge demonstrates its utility and shows that it is possible to develop and make it explicit to a large extent, even if only by extracting and systematizing it. It bears noting, however, that the development of this technology may cause reassessment of other aspects of administrative technique. The organizational structure used for administration might require fundamental revision before such a technology can be utilized.

The Problem of Transition

It may be well to conclude by raising again the first question: Are we as a society and political system going to make the transition into a state of purified politics which would give relevance to the concept of adaptation by confrontation? Even assuming that the forces working toward such change have overrun counter-tendencies toward the status quo, it is not obvious that the transition will take place. For in this transition we would suffer a severe crisis of legitimacy in our basic institutions and the protest raised would be confused and unproductive to a dismaying extent. This crisis is occurring already. Deference to institutions

[32]See Sjoberg, Hancock, and White, *op. cit.* Also, see Orion F. White, Jr., "The Dialectical Organization—An Alternative to Bureaucracy," *Public Administration Review* (January-February, 1969), pp. 32–42.

[33]See Warren G. Bennis, *Changing Organizations* (New York: McGraw-Hill, 1966); and Edgar H. Schein and Warren G. Bennis, *Personal and Organizational Change Through Group Methods: The Laboratory Approach* (New York: John Wiley and Sons, 1965).

is diminishing rapidly and in much of the protest now going on one can see new content in old forms with a confused *conflict* as a result. The resolution of such instances does not ameliorate the problems which gave rise to them. This eventuality raises an alternative of social change which has not been discussed here, and the outlines of which are not clear. It would seem to be, however, a movement into a situation where suppression is widely used to maintain society at an evolutionary stage which was satisfactory in the past and is no longer so, but where reaching a happier alternative seems impossible. This alternative is vague, but it does not seem a happy prospect and, at any rate, if it develops, all that has been said here about a technology of confrontation will be superfluous. Administrative institutions will play a large role in determining whether we move into a politics of contract, love, or suppression. One can only hope that by developing appropriate techniques for changing conditions we can effectively make a transition which will avoid a societal state in which suppression is widely used.

Comment: Contract, Love, and Character Building

Matthew A. Crenson

Orion White's paper reached me at about the time of the Democratic Convention, and I confess that I read it for the first time during commercial breaks in television coverage of the doings in Chicago. The convention was a credit to his work. Just after reading that the revolution in communications had contributed to the merciless unmasking of American institutions, I looked up to see a newsman on the convention floor mercilessly unmasking some backstage attempt to monkey with the convention's order of business. It went that way for most of the evening, with the television newscasters providing illustrative material for White's essay. I hope that my remarks will serve a somewhat similar purpose. I'm going to attempt to elaborate on the notions that he has outlined, and to suggest some of the implications that I think they have for both the study and the operation of

public bureaucracies. My remarks are—as White's were—
highly speculative.

The Politics of Contract

First, let me say something concerning the nature of those
possible political changes that White has identified and labeled.
He has captured the essential uncertainty of our present situation by describing two alternative trends and by allowing for the
possibility that one or the other or an amalgamation of both
may finally sweep through the American political system. One
of these emergent political tendencies—the politics of contract—
is described as a philosophical and empirical offshoot of a free-
enterprise economic system. In White's account, the politics
of contract promotes the notions of individual autonomy and
specific, negotiated connections between individuals. I would
add that it represents a reaction—not only of economic man, but
of bureaucratic man—to a time of troubles. In fact, it may be
that modern bureaucracies—both public and private—lie somewhere near the origin of this political tendency.

The kinds of phenomena that I associate with the politics of
contract, as White describes it, all suggest that there is something essentially noncompetitive in this political orientation. Its
representatives have, by and large, disavowed the quest for profit
maximization and taken up the cause of social stability ("law
and order," to use the current slogan). They yearn for the kind
of individual autonomy that we associate with the free market,
but they do not readily accept the uncertainty or abrasiveness
of free-market competition. The earmark of this political tendency is a preference for social and personal insulation: a desire
not to be bothered, disturbed, upset, or even excited. The inclination is today most evident in the lower-middle levels of
American society. And I don't think it entirely accidental that
many observers have perceived something very much like it
in the lower-middle levels of large, bureaucratic organizations.

Max Weber, for example talks about the obstruction of
bureaucratic rationality by the "average official" who longs for a
civil-service law that will secure his old age and provide guarantees against his arbitrary removal. Once he acquires these

protections, he has diminished the degree to which he is dependent upon his bureaucratic superiors. This example demonstrates the kind of power equalization that White discusses, as well as an increase of individual autonomy.

There is an even more striking resemblance between the politics of contract and Michel Crozier's description of strata isolation within bureaucratic organizations.[1] Middle- and lower-level bureaucrats, Crozier points out, seek to protect themselves from the "interference" of their superiors through the rigid interpretation of formal, bureaucratic rules (seniority rules, for example). These formal barriers to the exercise of discretion by superiors serve to liberate bureaucrats from the need to seek the informal protection that is provided by their equals. The result, as Crozier describes it, sounds remarkably like the politics of contract. There is a decline of diffuse, informal connections among fellow workers; an increase in individual autonomy and in the prevalence of specific, limited social relationships; and an equalization of power between superiors and subordinates. Finally, I detect that the bureaucratic situation which Crozier describes is characterized by a certain general belligerence or animosity. Strata isolation makes for a testy society.

In short, I would argue that there may be a logical convergence between the politics of contract and the politics of latter-day bureaucracy. There is also an empirical convergence between the two phenomena. Among the most militant practitioners of the politics of contract are the members of today's public-employee unions. Their aim, if I interpret it correctly, is to insulate themselves from both their clients and their bureaucratic superiors. The New York City police exert their political energies to slay the Civilian Review Board and their Commissioner openly snubs Mayor Lindsay and the Mayor's agents because he feels that he must protect the Department from "political interference." Similar examples from other kinds of public organizations would only cover familiar ground. The point is simply this: The politics of contract, as Orion White sees it,

[1]Michael Crozier, *The Bureaucratic Phenomenon* (Chicago: University of Chicago Press, 1964).

may be interpreted in part as a generalization of bureaucratic politics (or perhaps of postbureaucratic politics). As more and more Americans get absorbed into the lower-middle levels of large bureaucratic organizations, more and more of American politics gets assimilated in the bureaucratic pattern. The important thing to note is that bureaucracy has not merely responded to the existence of a political temperament, but may also have contributed to the creation of that temperament.

The Politics of Love

Now, what about the other political tendency: the politics of love? So much has been said concerning the various partisans of this political alternative—the hippies, the yippies, and all the rest—that I will keep my remarks brief.

First, I would revise Orion White's conception of this political orientation. It seems to me that the politics of love is not founded upon a belief in the essential goodness of humankind, but on a conviction that men are essentially malleable. Their values, sentiments, and behavior are thought to be molded by their social and political institutions. Change the institutions, the argument goes, and you will change the men. Get rid of the war machine, for example, and men will cease to be warlike. Partisans of the politics of love, I think, see an intimate connection between political institutions and human character. (Partisans of the politics of contract seek to sever that connection.) The idea that there is and ought to be such a connection is not new. In fact, it is ancient. The Greeks seem to have seen this same intimate relationship. An ordinary citizen who was denied membership in a political community was denied his selfhood. If he couldn't be a political animal, then he was *just* an animal. It is therefore understandable that the Greeks formed passionate attachments with their communities. But strangely enough this passionate loyalty appeared in conjunction with a shockingly high incidence of treason. Herodotus, for example, cites many Greeks who fought on the Persian side against their own home towns. And there was not only treason, but assassination, revolution, and treachery of all sorts. What the Greeks practiced was not simply the politics of love, but the politics of love-hate. I believe that we may be seeing a revival of such a politics today.

A man who believes that political events are somehow bound up with his own person is likely to have a stormy political life. He feels passionately attached to the political system, but at the same time it is capable of evoking passionate hatreds in him. He sees politics as an avenue of self-fulfillment, but it also poses the threat of self-destruction. For him, politics ceases to be a merely instrumental activity. It becomes an expressive—almost an artistic—enterprise by which he strengthens, displays, and even changes his own character.

The administrative impact of the politics of love turns, I think, on a change in the significance of participation. Participation is no longer just the means by which people influence politics, but a way for politics to influence people. Many citizens no longer regard political action as a mere instrument for affecting public policy. Even when there is little prospect of affecting policy or improving governmental effectiveness, they insist on taking action. The reason, I think, is that it's not the policies or the programs that they want to influence, but themselves. Political action has come to be regarded as a character builder. It's not necessary to look as far as the New Left or the black militants for examples of this sentiment. The participatory rationale of the Poverty Program contained a strong element of it. "Maximum feasible participation" was presented not simply as a duty of good men, but as a means by which good men can be fashioned.

The bureaucratic consequences of this point of view are not entirely clear. But I would guess that the demand for an expressive sort of participation would lead toward administrative decentralization. Herbert Kaufman has discussed this decentralizing tendency, and I recommend his discussion to you.[2] But if this movement toward decentralization materializes, I think it will look very unfamiliar to us. Until now, we have tended to see administrative and political decentralization as one of a constellation of political properties. Now that constellation is likely to be broken up. Decentralization, for example, has been associated—

[2]Herbert Kaufman, "Administrative Decentralization and Political Power," *Public Administration Review* (January-February, 1969), pp. 3–14.

at least in the minds of many political scientists—with incremental decision making. The fragmented character of American politics is seen as preventing any great leaps forward in the United States. We make "small" decisions and avoid radical departures from current practice. But, in a regime characterized by the politics of love, decentralization and incrementalism would be likely to part company. The same impulses that lead toward decentralization in this case lead away from incrementalism, or at least toward a different order of increments. The tendency toward expressive or symbolic political action is likely to produce a preference for the politically dramatic, for the radical initiative. Briefly, the kind of administration that I foresee under a politics of love is decision making by demonstration project: radical departures, but on a small scale.

Public Administration and the Making of Citizens

I think that the politics of contract and the politics of love both suggest a new focus for studies of Public Administration. Until now, students of public bureaucracy have occupied themselves with the task of explaining why bureaucrats behave as they do. They have paid relatively little attention to the consequences of administrative action in terms of impact upon the characters and attitudes of citizens. The presuppositions of the politics of love call attention to precisely these consequences. And the politics of contract may be one of those consequences: a case in which the public's experience with bureaucratic organization may have helped to shape the public temperament. Public administration is not merely the instrument for executing public policy, but one determinant of the way in which the public sees the world—particularly the political world—and their own place in it. The relationship between the everyday operations of public bureaucracies and the foundations of political order may be closer than we think. Perhaps we ought to be paying more attention to that relationship than students of Public Administration traditionally have. We ought to find out, for example, how the operations of welfare agencies affect the attitudes that welfare recipients have concerning public officials and themselves. We ought to know how the activities of police departments influence the opinions that people have concerning public authority and its exercise. In short, it is important to find out how citizens have been changed by their encounters with administrative authroity.

Editorial Note

The open discussion of the essays in this chapter tended to cluster around two points: the dangers in the promise of "confrontation" and the client-bureaucracy interface.

The discussion of the possibilities of confrontation was closely linked to Edward Friedland's comments upon the prevalent optimism at Minnowbrook and the awful potential of humans, as well as to the discussion about the probability of uncompromisable struggles and repressive social action. One question—"What about when in all honesty I think that you should be annihilated?"—stimulated the following exchange:

A: I think that in the politics of confrontation you could run into the very fundamental problem of two groups standing off and being honest about their desire to annihilate one another, that is, the confrontation might develop an insufferable breach. That's part of human reality; we know that sort of thing can happen. I have faith that it won't happen, but I admit it is always a possibility. If an insufferable breach developed perhaps we would develop an inconsistent ideology. On the other hand, suppose we trace out our values by being honest and we develop a system of action consistent with the resultant ideology. Then the questions become, will the transformation then be back to the "politics of contract" or will the evolution keep going and lead constantly to confrontation? The latter seems possible to me because it seems to me that human reality keeps changing. My personal way of looking at human and social reality is from a Meadean social-psychological perspective that reality in nature changes with almost every act. That presses upon you the need to be sensitive continuously to the development. In short form, this is the notion of developmental social reality which one can link to Maslow's hierarchy of needs which is touched on by the Kirkhart and Harmon papers.

B: This group seems completely at ease discussing confrontation without the slightest apparent concern for where confrontation might lead. Don't we have any fear that confrontation might lead to a new set of political realities where confrontation is replaced by the question "Whose side are you on?" and where there would be no more room for any kind of confrontation or disagreement?

A: I don't fear confrontation. I fear what seems to be the alternative: conflict. It seems to me that conflict comes out of very deep misunderstanding. That misunderstanding comes out of the failure to be honest. In bargaining, people cannot trust one another and we have developed in the bargaining process all kinds of involuted ways of trying to guess what the other party really wants or means. And we must develop ways of breaking this down so that we can deal with one another openly and honestly in terms of what we really want, in terms of what we really think, without the necessity to play so many of the games that are involved in bargaining.

This exchange, of course, was not the extent to which "confrontation" and the "politics of love-hate" were discussed by the participants. It does, however, give something of the flavor of one of the most persistent debates which grew out of Orion White's paper.

The second chief topic which developed from White's paper—the relationship of bureaucracies to their clients—was persistently pursued, partly because it was so closely related to other Minnowbrook papers. The following discussion about client-focused bureaucracies is suggestive of the variety of concerns aired and sentiments expressed:

A: The seduction of Public Administration by administrators [i.e., the control of the whole of Public Administration's development and concerns by the narrow and uncritical view of the practicing administrator whose plea is that Public Administration ought to be relevant to him and his problems] works against Public Administration. Administrative institutions establish structure to implement policies without realizing that the structure itself is an aspect of that policy. At my university they recently interviewed some students and one of the things that they found out was that students didn't have specific complaints exactly. Rather, they were against the whole system; they were saying, "What this university is doing is not education." Essentially, I think it's the idea that the medium is the message, and that's what administrative institutions are doing to all kinds of clients. They are establishing a structure for the implementing of policy without realizing that the structure itself is an aspect of that policy.

B: The administrator, though, very often finds himself in the middle, especially when he identifies closely with the objectives of the client. The best example I can think of is a neighborhood youth director in New York City who as an administrator was responsible for implementing an entire program; however, he identified with the problems of his client group and the big proglem was that there wasn't enough money to get the jobs done as he perceived his role. So he worked to help the clients get together and demonstrate for more money; of course, he was suspended. The dilemma is serious for the administrator; on the one hand he is trying to administer a program, and on the other he is identifying with his clients and trying to bring about changes which he believes are right and proper.

C: I think that the kind of interaction that White was speaking about probably already takes place at the lower levels of most of our government agencies now in terms of the services they are dispensing. We are, because of the increased professionalization at these lower levels, achieving better relationships between clients and the professionals in the agency. Where the difficulty comes in, it seems to me, is working up through the entire organization with this attitude. We have centralization of input (men, money, and so on), and decentralization with regard to the products and services we dispense. In a university, for example, a teacher has quite a bit of freedom about what he is going to teach his students, but very little control of the facilities and so on that he is going to have for teaching them. The individual higher up in the university administration, on the other hand, doesn't care about what's being taught to the students. His only concern is how much money and facilities we are giving the teachers. The consequence is a real lack of communication between these two ends of our structure.

D: I have great reservations about the notions of the politics of love and the politics of contract, and some of these reservations have to do with client interaction with organizations. I think these concepts define the nature of conflict in highly individualized personal fashion and demonstrate a propensity among American intellectuals to view conflict in psychological and social-psychological terms. I also think that this has a concrete impact, both in terms of policy and how we affect organizations' relationships with their clientele. I think of this in terms of the difference between the instrumental and expressive dimension of politics. And again, I would like to relate to the practitioners here. I would like it clear that this affects practice. I would argue, for example, that certain types of clients are demanding to be treated in terms of their role as citizens, that what they are demanding is not an attitude of "trust" or "honesty" on the part of organizations but rather some expression *in political terms* of concern for the demands being made.

The necessity to respond *in political terms* may have very different consequences for organizations than we have been suggesting here. For example, we may find that the types of solutions we may have to use to deal with clients who feel themselves deprived may not be food stamps. On the other hand, they may not be—and I think this is the trend today—a demand to recognize the dignity of the clients. What I have in mind is the experience of less developed countries and also our own in an earlier period of our history. What may be required today is a political type of bureaucracy similar to the type of experience, say, that the Mapia party in Israel has had in dealing with immigrants unassimilated and yet mobilized, and the political machines that the United States had in dealing with the expressed demands of certain clienteles in directly political terms. They would not, of course, be appropriate in the form in which they existed in the early twentieth century. What we may need now in the United States is some system of dual bureaucracies. These might be capable of dealing with certain demands of expressive clients today. Of course, the United States may be incapable of developing this kind of response; if so, then we have much more reason to be pessimistic than optimistic.

4

Adaptation Capacity and Organizational Development

In his discussion—"Some Implications of Adaptation for Organizational and Political Development"—Robert Biller supports and supplements the general view of the state of affairs and the art which La Porte and White suggested. Biller's labor on the road to theoretical and practical improvement centers on the concept of development, but along the way he stops to explore several dilemmas of the study and practice of Public Administration, including a redefinition of "public" which incorporates turbulence as an essential element. S. B. Joedono, in his comment "Development, Learning, and Models," treats mainly the epistemological issues raised by Biller's discussion.

Some Implications of Adaptation Capacity for Organizational and Political Development

Robert P. Biller

Both as a discipline in which certain problems have been studied and taught, and as a profession in which certain practices have been brought to bear on problem solving, Public Administration gives evidence of encountering serious difficulties.

We run the risk of increasing disengagement from the most basic social facts of our time. By simply doing what we know how to do in a period where that makes increasingly less sense, we continue to pave the way for either languishment in irrelevance or greater contribution to the compounding rather than the solving of problems. The period in which we now live may mark a watershed as profound in its consequences for human existence as were the Agricultural and Industrial Revolutions. Yet we continue to treat the manifestations of a fundamental transition as if they were incidental anomalies to a continuous social order that will accommodate and persist. This paper considers briefly how we came to be where we are and some of the elements of the transition we are undergoing, and then focuses upon a concept of organizational and political "development" to see whether there might be a more salutary basis and direction for some of our disciplinary and professional activities.

The Historical Roots of the Present

The United States' experience with Public Administration has had two themes.

The first theme has been an inward-looking one in which we demanded that the public's business be conducted with competence, efficiency, and care. This reformist commitment—forcefully expressed in the latter half of the nineteenth century, solidified in the early twentieth, and continuing down to the current Senate interest in another "Hoover Commission"—assumed that a process of improvability through rational analysis was both possible and necessary. The hope was that this spirit would permeate all administrative units in the public sector. Both the importance of ensuring accountability and the evidence of antichange inertia, however, tended to enhance an external-change strategy: Reform was attempted through such devices as legislatively appointed commissions, task forces of experts, consultant reports, and separate analysis units in large organizations.

The commitment to values such as productivity, efficiency, and accountability were highly consistent with the industrializing experience which the society was undergoing. Certain underlying assumptions upon which these values were based appeared true enough to warrant action. Three of the most fundamental of these assumptions were (1) What ought to be done is known or determinable; (2) How it can be done well is determinable through analysis and planning; (3) To ensure that desirable things are done well, arrangements must be made so that public organizations and their members are both controlled in and held accountable for their actions. The strategies employed to implement these assumptions included such social inventions as hierarchically designed organizations, external control through politically responsive legislative and executive channels, internal control through Scientific Management procedures and its latter day Human Relationist revisions, and change strategies based upon externalized definitions of adaptation requirements when sufficient anomalies had accumulated to indicate a problem to be corrected.

The second theme underlying United States' experience with Public Administration has been an outward-looking one in which we have felt a responsibility to share the fruits of our success abroad. Though present to a limited extent earlier in this century, this theme has gained impetus in the last two decades with the emergence of the "third world" in articulate form and our self-recognized status as a great power. As with other sectors of our society, Public Administration has responded with objectives as disparate as the following:

International politics—"This is a large and potentially hostile world so let us do those things which are likely to make you stable, hopefully friendly, but at least not enemies."

Dispassionate humaneness—"We respect your autonomy as nations and individuals, but our consciences simply cannot tolerate your starving, dying prematurely, and unnecessary poverty, so let us help."

Missionary zeal—"We have discovered ways to meet your aspirations for political democracy and the technologically good life, so let us show you these ways."

Truth seeking—"We can know ourselves better and the nature of reality more accurately if we are less culture bound in our researches, so let us come study in your midst."

With this theme also, there has been a variety of underlying assumptions and a number of strategies adopted in its furtherance.

Though these are discussed in detail below, it should be noted that they are not dissimilar to those noted in the first theme: that is, we know or can determine what ought to be done, we can figure out how to do it well, and we can control what we do to ensure that what we have determined ought to be done is done. Let us now consider where Public Administration is in relation to these two major themes.

The Transition to a Postindustrial Society, or Where Are We Now?

We are experiencing serious, sustained, and fundamental dilemmas on both fronts. On the outward-looking theme we have encountered crises of aspirations, procedures, and assumptions. In terms of aspirations we appear to be experiencing a significant disillusionment as the resources required for—and the probabilities of dramatic success of—technical assistance become clear. Procedurally, we lack confidence about what to "export," much less how to do it in ways that have high probabilities of "success." It is, however, at the assumption level that we may face our greatest dilemma. The United States has felt that it could "lead" from strength; that we were a developed society with a message worth giving to others. We now find ourselves as a society with developmental exigencies as profoundly difficult to solve as anything we encounter in the "third world." We find our energies being redirected toward our own society, and our confidence about the future which we can hold out as a model to other societies diminished. In a sense, then, our interest in the outward-looking theme has been derived from our sense of confidence about our own society's adequacy, success, and desirability. Since what we are able and interested in doing abroad is so strongly related to what happens at home, we must ask how the inward-looking theme is faring in our society today.

It has now become painfully visible to our society that it is the owner of decaying cities, racial inequities, civil strife, accelerating economic disparities, generational cleavages, diminishing time periods in which to adjust to the consequences of rapid technological change, inadequacies in the quality and responsiveness of a large array of governmental services, and so on. As these problems mushroom, we appear simultaneously to be experiencing a set of changes that casts doubt upon the adequacy of those assumptions which have previously informed our activity. The consequences of these changes may in fact be so quantitatively large as to be best described with a qualitative description such as Postindustrial Revolution.

The complexity and specialization of our society increase. The scale of attempted enterprise increases. The intensity of the interdependencies occasioned by and resulting from complexity increases. Through such an increasingly complex and interdependent society the consequences of change seem to reverberate and ramify—facilitated by an ever more sophisticated and penetrating communications network—with mounting intensity, scope, and unpredictability.

Such processes do not seem to be simply extensions of ones we have already experienced. Bizarre and unexpected anomalies appear that test the adequacy of understanding drawn from earlier experiences. The growing complexity and interdependency of our society does not appear to be leading towards the monolithic rationalization and stability envisioned by a George Orwell, but rather toward the institutionalization of impermanence.[1] The half-lives of technological inventions; amortization times for rationalizing investments; length of time in occupations, careers, statuses, and residence in given geographic locations; and other factors all appear to be shrinking rather than expanding. Evidences of transiency, tentativeness, and impermanence increase apace with our attempts to plan with longer time spans and to control larger programs and segments of the socioeconomic system. Product obsolescence came to be recognized as an attribute of industrialization; perhaps an increased temporariness of those social arrangements we describe as organizations will come to be recognized as an attribute of postindustrialization.

At one level we see evidence of the increasing homogeniza-

[1] I am indebted to Warren G. Bennis who first stimulated me to think about the ways in which rapid and extensive change might cumulate into something like "permanent" temporariness. A number of the ideas noted in this paragraph are drawn quite directly from his work, and other notions in this paper have certainly been affected by my reading of his papers. See for example his recent volume with Philip E. Slater, *The Temporary Society* (New York: Harper and Row, 1968).

tion of our society through common socialization experiences such
as television, standardized primary and secondary education, and
a "natural" culture of laws, norms, and material products. At
another level we see evidence for an increasingly heterogeneous
society with professional and occupational specialization, a pro-
liferation of the bases upon which persons may establish their
security and autonomy of action, increasing resources available
for leisure and other activities, and the potentially widening
cleavages along racial, economic, age, and other lines. Whereas
we formerly feared the conformity of values and stagnation of
aspirations which the affluence of technical industrialization might
bring, we now fear for the capacity of our society to deal with
the fluidity of values and the avalanche of conflict over aspirations that seem to be upon us. In short, something revolutionary
may be upon our society for which our experience may not have
been particularly preparatory.

Whereas it has taken several thousand years to explicate the
implications of the Agricultural Revolution, and several hundred
years to explicate the implications of the Industrial Revolution,
we now seem to be attempting in a matter of decades a transformation as profound as either of the earlier ones. This tele-
scoping in time is further compounded by the residual work that
continues on the two prior transformations: with the Agricultural Revolution, the continuing automation of food production
with the attendant rural to urban migration; and, with the Industrial Revolution, the continued rationalization of wealth production and distribution through automation, PPB (planning-
programming-budgeting system), and other related phenomena.

In an increasingly complex, changing, and interdependent society, it becomes increasingly difficult to assume that conditions
exist to support the assumptions that we know or can conclusively
determine what is to be done, how it is to be done, or how its accomplishment is to be controlled. As the utility of such assumptions declines, the attempt to respond to problems by greater and
greater efforts along the old lines is to risk a political and social
bankruptcy spiral. Having frozen the assumptions, one would
expect those problems not fitting the solutional systems inferred
from these assumptions to accrete and ramify faster than one's
ability to ameliorate symptoms. This imbalance would be the

case even though each individual unit member sincerely hoped for the best, tried hard, and did what he could. In such a situation one would predict that repression would probably be attempted in order to simplify arbitrarily the issues of order within complexity. There is reason to believe that public Administration is in danger of being thwarted and ineffectual abroad and of reaching a cul-de-sac at home. Does the concept of "development" and commitment to it offer any resolution to either dilemma?

Considerations in the Relationship of "Development" and "Public" Administration

An exploration of the concept of "development" in relation to Public Administration requires a prior consideration of at least five things. One needs to know what unit one is talking about; what the environment is within which that unit is sited, and the relationship between the unit and environment; what, if anything, the concept of "publicness" contributes to an understanding of things; the criteria by which change in the unit, the environment, or their relationships is going to be inferred; and what set of normative criteria will be used to evaluate the inferences about change. Let us review each of these in turn.

The Units

We are concerned with the systems of human interaction ranging in scale from what are commonly called organizations to political nation-states.[2] Such systems share certain features in common.[3] They are defined by boundaries which analytically distinguish members from nonmembers. Their members and subsets of members engage in patterned and interdependent interaction. When such patterned, interdependent interaction is sustained we may choose analytically to infer the presence of structure. To the extent that the members' sets of objectives overlap we may choose analytically to infer purposiveness or goal

[2]The similarities in concern between the theories of organizations and politics has been commented upon by Herbert Kaufman, "Organizational Theory and Political Theory," *American Political Science Review* (March, 1964), pp. 5–14.

[3]An excellent recent source book in general systems theory is Walter Buckley (ed.), *Modern Systems Research for the Behavioral Scientist* (Chicago: Aldine Publishing Co., 1968).

directedness. The conversion of input resources into outputs—as well as other internal transactional processes engaged in by system members—are presumed to be responsive to certain reciprocity, processes analytically described as dynamic equilibrium.

Such system units may be both clear to an analyst and real to those persons affected by them, but they are in the final analysis figments of our imaginations. Each of us finds it useful as a simplifying device to aggregate our knowledge about patterning of interactions, mutuality of expectations, shared perspective and information, and other such matters under those names by which organizational and political systems are labeled.[4] Yet such systems do not exist; people exist.

We must therefore recognize in dealing with the "development" of such units that we are working with an inevitably simplified and abstracted version of a complex, interdependent, amorphous network of human interaction. Information upon which the development of such units may be contemplated is hard to acquire. For even the smallest systems, such information tends toward the simplistic (in which the interdependencies of complex interactions are necessarily ignored) or the abstract (in which gross generalizations are made at an unhelpfully broad level). If the development of such units depends to some degree on adequacy and quality of information we must not only exercise caution but find some way of dealing with this issue.

The Environment

While the environments of units may be defined as external things which affect the unit, it is more useful for our purposes to focus on the human aspects of environments. In these terms a unit's environment is composed of those persons—or clustered aggregations of persons—outside of the unit with whom unit members interact in ways salient to the unit. We are only now beginning to comprehend the extent to which our understanding of system units has tended to ignore environmental effects.[5]

[4] In addition, caution is called for in our labeling practices. Some portion of those units now labeled "organizations" or "political nation-states" may meet so few of the definitional criteria noted above that they are so named only to the analyst's peril.

[5] Such effects, among all organizational phenomena, have been under-studied. The recent development of this literature is reflected in the essay by Shirley Terreberry, "The Evolution of Organizational Environments," *Administrative Science Quarterly* (March, 1968), pp. 590–613.

Much of the work in Public Administration responsive to the inward-looking theme assumed that external questions were either "political" or generically common enough to warrant little attention. When seen as political they tended to be accepted as given constraints or studied independently and partially, as in the case of organization interest-group studies. When seen as pervasive, they became irrelevant. As long as one could assume that all Americans roughly agreed on what "good government" was and that it ought to be achieved, it is understandable that most effort focused on internal questions of how to reform units so that "good government" would be achieved.

To talk about the development of units without talking about the environments in which they are sited, however, is impossible. It is the environment which possesses the sets of constraints and opportunities, resources and demands, which ultimately condition the terms under which unit members may act. If developmentally relevant information is hard to come by in regard to units because of their complex and amorphous character, however, we appear to be confronted with a question an order of magnitude greater in regard to such information about environments and the relationships between units and environments. To enumerate—much less to comprehend—such information about the smallest systems becomes a staggering task. It would require information about the cognitive, affective, perceptual, and expectational "maps" employed by the participants in such interaction. It is no wonder that our information about such matters tends toward the limited and unordered specific or the generalized but often irrelevant abstract.

To compound this problem further, our need for such information appears to be inversely related to our ability to gather it. Emery and Trist have suggested a useful classificatory scheme for visualizing the environments of the human interactional units we are discussing.[6] They propose thinking about environments in terms of the complexity of connectedness and stability of environmental elements as analyzed from the focal unit's perspective. A continuum of environments is derived ranging from placidity to turbulence. Systems sited in the ideally placid environment

[6]F. E. Emery and E. L. Trist, "The Causal Texture of Organizational Environments," *Human Relations* (February, 1965), pp. 21–32.

("placid-randomized") have no need for accurate and predictive information about their environments since a random-walk strategy is the most efficient procedure for dealing with a set of disconnected, relatively unchanging, and randomly distributed opportunities and constraints. Systems sited in environments characterized by a relative stability of environmental elements, but an uneven distribution or clustering, need enough accurate and predictive information about these environments to deal with tactical questions concerning opportunities and constraints. In both of these types the environment's relationship to the system is essentially passive. The system's only requirement for information derives from the questions of how best to proceed within the given constraints and available resources provided by the environment.

In the second two ideal types, the environment's relation to the system is an active one. Systems sited in "disturbed-reactive environments"—characterized not only by clustering but also by the presence of other complex systems with which cooperative or competitive relationships are negotiated—need enough information about these environments to deal with questions of tactic and strategy. The "hosted" system gathers accurate and predictive information to anticipate alternative responses and contingencies from environmental elements that might be occasioned by system action. The key point here is that such an environment is still finite enough and stable enough to be "knowable" by the system in these terms. The consequences of system action can be predicted with a fairly high probability of success. Systems sited in the final type of environment ("turbulent-fields"), however, find themselves confronting an apparently endlessly ramifying network of interconnected effects and consequences. The diversity and complexity of such an environmental network; its capacity to amplify, reinterpret, or damp the hosted system's actions or nonactions (often at unexpectedly "distant" points); its ability to dissolve and coalesce in new ways on issues salient to the hosted system on the basis of data far removed from that system's information scanning mechanisms makes it extremely difficult if not impossible for the system to definitively predict, much less control, its environment.

A unit's environment is the "owner" of those constraints and opportunities that ultimately condition the terms under which the unit members may act. Therefore, discussion of the "development" of units requires some information about and analysis of the environment within which the units are sited. Yet the above discussion of environments implies a rather stark discontinuity. In the case of placid-random environments, units require little if any environmental information because it would be irrelevant. In the case of placid-clustered environments, units require enough environmental information to enable them to develop intelligent tactics, and they have a good chance to acquire such information. In the case of disturbed-reactive environments, units require a higher order of environmental information to enable them to develop both intelligent strategy and tactics, but the problem is still finite enough to lend itself to solution. In the case of turbulent fields, however, to develop equivalently high probability-of-success strategies and tactics would require a quantity and quality of information that is not only beyond the realm of practicality, but which may simply not exist until something is "tried."

In such a complex, interdependent, and potentially changeful field one may be able to create information—through acting and then observing—in a more accurate and timely fashion than one can gather information through observation and prediction. The "development" of any unit "hosted" by such a turbulent field may therefore require a different set of assumptions and strategies than those indicated for the less complex types of environments. The importance of this possibility is underscored by the extent to which those exigencies faced by Public Administration in both its inward-looking and outward-looking themes are aptly described as problems situated in turbulent fields.

The Concept of "Publicness"

To link a concept of development with the field of Public Administration requires an analysis of both referents and their linkage. Development and administration are addressed below. There is an obligation at this point, however, to state whether the adjective "public" bears any relationship to the analysis. That is, is the description of certain forms of administration as "public" gratuitous or does it imply a difference that makes a difference?

Though various meanings have been attributed to the concept of publicness, it is unclear whether such meanings can stand analytic or practical tests. Let us review some of the approaches to the notion of publicness and see whether—in terms of the argument to be advanced here—a satisfactory base for this concept can be inferred.

At various times publicness has been attributed to organizations on the basis of their status as agents of sovereign (that is, governmental) power, their responsibility for the definition and advocacy of the public interest, their presumed accountability to the public at large, their presumed responsiveness and representativeness, their location in noneconomic markets, a classification of their functions into public and nonpublic categories, and other such criteria.

Some of these are more aspirational than definitional; others do not hold up well when applied. The coercive power implied by sovereignty is seldom employed, and its threat is seldom a realistic alternative. Depending upon which definition of the "public" interest one chooses to adopt, there always seem to be examples of "private" organizations that are more responsive than "governmental" ones. Organizations we intuitively classify as public seem all too often to be among the less responsive and representative ones. Political markets appear to have all of the essential features characterizing economic ones. Public and private decisional processes seem increasingly to interweave. Governments contract out functions previously regarded as public while at the same time they are investing risk capital in functions previously regarded as private. Is the distinction contained in the concept of publicness losing analytic or practical significance?

The discussion of environment in the preceding section is relevant to this question. What is distinctive about public organizations is that their boundary-layer transactions are inherently subject to ambiguity, diffusion, and destabilization. Private organizations are able to make rather accurate and predictive statements about the relative salience of elements of their environment (that is, customers and suppliers). Public organizations have environments in which predictive statements about relative salience based on the organization's definition are subject to change or reversal by political actors with legitimate, but heretofore unknown or unexplicated, claims. The basis upon which the legitimacy of such environmental entrants is established tends to be both "easy"—birth, citizenship, residence—and difficult for any organization to affect significantly. Methods for affecting legitimacy of entrance are available—for example, incarceration, expulsion, class legislation, disenfranchisement—but use of these tends to be either too selective or too encompassing in their consequences to allow for timely or modulated response.

Publicness, in this view, is not an attribute of an organization but of an organization's relationship to its environment. The inevitable lack of congruity between any organization's definition of salient environment and the potential configuration of that environment—given the recruitment or reconfiguration of all possible sets of political actors in any political system—would make it appear that any such organization would either be continuously hosted by a turbulent field or be subject to this possibility. *The proposition is therefore made that any unit is public to the extent that it is hosted in a turbulent field.* Public units are ones that either routinely exist in such turbulent fields or are with some frequency catapulted into them.

The "privateness" of any unit is proportional to the extent that it finds itself hosted by—or is able to successfully simplify its environmental relationships in ways that approximate—a less turbulent field. For example, to the extent a governmental commission, bureau, police department, or other unit is able to simplify its potential environment, it might more accurately be classified as a relatively private organization. The desirability of such a strategy is of course open to extremely serious question. On the other side of the question, the proposition would imply that any unit—whatever its other attributes—shown to be functioning in, or with some frequency catapulted into, a turbulent field ought to be treated to that extent as a public organization. This proposition raises some extremely critical questions for any concept of development, if there is truth in the earlier proposition that turbulent fields—because of the difficulty of gathering and assessing information relative to predictive planning—pose fundamentally different unit-development issues than those posed by less turbulent fields.

The Concept of Change

Since the concept of change is so closely linked with our ideas about development it is necessary that we address two questions concerning it. The first has to do with the meaning of the concept. The second has to do with our expectations about its occurrence.

Change is an elusive concept.[7] It is an abstraction imputed to reality rather than an inherent attribute of reality. The concept cannot be expressed in absolute terms but only in relational or relative terms. When we say a change has occurred we typically mean that some state has been altered relative either to a previous state of that object or some other object to which we have inferred a relationship. Both of these meanings have difficulties. For example, change attributed to a unit that has existential meaning only in terms of some pattern or cycle is more likely to be an artifact of the observer than a characteristic of the observed. When change is inferred from a comparison of the states of different units we have no ultimate way of assuring ourselves which of the two objects has changed, or how much.

If we attempt to simply equate change with some conception of movement, we lose any capacity to make relational statements. For example, any unit may, by any movement measure, have remained unchanged over some period of time. If, over this same period of time, that unit has experienced increased demands from its environment, it would appear that lack of movement was associated with potentially radical change.

Inferences about the directionality of change are equally hard to make. Three similar units could each have doubled on some performance measure in the same time period. The inferences we would draw from such information would be quite different, however, should we also know that the demands for this performance placed on these three organizations by their environments had in one case halved, in a second case remained constant, and in the third case doubled. We might be inclined in the third case to infer maintenance, in the second case retrogression, and in the first case development. In no case, however, would information about internal movement be sufficient to draw such an inference. In discussing change we are of necessity dealing with an abstract con-

[7]The next three paragraphs are drawn from Carter Zeleznik, "Some Reflections on Change," *Kyklos*, (1960), pp. 373–385.

struct with which we must carefully specify the relational refer-encing used in the drawing of any specific inference.

Our expectations about the occurrence of change also bear examination. For many reasons discussed in the available litera-ture, we have come to expect system units such as those addressed in this analysis to be normally characterized by stability.[8] While there is compelling evidence for the equilibrating characteristics of such units this would seem to be inadequate as the paramount explanation for the data available about such units. Figure 1 de-

FIGURE 1. EQUILIBRATING ASSUMPTIONS

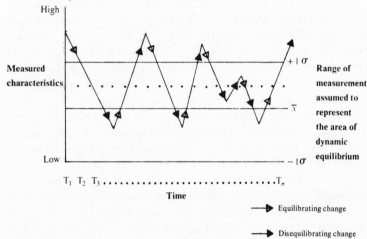

picts a hypothetical graph in which some unit characteristic (ordinant) has been measured over time (abscissa) as indicated by the solid line. The dotted line indicates the range most often encountered and which is commonly referred to as the area of dynamic equilibrium. The darkened-arrow symbols depict those directions of change which—in this after-the-fact fashion—are in-ferred to be equilibrating. To infer this range we have simply per-formed a statistical aggregation process in which a process of continuous change has been summarized by measures of central tendency and variability. The reification of such an aggregation

[8]A recent source citing much of this literature is Walter Buckley, *Sociology and Modern Systems Theory* (Englewood Cliffs, N. J.: Prentice-Hall, 1967). Also see Ralf Dahrendorf, "Out of Utopia: Toward a Reorientation of Sociological Anal-ysis," *American Journal of Sociology* (September, 1958), p. 23.

process may then result in its use as evidence indicating the presence of a stable base and in primary attention being directed toward those segments of the measurement line depicting movement toward the dynamic-equilibrium range as in some sense descriptive of a normalizing or stability-seeking tendency. If we choose to retain the concept of equilibrium it would appear equally logical to infer that at any randomly chosen point in time the characteristic would be as likely to be disequilibrating as equilibrating.

Hence to assume that units are inherently stabilizing and that the change phenomena they reflect are unusual or anomalous is at best a partial statement. The further possibility of positive feedback cycles[9]—more accurately described as deviation amplification than damping—also indicates the wisdom of remaining cautious about expectations of stability. From this perspective it would be no more reasonable to expect stability than change in any given situation. The fact that the potential for any unit to continuously disequilibrate has not generally been recognized. The preponderance of research and pejorative writing, for example, has dealt with "how to overcome resistance to change" rather than on "how to overcome resistance to stability."

The extent to which our world views lead us to expect order and stability rather than disorder and change is probably a more deeply embedded artifact of our culture than any of us can appreciate. Most of us feel uncomfortable enough with the concept of inertia that indicates it takes as much force to stop a rolling ball as it does to start a ball rolling. The suggestion that some significant portion of what we know about a stable and ordered world is simply the collective operation of many individual "imaginations"—each endeavoring to make sense out of individual perceptions and cognitions through the use of language and other cultural agreements—is unlikely to be quickly assimilated.[10]

Normative Criteria

It is an odd commentary on Public Administration that normative issues have been shunned on the grounds that they are in

[9]Mogorah Marayama, "The Second Cybernetics," *Industrial Research* (July-August, 1964), pp. 48–56.

[10]For a particularly lively account of the way we deal with the world in terms of images see Kenneth Boulding, *The Image* (Ann Arbor: University of Michigan Press, 1956).

some sense less ascertainable than are facts about organizations, administrative processes, and other such matters. Upon reflection this may be simply and absolutely untrue. The decision to emphasize the study of administration over values, on the assumption that the former poses problems more amenable to solution than the latter, may have been ludicrously inconsistent in terms of the criteria employed. As we have already noted, such apparently factual matters as the nature of units and environments are extraordinarily chimerical. In the last analysis they represent rough approximations of elusive and shifting sets of information, perception, expectation, interaction, and other such manifestations of the processes of human cognition and behavior, often framed at unhelpfully simplistic or abstract levels. Though by inclination and training committed to what might be called empirical research on public organizations, I am at times awestruck by the lack of responsiveness of my own and others' research to those public-policy issues in which questions of value are central, and which are desperately in need of solution.

I believe we have a clearer understanding of, agreement about, and commitment to certain values by which we assess the adequacy of public-administrative processes than we admit to ourselves or each other. If such understanding and agreement exist, they might serve as a test, both for the adequacy of the current polarization of the field of Public Administration, and for the desirability of a development model for the consideration of that field. To pursue this thought further, consider some of the tensions apparently inherent in the ideas of freedom and democracy.

Freedom and democracy have both been given a variety of content meanings. Various descriptions of personal circumstance and arrangement of governance have been offered as answers to the questions of: "I would be free if . . ." or, "We would be democratic if . . ." A content-oriented definitional approach appears, however, to miss the most important element of both concepts. Both are essentially process-oriented ideas and should be so defined. At least with our present knowledge, both represent explorational avenues rather than finitely definable end-states. In this sense one could not *be* free, but one could be *becoming* free. While it is impossible to know with absolute certitude that one *is* free (that is, "Am I bound in ways I cannot now comprehend?"), one can on the basis of finite judgments determine the liberating or binding consequences of particular events or conditions. The concepts of freedom and democracy are thus highly analogous to our concept of the null hypothesis.[11] Democracy, for example, can be analyzed as a method of "truth finding" based on the epistemological idea that, though nothing may be ultimately provable, any number of things may be subjected to disproof tests sufficient to enable one to act with an extremely low probability of error. The concepts of freedom and democracy are not content free, but the content of their meaning is accreted in a very particular (and essentially negative) mode of process discovery.

Both concepts are paradoxical in that, while each is intendedly aspirational, the process of their discovery and explication appears blocked rather than facilitated by any but the most tentatively advanced positive prescriptions. While such positive prescriptions are tentatively advanced for potential disproof, the accretion of content is expressible by negative statements. While it is possible to say that it is not democratic to deny decisional access to the governed, it is with greater tentativeness that we attempt to state that it is democratic to provide a certain specified amount of influence on any particular decision. In the case of freedom we may aspire to something like "maximization of life choices," but since we do not know either what all of these are or how they are to be realized, we say rather that known and available life choices should not arbitrarily be denied. Thus, while the essential idea is defined in process terms, we constrain that process as we discover things contrary either to the concept's intent or to the process by which further discovery may occur.

Both the concepts of freedom and democracy involve certain tensions concerning assumptions about man's nature and social condition. These tensions are reflected in such pairings of ideas as autonomy and interdependence, individual freedom and social responsibility, minority and majority rights, opportunities for the individual and social constraints to be placed upon the individual. We tend to assume that each side of any such pairing is implicitly and necessarily constrained by the other side and that their integration requires some form of balancing.

[11] I am indebted to my friend and colleague Professor Todd R. La Porte for first cudgeling this idea into me in the course of many stimulating discussions. A number of the other ideas discussed in this paper either would not have come up, or would have come up in even cruder form, had these exchanges not occurred.

To assume the need for such a balancing of constraints leads to negotiation over their construction and explication. To doubt the need for such a balancing leads to negotiation over the times and places where they may be dissolved. A discovery-process concept of freedom or democracy would appear more compatible with the latter than the former.

To assume, for example, that individual freedom and social responsibility are in some fundamental sense incompatible is to draw an inference beyond the available data.[12] Since we know the meaning of both in only proximate ways, data about their apparent present or past incompatibility is useful only in determining the degree of confidence with which we would undertake risks involved in their fusion. Thus, to remain agnostic on this point is to cultivate the possibilities of discovery implicit in the concepts of both freedom and democracy. Responsible anarchy, for example, may be less inconceivable than we now suspect.

This discussion of normative criteria was undertaken to see whether we could infer a value basis to test the desirability of a development model for the field of Public Administration. If there were agreement on the propositions introduced thus far, such a test would include the following characteristics. It would be more committed to the process of freedom and democracy discovery than a particular content-specified definition of these concepts. Its prescriptive implications would be stated negatively while its elicitive implications would be stated positively in ways subject to disproof and amendment. It would be tentative about the specification of substantive goals but certain about the denial of procedures that have been discovered to be value denying. Its operation would be likely to increase the probability that affected persons or units would find the process of becoming free or democratic expanded.

Development as Process: The Capacity for Adaptation

Development is defined as that process by which the adaptation capacity of any unit is increased. The concept of development is process rather than content oriented and is on this basis

---

[12]Herbert Shepard has discussed the organizational implications of the proposition with considerable insight in "Changing Interpersonal and Intergroup Relationships in Organizations," James G. March (ed.), *Handbook of Organizations* (Chicago: Rand McNally, 1965).

to be distinguished from the concept of modernization.[13] Development refers to the interactional process through which individuals associated in unit networks learn how to articulate and solve problems. Modernization refers to those symbols, products, and modes of life associated with modernity—primarily defined in terms of technology at this point—which a unit or its members may acquire. As a process-oriented concept, development is focused on questions of level. Questions such as the rate of change may be addressed by either development or modernization, but the referent would be different for each. With development it would refer to the rate at which problem-solving capacity was increasing or decreasing, while with modernization it would refer to the rate at which symbolic content was being accreted. Let us clarify the sense in which each of the major terms is used in this definition of development.

Development is defined as a process, not as a state. States are descriptive of content while processes are descriptive of those steps by which states are created. In this sense both process development and content modernization could be reflected in such a statement as, "We wanted to cross the river so we built a bridge." A developmental component would be present if—in that process by which a need was articulated and translated into those social arrangements necessary to produce the bridge—any unit learned how to deal with such an exigency more skillfully in the future. A modernization component would be present if the acquisition of the bridge represented a symbolic addition to the sense of being identified with modernity on the part of those affected. That is, a developmental process is one that enlarges the problem-solving routines of a unit, while modernization enlarges the pool of symbols judged to be modern. Developmental process is thus a unit analog to individual learning. This analogy is not intended as a reification of some notion like "group mind." It simply reflects a description of the cumulative interactional

[13]The concept of development is also to be distinguished from the idea of industrialization. Industrialization is also a process idea but with its referent established to a particular form of problem-solving skills. Since we have reason to suspect that industrialization represents a phase rather than the culmination of our own and other societies' development, it would seem of little use to intimately link the more general process of development with this more limited class of problem-solving activity.

learning that unit network members acquire in the form of expectations, sets, conventions, knowledge, and so on.

As a process, development is intendedly open ended. On the assumption that meeting needs (solving problems) serves as the base upon which new aspirations may emerge, one could not sensibly describe any unit as developed. One could describe a unit as developing, de-developing, or stabilized. Since individuals, not units, aspire, development as a process implies no assumption about unit survival. Depending upon the nature of the problems about which a unit coalesces, its development may lead it towards survival or nonsurvival. Oddly enough, unit nonsurvival may ultimately provide the only measure of development as a state rather than as a process. The unit that evanesces because members of the unit and its environment are satisfied that the problems by which it was defined are solved could be said to have developed.

"Adaptation" is given no meaning beyond that of problem solving. As a word it is used with some reluctance because it is not meant to imply simply *re*active, *re*sponsive or *re*formist behavior. Though our vocabulary is still limited in this regard, the concept of problem-solving adaptation is meant to be equally descriptive of those activities best described as *pro*active, *pro*sponsive or *pro*formist.[14] In this definition it is used as an adjective, not as a noun: It is meant to be descriptive of a unit capacity—for example, to distinguish it from a concept like performance capacity—not those outcomes or "adaptations" that may result from the operation of the capacity.

The concept of capacity is meant to denote problem-solving capability. It is a latent rather than a manifest construct. One can observe capacity only as it is manifested in behavior. Therefore, though two separate concepts have been defined—process-oriented development and content-oriented modernization—it is clear that they are related. When one begins to analyze or practice various strategies of change, however, their clear distinction becomes imperative.

The "unit" concept denotes those systems of human interaction discussed earlier in this paper. A common process-

[14]Gordon W. Allport, "The Open System in Personality Theory," *Journal of Abnormal and Social Psychology* (November, 1960), pp. 301–311.

oriented development concept is proposed as equally explanatory and useful whether one is dealing with those units usually
labeled organizations or political nation-states. The same dynamics characterize the development of both. While the definition of development is meant to be applicable to all units meeting
the definition of human interactional systems, the development
of public units implies some unique difficulties and opportunities
due to their location in turbulent fields.

The word "increased" is used in both a relative and relational
sense. It is relative in the sense that a unit's learning is to be
understood not in any isolated or absolute sense, but relative to
that learning base established prior to some developmental
experience. It is relational in the sense that a unit learns in
proportion to those learning exigencies (problems) with which it
is confronted, and that a unit's ability to do this is at least partially proportional to the problems, constraints, and opportunities presented to it by its environment.

In summary, this concept of development places more emphasis on what a unit is learning how to do through solving problems than on its symbols of modernity.

Implications of the Concept of Development
for Public Administration

Let us now turn to a necessarily brief exploration of some of
the derivative implications that this development concept might
have for Public Administration.

Inward-Looking Theme

In terms of the inward-looking theme of Public Administration one could inquire about the capability of our public units in
developmental terms. That is, what is the extent to which our
public units are developing in response to the set of problems
within which they are embedded and those indications of
changed circumstance and condition implied by a Postindustrial
Revolution? In a sense, this is the question of how we fare in
terms of the development of our own administration. Let me
admit at the outset that I am not particularly sanguine about
this question even though I have been able to think about development in the ways suggested so far only as a result of con-

sidering those events that strike me as desirable and hopeful. This personal judgment is offered as reason for the brevity of the overassertive and underqualified statements that follow.

Environmental turbulence and fluidity, along with complexity and interdependence, are increasing. Yet in our most critical relational areas—interfaces such as legislation/administration, higher administration/lower administration, headquarters/field, organization/client, and intergovernmental relations—we still are investing more resources in attempting to overcome these dilemmas by trying harder to do that which we know how to do than in discovering the ways in which these tensions could be turned to advantage. The latter might be done by using the null-hypothesis value testing process to convert positive control procedures into negative constraint procedures, and by constructing "rich" networks of diversity which could approximate in their randomized error-correction capacity the lower-risk characteristics of more placid environments.[15]

The requirements for and utility of development vary positively with the degree to which a public unit has goal uncertainty, environmental turbulence, and requirements for situationally reprogrammable interdependencies.[16] Although these conditions are increasingly characteristic of public units, there are relatively few development strategies being considered or implemented in response to them. At the unit level we still assume that development means learning how to do something rather than the more fundamental learning how to learn. As a consequence we still employ personal or organizational change strategies where organizational-unit development strategies might be more appropriate.

Content-oriented solution systems are allowed to dictate the problems we try to solve and the procedures by which we attempt to solve them. The probability is that any problem whose symptoms do not fit the solution-oriented category system (which

[15]Many of the attacks on Lindblom's concept of Partisan Mutual Adjustment do not, I believe, fully appreciate the error-correcting potential represented in this process. See for example his *Intelligence of Democracy* (New York: Free Press, 1965).

[16]For an excellent analysis of these concepts see James D. Thompson, *Organizations in Action* (New York: McGraw-Hill, 1967); and Chris Argyris, *Integrating the Individual and the Organization* (New York: John Wiley and Sons, 1964).

inevitably was defined at some prior time in response to a some-what different problem array) will tend to go unperceived or unaddressed until it reaches catastrophic proportions.

Organizational forms (structures) and procedures (processes) vary in the degree of development they are likely to elicit. Yet most of our assumptions, expectations, and control procedures work to ensure the perpetuation of that form of bureaucracy which—though well enough suited to certain purposes and con-ditions—is at least able to support the reprogramming adapta-tion fluidity required to deal with uncertainty and flux. Such arrangements as matrix or functional-team organizations tend to be developed only covertly and with inadequate facilita-tive support.

Commitments of trust in procedural safeguards necessary for the toleration of deviation, conflict, and confrontation are necessary for developmental capability. Yet most units still in-vest more resources in conflict suppression than conflict elicita-tion, in confrontation avoidance than confrontation, in devia-tion control than nurturance.

Outward-Looking Theme

The outward-looking theme of Public Administration sug-gests questions about the capability of public units in contributing to the developmental processes of other units. Though histori-cally we have treated the development of administration largely with an overseas or "third world" focus, it would appear that there are both similar and equally serious issues facing us in terms of our own development. Though certainly not true at the turn of the century, nor probably until this decade, it now seems evident that we are as perplexed about what to do as a nation vis-à-vis a situation like Watts as we are about a situation like Nigeria.

The history of our society's experience with change phenom-ena has been a reformist one. We have tended to assume that change is an externally stimulated process, that external stimula-tion leads to the accomplishment of particular changes. That a unit, as a result of such an experience, would be more capable in the future of recognizing its own change aspirations or dealing with them has been an implicit objective that has not occasioned much attention. We have invested considerable energy in perfecting sales techniques for introducing change but not in considering those circumstances in which a process of self-sustaining change process might be established. The process concept of development discussed here is therefore not a model of change but of changing or changefulness.[17]

To a significant extent, therefore, the change theory we tend to have employed both within this society and in our technical-assistance relationships abroad has been more compatible with modernization than development. It tends to focus primarily on the transfer of certain symbols of modernity or progress from donor units to recipient units. While the perils of this sort of spatial transfer have been recognized—for example, the need to establish a supporting infrastructure and to deal with "cultural" differences—its more fundamental limitations have not. The theory is based on the assumption that the primary contribution of the transfer agent is the technical content of his skill or device. It tends to start with solutions and either find or infer the evidence of problems. By playing a critical if not paramount role in goal specification, the assumption of the transfer agent that the information least accessible to him (recipient-unit data) must be less relevant than that information most accessible to him (the "technique" which he has to offer) leads to a situation in which error correction can occur on technical considerations but with much less probability on recipient-unit considerations. The dependency relationship that tends to be established during the actual transfer tends to reinforce this process. If the attempted transfer is unsuccessful, the transfer agent tends then to proffer explanations about the recipient-unit inadequacy, while at the same time withdrawing into an increasingly technical definition of his own role as his *raison d'être* is threatened.[18] If the transfer succeeds, the agent tends to proffer explanations in terms of the newly confirmed technical excellence of whatever has been transferred.

[17]Robert Chin, "The Utility of System Models and Developmental Models for Practitioners," *The Planning of Change: Readings in the Applied Behavioral Sciences* (New York: Holt, Rinehart and Winston, 1961), pp. 201–214.

[18]William B. Storm and Jason L. Finkle, *American Professionals in Technical Assistance: A Preliminary Report* (Los Angeles: School of Public Administration, University of Southern California, 1966).

The theory of changing implied by the development concept is quite different in its essential features. It is not focused on spatial change (transfer) but on temporal development (adaptation increase over time). The primary contribution of the change agent lies in interactional skills, not content skills.[19] He acts as a catalyst in need articulation and problem definition. While the transfer agent's behavior styles are primarily those of telling, stating, and deciding, the change agent's are those of listening, restating, and inquiring. His objective is to ensure that unit members make accurate information available to one another and that potential solution responses are determined by those who are considering the investment of energy or who will be affected by some ultimate change. Neither of these intervention styles is played with the degree of simplified single-mindedness reflected in these descriptions. They do, however, represent two different modes of approach to intervention for the purpose of change.

It was noted earlier that, though the concepts of development and modernization could be analytically distinguished, they are necessarily related. The former finds expression in the latter, and the latter implies the operation of the former. It is the nature of this relationship which is critical. A considerable portion of our technical-assistance efforts may have been less effective than possible because we have misread our own history. We have tended to accept the definition that we are relatively more developed because we are technologically advanced. Should any causal statement be advanced it would more probably be the reverse: We are technologically advanced because we have chosen to apply our developmental capacities to this sector.

A Proposed Strategy

Can anything be said about a desirable interventional strategy of the administration of development? It is proposed that a strategy based on the following elements would be effective in dealing with the normative commitments outlined earlier and the imperative content-oriented aspirations.

First, the strategy would be intendedly and primarily develop-

---

[19]See for example Ronald Lippitt, *et al.*, *Planned Change* (New York: Harcourt, Brace and World, 1958).

mental. This primary orientation would, however, be constrained both positively and negatively. The process of developmental change—since it is based on need articulation and mobilization of social and political resources—is an inherently destabilizing one. But all units appear to have finite absorptive capacity for entrance of new actors and demands; exceeding that capacity would probably be associated with repression, and this threat disinclines units toward the necessary confrontational behavior. The level of investment in developmental strategies would be no greater than that which would occur without repressive response.

The investment in developmental change would, negatively, be no less than that differential between total available change resources and that proportion required for minimal legitimizing modernization investments. Modernizing investments in this sense serves as the legitimatizing explanation that protects the developmental investment. Donor units can see some immediate return on their investment, as well as avoiding the recipient charge of neocolonialist policy.[20] Such a modernization investment would also provide some level of symbolic payoffs to deal with the issue of rising expectations. Finally, those investments in modernizing content would be chosen and implemented wherever possible with procedures designed to give support to parallel developmental investments.

Conclusions

Public Administration in both its professional and disciplinary dimensions must discover a new basis upon which to define itself and guide its central contributions. Assumptions descriptive of a period when rationalizing industrialization held undisputed sway no longer hold. Procedures derived during a

[20]That is, "You have something we value. You give lip service to helping. But you patronize us by not giving us what you yourselves value most highly on some assumption that we are not ready for it." This is an odd situation because in fact there is no policy more neocolonialistic than only modernizing transfers. Because the donor unit is likely to generate new symbols faster than the recipient society can generate—through random spill-overs and self-development starting from lower capacity thresholds—capacity for self-sustaining modernizing symbol production, such a policy simply commits the recipient unit to a continued dependency relationship.

period characterized by certain essential stabilities now appear in many cases not simply irrelevant but also positively wrong. Aspirations early seen as progressive now are perceived as regressive by large segments of a fluid society. We are in need of a redefinition that would be geared to uncertainty, based on assumptions of change rather than stability, capable of dealing with situational interdependencies, able to convert complexity into error-correction capacity, and facilitative of those process-discovery procedures which would not block the realization of human values.

We need to create public units capable of dealing with turbulent fields. Such units are more likely to have situationally determined patterns of leadership, influence, communication, authority, and decision than the more permanent structures now predominant. The last decades of Public Administration have dealt with public units in terms of the desirability of amalgamation, merger, economies of scale, and so on, but the next decades are more likely to emphasize situational-devolutionary strategies. Having seen the incorporation of the suburbs we may now see the deincorporation of central-city neighborhoods. Public units are likely to invest considerable energy in learning how to absorb, explicate, cultivate, and use for problem-solving purposes those sources of deviation and conflict available to them. Finding ways of liquefying solution systems in order to encourage problem-oriented behavior is likely to be a source of major tension, especially since the continuing professionalization process appears to work toward the opposite end. Proportionately greater development investments will go into unit-network training and development activities. Such units will be attempting to find ways of learning from experience rather than being bound by it.

Parallel to those changes in public units and responsive to the same destabilizing factors, certain changes would appear to be indicated within the profession and discipline of Public Administration. Within the profession the proportion of explicitly educated policy actors and developmental change catalysts should increase. Both these approaches should be extended to other professional fields as the distinguishing contribution of collateral education offered by Public Administration faculties. Hopefully we shall be able to treat the educational processes available through colleges and universities as a basically self-organizing, continuously available experience. The proportional volume of action and policy-oriented research will hopefully increase. To the extent they are retained, internship experiences should be converted from rotational organizational internships to public-problem, public-policy, or organizational-development experiences. Perhaps the most fundamental change that will occur is the reengagement with questions of value. Many of the public units we have constructed appear to be more value destroying than value enhancing. These issues of value, and how they are to be realized are critical, are becoming more critical, and are worthy of more self-conscious attention on our part.

Comment: Development, Learning, and Models

Satrio B. Joedono

I shall address myself to three issues raised in Biller's paper: his idea of the development of Public Administration as a field of study, the notion of learning developed in the paper, and the role of models or systems in thinking and behavior.

Development of Public Administration as a Field of Study

Biller's idea of the development of Public Administration as a field of study is strikingly reminiscent of T. S. Kuhn's theory of the development of natural science.[1] Very briefly, Kuhn holds that every scientific endeavor is based on some pretheoretical assumptions about the nature of reality that forms the subject matter of the science; that the scientific community tends to find anomalies—events or phenomena that cannot be accounted for *if* the original assumptions were true—and that this leads to attempts to redefine the original assumptions about the nature of reality.

It seems to me that Biller's discussion of the development of

[1]Thomas S. Kuhn, *The Structure of Scientific Revolutions* (Chicago: Chicago University Press, 1962).

Public Administration follows these ideas very closely. He has stated some of the assumptions underlying Public Administration in the United States. He has also indicated some of the anomalies that Public Administration encounters today. Lastly, he advances a specific suggestion as to how present American social and political reality should be viewed, and this suggestion has some very fundamental implications for theory building in Public Administration.

This suggestion leads to the question of whether a paradigm exists in Public Administration, and more specifically, the question as to whether the two themes—"inward-looking" and "outward-looking"—are *in fact* included in such a paradigm. We should address these questions more explicitly. We could do this by building up an inventory of propositions such as Kronenberg suggests in Chapter 7 below. This inventory could then be analyzed to make explicit Public Administration's assumptions about reality and how best to approach it. The result of such a study would then indicate whether or not students of Public Administration have, in fact, followed a common paradigm, and whether or not the two themes identified by Biller have been part of such a paradigm.

Development as Learning

One of Biller's main arguments is that a fundamental characteristic of contemporary American social reality is change; that therefore we should conceptualize such reality in process—"change" terms and "development" terms; that development is basically learning (that is, the capacity to cope with problems); and that consequently American Public Administration should be "developing" administration (Public Administration that is capable of keeping up with the manifold problems of change).[2]

The crucial notion in this chain of reasoning is the notion of learning. Apparently, what is meant by "learning" here is a process of arriving at the meaning of terms not through definitions but by a process analogous to the procedure of the null

[2]I should add that I find very helpful the distinction between "modernization" and "developing" which enables one to view social organizations as both "modern" (equipped with all the trappings of modernity, such as computers), *and* "un-developing" (losing their capacity to handle problems).

hypothesis. This latter process consists of successively *accreting* substantive meanings to the term by positing and testing statements of what the term does *not* mean, or more precisely, what conditions or situations the term does *not* imply.

I must confess to having difficulties with this notion of learning, and these center on the following problems: Of what does the testing of statements consist? Who does the testing and who judges the validity or truth value of the results? And more fundamentally, how is it possible for one to know what conditions a term does *not* imply without knowing at the same time, or even before, what conditions it *does* imply? (Is it possible for one to say "A is not P" or "A implies not X" without knowing, at the same time or before, what "P" and "X" are, or stand for?)

This notion of learning bears more speculation and further development. Basically, I like the notion, if only for the simple reason that upon reflection it seems I have been using the same procedure in arriving at the meaning *for me* of ideas such as "the good life." I do not know the *definitive* meaning, even for myself, of "a good life." However, I *have* arrived at some notion of what the term "a good life for me" means through involving myself in life situations and then "feeling," or "testing," my "gut reaction" to those situations. Biller would say that I have successively accreted the substantive meanings of the term "a good life for Joedono." I would agree. He and I would further agree that this accretion indicates that we can never, at any point in our lives, know the *definitive* (that is, the "true-for-all-times") meaning of such terms as "the good life for me." Rather—he and I would say—it makes more sense to say that each of us *learns* through involvement in life situations what the term means for us. But he feels that the successively accreted substantive meanings of a term arrived at through learning can be more accurately expressed by *negative* statements, whereas I feel that while this may be correct for what might be called "the testing of future meanings of terms," it must be rejected on logical grounds. For purposes of testing the meaning of terms in future situations it makes sense—and here the analogy with the null hypothesis is very apt—to state what Biller calls the "base" in negative terms, but it seems to me that this requires a prior positive knowledge of what that base involves.

Models and Systems

Speaking of the role of models or systems in thinking and behavior, Biller states:

Such system[s] . . . may be both clear to an analyst and real to those persons affected by them, but they are in the final analysis figments of our imaginations . . . . [S]uch systems do not exist; people exist.

I regard this statement as somewhat misleading. First—fully realizing my pedantry at this point—I would insist that these models *do* exist. They exist as figments of our imagination. Moreover, they are important, not only for their obvious functionality in all scientific activity, but also because they tend to be predictive of our behavior. Our behavior is largely determined by our figments of imagination: We act on the basis of what we *believe* to be true. As Berger and Luckmann have indicated, what we call social reality is the externalization of these figments of our imagination in action through roles.[3] Through learning and other forms of socialization we internalize these models of the reality around us. They give meaning and structure to reality. Once having internalized these models or systems we then "act them out"; we realize them in the sense of making them real through and by our action. Seen from this perspective, our imaginations are at the basis of what we call social reality, because as someone put it, "in the last analysis a society is only possible because people have pictures in their heads about what that society looks like."

Editorial Note

In the discussion following the essays of this chapter, participants returned once more to the notion of "confrontation" which they had found intriguing in their discussion of White's essay:

A: Biller's essay is premised on participatory and confrontational procedures. I think the difficulty here is the way in which we are dichotomizing confrontation and nonconfrontation procedures. To convert nonconfrontation procedures to confrontational ones represents risks of enormous proportions. But I think we have been talking about

[3]Peter L. Berger and Thomas Luckmann, *The Social Construction of Reality* (Garden City, N. Y.: Doubleday, 1966).

the conversion as though it would be inconceivably abrupt. You obviously don't convert from one to the other immediately. Rather, you convert by engaging those issues which are confrontational in nature. In the engagement of such issues, it seems to me, the participants in the confrontation are probing the level of risk they are prepared to tolerate in the confrontational arena. It is irrational to expect anyone to move abruptly from a low risk to a high risk policy. But it seems reasonable to assume that as you discover things about which you need not be fearful, this establishes a context in which you may develop an ability to countenance risks which presently seem unacceptable. And if positive experience does not accumulate, you just don't increase your acceptable risk level.

B: No social goal is likely to be realized at any level greater than that of the information that informed its definition. How do you inform a definition with high-quality information? It seems to me that you attempt to maximize information-entry processes, and there is no easier way to do that than through confrontational politics. The problem is that the system has to be configured in ways that support and allow confrontational politics. This seems to me to imply a process commitment, on the part of Public Administration both as practice and study, to confrontation elicitation. But our system tends to be characterized by confrontation suppression.

The notion of turbulent environment as an element in the definition of "public" organizations stimulated a lengthy discussion, of which the following snatches are characteristic:

A: The proposition was that the more indeterminate the environment the more public the organization, and that over time organizations move from private to public depending upon the character of their environment. I see this as doing away with the distinction between private and public. We can no longer say this is a public organization, or this is a private one, rather only that there are degrees of publicness in all organizations.

B: I think it goes further than that. One way of understanding some of the dilemmas of organizations which we now classify as public is by looking at this sort of dimension. An organization—say a police department—may attempt to make its environment determinate by establishing its legitimacy and support with particular segments of the political system to an extent that makes it difficult for other elements entering the system to intervene. Now, to the extent to which the organization has simplified its environment by treating itself as more private than public, it is not "public" in the sense of the continuum suggested, and some of its difficulties can be seen in terms of this dilemma.

C: This is the first time that I have gotten the sense that perhaps the phrase "new Public Administration" really means something. Because such ideas mean that new Public Administration will be the study of organizations in rapid change. The interest in public organizations would be one of continually shifting concern or focus. And theories would not be about stable organizations, but rather about organizations situated in turbulent environments.

D: There seems to be a kind of conflict between, say, what Galbraith sees as the role of government, and what Biller would seem to be arguing for (and I agree with him): that administrators have an obligation not to arbitrarily reduce ambiguity and indeterminacy but rather to try to set up systems which can account for or allow for free interchange of exercises of power.

B: It seems to me that you can make some kind of proposition such as "organizations are uncertainty-reducing mechanisms." All of the efficiency models and all of our procedures for doing that, in a sense, plainly have organizations that are designed for uncertainty reduction in mind. When you have an environment which is ultimately indeterminate, you have a problem. You either develop the kinds of procedures which Orion White was talking about or you fall back on simplifying the environment somehow arbitrarily (and probably inappropriately). It seems to me that the dilemma here is that government as a whole is attempting to act as a social change agent. It is clearly using inappropriate instruments to do that: it is using uncertainty-reduction instruments to increase uncertainty. Furthermore, the consequences of its actions are destabilizing rather than stabilizing. To attempt a cooperative strategy and say we are going to deal with Blacks by a set of side payoffs, transfer payments, and then they are going to be happy is absurd because these side payoffs ultimately increase rather than meet aspirations.

E: I think here of the Department of Agriculture which every year does a survey of farmers to find their perceptions as well as quotas and other things, and they play the side payoff game. They create a symbiotic situation which really stabilizes and which no outsider can crack. Is this what you are suggesting public organizations ought to do?

B: No, I am suggesting that to the extent that the Department of Agriculture has simplified the environment in which it exists—which is the political system of the United States—perceiving only farmers as the relevant environment, it is more private than public and is in trouble in the system.

C: And its trouble is indicated partly by a sort of latent clientele such as the hungry poor which is now pressing for notice.

D: It seems to me that one could infer a proposition about the public interest from Biller's comments which would tie in quite well with Michael Harmon's paper. That is, public administrators or public organizations operate within the public interest to the extent their degree of openness or allowance for confrontation is consistent with the amount of actual publicness as defined by the amount of turbulence in the environment.

5

Public Administration and Selected Developments in Social Science

Larry Kirkhart's discussion—"Toward a Theory of Public Administration"—and Frank McGee's comment—"Phenomenological Administration—A New Reality"—represent a slight shift in focus. Whereas the earlier three chapters had taken as their primary focus the relationship of Public Administration to our changing society, the present chapter is the first of three which focus primarily upon the relationship of Public Administration to social-scientific theory. Kirkhart finds that many of the difficulties of defining or building a theory of Public Administration are related to the history and context of the social sciences. He traces out some of the newer trends in social science—with special reference to philosophy, sociology, and psychology—and attempts to discern their implications for theory of Public Administration.

Toward a Theory of Public Administration

Larry Kirkhart

There are few problems in Public Administration more difficult to cope with than the question of what Public Administration is and where it fits into the theoretical landscape of social science.[1] This problem is particularly acute because one of the most striking features of Public Administration is its lack of conceptual boundaries. The only theme that consistently recurs in the literature which attempts to define Public Administration is a concern for organization questions.[2]

In part, this problem is a consequence of the dominant role that political scientists played in the inception and development of Public Administration. During the early period (1870-1927) there was very little emphasis on conceptualizing the field because it was considered to be a subpart of the "discipline" of political science. This situation was complicated by the fact that many political scientists were much more than a little dismayed that their colleagues would engage in such mundane problems as administration, budgeting, and personnel reform.

For the student entering the field, this condition of conceptual destitution generates anxiety. He begins with the reasonable expectation that people who are already within the enterprise have a fairly thoroughgoing grasp of the parameters of their field, but he is apt to encounter only statements like "Public Administration is what public administrators do" or "Public Administration is the execution of public policy," and the like. Part of the problem "What is Public Administration?" can be alleviated by reading the historical analyses which are available.

This chapter addresses a different dimension of this riddle by assessing selected developments in other fields of social science

[1]To the extent I am liberated from the artificial and distorted boundaries generated by academic fields of endeavor and to the extent I am aware of the heritage of social science in a global sense, I am indebted to Alberto Guerreiro-Ramos— one of a very small number of social scientists who can place their own field of interest in brackets. I dedicate this essay to the spirit and enthusiasm of the *engagé* experience I have shared with him, the present experience, and the future.

[2]For historical perspectives on the field of Public Administration, see John M. Gaus, Leonard D. White and Marshall Dimock (eds.), *Frontiers of Public Administration* (Chicago: University of Chicago Press, 1936); Dwight Waldo, *The Administrative State* (New York: Ronald Press, 1948); Paul P. Van Riper, *History of the United States Civil Service* (Evanston, Ill.: Row, Peterson and Co., 1958); Frederick C. Mosher, *Democracy and the Public Service* (New York: Oxford University Press, 1968). Also, there are a number of excellent articles; see John M. Gaus, "The Present Status of the Study of Public Administration," *American Political Science Review* (February, 1931), pp. 120-134; Dwight Waldo, "Public Administration," in Edward Shils (ed.), *International Encyclopedia of the Social Sciences* (New York: Macmillan, 1968), pp. 145-156.

which have the potential of affecting theory in Public Administration. Three major points are advocated. First, part of the problem of defining a field in the social sciences is a consequence of the organization of the academic study which lends itself to poor communications, departmental and disciplinary rivalries, and other intricate behavior patterns which have nothing to do with the social scientist's *raison d'être*. Second, there are "new" currents in the social sciences' disciplines most closely related to Public Administration which perhaps offer the prospect of closer integration of the disciplines and may offer insight into likely developments in the social sciences. Third, Public Administration can further its own conceptual refinement in the general development of social science by considering what contributions and modifications to the theory of formal organization are suggested by such recent and perhaps impending developments in other social-science disciplines. The remainder of this discussion is divided into three major divisions corresponding to these points.

The Ecology of Social-Science Disciplines

The artificiality of divisions in social science is apparent in the way the several fields emerged. For example, it was not until the twentieth century that sociology was recognized as an independent field of study and this was largely due to the determined efforts of Emile Durkheim. Political science was encompassed within history departments in the United States until the last two decades of the nineteenth century. Even today, social psychology enjoys an ambivalent status between psychology and sociology departments. Public Administration was not represented by independent schools until 1927 and 1928 when Syracuse University and the University of Southern California established special programs. Although *Public Administration* was published in Britain as early as 1923, it was not until 1939 that a comparable journal, *Public Administration Review,* was produced in the United States. It is interesting to note that while numerous disciplines have emerged during the twentieth century, few have disappeared from academic programs.[3]

[3]The School of Administration of the University of California at Irvine is one of the exceptions to this statement; it reflects an absorption of Educational Ad-

The pattern of growth of separate social-science disciplines seems strikingly similar to the behavior of bureaucratic structures and suggests that the emergence of fields in social science may be largely a consequence of the ineffectual handling of conflict.[4] Since most of the material written about a field is produced in an academic setting, an analysis of the academic context may provide a useful perspective on relationships between Public Administration and other fields.

Like many other contemporary organizations, universities are confronted with interpenetrating demands from the environment—represented by racial, political, and student upheaval. These demands call for an understanding of the nature of existence in a complicated organizational society that is increasingly being laced into an emerging world society[5] and having to deal with the omnipresent factor of technological change.

Finally, additional pressures are created by an expanding body of technical literature. Each field of the social sciences has been undergoing continued differentiation into narrower and narrower areas of inquiry, and as this has occurred a league of specialized journals have arisen to meet the communication needs of the subspecialties. For example, within the last eleven years, there have been over twenty-five new social-science journals published.[6] A very conservative estimate of the number of social-science journals available, *excluding* philosophy, law, and history, as of 1966, was 114.[7]

---

ministration, Business Administration, Public Administration, Welfare Administration and Planning under the all-embracing concept of administration. This school is an example of the triumph of a controversial concept—administration as a generic phenomenon—that for many years played an important role in all of the previously mentioned fields and is now represented by the emergence of a new academic program.

[4]See Daniel Katz, "Group Process and Social Integration," *Journal of Social Issues*, (January, 1967), p. 8.

[5]See Barbara Ward, *Space Ship Earth* (New York: W. W. Norton, 1966); and Karl Deutsch, "Nation and World," *Contemporary Political Science* (New York: McGraw-Hill, 1967), pp. 204–227.

[6]Peter Lengyel, "Introduction [to the Social Science Press]," *International Social Science Journal*, (1967), p. 147.

[7]Daniel Bell, "United States of America," *International Social Science Journal*, XIX, No. 2 (1967), pp. 245–246.

Bureaucratic Patterns

Most universities are decentralized bureaucracies, and like most decentralized bureaucracies, the operating units (the departments) are cloaked by the tradition of autonomy in most of their undertakings except finance. In matters of finance the university system utilizes competition between the departments as a control device. Since the nonacademic managerial hierarchy knows next to nothing about the academic programs this interdepartmental competition is a rather efficient means of developing information which can be used to determine which department will receive an incremental increase or decrease in funds each year.

Spirited competition born out of this control structure does not languish between funding periods. In fact, there is every reason to believe that rational behavior in this context calls for developing greater insularity between one's own department and others. In addition to interdepartmental insularity, a self-aggrandizement spiral tends to be supported in each of the departments; this spiral is partially a product of insularity and partially a product of the dynamic of competition.

Because of the structure of the organization there is little sharing of problems, issues, or questions between the various departments or disciplines. It is virtually impossible for any unit to perceive the total system and discover points of commonality. Merton has described a situation where "individual members of a group assume that they are virtually alone in holding the social attitudes and expectations they do, all unknowing that others privately share them . . ." as *pluralistic ignorance*.[8] It is this condition precisely which is built into the decentralized academic bureaucracy. The only difference between this structure and a standard bureaucracy is a certain level of autonomy around *some* aspects of the subunit behavior. This delimited autonomy is permitted because competition, which serves as a control device, is thereby increased.

In short, the emergence of the various academic disciplines

[8]Robert K. Merton, "Instability and Articulation in the Role-Set," in Bruce J. Biddle and Edwin J. Thomas (eds.), *Role Theory* (New York: John Wiley and Sons, 1966), p. 285.

has been episodical with a distinct tendency for new fields to emerge from existing enterprises. This trend suggests that the emergence of new fields and the relationships between existing fields may be as much a consequence of the structure of the academic setting as it is intelligent analysis and purposive structure. Since universities tend to be decentralized bureaucratic structures which support a condition of pluralistic ignorance, the result is poor communications and intellectual awareness both between and within departments and disciplines.

Evolution of Disciplines

All of the fields of social science have undergone an amazingly similar pattern of development. A general rejection of macrotheory was prevalent in all fields at the turn of the century; this was followed by an emphasis on concrete units of analysis—institutions such as the family, local community, the Congress and schools—and the celebration of the triumph of positive science, however ill-defined the latter may have been.[9] In general, this period of approximately seventy years was marked by an immersion in the "facts" of social existence, a rather ambivalent attitude toward theory, and a chaotic attempt to reformulate traditional doctrines. No new theories were propounded, no revolutionary doctrines emerged. Novelty remains more or less in the area of systems theory, which has recently become the new ground of empirical study but the roots of which can be traced at least back to Kant who, like contemporary systems theorists, was deeply concerned about the logical category of totality.

It is not difficult to find spokesmen within any of the fields of social science who feel that despite advances in analytical techniques and a growing volume of literature, theoretical developments are somehow constricted, limited, and scientifically unsatisfactory. This condition of malaise is notable today because

[9]The following articles all trace the same general pattern of historical development: Dwight Waldo, "Public Administration," op. cit.; Carl Rogers, "Toward a Science of the Person," in T. W. Wann (ed.), Behaviorism and Phenomenology (Chicago: University of Chicago Press, 1964), pp. 109–32; Robert E. C. Paris, "The Discipline of Sociology," in Robert L. Faris (ed.) Handbook of Sociology (Chicago: Rand McNally, 1964), pp. 23–25; David Truman, "Disillusion and Regeneration: The Quest for a Discipline," American Political Science Review, (December, 1965), pp. 865–873.

it is being verbalized by a number of *leading* authors, not marginal members who may be projecting their own experience of marginality to a field. Carl Rogers in psychotherapy,[10] Abraham Maslow in psychology,[11] Herbert Blumer in sociology,[12] Abraham Kaplan in philosophy,[13] James Rosenau in political science[14] and Dwight Waldo in Public Administration[15] have addressed this issue.

The reasons for disclaimers are not precisely the same in all of these fields. Waldo, for example, is quietly arguing that the remaining segments of the umbilical cord between political science and Public Administration be severed. Rosenau is critical of the way theory is battered about by political-science departments so that it becomes, simultaneously, meaningless and unavoidably utilized by everyone.

Blumer, Rogers, Maslow, and Kaplan all reflect similar complaints—an unnecessarily narrow definition of their fields that is a consequence of a positivist orientation. Kaplan, whose protest is the mildest, feels that analytic philosophy (logical positivism), while clearly a powerful philosophical outlook that has contributed numerous innovations in logic and semantic analysis, is too withdrawn from contemporary life and its manifold problems. In a word, he accuses this outlook of aloofness.[16]

Underlying some of the complaints lodged by the authors mentioned here as well as other social scientists is a questioning of some aspects of the positivist philosophical tradition which has held a dominant position in Britain and the United States for at least the last thirty years. Why this philosophical position

[10]Carl Rogers, "Psychotherapy Today or Where Do We Go From Here?" in Walter D. Nunokawa (ed.), *Human Values and Abnormal Behavior* (New York: Scott, Foresman, 1965), p. 86.

[11]Abraham Maslow, *Toward a Psychology of Being* (New York: Van Nostrand 1962), p. 77.

[12]Herbert Blumer, "Foreword" to Severyn T. Bruyn, *The Human Perspective in Sociology* (Englewood Cliffs: Prentice-Hall, 1966), p. vii. Also, see C. Wright Mills, *The Sociological Imagination* (New York: John Wiley and Sons, 1960).

[13]Abraham Kaplan, *New World of Philosophy* (New York: Random House, 1961), pp. 53–90.

[14]Neil A. McDonald and James N. Rosenau, "Political Theory as Academic Field and Intellectual Activity," *Journal of Politics* (May, 1968), pp. 312–313.

[15]Dwight Waldo, "Public Administration," *Journal of Politics* (May, 1968), pp. 443–479.

[16]Kaplan, *op. cit.*, p. 90.

should be losing its tenaciousness—if indeed it is—is a question of fundamental importance.

New Currents in Social Science

Complete abandonment of logical positivism clearly will not occur, but it is likely that the perspective beginning to be articulated in Britain and the United States will widen the scope of social science. The perspective is phenomenology. It is by no means a new orientation in philosophy but it is relatively new to the United States and Britain.[17] The impact of this and related perspectives upon philosophy, sociology, and psychology is especially relevant to Public Administration.

A Philosophy of Philosophy

Despite the problem of precisely defining phenomenology, there is no doubt about its basic theme: Only through a rigorous analysis of the structure of consciousness is it possible to establish a basis free of presuppositions for philosophy. This attitude is known as critical (as contrasted to the more familiar "natural" attitude).

Conventional assumptions about the objectivity of sense data which are supposed to rest in a rational context, susceptible to lawful explanation, and the idea of a subject that is a pure consciousness, fully transparent to itself, is not acceptable. Husserl calls this dual orientation the "natural attitude."

The dominant tradition of positive science, in which we have been educated, has imposed on us certain prejudices regarding the supposed object of experience. It claims that this object is the object as it manifests itself through the exact description and determination of the sciences. In fact, however, the object of positive science is an abstraction

---

[17]The founder of phenomenology, Edmund Husserl, began to publish as early as 1900, and his article "Philosophy as Rigorous Science," published in 1911, is one of the earliest statements of the problem raised by phenomenology. Husserl pursued the development of this method from approximately 1900 to 1938 and only an extremely small part of the material he wrote has thus far been published. This is one of the reasons why this orientation remained confined to continental Europe. Today, though, a number of authors have begun to publish Husserl's essays and to translate the phenomenological material from German to English. "Philosophy as Rigorous Science" has been translated and reprinted in Quinten Lauer, *Phenomenology and the Crisis of Philosophy* (New York: Harper and Row, 1965), pp. 71–147.

and an artificial structure in reference to the world of our original experience.[18]

In contrast to this position (held by all forms of positivism), Husserl argued that only ideas can have certainty; facts are always contingent. If philosophy is to be scientific it must develop a means of insuring that the basis of its knowledge is as certain as possible. According to Husserl, insuring this certainty can be accomplished only through an analysis of the structure of consciousness. Phenomenology is the method of dealing with this problem.

Despite some rather cumbersome language and alarming terminology (essences),[19] Husserl has identified an absolutely critical weakness in conventional philosophical analysis. However, he did not propose an alternative philosophy; his goal was a methodology with which a presuppositionless and therefore scientific philosophy could be erected. Turned another way, phenomenology is a device for understanding the nature of creativity. Husserl is in effect saying that all important insights occur in a manner represented by his technique; thus, phenomenology can be seen as applied creativity.

Contrary to much of the literature in philosophy and social science, phenomenology is based on a rather heroic model of man—one which assumes the possibility of rationality rather than impulsiveness and irrationality. It is interesting to note, however, that traditional existentialism is based on phenomenology and yet postulates that absurdity is the defining characteristic of man's existence and contingency is the omnipresent experience. For the purposes of this essay, it is not necessary to pursue this set of ideas; there is a movement under way which has the potential of developing a more open-ended, less constricted philosophy of existence.

Colin Wilson is a contributor of "New Existentialism" in the United States and has at least one counterpart in Britain, Michael Polanyi.[20] Both of these philosophers portray man as having an

[18]Joseph Kocklemans, "Some Fundamental Themes of Husserl's Phenomenology," in Joseph J. Kocklemans (ed.), *Phenomenology* (New York: Doubleday, 1967), p. 33.

[19]That is, alarming to a positivist; and who isn't a positivist in our culture?

[20]See Colin Wilson, *Introduction to the New Existentialism* (Boston: Houghton Mifflin, 1967); and Michael Polanyi, *Personal Knowledge* (New York: Harper and Row, 1964).

instinctive desire for knowledge rather than as a guileless creature that is completely a function of his environment. Polanyi demonstrates that the passionless model of science depicted in the literature of the philosophy of science could not be less accurate. He shows, through a plethora of examples, that even if the assumption of complete objectivity or passiveness is attributed to the scientist the language of science is incapable of fully representing the state of knowledge as it existed at the time the "facts" were presented. This condition exists because it is impossible to translate the tacit, the uncommunicable—and in many ways, the most profound—aspect of the scientific act:

We can know more than we can tell and we can tell nothing without relying on our awareness of things we may not be able to tell.[21]

Colin Wilson considers the role of subjectivity from a different perspective. Drawing from the work of Michael Polanyi and Abraham Maslow, Wilson shows that (traditional) existentialism evoked an unnecessary constriction in its development—contingency. Wilson, in contrast, reasserts that ". . . consciousness *is* intentional."[22] And, if consciousness is intentional, then the scope of perception is the consequence of intentional acts. Therefore, through disciplined effort it may be possible to break the intentionality of limited perception.

Wilson is not overwhelmingly optimistic about the prospects of simply eliminating the problem, though. Part of the difficulty is that even if man chooses to expand his consciousness, there is a singular absence of language—a necessity for sharing and describing an experience with others—to describe the experience. Building a new language to communicate the experience of expanded consciousness is, as Wilson says,

analogous to building a road into the wilderness. Our ordinary language is definite because it has a *scaffolding* of everyday experience around it, and this scaffolding acts as a co-ordinate system, enabling one to define any point with a certain precision. But to give a new word a definite meaning, one has to erect a system of scaffolding to support it.[23]

Because of the important role that language plays in this process, Wilson feels that the New Existentialism will involve an integra-

---

[21]Polanyi, *ibid.*, p. xi.
[22]Wilson, *op. cit.*, p. 99.
[23]*Ibid.*, p. 138.

tion of analytic philosophy, with its attention to linguistic analysis, and phenomenological existentialism.

Sociology

Like philosophy, sociology in the United States is only beginning to formally recognize the relevance of phenomenology. As this recognition occurs, European scholars such as Georges Gurvitch, Max Scheler, Alfred Schutz, and Alfred Vierkandt will begin to play a more direct role in shaping the sociological tradition in America. Of these several authors, Alfred Schutz, who spent many years in this country teaching and writing, comes closest to having played a significant role. Yet, despite his presence, it was not until 1967 that his classic volume, *The Phenomenology of the Social World* (originally published in 1932) was available in English. In general, most of the sociological material explicitly related to phenomenology has been published for the first time in English during the last ten years.

Schutz's work is undoubtedly the most profound integration of Husserlian and Weberian analysis; it was written with the explicit goal of further developing Weber's *Verstehen* sociology. According to Schutz, Weber's formulation of social action,[24] while extremely promising, was not developed any further than was absolutely essential to his comprehensive sociological theory. Thus, social action, a primitive in Weber's theory, becomes a highly elaborated concept in Schutz's analysis. Although Schutz makes five specific criticisms of the concept of social action, the most telling points are that (1) Weber did not differentiate action (something in process) and a completed act and (2) he did not seriously consider the matter of intersubjectivity—self-understanding and the understanding of others.[25]

In order to deal with the first of these issues, Schutz analyzed the problem of the constitution of meaning in social action and demonstrated that it is a consequence of lived experience. Con-

[24]"Action is social insofar as, by virture of the subjective meaning attached to it by the acting individual (or individuals), it takes account of the behavior of others and is thereby oriented in its course." Max Weber, *Theory of Social and Economic Organization*, translated by A. M. Henderson and Talcott Parsons (New York: Free Press, 1947), p. 88.
[25]Alfred Schutz, *The Phenomenology of the Social World* (Northwestern University Press, 1967), p. 8.

sequently, the problem of meaning is fundamentally a time prob-lem.[26] An act which is projected in the pluperfect sense—as an accomplished fact—is the basis of the concept of project; the meaning of action (something in process) is the projected act.[27]

Motivation in a project is describable in terms of *in-order-to* motives which are the rationale for action and are carefully dis-tinguished by Schutz from *because* motives which are the *primum mobile* of an act.[28] Because motives are always cloaked by tem-porality and experience—the present situation, past experience, and anticipated possibility. The classic example of in-order-to motives is when a person is asked why he opened his umbrella in the rain and replies "to keep from getting wet." In contrast to the in-order-to motive, the because motive is related to experi-ence with moisture and fabric which results in wrinkles, stains, or mildew.

Schutz distinguishes three types of social worlds which can con-stitute the context of individual projects and intersubjective re-lationships especially: the world of contemporaries, a world in which the subject can be both an actor and an observer; the world of predecessors, in which a subject can be an observer but not an actor; and the world of successors, which is very difficult to grasp and, in fact, is usually assumed to be the same as the social world of contemporaries.

For our purposes, only the world of contemporaries needs to be scrutinized. This social world includes all persons with whom it is *possible* to have a direct experience—in other words, all living human beings. A subset of this concept is the world of *consociates:* persons with whom one interacts directly. In this setting it is possible to have a number of different types of direct relation-ships, such as a *Thou* relationship in which the other is seen as a subject rather than an object, a *We* relationship in which the subject-to-subject orientation is reciprocated, and, finally, a *They* relationship that is inevitably involved when interaction is rare or when others are viewed anonymously.[29]

The We relationship stands at the nexus of the problem of in-

[26]*Ibid.*, p. 12.

[27]*Ibid.*, p. 61. *Note*: The concept of action is distinguished from the broader concept of behavior by the fact that action is related to a project.

[28]*Ibid.*, pp. 88–92.

[29]*Ibid.*, p. 183.

tersubjectivity; in the pure We relationship the Other is related to as a subject whose life-world is sympathetically participated in. The unique aspect of this relationship is not, however, the reciprocal structure of the face-to-face transaction *per se,* but the disclosure of motives. This disclosure occurs in the We relationship because adjustment to the behavior of others can occur with maximum facility and because the nature of the interpenetration of because and in-order-to motives of actors can form a direct source of accommodation without a reflective act in which the other is viewed as an object.

Pure intersubjective motivation is closely approximated in the We relationship of consociates. All other forms of social relationships involve less and less concrete information, and this reduction in turn forces individual actors to resort to increasingly abstract representations of the Other. This abstracting process occurs because each step beyond immediacy results in a marked decrease in the number of perceptions and the breadth of perspectives within which the Other is viewed.[30]

Since knowledge of the social world unavoidably involves some degree of interpretation due to varying degrees of explicit knowledge, there is an increasing need for interpretative schemas to understand the phenomena of behavior as one shifts from We relationships to They relationships. It is precisely this situation that gives rise to the use of *ideal types.*

Two basic forms of ideal types are distinguished by Schutz: course-of-action types and personal-ideal types. The former is derived from objective-meaning contexts that call for specified behavior. Personal ideal types are based on subjective meaning associated with an action and are always derivatives of course-of-action types. This derivative quality holds because the "typical" subjective meaning of a pattern of behavior requires a course-of-action (goal-oriented) context.[31]

As the relationship shifts to an Other or to a They, these ideal types tend to become more and more anonymous. And as this anonymity grows, the actors whose behavior is typified become more and more deterministically represented, and increasingly related to objective-meaning context rather than subjective con-

[30]*Ibid.,* p. 177.
[31]*Ibid.,* p. 187.

texts.[32] And finally, ideal types can be divided into those that are empirical, that is, derived from the senses, and those that are eidetic, or "derived from essential insight."[33]

Thus, as this section has demonstrated, some of the sociological literature in the United States is beginning to be oriented toward existential phenomenology. Of particular interest to Public Administration is the fact that one of the most advanced treatments of sociological theory from a phenomenological viewpoint—Alfred Schutz's *Phenomenology of the Social World* —is expressly formulated as an extension and modification of Weberian theory.

Growth Psychology

More than any other field, psychology has been affected by existential phenomenology. This influence is represented by a movement bearing several titles—Third Force, Humanistic or Growth Psychology.[34] All of these titles are more or less synonyms for an existential orientation. Exponents of the Third Force argue that previous psychological orientations are not capable of dealing with growth. While Freudian psychology and positivistic behaviorism have both developed a body of important knowledge about certain characteristics of human behavior, these theories taken separately or together are not sufficient to deal with the totality of human behavior. In a very rough sense, the early theories were only dealing with either the subjective or the "objective" aspects of human behavior.

Carl Rogers has argued that the phenomenological way of knowing lies between the two polar extremes of subjective and objective knowing.[35] The problem with subjective knowing is that there is no way of verifying the experience; this mode involves an individual's subjective assessment of the feelings he holds about some situation or person. The reference is entirely subjective. Objective knowing (verified by psychological tests

[32]*Ibid.*, pp. 194–195.

[33]*Ibid.*, p. 244.

[34]A 177 item bibliography on material in this area can be found in the following article: Joseph Lyons, "A Bibliographic Introduction to Phenomenology and Existentialism," in Rollo May (ed.), *Existential Psychology* (New York: Random House, 1960), pp. 101–126.

[35]Carl Rogers, *op. cit.*

or experimental manipulation) does not consider the subjective orientation of the individual; preconceived variables are used to explain manifest behavior and a professional reference group acts as a judge of the correctness of the procedure and theory described by the researcher. This approach assumes that the variables being assessed are relatively unchanging, which in turn enables others to replicate the study and verify the experimental knowledge.

The third way of knowing is interpersonal. It requires that the reference point is the other person related to as a subject, that is, empathetically. Hypotheses about the experiencing of the Other can be tested by asking the Other how he feels and by observing the forms of expression he uses: words which imply hostility, fear, love, and so on; gestures that reflect tension, relaxation, surprise; or the feeling-to-feeling dimension where the Other's presence is sensed in a nongesture, nonverbal, physiological manner that is very much like, shall we say, radio waves which bridge the gulf between the two subjects but cannot be seen or heard unless the "receiver" is working.

Sidney Jourard argues that the interpersonal way of knowing is critically dependent upon self-revealing behavior.[36] According to his theory, once one person is able to muster the *courage* to reveal himself to another, a circular pattern of interpersonal relations tends to occur. In other words, self-revealing behavior usually results in the other's revealing himself also. As this occurs, both parties are likely to experience psychological growth. Less and less energy is expended in the maintenance of psychological masks to keep the other from knowing one's true feelings. This unmasking in turn frees the individual for other activities and increases the probability of authentic feedback.

The theory of client-centered therapy is an older, one-dimensional statement of the theory presented by Jourard. Unlike the reciprocal revealing that Jourard talks about, the client-centered theory is focused on the exposure of only one party's feelings. The distinguishing feature of this theory, as developed by

[36]See Sidney Jourard, *The Transparent Self* (New York: Van Nostrand, 1964), and "Growing Awareness and Awareness of Growth," in *Ways of Growth*, Herbert Otto and John Mann (eds.) (New York: Grossman Publishers, 1968), pp. 1–14.

Carl Rogers, is that the therapist, in addition to providing a trustful and loving climate for the client, attempts to become nonjudgmentally involved in the client's life-world. The role requires that the therapist act as an empathetic "mirror" and reflect the *themes*—the recurrent strains of anguish or joy—that the client expresses.

One of the most interesting aspects of the client-centered theory, which is widely accepted and practiced today, is the demands it places on the therapist. It takes a fully functioning person to be able to transcend his own self-needs in a relationship and pour himself completely into the other's life-world in a trusting and helpful way. And it takes a great self-trust to enable one to throw himself into the psychological realm of the Other which will, more than likely, contradict the therapist's life rules. It could be argued that the counselor does not really assume any risks because he has been carefully trained to be aware of virtually all of the psychological problems people can have and that he has been exposed to them personally. This is undoubtedly true but it is also true that to be effective the therapist must meet the client on his own terms as a subject, not an object of general familiarity. From this point of view the risk is clear; the counselor must have an inordinate trust in his ability to meet his own needs and anxieties as they arise in the encounter and at the same time provide a climate in which the client can let his inner feelings pour out.

The extraordinary demands which client-centered therapy places upon the therapist call to mind Abraham Maslow's statement of the need for a self-actualization. Compared to the first four needs in Maslow's hierarchy of needs that all human beings share—physiological need, the need for safety, social need, and, the need for self-esteem—the need for self-actualization has been relatively unexplored in the psychological literature.[37] It is extremely interesting to note that the last need was developed simply because Maslow chose to study relatively fully functioning people rather than persons who were clearly poorly functioning. In the precess of studying the former, he discovered that there was a

---

[37]Maslow present these needs as "instinctoid" and arranged hierarchically so that the first is prepotent to the second, and so on, until the last need—self-actualization—is operant.

distinct tendency for these people to be self-transcendent, able to move beyond their own needs and fuse their interest with the interest of others. And, in a sense, these people were found to be unmotivated; that is, they were not concerned about the need for safety, love, self-esteem, and so on, and therefore did not manifest a striving or desiring orientation.[38] "It was also possible to describe self-actualizing people as expressing rather than coping, and to stress that they were spontaneous, and natural, that they were more easily themselves than other people."[39] All of these people identified with a vocation that was very much a part of their self, their identity, and was a source of profound interest and concern. The real motives for self-actualized persons are apparently the metaneeds of beauty, truth, meaningfulness, perfection, and the like, which are usually relegated to the realm of metaphysical or utopian speculation.

Thus the seemingly extraordinary characteristics demanded by client-centered therapy and self-revealing behavior are, in Maslow's view, features which man has within himself as basic drives and which will emerge naturally if they are not overwhelmed during childhood or by the context of adult existence:

When the philosophy of man (his nature, his goals, his potentialities, his fulfillment) changes, then everything changes, not only the philosophy of politics, of economics, of ethics and values, of interpersonal relations and of history itself, but also the philosophy of education, the theory of how men become what they can and deeply need to become. We are now in the middle of such a change in the conception of man's capabilities, potentialities and goals. A new vision is emerging of the possibilities of man and of his destiny, and its implications are many. . . .[40]

Theory of Organization

Changes in the social sciences—assuming that the phenomenological and existential influences discussed above actually represent potential changes—will have implications for organization theory. The study of complex organizations is one of the most rapidly growing areas of social inquiry. But despite the flood of books and articles, one cannot read this literature without feeling that it has reached a cul-de-sac.

[38]Maslow, *Journal of Humanistic Psychology*, p. 93.
[39]*Ibid.*
[40]Maslow, *Toward a Psychology of Being*, p. 177.

Every empirical study and most theoretical summaries explicitly or implicitly rest on the Weberian concepts of formal organization.[41] Even Katz and Kahn's *Social Psychology of Organizations*,[42] which is clearly the magnum opus of this decade, is tied to these ideas. The Weberian base is not immediately apparent in this case because the authors begin their treatise with a comprehensive survey of systems and role theory which leads one to believe that their formulation will be markedly different. However, it is not. The hierarchical pattern of bureaucracy which underlies their analysis is revealed in their conceptualization of leadership. In their framework, the introduction of structural change to achieve organizational goals is initiated at the *apex* of the role system; the middle leadership level is concerned with elaborating and adapting a given structure to achieve *given* goals (interpolation); and finally, the bottom of the leadership system is concerned with the use of the given structure. There are a number of empirical studies which explicitly utilize the Weberian model and demonstrate that organizational reality seldom correlates very closely with the parameters of the "model." Typically, the *deviations* from the "pure" consequences of this arrangement are explored and conceptualized, but the basic paradigm is not fundamentally questioned.

In no way is reliance on the bureaucratic ideal type transcended by the utilization of the "cybernetics" model or by systems theory, the two most prominent analytical schemes available in the literature.[43] Both of these approaches are, at their present stage of de-

[41]Warren Bennis, *Changing Organizations* (New York: McGraw-Hill, 1966), is an exception.

[42]Daniel Katz and Robert L. Kahn, *The Social Psychology of Organizations* (New York: John Wiley and Sons, 1966), pp. 42–46, 210, and 308–334. Rensis Likert's *Human Organization* (New York: John Wiley and Sons, 1967) follows a similar pattern.

[43]See Chapter XXIV in F. J. Roethlisberger and William Dickson, *Management and the Worker* (Boston: Harvard University Press, 1939). The idea of viewing a formal organization as a system was first utilized over *thirty* years ago in the Hawthorne study. Today there are several promising trends in systems theory but even these are dealing with the concept of structure in dichotomous terms rather than a formulation which deals directly with change and the nature of structure. Walter Buckley's *Sociology and Modern Systems Theory* (New York: John Wiley and Sons, 1967) is the most advanced treatise on systems and also an example of the dichotomous treatment of structural change.

velopment, incapable of dealing with the problems of *structural change*. Secondly, in their application to organizations, this approach—or these approaches, if one sees them as substantially different—always rests on the structural variables involved in the bureaucratic ideal type.

Since Public Administration is traditionally associated with the problem of bureaucracy and has consistently voiced a concern for organizational problems, this theoretical embolism offers the possibility of stimulating the conceptual refinement of the field and of contributing to the larger body of knowledge in the social sciences. It is remarkable that the reviews of the Weberian bureaucratic ideal type are usually limited to only a few of the descriptive features of this model of organization; apparently, the presumption is that one can yank a small piece out of a larger theoretical framework and utilize it as a systematic statement. In fact, Weber's conceptualization of formal organization is only partially intelligible when this limited treatment occurs.

In order to gain a foothold on this problem, it is necessary to reexamine part of the Weberian conceptual framework. This examination will entail (1) an assessment of *some* features of the general framework that Weber developed, (2) an exploration into the meaning of the "ideal type" or "pure type" and, lastly, (3) an explication of the structural features of the bureaucratic ideal type.

A Perspective on Max Weber

When Max Weber wrote,[44] social science in Germany was split into at least two philosophical positions—positivism and neo-Kantianism.[45] The former was based on the idea that the social

---

[44]Despite the attractiveness of Weber's work, it is very difficult to obtain a systematic presentation of his material in English. Pieces of his articles and books have been separately translated and the problem of the lack of a comprehensive translation is thus compounded by overlapping in the material that is available. (See Alfred Diamant, "The Bureaucratic Model: Max Weber Rejected, Rediscovered, Reformed," in Ferrel Heady and Sybil L. Stokes [eds.]. *Papers in Comparative Administration* [Ann Arbor, Michigan: Institute of Public Administration, The University of Michigan, 1962], pp. 59–96.) Moreover, since Weber was continually in a process of intellectual reformulation, it is hard to precisely define his methodology; therefore, one is forced to work with translations of translations of translations of his methodological orientations.

[45]Don Martindale, *The Nature and Types of Sociological Theory* (Boston: Houghton Mifflin, 1960), pp. 377–381.

sciences (and in particular sociology) could be developed by employing the methods and philosophical orientations of the physical sciences:

> . . . positivism could claim, as Compte put it, to be the philosophical integration of human knowledge; the integration was to come through the universal application of scientific method and through excluding all objectives that, in the last analysis, could not be verified by observation.[46]

While it is difficult to generalize about the Neo-Kantians, there is at least one position they all shared: The social world was *not* understandable simply on the basis of observation as utilized in the physical sciences.[47] There were varying degrees of sharpness in the division made between the physical or natural sciences and the cultural sciences. Some theorists such as Rikert argued for an extremely sharp division and others such as Dilthey thought that even though different methodologies may be necessary, there was a broad common ground which could not be ignored. Dilthey raised the issue of the impact of the cultural milieu on the researcher and argued that understanding requires entering another age or person's point of view through the ideas and values of the researcher; consequently, there is always a degree of relativity structured into the social sciences. He argued emphatically that social research must begin with the meaning that is given to life by humans; in other words, that the method of *Verstehen* must be employed.[48] This same approach was advocated by Rikert to the extreme in that he thought cultural knowledge was not subject to "lawful" explanation at all, but was always completely individualized and culturally situational.

Weber developed his methodology with an awareness of the gulf between these two philosophies; he foresaw the possibility of integrating the problem of meaning in social behavior in a way that would satisfy the canons of science and simultaneously avoid the narrowly conceived parameters offered to social science by

[46]Herbert Marcuse, *Reason and Revolution: Hegel and the Rise of Social Theory* (Boston: Beacon Press, 1960), p. 327.

[47]Nicholas S. Timasheff, *Sociological Theory*, Revised Edition, (New York: Random House, 1957), p. 168. Also, see Max Weber, *Theory of Social and Economic Organization* (New York: Free Press, 1947), pp. 8–9.

[48]See H. P. Rickman, "Wilhelm Dilthey," in Paul Edwards (ed.), *Encyclopedia of Philosophy*, II, (New York: Macmillan Co., 1967), pp. 403–407; Lewis White Beck, "Neo-Kantianism," in *Encyclopedia of Philosophy*, V, pp. 468–473.

the positivists. Nicholas Timasheff says that Weber

shared the belief that the social and natural sciences were quite different. In the natural sciences, human interest is directed toward control: he who knows the uniformities can dispose of the forces of nature.
On the contrary, in the social sciences, human interest is directed toward valuation. The concept of culture itself is a value concept. Empirical reality becomes culture to us because, and insofar as, we relate
it to values. The validity of values is a matter of faith, not of knowledge, according to Weber; therefore, the social sciences must investigate values but cannot provide binding norms and ideals from which
directives controlling practical activity can be derived. Accordingly,
in Weber's opinion, the social sciences (including sociology and history)
must be *value-free*.[49]

Preliminary Concepts

The integration of the two philosophical orientations is apparent in Weber's basic concept of *action*. This term is meant
to describe "all human behavior when and so far as the acting
individual attaches a subjective meaning to it."[50] For the moment,
let us place in suspension considerations of methodology and
simply note that according to this definition, action includes
occurrences which are not necessarily manifest. Action is therefore a very broad concept which encompasses virtually all of
human behavior and all of the various fields of social science.

In order to establish some definitional parameters to sociology
and the breadth of his inquiry, Weber chose to concern himself
with *social action*. "Action is social insofar as, by virtue of the
subjective meaning attached to it by the acting individual (or individuals), it takes account of the behavior of others and is thereby
oriented in its course."[51] Given this focus, the problem for the
sociologist is to develop an understanding of social phenomena at
the level of causal adequacy and meaning. "An interpretation of
a sequence of events is causally adequate if careful observations
lead to the generalization that it is probable that the sequence
will always occur in the same way."[52]

Interpretation requires two simultaneous orientations. First,
in direct observation the observer attempts to understand the

[49]Timasheff, *op. cit.*, p. 169.
[50]Henderson and Parsons, *op. cit.*, p. 88.
[51]*Ibid*.
[52]Timasheff, *op. cit.*, p. 170.

meaning that another person gives to an action by examining his own *intentions* when engaged in a similar kind of behavior; meaning in this instance is a consequence of the rational framework that the observer attributes to the observed. The second type of understanding at the level of meaning is to attempt to empathize with the actor in order to understand his motives.[53] The social scientist, unlike the physical scientist, can check his understanding of a particular pattern of behavior against the field of his own intentions in a similar situation or against his subject's description.

Thus, the task of the social sciences is to develop a body of knowledge which is sound at the level of *both* causal adequacy and meaning. Causal adequacy is not dissimilar to that of the physical sciences; *meaning* (*Verstehen*) is distinctly different. Meaning involves an understanding of the goal orientation (intention) of the actor and the motives from which the goal-directed or purposive behavior springs. These two parameters of understanding play an important role in the development of *pure types* or *ideal types*.

Methodology of Ideal Type Construction

A perennial problem in social analysis is explicating concepts without making the positivist error that a concept is a reflection of reality. The concept of ideal, or pure, types[54] is one way of attempting to make one's analytical framework as clear as possible; it involves the selection of a set of variables from the matrix of possible factors which are involved in an event or could be utilized to assess a particular problem. The very term *ideal* calls attention to the fact that an abstracting process is implied.

The purpose of an ideal type is to portray behavior patterns in their pure form, unaffected by situational modifications; in other words, it is a tool for comparative analysis. "It is not a description of reality but it aims to give unambiguous means of expres-

---

[53]"A motive is a complex of subjective meaning which seems to the actor himself or the observer an adequate ground for the conduct in question." Martindale, *op. cit.*, p. 386.

[54]Because the term "ideal" connotes desirability or perfection to some people, the concept of "pure type" is less value loaded. To Weber, ideal type was not a matter of values but a consequence of methodology (as we shall see). The terms ideal type and pure type will be used interchangeably in the text.

sion to such a description."[55] The pure type is simply a methodological device to be utilized in the process of understanding a
given phenomenon; it does not require the belief that reality is
rational.

The development of the unified analytical construct begins with
the selection and accentuation of relationships which are suspected
or discovered to exist in reality. Accentuation often helps to
bring additional relationships to the attention of the researcher,
who can carefully explore them in order to understand the bearing they might have on the phenomena. This process, according
to Weber, must proceed in a manner which is consistent with the
canons of understanding discussed previously. Imagination and
conjecture are essential, since an ideal type is *not* intended to be
an isomorphic representation of reality. It requires the "synthesis of many diffuse, discrete, more or less present and occasionally absent, concrete individual phenomena."[56]

The second methodological criterion is that the pattern or configuration represented by the pure type must be *objectively possible*. In other words, the relationships posited by the pure type
must not contradict the known laws of nature or the facts of a
concrete situation.[57]

Finally, the pure type must be capable of sustaining the test of
causal adequacy (in one sense this is a question of economics).
That is, any item in the type should be causally relevant to the
total pattern of behavior depicted by the type. After constructing
the ideal type(s) relevant to a particular set of phenomena, the
researcher compares the different empirical situations with one
another based on the perspective provided by the ideal type. This
comparative function has a number of implications for the administration literature; usually bureaucracy is assumed to be
an *isomorphic model* of reality, not a carefully accentuated and
differentially emphasized unified construct used to compare *different* empirical situations.

To summarize, ideal types rest on the following assumptions:
(1) Reality is never completely unambiguous. Therefore sim-

[55]Max Weber, *The Methodology of the Social Sciences*. Translated and edited
by Edward Shils and Henry A. Finch (New York: Glencoe Free Press, 1949), p. 90.
[56]*Ibid.*
[57]See Martindale, *op. cit.*, p. 383.

plified artifacts must be developed to ascertain an insight into a particular context. (2) A more profound knowledge of the empirical world can be gained by segmenting parts of it and developing unified constructs to represent these segmented parts. (3) Ideal types must be constructed so that they can be utilized as a framework for comparing different empirical situations, the relationships posited in the type manifest causal adequacy, and the configuration or pattern of relatonships is objectively possible.

It might be possible to argue that the utilization of the bureaucratic ideal type as a model—a utilization which has empirical support in the literature[58]—is why it remains embodied in the literature of Public Administration and organization literature in general. It is also tempting to assume that it was because the bureaucratic ideal type seemed to be such a rational and efficient way to organize that it was adopted by positivist American scholars—and, in particular, those in Public Administration—as a *goal* to achieve. These speculations are premature; the point here is simply that an ideal type is a methodological tool with certain characteristics which, in turn, define the area of its legitimate use.

An Ensemble of Ideal Types:
The Conceptual Trip to Bureaucracy

One more aspect of the Weberian framework—the *transitional* concepts which constitute the bridge between the construct of action and the construct of bureaucracy—must be examined before an assessment of the conceptual roots and import of the bureaucratic ideal type can be made.

Earlier, Weber's definition of action was provided (behavior to which an individual attaches a subjective meaning) and it was indicated that he limited his attention to the subdivision of *social action* (behavior in which an individual takes into consideration the action of others). Based on this narrowed point of analysis, Weber developed the following four ideal types of *social action* (see Table 1).

---

[58]An article by Richard Hall presents an excellent example of the use of the "type" as a model. See Richard D. Hall, "The Concept of Bureaucracy: An Empirical Assessment," *American Journal of Sociology*, LXIX (July, 1963), pp. 36–41.

TABLE 1. TYPES OF SOCIAL ACTION

Affective	_Traditional_	_Rationally Purposeful_	_Rational in Terms of Values_
Emotional factors determine means and ends of action	Both means and ends are fixed by custom	Action addressed to a situation with a plurality of means and ends in which the actor is free to choose his means purely in terms of efficiency	Means are chosen for their efficiency but the ends are fixed in advance

Source: Adapted from Don Martindale, _The Nature and Types of Sociological Theory_ (Boston: Houghton Mifflin Co., 1960), p. 388.

The typology depicted in Table 1 is adequate only for individual behavior; it suggests that at the individual level of analysis behavior can be considered in terms of these four pure types of action, none of which would be sufficient to yield full understanding.

In order to work with social structures, Weber developed another typology for what he called _social relations_: a model pattern of behavior which may prevail when a number of actors are observed. In effect, this typology involves a more abstract unit of analysis, that is, a number of interacting individuals viewed as a collectivity. The interactional framework of Table 1 (the analysis of two or more individuals interacting) becomes more and more difficult to utilize because as the number of actors increases arithmetically, the number of possible interactions increases geometrically. The observer is forced to shift to a less concrete level in order to assess the phenomena.

Table 2 indicates the types of social relations which encompass the various types of social action in Table 1. The first pure type—usage—encompasses all of the other types; it is the limiting case of absolutely similar actions. The other types follow a pattern that is more or less derived from the typology of action. Custom and fashion (2 and 4) are derivations of traditional action; rational usage (3) is conceptually similar to rationally purposeful action. Convention and law (5 and 6) are analogous to social action that is rational in terms of values. Construed more broadly, one could work either way between these typologies; for example, a pattern of behavior identified as "law" could be subanalyzed to assess the extent to which any of the various types of social action are or are not manifested.

TABLE 2. TYPES OF SOCIAL RELATIONS*

1	2	3	4	5	6
Usage	*Custom*	*Rational Usage*	*Fashion*	*Convention*	*Law*
Actual uniformity of social relations	Usage on long familiarity or habit	Uniformity determined by the rational actions of actors under similar conditions	Usage determined by the presence of novelty in the corresponding behavior	Usage springing from desires for social prestige, usage determined by normative patterns	Usage determined by the presence of designated enforcing authorities

Source: Adapted from Don Martindale, *The Nature and Types of Sociological Theory* (Boston: Houghton Mifflin Co., 1960), p. 189.

*There is considerable confusion about the exact number of precise definitions developed by Weber in this area. See Parsons, *The Structure of Social Action*, Vol. II, pp. 650–651. I have arbitrarily adopted Martindale's definitions because they seem more plausible.

In addition to exhibiting pattern, social relations are also characterized by an orientation to an *order*; thus, social relations may be predicated on a subjective identification with custom, fashion, and so on. If an action is perceived by the members of the order as that orientation which is most desirable for all members (normative validity), then the relations are called a *legitimate order*.[59] It is by these two criteria—orientation to a particular set of values and the presence of order—that one can begin to classify groups.

[59]Martindale, *op. cit.*, p. 390.

An additional factor necessary to explain differences between groups is the way members of an order are distinguished from nonmembers. Two types of relationships were defined by Weber: *open* and *closed* relationships.

A social relationship . . . will be spoken of as "open" to outsiders if and insofar as participation in the mutually oriented social action relevant to its subjective meaning is, according to its system of order, not denied to anyone who wishes to participate and who is actually in a position to do so. A relationship will, on the other hand, be called "closed" against outsiders so far as, according to its subjective meaning and the binding rules of its order, participation of certain persons is excluded, limited, or subjected to conditions.[60]

The type of closed relationship described in this quotation is of particular importance to Public Administration; it is the closed type of social relationship which forms part of the basis for what Weber calls the "corporate group." More than a closed quality is necessary, however, for the existence of a corporate group. In addition, there must be present *specific* individuals whose action reinforces the order of the closed group on a regular basis and often this also includes an administrative staff. The persons who are responsible for enforcing the order "normally also have representative authority.[61] This is another way of saying that one or more individuals will be held responsible for the behavior of the larger collectivity with regard to how adequately the order of the corporate group is reinforced. If those who are representatives are successful in this task, they will receive the credit, and if unsuccessful, the blame.[62]

The next level in Weber's terms is the concept of *organization*. "An 'organization' is a system of continuous purposive activity of a specified kind."[63] If an administrative staff is added, the result is a *corporate organization*.

All of the relationships thus far are more or less related to the generalized features of the corporate group without specifying the internal processes or action patterns which hold the system together. For this purpose, it is necessary to begin with the concept of power, which was implied when it was noted that typically

---

[60]Henderson and Parsons, *op. cit.*, p. 139.
[61]*Ibid.*, pp. 143–144.
[62]*Ibid.*
[63]*Ibid.*, p. 151.

some person or persons are responsible for reinforcing the order (norms) of the corporate group. Now, more specifically: "Power is the probability that one actor within a social relationship will be in a position to carry out his own will despite resistance, regardless of the basis on which this probability rests."[64]

Imperative control is an extension of the concept of power from an interpersonal relationship to that of group (this concept is very similar to that of authority in the contemporary literature), and has to do with this probability that orders or commands from a specific source will be obeyed. A subpart of the concept of imperative control is habit. Weber assumes that discipline is partially a consequence of habit and partially a consequence of an interest in obedience which is manifested through voluntary submission.[65] Therefore, Weber's definition is that "discipline is the probability that by virtue of habituation a command will receive prompt and automatic obedience in stereotyped forms, on the part of a given group of persons."[66]

If in turn imperative control, that is, authority, is applied to a corporate group whose members, by virtue of their membership in the group, are subject to the exercise of legitimate authority, then Weber calls this an *imperatively coordinated group*.[67]

An imperatively coordinated corporate group will be called "political" if and insofar as the enforcement of its order is carried out continually within a given *territorial* area by the application and threat of physical force on the part of the administrative staff. A compulsory political association with continuous organization will be called a "state" if and insofar as its administrative staff successfully upholds a claim to the *monopoly* of the *legitimate* use of physical force.[68]

This definition of the state is not unlike the one which is supported in the contemporary literature of political science.[69] Both sociology and political science see the question of legitimacy as

[64]*Ibid.*, p. 152.
[65]*Ibid.*, p. 324.
[66]*Ibid.*, p. 152.
[67]*Ibid.*, p. 153.
[68]*Ibid.*, p. 154.
[69]See David Easton, *A Framework for Political Analysis* (Englewood Cliffs, N.J.: Prentice-Hall, 1965), pp. 21, 96; Robert A. Dahl, *Modern Political Analysis* (Englewood Cliffs, N.J.: Prentice-Hall, 1963), p. 12. Dahl states that he is using the Weberian definition.

essential to the modern definition of the state. And this question is crucial too for the conceptualization of Public Administration.

Before turning directly to this problem let us review the conceptual framework that has been presented. Weber began his sociological analysis with the concept of social action which was the basis for a typology encompassing four *types* of action: affective, traditional, rationally purposeful, and rational in terms of values. He then moved to a slightly more abstract level of analysis, social collectivities, and developed this typology of social relations, which included six ideal types of social relations. This typology provided half of the conceptualization of a social relationship: the typification of value orientations which may be held in relation to an order. The second half of this concept was the way in which participation was defined. If participation was not restricted, an *open* social relationship was said to exist. If it was restricted, a *closed* social relationship was considered to exist. Weber defined a closed social relationship whose order was reinforced on a regular basis and whose activities were oriented to specific purposes as a *corporate organization*. This definition, in turn, was the basis for his definition of an imperatively coordinated group which contained all of the characteristics of a corporate organization plus the legitimate exercise of power utilized to maintain the internal processes of the system over time. Finally, an imperatively coordinated group that maintained itself within a given territory through the legitimate monopoly of the exercise of physical force was called a *state*.

Public Administration and Weberian Theory

The role of Public Administration is clearly spelled out by Weber: It is to maintain the legitimacy of the state as the social system with a monopoly on the claim to the legitimate exercise of physical force. This conceptualization is considerably richer than a politics-administration dichotomy or the idea of Public Administration as another political process, or simply the identification of the field with government administrators. It is possible, by drawing from Weber and Schutz to say:

Public Administration as a type of social action is defined insofar as, by viture of the because motives of the acting individual (or individuals), it takes into consideration the behavior of others and is thereby oriented in its course to the maintenance of the political order's monopoly of the legitimate exercise of physical force.

Given this definition of Public Administration, what kind or kinds of organization are appropriate? Weber's answer is well known: He postulated the monocratic form of bureaucracy as the most rational form of organization. In addition to the characteristics of the bureaucratic ideal type which is usually provided in the literature, Table 3 displays Weber's criteria of effectiveness and the consequences he thought bureaucracy would have for society.

TABLE 3.   LEGAL RATIONAL AUTHORITY WITH BUREAUCRATIC STAFF

Criteria of Effectiveness

1. Any legal norm may be based on
   a. agreement
   b. imposition
   c. expediency
   d. rational values
   e. rational values and expediency

   and is accompanied with a claim of obedience on part of numbers of corporate groups.

2. Every body of laws is an intentionally established body of abstract rules. Administration is rational pursuit of interests specified in order governing corporate groups, limited to
   a. limits in legal precepts
   b. using principles capable of generalized application—approved or at least not disapproved by order governing group

3. Person in authority occupies "office"—subject to impersonal order which governs "office" and to which his action is oriented.

4. Person obeys authority only in his capacity as a member of corporate group and what he obeys is only the "law."

5. Obedience to person in position of authority not because of individual but because of obedience owed the impersonal order.

Structural Characteristics

1. Continuous organization of official functions bound by rules.

2. Specified sphere of competence:
   a. obligations to perform functions which are part of systematic division of labor
   b. provision of necessary authority to carry out functions

[Continued

Table 3. *Continued*

Legal Rational Authority with Bureaucratic Staff

Structural Characteristics

    c. necessary means of compulsion are clearly defined and their use is subject to definite conditions

    d. discipline, a stereotyped response to a command, rests on habit and voluntary submission

3. Organization of offices follows principle of hierarchy

    a. each lower office is under control and supervision of higher office

    b. right of appeal and statement of grievances from lower to higher—responsibility for handling subordinate grievances may be higher in hierarchy or remain at same level

4. Technical rules or norms regulate the conduct of office. Specialized training is necessary.

5. Administrative acts, decisions and rules are formulated and recorded in writing.

6. Members of administrative staff are separated from ownership of means of production or administration.

7. Complete absence of appropriation of official position by incumbent.

8. Selection of Office Holders

    a. based on free contractual relationship

    b. selection on basis of technical competence

        1) tested by examination or guaranteed by diploma

        2) persons appointed, not elected

9. Conditions of office

    a. sole or primary occupation of incumbent

    b. occupation constitutes a career

        1) system of promotion based on seniority or achievement or both

        —promotion dependent on judgment of supervisors

        —insures that subordinate is dependent on superior

10. Remuneration based on fixed salaries in money, plus right to pension.

    a. only under certain circumstances can employer terminate appointment

    b. official always free to resign

    c. salary based on position in hierarchy

[*Continued*

Table 3. *Continued*

Legal Rational Authority with Bureaucratic Staff

Social Consequences of Bureaucratic Control

1. The tendency to "leveling" in the interest of the broadest possible basis of recruitment in terms of technical competence.
2. The tendency to plutocracy growing out of the interest in the greatest possible length of technical training.
3. The dominance of a spirit of formalistic impersonality, . . . without hatred or passion, and hence without affection or enthusiasm.

Source: Adapted from Max Weber, *Theory of Social and Economic Organization,* trans. A. M. Henderson and Talcott Parsons (New York: Free Press, 1947), pp. 329–334 and 340.

The Weberian ideal type of bureaucracy has, of course, met with its critics. One of them is Warren Bennis who is exceptional because he is trying to develop an alternative to the bureaucratic model. In his book, *Changing Organizations*, Bennis develops some parameters of the nonbureaucratic organization.[70] There are difficulties, though, with Bennis' theory. In my opinion, he places too much reliance on professionalization; very few professional schools promote risk-taking behavior or interpersonal competence. It is unlikely—and this may be fortunate—that in the near future everyone will be a professional. Moreover, some of the values of professionalization are not supportive of the risk-taking environment that Bennis describes as based on the presence of professionals. In other words, Bennis overstates the case for the virtue of professionalization and overestimates the degree to which the population is likely to be professionalized in the future. In addition, because his theory is very dependent on the role of professionals, it does not take into consideration the manner in which the total organization will be tied together with systematic rules of the game and the conditions within which these rules could be operant.

Consociated Ideal Type

The consociated ideal type elaborated in Table 4 is an attempt to provide a more systematic conceptualization of one non-

[70]Warren Bennis, *Changing Organizations* (New York: McGraw-Hill, 1966).

bureaucratic variant.[71] In many ways the consociated ideal type parallels and builds upon Bennis' ideas; in other ways it diverges rather sharply.

Table 4. Legal Rational Authority with Consociated Staff

Criteria of Effectiveness

1. Any legal norm may be based on
   a. agreement
   b. imposition
   c. expediency
   d. rational values
   e. rational values and expediency

   and is accompanied with a claim of obedience on part of numbers of corporate groups.
2. Every body of laws is an intentionally established body of abstract rules. Administration is rational pursuit of interests specified in order governing corporate groups, limited to
   a. limits in legal precepts
   b. using principles capable of generalized application—approved or at least not disapproved by order governing group
3. Situational adaptability of organization
   a. as a total system
   b. in terms of subsystems
4. Noncompetitive, trusting social relationships
5. Attracting capable personnel
6. Client-centered services
7. Eliminating need for organization's services

Structural Characteristics

1. Basic work unit is project team.
   a. financial autonomy
      1) lump-sum budget
   b. situationally provided technology
      1) tailor-made information and feedback system—computer based
   c. interdependent with other project teams   [*Continued*

---

[71] I have benefited greatly from the penetrating insights of Professor Neely Gardner, School of Public Administration, University of Southern California, with regard to the importance of project teams, decentralized budgeting, trustful relationships, and the like, but would not want to "saddle" him with the type depicted above. Nevertheless, our encounters were a necessary precondition of the conceptualization of the consociated ideal type.

TABLE 4. *Continued*

LEGAL RATIONAL AUTHORITY WITH CONSOCIATED STAFF

Structural Characteristics

2. Multivalent authority structure
   a. no permanent hierarchy
   b. situational leadership
   c. diverse authority patterns among various project teams
3. Total organization based on time imperatives.
   a. established to solve a particular problem within specific time limits
      1) subunits on shorter term time parameters
4. Diverse subunit (projects) programs to deal with same basic problem.
   a. assumption of equifinality of means to goals
5. Social relationships characterized by high degree of independence and interdependence.
   a. direct, authentic interpersonal and intergroup communications
   b. disintegration and redevelopment of project teams facilitates direct communications
   c. most permanent project team responsible for team building and basic encounter training
      1) used to build trust, noncompetitiveness and interpersonal competence
      2) team-building training prior to initiating project
      3) basic encounter training used following disintegration of project team units
6. Clientele served is represented in organization.
   a. cross section of clientele
   b. authority *equal* to professional members
   c. to obtain better information on service needs and, whenever possible, to provide organizational experience to youth prior to college
      1) latter is to help generate interest in post-college work in organization
7. Organization is place of temporary employment, not a career.
   a. career associated with professional reference group outside organization
8. Record keeping is computer based.
   a. performance goals of each project team shared with all others
   b. requests for progress data automatically shared with others

[Continued

TABLE 4. *Continued*

LEGAL RATIONAL AUTHORITY WITH CONSOCIATED STAFF

Structural Characteristics

9. Professional role requires
   a. technical skills
   b. skill in preventing emergence of more than *minimal* social stratification
      1) promotes interdependence
      2) promotes ambiguity useful in problem solving
      3) maintenance of ambiguity builds greater trust between team members

Social Consequences of Consociated Control

1. Social diversity and independent personal styles is facilitated.
2. Persons derive minimal alienation from organizational experience.
3. Tolerance for conflict and ambiguity is increased.
4. Basis for joining formal organization is public values it supports.
5. Problem of structural rigidity is reduced through intentional elimination of organizations.

It is very important to meet the bureaucratic model on its own terms. Many people believe in the virtues of bureaucracy and are not likely to be convinced it is possible to have a rational organization unless it more or less follows the parameters depicted by Weber. Before this matter is reviewed, there are several caveats that need to be issued about the extent to which current social conditions differ from those Weber observed.

Perhaps two key variables have changed sharply. One is that interorganization mobility is no longer frowned upon. When Weber was writing, one of the most important measures of personal responsibility was how long one had worked for an organization; movement from organization to organization was considered a mark of irresponsibility. The second factor is the emergence of a remarkable degree of geographical mobility. This factor in turn means that individuals in organizations must learn to deal with a much more elaborately differentiated pattern of subcultures. Fifty or sixty years ago, a person began his career in an area, raised his family, established his community image and died in the same town where he began.

Both of these variables have an important effect on career structure, which is one of the major concepts in the bureaucratic ideal type. The Weberian model assumes that once a person enters the organization he will remain for the balance of his career, fight his way upward through competitive examinations, and in middle age assume a position of authority in the upper strata of the hierarchy.

The consociated model, in contrast, does not assume that the individual sees his career in terms of one organization. The model assumes that movement from one organization to another is a prominent feature of organizational patterns. This assumption in turn implies that the orientation, goals, and values upheld by an organization will play an increasingly important role. Therefore, the reward structure is oriented toward promoting the self-esteem of the professional members through intentional provision of financial and material support. A related factor is the attempt to bring young people from client groups into the organization. By involving the client group it is possible to gain more knowledge of the idiosyncratic features of the culture that is confronted *and* increase the likelihood that the clientele representatives will experience considerable satisfaction from holding a job with responsibility and return later to be professional employees.

Another matter that is very important to both the bureaucratic and the consociated models is control. In Weber's formulation, control is accomplished through a chain of command in which the subordinate is in a dependent relationship to the superior and thus susceptible to the commands of his superior. The competition built into the structure serves as a control device by introducing greater impersonal objective examinations, carefully designed jobs with a precise description—which makes the prize that one is competing for much clearer—and carefully designed regulations for each of the offices. The primary reference group for the officials of a bureaucracy is the organization itself. This formulation stands in contrast to the consociated type where control is achieved through the promotion of ambiguity, rather than specificity, and trust, rather than competition. Both of these conditions are consciously pursued in order to keep the structural patterns of the organization as susceptible to change as possible. This provision is assumed to be necessary because organizational forms are based on limited time dimensions and increasingly complicated clientele problems.

In order to deal with the clientele problems, the structure of the consociated model incorporates selected, nonprofessional personnel who *share* decision-making power with the professionals. This situation insures that the clientele obtains the services it desires and that the professionals can bring their technical expertise to bear as precisely as possible. Team development and basic encounter groups are undertaken to help unfreeze interpersonal rigidities which would reduce the ability of the team to develop the parameters of the services which are to be offered to the larger community and which are legitimate in terms of the political order.

Finally, the consociated model attempts to present an image— a *value pool*—which will accomplish three purposes: attract capable personnel to serve in the organization, invest in the future and the present through the involvement of community or clientele members, and promote organizational effectiveness by establishing the total organization and subsystems on specific time parameters (an explicit recognition that the task of an organization is to put itself *out* of business).

These considerations are increasingly important in the contexts of the United States and Canada which are well into the development of postindustrial society. As this process continues (assuming that it does) the environment of any given organization is likely to be similar to that described by Emery and Trist in their now classic article, "The Causal Texture of Organizational Environments."[72] They demonstrate the incredibly complex and contradictory demands for organizational adaptiveness in postindustrial society. These demands arise from the character of the environment which is highly unstable, not only at the microlevel of particular sets of interacting and interrelated organizations, but also at the level of the *total* society. The environmental totality is itself as mobile, dynamic, and changeful as environmental subsets are in industrial society.

Already "organizationally relevant uncertainty" is a very im-

[72] F. E. Emery and E. L. Trist, "The Causal Texture of Organizational Environments," *Human Relations* (February, 1965), pp. 21–32.

pelling fact for many organizations; as society moves deeper into postindustrial development, this will escalate and spread. It can be seen today that

the consequences which flow from . . . actions lead off in ways that become increasingly unpredictable; they do not necessarily fall off with distance, but may at any point be amplified beyond all expectation; similarly, lines of action that are strongly pursued may find themselves attenuated by emergent field forces.[73]

Such environmental turbulence and complexity requires a strategic response which results in simplifying and significantly reducing environmental ambiguity. Emery and Trist propose that this can be accomplished through the development of interorganizationally shared values which can serve as guidelines for action. It is in this sense that the value-pool concept is an important step in the direction of evoking consequences which would have a temporary stabilizing effect.

On the other hand, the consociated model is not intended to be *the* organizational model for postindustrial society—a proposition both infinitely grandiose and infinitely undesirable. It is intended to portray one of the *N* + 1 *objective possibilities* which would be reasonable responses to the problem of organizing for adaptability and changefulness.[74]

Comment: Phenomenological Administration— A New Reality

Frank McGee

Maybe man's needs are arranged "hierarchically"—that is, the more fundamental our needs are with respect to existence the more proximate they are to our consciousness—as Abraham Maslow, the psychologist, implies. If it is assumed that human problems are solved progressively with little or no slippage, then it is sufficiently difficult to match public organizational response to the level of need at hand. However, when you admit regression —when man does not just make himself totally miserable again

[73]*Ibid.*, p. 26.

[74]For a superb analysis of the concept of objective possibility, see Max Weber, *Methodology of the Social Sciences*, pp. 164–188.

at a higher level of need but also creates real problems of different types at different levels of need in the process of consciously "solving" or satisfying *a* particular type of need at some level— then the problem of matching the *correct* organizational response to human problems becomes formidable. Certainly, if it is assumed that government is responsible for satisfying human need in part or in whole, then its responses *should be* a function of the problems.

The objectification of social relationships coupled with the paramilitary work ethic has borne fruit in this country over the last few decades in the form of technological advancement, material abundance, and almost limitless opportunity to *acquire*. And the result approaches social disaster. Relative affluence has become a poor surrogate for the solution of all sorts of problems— such as alienation, whether it be generational, spiritual, or racial—whereas traditional theory assumed that problems would be solved by material well-being.

Alienation grows in part from apartness: from being alone, being a minority, being bought off, being too competitive. There are many degrees of alienation, from the benign to the malignant, from the tolerable to the intolerable, from the necessary to the debilitating. One symptom of alienation is the inability or unwillingness to communicate. For example, *measurement* can be a pretty poor way to understand the nature of social problems. People are tired of being objects of research and experimentation. They are sick of being probed, measured, objectified, and therefore dehumanized. People are not aggregates or other abstractions; people are people. Among students there is a strong antibehavioral trend to the extent that behavioral study is equated to the positivistic process of isolating a few observable variables for "objective" measurement. In terms of social research, it is a "cop-out" which applies positivistic tools of analysis to what are necessarily the wrong questions in order to achieve irrelevant solutions. The comments "Picture yourself in his shoes" or "Lend a sympathetic ear" are not alien to us or our culture, but these responses have been reserved by us for very few.

The "growth" of phenomenology as an intellectual pursuit in American academe is, in part, a result of the reality of today. It could be said that this growth is the beginning of a legitimizing process almost in an Orwellian sense; it is not so much that history is being rewritten, or even reinterpreted, but rather it is being reemphasized. After all, phenomenology has had a long though obscure history which can be traced back to the Renaissance.

Phenomenology is perhaps the supreme philosophy of relativism. It asserts that there are many paths that lead to and build understanding. Only ideas are certain, comprehensible, and static. Reality is contingent, uncertain, and dynamic. Undeniably, we can know enough to create satisfactory "realities" in terms of human need. Again, however, human need is like the shifting sands, and acculturated "realities" often become unreal. Phenomenology suggests that one can proceed to a "new reality"—that is, an understanding of the self and of other people. Achieving this reality takes communication which often transcends the medium of linguistic symbols and sounds but includes much more, such as feeling.

The "advent" of phenomenology as sociological insight, or psychological approach focuses on knowing in another dimension which is often slighted in our culture. This way of knowing has to do with the wholesomeness of interpersonal relations: treating individuals as people and not just entities. Phenomenology is consciousness expansion: "seeing" what is often known intuitively, transcending cultural categories of knowing, gaining new perspectives of ourselves and others. This expansion does *not* rule out the proper use of measurement based on observed and participated-in behavior, but rather makes it possible to utilize it appropriately and in proportion to the nature of the social problem at hand.

Phenomenology and Administration

Organizations have often been considered analogs of engines. For example, when the question of which engine design should be implemented was asked, the answer was usually that design which maximized output of energy per unit of fuel. In this tradition, Americans attempted to build the most efficient organizations based upon maximizing profit. People in these organizations were viewed as components of the production process: as units of input.

When Weber's formulations of ideal types of social action—the state and bureaucracy—were translated into English, these conceptions had been goals of long standing rather than aids to comparative analysis. Attempts had been made to actualize much of the Weberian bureaucratic typology. What was meant to be a methodological tool, in fact, for many became normative theory.

It is clear that Weber was concerned about the either/or positions which were held by German philosopers of his day with respect to positivistic generalizing and subjective individualizing. He tried to bridge the gap by representing subjective valuations—motives for social action—by categories of social action. He called his approach *Verstehen*, meaning "understanding." He realized that his typological categories were not all-inclusive with respect to causes of human motivation, but rather incorporated what were to him the more obvious, indicative motives. As presented in Kirkhart's account, Weber's *Verstehen* seems to have little bearing, other than being a presupposition, on the latter's bureaucratic typology. One gets the impression that *Verstehen*, though applied by Weber to many levels of social reality, bears only indirectly on bureaucracy. In other words, it seems that Weber did not *directly* relate his *Verstehen* sociology to the internal "mechanism" of administering the state, that is, bureaucracy.

In Kirkhart's presentation, one makes a quantum leap from Shutz's integration of Husserl and Weber's typologies of social action—that is, the expansion on the concept and meaning of social action—to the consociated ideal type. One cannot help but wonder about the correct role of Weber's material in this presentation since Weber did not expand his definitions of social action. But even if Weber had expanded these definitions in a phenomenological direction, it almost certainly would not have changed the development of his ideal types because his typologies were, again, methodologies which incorporated the most manifest characteristics of governmental organization in his time for analytical-comparative purposes.

In late-twentieth-century America, one really has to strain—indeed to fantasize—in order to built a consociated ideal-type methodological instrument based on manifest characteristics of organizations. But then, most of us are culture bound and have not questioned many of our presuppositions and categories: we see what we are conditioned to see. Perhaps Weber had this problem too. As Kirkhart presents his material, there is a normative ring to the consociated ideal-type, for it is not *just* a methodological tool but "wish-thought." It is all well and good to strive for a state of organizational affairs in which one can "see" manifest qualities such as trust, ambiguity, and a distinct problem orientation. But let's not suppose that this consociated type would be useful as a methodology exactly as Weber meant ideal types to be, unless the normative quality is deemphasized.

In our culture, attempts have been made to actualize much of the bureaucratic ideal type; it has been viewed as prescription, consciously and unconsciously. Almost all organization-theory literature, as Kirkhart notes, alludes to bureaucracy implicitly or explicitly. The notion has become, in fact, an unchallenged premise, an unconscious organizing framework. Acknowledging the strength of this influence is not to imply that the translation of Weber into English about 1948 has been the prime mover in the increased bureaucratization of national life. Indeed, bureaucracy, hierarchical relationships, impersonal roles, superordination, and subordination have been around at least since military organization and the Captains of Industry became imprinted on the consciousness of the American collectivity. Bureaucracy was and is very real in that human interaction is real, and many characteristics of this type have been needed in the solution of very definite kinds of problems.

Organizations and Problems

Generally, the consensus would seem to be that organizations should merely be responses to problems—to commonly adhered to value imperatives. Unfortunately, most people are too organization conscious. That is, they focus on organizational survival, job survival, job definition as discrete plums in a competitive environment. In a very real sense, organizational clienteles are *within* the organization as well as *without*. Some extremely large organizations produce "output" which is not clearly beneficial to any external clientele or "public," but rather serves that figment called "the public interest" or "national security." Who is to deny that some organizations provide *raisons d'être* for thousands upon thousands of "within" people. And not just *raisons d'être*, but other tangible and intangible benefits are provided as well, such as income, satisfaction, and pride. Perhaps we should in some ways be quite happy that organizations to a greater or lesser degree *are* self-serving.

However, because most of the critical problems facing us as a society are very human problems in a direct sense—such as health, education, and welfare—a redirection of our positivistic inclinations is in order, at least in the sense that a redirection toward the conscious building of organizational responses to problems is mandatory. This need for responsiveness calls for organizations or parts of organizations which will focus on the troubled and disadvantaged as whole people, and which will be composed of people who work effectively both together as professionals with substantive knowledge and with their clients for the solution of particular problems. In many ways, the clients would solve their own problems with catalytic or professional aid.

Kirkhart's phenomenological approach has great impact at two levels. First, it forces one to question the very nature of social problems. One sees solution not solely through aggregations, but also through individual response. One sees a need for more *wholesomeness* and empathy in professional life. Second, and perhaps more central to Public Administration, it is imperative that thinking be centered on the creation of *wholesome* environments: environments in which professionals can work in thorough communication with other professions and with clients. This statement is pregnant with action implications. Academicians, for example, should become more "applied" and less "pure" with respect to social ills. Organizationally this means at least two things. One, it could imply a superstructure of political executives hedging a very empathetic rather than technical environment. In other words, one would see a more or less bureaucratic administration "protecting" a consociated environment. Or, two, it could imply that it would be fitting to create a more or less consociated organization en toto.

Again it would be the same old trap if one became too enamored with this organizational approach to problem solving in the sense that one might conclude that it is *the* organizational response to all problems or the way *all* organizations should be developed. For example, one might take too seriously the contention that all organizations—or even all of *one* organization— should be developed adhering closely to Kirkhart's consociated type based on organizational development. In such a case one would predict probable chaos with respect to an organization of any size. Scheduling, coordination, just plain logistics, cannot be ignored. Most probably, some parts of an organization would be best developed along bureaucratic lines, and other parts— especially with respect to direct professional service to clients— in a more consociated manner. Neither of the parts, bureaucratic or consociated, would be manifest in toto. You would still have formal relationships of great importance in the former and leadership and coordination problems in the latter.

Conclusion

If Kirkhart's intention is to stimulate interst in the development of a consociated type by investigating Weber and other traditions or precedents in the process of explaining or describing human action with respect to types of organizational possibility, then he is to be applauded. Similarly, he is to be applauded insofar as his discussion suggests the possibilities that there are different ways to deliberately proceed to *know* human problems; that there are other legitimate and respectable ways to understand besides the positivistic way; that there may be other and more relevant organizational responses to human needs within and outside organizations besides that of objectification and measurement; that many so-called problem solvers are inherent parts of the problem; and that our most basic concepts of organization may be culture bound and based on unchallenged premises.

Among the mildly cacophonous vocalizing at Minnowbrook, those voices espousing the serious questioning of very basic value premises from which many administrators have traditionally operated seemed to predominate. Kirkhart's message was clearly in line with the above. He was not just presenting a new slant on a methodological approach, but was intimating, it seemed, a very normative framework for administrative action. It cannot be denied that Public Administration *is* in a time of turbulence. Perhaps Kirkhart has supplied us an initial typology by which one can gauge the effectiveness and responsiveness of organizations, and particularly public ones, to these times and to the recently comprehended tide of latent social problems.

Editorial Note

General discussion tended to focus upon the consociated model of organization, especially as the model related to other Minnowbrook discussions, contemporary administrative practices, and the implications for Public Administration. The following excerpts indicate some of the directions taken:

A: If a consociated model would work, it would have a lot of characteristics that an organization or agency would want to have if one accepted Biller's identification.

B: There is not one element or feature of the consociated model which is not now in operation in real organizations, some of which are in the public sector, and some of which come very close to approximating at this moment the entire set of characteristics of the consociated model. These organizations tend to be invisible to us because we are not sensitized to observing appropriately.

C: Admitting that the consociated type is possible as well as desirable, the fact remains that everything about Public Administration in the technical sense as we know it, works to make the development of the type difficult. Look at classification systems, certification systems, incentive systems—any system you like—they are based upon assumptions fundamentally opposite from those of the consociated model. To the extent that the consociated type of organization now occurs, it is only because of great effort on the part of people who somehow find a way to tolerate tremendous external pressures. And that's not right!

6

Normative Theory

In this chapter, Michael Harmon approaches the topic of normative theory in Public Administration through the problem of administrative responsibility. In a tone consistent with earlier papers, he finds our ideas of administrative responsibility quite inadequate in terms of our present social and political state. Harmon believes that some recent thinking introduces ideas which are promising and no more devoid of empirical support than traditional notions. The implications of these ideas for Public Administration—both in the faculty and in the field—are substantial. John Paynter comments on Harmon's argument.

Normative Theory and Public Administration: Some Suggestions for a Redefinition of Administrative Responsibility

Michael M. Harmon

The dominant issues in normative theory of Public Administration in the past several decades have been responsibility and freedom. Theoretical discourse on the nature of administrative responsibility has for nearly thirty years ranged roughly between the position of Herman Finer, who argued that loyalty to legitimate political authority is the criterion of responsible behavior, and Carl Friedrich's position that responsibility requires the active participation of administrators in sensing and responding to public needs. The question for each was, How can we assure, or at least reasonably expect, that administrators will behave in ways that are responsible to one or another version of the public interest? To Finer such assurances rested in the law and other formal devices enforcing accountability. For Friedrich, the "inner check" provided by the professional values inculcated in administrators during their formal training justified a departure from the narrow legalism of Finer's perspective.

While essential agreement with Friedrich's view of the responsibility issue has been regarded as a crude measure of one's administrative liberalism, it is significant that both interpretations assume a fundamentally negative stance on the nature of man in general and of public administrators in particular. Although Finer and Friedrich arrive at differing conclusions, the same premise about human nature underlies each argument: Without the checks provided by either the law or the processes of professional socialization, the resultant behavior of administrators would be both selfish and capricious. This pessimism, it will be argued below, stems from the peculiar and unnecessarily restrictive assumptions on which administrative responsibility is conceptualized in the literature of Public Administration and political science.

Similarly restrictive is the manner in which the issue of freedom and the public administrator has been treated in the literature. As long as the concern is with how administrators preserve and protect the freedom of others, we are on quite safe and manageable grounds. Issues that arise in this context can be managed through the use of utilitarian formulae of one sort or another. When, however, the administrator inquires about his own freedom, such as the freedom to exert greater influence on public policies, he is confronted with the presumed dilemma between his exercise of free choice and his responsibility to serve the interests of others. Resolution of these conflicts is most often achieved either by the administrator's acquiescence to a higher authority or by striking an expeditious "balance" between his interests and those of the public (or some segment of it). While it is conceded that courageous and risk-taking administrators have not been universally vilified by students of the discipline, the bases on

which such administrators are given approval have not been consciously integrated into contemporary theories of responsibility
and freedom in Public Administration.

The purposes of this chapter are to show how our assumptions
about responsibility and freedom have inhibited the development
of normative thinking in Public Administration and to offer the
basis of a more affirmative and activist theory of administrative
responsibility.

A half century ago answers to normative questions in Public
Administration were rather easily proffered. The American era
of reform to which the central values of Public Administration
were tied emerged from the excesses of Jacksonian Democracy.
During this reform era the doctrine of separation of powers and
checks and balances was forwarded with renewed zeal in the form
of a simplistic distinction between politics and administration
which made the issue of administrative responsibility seem unambiguous. Administrative activity was considered to be responsible to the extent that it reflected the wishes and dictates of
elected representatives. Beginning with Dimock,[1] critics of the
dichotomy between politics and administration argued that such
a view avoided the realities of the governmental process. Administrators, they said, are inevitably involved in political activity and should, therefore, be aware of its subtleties. While this
point is now largely conceded, leadership by administrators in the
formulation of public policy is still grudgingly regarded as a
pragmatic necessity rather than as a positive and integral part
of that process.

The belief that policy should be formulated exclusively by
elected officials can be traced to the assumption that they are the
only actors in the political system who can be held accountable by
the democratic constraint of election. Supporting this assumption
is the view that democracy is fundamentally a balance between
majority rule and minority rights, the former enforced through
voting and the latter through the courts. But majority rule and
minority rights are only two of a number of features possible in a
democratic system; they are not its essence. Keeping the way open

[1]Marshall E. Dimock, *Modern Politics and Administration* (New York:
American Book, 1937).

for change with respect to social goals is its essential imperative.[2] To view democracy as more than a balance of majority rule and minority rights is especially crucial when relatively little activity in government is actually subject to the vote or scrutiny of elected officials. Given the paramount role of administrators in policy making, the ways in which we—and especially *they*—view their appropriate roles are of central concern.

At the same time that discomfort about the politics-administration dichotomy was being expressed, efficiency as a dominant value in Public Administration came under fire. Dwight Waldo, while not denying the importance of efficiency, pointed out that it can be measured only in terms of purpose and "that the less mechanical and routine the instruments and procedures, and the more important *or more nearly ultimate* the purposes they serve, the less likely is their efficiency to be constant":[3]

. . . there is a realm of "science" where "objectivity" is possible and "efficiency" can be measured. On the other hand, . . . increasingly, as one's frame of reference widens and disagreement about ends becomes important, "science" and "objectivity" are more difficult, judgments of "efficiency" less accurate, more controversial.[4]

Further, while efficiency has some legitimate appeal, the vast resources of a wealthy nation tend to diminish its relative importance. With the demise of old values and assumptions about governmental activity comes the necessity to alter thinking about administrative responsibility. We are forced to regard a theory of administrative responsibility which relies heavily on efficiency as insufficient for this period in our social and political development.

The Ethic of Administrative Neutrality

Because of its commitment to the doctrine of separation of powers and legislative supremacy, the traditional American view of democracy affirms the ethic of administrative neutrality in matters of substantive policy. At the root of the contention that

[2]Thomas Landon Thorson, *The Logic of Democracy* (New York: Holt, Rinehart and Winston, 1962).

[3]Dwight Waldo, *The Administrative State* (New York: Ronald Press, 1948), pp. 204–205.

[4]*Ibid.*, p. 205.

administrators can and should remain neutral about policy lies the conventional distinction between freedom and responsibility. The argument in its most extreme form suggests that because administrators are not chosen by the electorate they are not free to act as advocates of policies or to allow their personal values to influence significantly the manner in which policies are implemented. Administrative responsibility in its traditional form requires that administrators be able to identify and account for their values so that they will not impinge on decisions of public policy. While the objectivity and clarity of perception necessary to behave with complete neutrality may have some theoretical desirability, such qualities are hardly descriptive of average or even exceptional administrators.

A more basic challenge to the freedom-responsibility dichotomy, however, has been leveled by philosophies outside the milieu in which normative issues in administration have usually been argued. From an existentialist's viewpoint, for example, it would be inappropriate to talk of activity purely in terms of responsibility to others, while ignoring responsibility to oneself. To the administrator this is a way of saying that sanctions assuring accountability which rest wholly outside his own values greatly reduce his sense of personal commitment and purpose. Additionally, freedom, in an existential sense, is not antithetical to responsibility. Thus, if the existentialists are correct in saying that freedom without responsibility is a meaningless kind of freedom, a definition of administrative responsibility based solely on the negative notion of accountability becomes untenable.

The "Dilemma" of Administrative and Political Democracy

Early writers such as Frederick W. Taylor recognized the importance, if not the precise nature, of individual motivation in organizations.[5] Conveniently, the primacy which Taylor ascribed to pecuniary reward as a value was consistent with the values then dominant in public and private organizations. Even the challenge posed to scientific management by the human-relations movement did little to undermine the belief in the essential congruence of individual needs and organizational goals.

[5] Frederick W. Taylor, *Principles of Scientific Management* (New York: Harper and Row, 1911).

Despite some disagreement in modern organization theory about the nature of individual motivation, a general concern is that individual and organizational needs may differ greatly, leading either to widespread employee discontent or the failure of organizations to achieve their goals. Etzioni, for example, has argued that the distinguishing feature of the modern or "structuralist" school of organization theory is that it stresses the inevitable existence of conflict between individual and organizational needs.[6] Transferred to the public sphere, the organizational dilemma posed by Etzioni assumes widespread proportions. Individual needs in this area must be matched against the interests of the general public rather than merely those of a single organization. Frederick C. Mosher recently raised the question of possible conflicts between individual self-actualization, brought about by a trend toward participative decision making in public agencies, and methods of administrative accountability in a democracy:

. . . there has already developed a great deal of collegial decision-making in many public agencies, particularly those which are largely controlled by single professional groups. But I would point out that *democracy within administration*, if carried to the full, raises a logical dilemma in its relation to *political democracy*. All public organizations are presumed to have been established and to operate for public purposes—i.e., purposes of the people. They are authorized, legitimized, empowered, and usually supported by authorities outside of themselves. To what extent, then should "insiders," the officers and employees, be able to modify their purposes, their organizational arrangements, and their means of support? It is entirely possible that internal administrative democracy might run counter to the principles and objectives of political democracy in which the organizations of government are viewed as instruments of public purpose.[7]

The dilemma which Mosher sees between administrative and political democracy is subject to serious question. The narrow professionalism in public agencies which he rightly fears is apparently assumed to be the result of a movement toward a more participative form of public management and greater self-actualization of professional public employees. But it is just as reasonable

[6]Amitai Etzioni, *Modern Organizations* (Englewood Cliffs, New Jersey: Prentice-Hall, 1965).

[7]Frederick C. Mosher, *Democracy and the Public Service* (New York: Oxford University Press, 1968), p. 18.

to assume that self-centered professionalism which ignores public needs is likely to manifest itself in organizational systems which rely on quite authoritarian, highly centralized methods of decision making. While the rise of professionalism in government and the growing acceptance of participative management have emerged at roughly the same time, they are not necessarily concomitants. The vision of professional administrators pursuing their own interests at the expense of the public denies the philosophical foundation of self-actualizing behavior. It assumes that administrators will act selfishly and irresponsibly unless forced to act otherwise by vigilant guardians of the public trust. Yet Abraham Maslow, for example, has predicted that the choices of self-actualizing people are more likely to meet the test of "responsible" behavior than those of less healthy people.[8] Maslow did not propose an elitist system in which self-actualizers are granted the exclusive privilege of making important public choices. He simply argued that such people are more likely than unhealthy people to recognize that their own freedom and the freedom of others are inseparable.

This point of view may be disputed on the ground that evidence is lacking to support the belief that individual self-actualization through participative decision making in public agencies will meet the test of responsible behavior in a political democracy. Admittedly, it is a difficult hypothesis to test. At the same time, however, it is also clear that the opposite assumption—that public administrators will act irresponsibly unless otherwise checked—is similarly devoid of empirical support. Yet the latter hypothesis underlies most contemporary political notions of administrative responsibility.

Certainly administrators are not always attuned to or act consistently with the public pulse. But surely corrupt or irresponsible behavior cannot be assumed to be the result of participative decision making and self-actualization until so demonstrated. One might carry the argument a step further by suggesting that the

[8]Abraham H. Maslow, *Toward a Psychology of Being* (Princeton, New Jersey: Van Nostrand, 1962). This theme is expanded further by Maslow in *Eupsychian Management* (New York: Dorsey, 1966) in which he discusses the concept of *synergy*. Briefly, synergy, as he defines it, is the reconciliation of the selfish and the unselfish, the rejection of the presumed dichotomy between freedom for oneself and freedom for others.

lack of trust in public administrators implied by a strict separation of policy formulation and implementation may, in some
instances, be a self-fulfilling prophecy. By too closely guarding institutional arrangments designed to check administrative discretion, a political system may likely be rewarded with precisely
the type of behavior it fears. Support for this view is meager in
the literature of Public Administration and political science. Yet
one need not stray very far into the literature and research about
human motivation to conclude that such a hypothesis is more
than idle speculation.

Suggestions for Redirection of
Normative Theory in Public Administration

In searching for the foundations of a new approach to normative theory in Public Administration, this essay has thus far
suggested two general guidelines: (1) That such a theory must accommodate the values and motives of individual public administrators to theories of administrative responsibility; and (2) that
the essential congruence of administrative freedom and political
freedom must be recognized. Stated in somewhat more generic
terms, the presumed distinction between freedom and responsibility (or between freedom for self and freedom for others)
should be rejected.

A third and closely related imperative is that the basic ambiguity and indeterminacy of complex social systems must be accounted for. While there are numerous predictions of probable
major trends in this country and in the world during the remainder of the century, it is clear that individual futures in the coming
years will be less predictable than they were in the past. Moreover, since clearly defined external sanctions to govern behavior
are becoming generally less evident, their existence cannot realistically be presumed in a theory of responsible behavior in any
sphere of activity. Instead, we are required to turn increasingly
to an existential concept of self-responsibility as the foundation of
a new theory.

This circumstance makes difficult the task of redefining
administrative responsibility. Guarantees of accountability traditionally provided by legal and bureaucratic machinery are a nec-

essary but certainly insufficient requisite of administrative responsibility under conditions of uncertainty and rapid social change. A theory of administrative responsibility based on responsiveness to diverse and changing public demands and advocacy of and commitment to programs designed to meet those demands can offer no such explicit guarantees.

Arguing for a more "affirmative" definition of administrative responsibility, however, does not necessitate total discard of traditional notions of accountability. The arguments offered here are simply a reminder that an exclusive reliance on devices to assure accountability has a tendency to create a "blinder" effect on public officials which causes them to ignore other aspects of responsible behavior. We can recognize that there is no necessary (although at times there may be a possible and even probable) conflict between accountability and positive responsibility, and at the same time retain elements of the former and speculate about the conditions under which the latter may be encouraged. We are not necessarily forced into an either-or proposition. My predilection toward creating conditions under which administrators may self-actualize—for example, by permitting them greater involvement in the advocacy and support of policy—is already apparent. If my interpretation of Maslow and other humanistic psychologists is correct, the risks involved in attempting to create these conditions do not appear to be excessive.

In accepting the existentialists' contention that ultimate and transcendental values do not exist, we are forced to confront the knotty problem of patterning administrative and political systems to accommodate this notion. Some valuable assistance in this regard has been rendered by Thomas Landon Thorson. After arguing against the existence of deductive and inductive proofs of the legitimacy of political systems, he argues in favor of democracy on the grounds of such nonexistence:

It is the very recognition of the fact that one cannot *prove* the validity of political proposals by induction or deduction which leads us to reject any claim to absolute truth, and thereby to reject any political system premised on such a claim. No one man, no group, whether minority or majority, is ever justified in claiming a right to make decisions for the whole society on the grounds that it knows what the "right" decisions are. Just because the "rightness" of a political decision *cannot* be proved—because its consequences, short- or long-range, cannot be predicted with certitude nor its ultimate ethical supremacy demonstrated—are we obligated to construct a decision-making procedure that will leave the way open for new ideas and social change.[9]

To Thorson, the key element of democracy is the admonition to keep the way open for change. This point is emphasized not because such openness permits the attainment of some preconceived objective, but because "proofs" for the legitimacy of denying free activity are by definition nonexistent in a democratic system. Thorson's argument that there is no ultimate correctness of normative propositions—which is his basis for justifying democracy—is somewhat similar to the existentialists' denial of universal social norms. Individual needs and values are presumed to be legitimate in part because of the lack of evidence to the contrary.

Ambiguity in Problem Definition

The ambiguity of problems which existentialists emphasize has been criticized by Wayne A.R. Leys as leading to a "cry-baby" attitude. "The existentialist cannot reduce the ambiguity of his problem, at least, prior to the deadline for action, and therefore he cannot rationally define 'the public interest' or anything else."[10] In recognizing their limitations in offering guides for administrative behavior, it should be noted that existentialists are not as universally pessimistic as Leys' comment suggests. Optimism is a dominant theme in much of the literature of humanistic and existential psychology and of what Colin Wilson calls the "new existentialism."[11] Even granting Leys' argument, it could be said that the existentialists' uncertainty in defining their own values and problems encourages them to refrain from defining those of other people in any dogmatic fashion.

The existentialist perspective suggests that the public administrator must attempt, however inadequately, to understand the relationship of his own values and motives to questions of public

[9]Thorson, *op. cit.*, pp. 138–139.

[10]Wayne A. R. Leys, "The Relevance and Generality of 'The Public Interest,' " in Carl J. Friedrich (ed.), *The Public Interest* (New York: Atherton Press, 1966), p. 253.

[11]Colin Wilson, *Introduction to the New Existentialism* (Boston: Houghton Mifflin, 1967).

policy, and to create a climate in which those to whom he is legally responsible are encouraged to do likewise and to assert their values in the political arena. Such a view meets the test of administrative responsibility in a conventional democratic sense; just as important, however, it recognizes that administrators are human beings rather than machines and that ethical neutrality is an abstraction incapable of providing a viable basis for administrative responsibility.

Some Implications for Education in Public Administration

Part of the difficulty in altering the normative basis of Public Administration can be traced, as suggested earlier, to the historical context in which the field has evolved. In the education of civil servants the values which emerged from the reform era still form the primary basis on which their administrative and managerial talents are developed. The context in which public organizations will operate in the final third of this century, however, differs distinctly from those of earlier decades. With a few notable exceptions, however, educational programs in Public Administration still are linked to questionable assumptions of relative stability in the environment and of high predictability as to the consequences of public policies.

As already noted, it is imperative for the field of Public Administration that it recognize ambiguity and uncertainty as basic conditions of administrative activity. This is a task to which education in Public Administration—both in universities and in midcareer executive development programs—has devoted insufficient attention. An ability to cope with ambiguity is more a function of personality, however, than a result of accumulated substantive knowledge. Public Administration's failure to develop a curriculum which accounts for this distinction is apparent by its treatment of problems and issues typically as matters of content rather than of process of behavior.

Illustrative of this viewpoint was the White House announcement of the formation of the Federal Executive Institute, a new executive-development program for senior career civil servants. The announcement specified three areas on which the FEI programs will focus:

—The major problems facing our society and the nature of the government's response to those problems.

—Ways of maximizing government organizations to increase the effectiveness of these programs.
—Ways in which administration of Federal programs can be improved.[12]

The stated objectives for the Institute, although obviously important, noticeably neglect the individual as an object of study. Instead, the announcement of the formation of the Institute stressed a "program" emphasis "to widen [the executives'] mastery of both the substance and administration of Federal programs."[13] Reflecting on this approach, FEI's first director, Frank P. Sherwood, commented:

Such a statement is capable of various interpretations, but it seems to suggest that breadth will be achieved through the input of data which lie outside the experience of the individual. The suggestion is that this will occur largely at the cognitive level. Second, there is the preoccupation throughout that the executive problem in the Federal service is essentially one of sub-optimization, in which executives are maximizing parochial interests at rather high system cost.[14]

While it would no doubt be desirable for federal executives to obtain a working knowledge of and commitment to the broad range of government programs, the nature of public policy making raises questions as to the possibility of achieving this objective. A preliminary document prepared by the United States Civil Service Commission states, "The main purpose [of FEI] is to augment the ability of the upper civil service to provide continuity and responsiveness in Government operations, and to insure that those near the top are identified with the government as a whole in pursuit of national goals."[15] Although the statement has some surface appeal, it seems to presuppose that there exists some more or less rationally defined set of national goals which government could achieve if only public executives were more fully aware of them. Yet it is almost pedestrian in a pluralistic society to say that a set of orderly priorities—the existence of which the FEI programs are apparently supposed to assume— does not exist. Moreover, the Commission statement suggests that higher civil servants have the powers both to grasp on a

[12]White House press release, May 9, 1968.
[13]*Plan for the Federal Executive Institute*, Prepared for the President by the U.S. Civil Service Commission (undated and unpaged).
[14]Memorandum from Frank P. Sherwood, Director of the Federal Executive Institute, to the Staff of FEI, July 1, 1968.
[15]*Plan, op. cit.*

continuing basis the intricacies of public programs relating to a broad range of national objectives, and to develop a much broader base of loyalties and commitments. The former suggestions seems questionable on its face. Regarding the latter, a good deal of literature indicates that loyalties in large organizations are seldom higher than the subgroup level at which employees can see some direct result of their endeavors. To think that personal commitments of public administrators can be expanded much higher than this point presumes, it seems to me, uncommon patriotism.

I am not proposing that narrowly defined self-interest should be the governing ethic of public administrators. The argument is simply that a knowledge of and commitment to a large number of specific goals and policies asks too much of administrators and is inconsistent with the incremental and fragmented process by which public policy is formulated. Rather, the breadth to be desired of public officials—or of anyone—is primarily a breadth of attitude. To quote again from the Sherwood memorandum:

In my judgment the executive of the future will have to tolerate far more ambiguity than has been true in the past. For a variety of obvious reasons change is becoming a way of life. Thus there will be an increasing number of uncertainties and incommensurables in the executive life space. If he is sensitive, he will feel acute discomfort, he will be open to learning. If he seeks to eliminate the discomfort by searching for certainty and stability, he will fear learning and will not engage in "creative leadership." Our task, then, is to move executives toward maturity, to work with tension by seeking more learning, as well as helping them to develop more insights into the nature of human cooperative processes. The concept of change is very important in this connection. For the executive must not only be concerned about how adaptive he is as an individual but how adaptive is the system for which he has responsibility.[16]

The requisite learning implied by this statement is of a more fundamental order of magnitude than the acquisition of new substantive knowledge. Since learning to be adaptive and to feel comfortable with ambiguity entails a rather immediate and sometimes threatening confrontation with individual values and modes of behavior, the risks involved in developing an educational program which focuses on this concept are substantial. At the same time, however, a strong case can be made that it is a more manageable task than attempting to provide public servants with suf-

---

[16]Sherwood, *op. cit.*

ficient substantive knowledge to perform their jobs well. If it is identifiable at all, such knowledge is enormously varied in the short run and continually changing in the long run. To design a general educational program for the public service primarily around inputs of substantive knowledge assumes both a static set of goals for public servants and their agencies and an infinite store of transferable knowledge. Lacking either of these conditions, an emphasis on "learning how to learn" and how to develop an adaptive capacity for public organization seems to be a comparatively modest and practical approach.

What is being proposed essentially is that public administrators learn how to become more democratic—democratic, that is, in the sense described by Bennis and Slater in their book *The Temporary Society*. "Democracy," the authors state, "becomes a functional necessity whenever a social system is competing for survival under conditions of chronic change."[17] Because of a decline in filial deference and the ever increasing mobility of people, fixed bases of human relationships will give way to temporary ones at both family and organizational levels. If Bennis and Slater are correct in predicting that we will live in a " temporary" society, it is important that education in Public Administration not be geared to assumptions of stability and certainty. Education for the public service—and normative theory in particular—must recognize the individual and organizational stresses generated by continuous and chaotic change. Change is not an unqualified virtue. It is, however, a fact of political and administrative life to which normative theory in Public Administration must be accommodated.

Comment: On a Redefinition of Administrative Responsibility

John Paynter

Michael Harmon's paper on administrative responsibility is a bold venture into a forbidding field. He makes an effort to *construct* in an area where old normative rationales have been the

[17]Warren Bennis and Philip E. Slater, *The Temporary Society* (New York: Harper and Row, 1968), p. 4.

objects of severely damaging critiques, and where most new work is still dominated or at least strongly influenced by a philosophic position that denies the possibility of doing normative theory. His constructions take seriously the major critique of the politics-administration distinction by considering the administrator as a politician, not only in his spare time (while a "citizen"), but in the very acts of "administering." And his redefinition is grounded in the two modern philosophic positions that contend most strenuously with logical positivism: existentialism and linguistic analysis.

Radical Intent and Conservative Theory

According to Harmon, one needs to go to philosophic foundations in order to properly redefine administrative responsibility because more has been defective in the past than our administrative understandings. The misguided notion that efficiency and neutrality should be prime administrative values is tied to the equally inadequate belief that democracy is "a balance between majority rule and minority rights." Only when the essence of democracy is properly understood can an adequate notion of administrative responsibility be developed. It is Harmon's intention to formulate such a thorough and comprehenisve redefinition of democratic administration.

In contrast to this obviously radical intention, however, he displays a surprising reluctance to relinquish the older understandings of democracy and administrative responsibility. Regarding a democratic regime, he asserts unequivocally that its essence is the imperative to keep "the way open for change with respect to social goals." But the sentence immediately following adds that democracy is "*more than* a balance of majority rule and minority rights" (my italics), implying that openness to social change is not the *whole* essence of democracy. Similarly, in redefining administrative responsibility he urges the public administrator "to understand the relationship of his own values and motives to questions of public policy," and "to create a climate in which those to whom he is legally responsible are encouraged to do likewise and to assert their values in the political arena." But he then adds that his view "meets the test of administrative responsibility in a conventional democratic sense." What he seems in fact to have formulated is not a wholly new definition, but an unresolved tension between new and old elements. An attempt to understand that tension and possible reasons for it may shed some light on the difficulties of the normative task in Public Administration.

The tension becomes clear when one spells out the new criteria for administrative action. In the case of the first standard, Harmon presumably means more than he says. The crucial question for an administrator is not whether he understands the relation of his values and motives to questions of public policy, but what bearing that understanding should have on his administrative decisons. From both the existentialist and postpositivist perspectives, the answer would seem to be that his decision should be guided by his own values, with some (undefined) recognition of the freedom of others and of the need to keep the way open for social change. The second criterion presents a similar case: The administrator presumably must do more than encourage political participation among those—but only those—to whom he is legally responsible. If he is to take the existentialist and postpositivist positions seriously, he must selectively urge anyone in the polity to participate whose action would enhance the possibility of continued social change. What remains unclear is how these criteria meet the conventional democratic test of administrative responsibility. In fact, Harmon's new standards would seem to undercut the traditional notion of administrative responsibility. The conventional criteria insisted that the policy decisions of elected officials, not the administrator's own values and motives, should dominate and guide administrative decisions, and that administrators should officially relate to and influence their "clients," not as whole citizens, but only within the sphere of their legally defined and authorized duties.

Of the many possible reasons for Harmon's retention of the conflicting old and new elements, two seems to me especially important for those of us who share his concern to redefine administrative responsibility. First, both elements may have been included because neither by itself yields an adequate understanding of administration. Harmon has indicated some of the defects in the older view, especially its failure to acknowledge the policy role of the administrator. He attempts to overcome that defect by viewing the administrator as something other than a mere implementer. In doing so, however, he virtually shatters the connection between administration and the rule of law. Proponents of the politics-administration distinction understood that connection in terms of the relation between legitimate legislators and obedient executors. The new position, in contrast, acknowledges two other criteria of right decisions: the administrator's own values and the imperative of openness to social change. If the latter is to entail anything more than promotion of the greatest quantitative mutation in human conditions, some additional standard is required for discriminating good from bad, or healthy from unhealthy, change. The imperative itself does not yield such additional standards, and, as existentialists acknowledge, neither will one's own values, as merely personal preferences, yield such socially binding rules. Consequently, the "conventional democratic sense" of administrative responsibility may have been reintroduced in order to provide a legitimate source for needed criteria of action, thereby avoiding the implications of administrative paralysis or political nihilism.

Democratic Administration?

Harmon's problematic effort at redefinition suggests a second possible reason for the difficulties in that position. It may be that the requirements imposed on government by a large, complex, and highly industrialized society make a genuinely democratic administration untenable. Harmon asserts early in his paper that the administrator today has "the paramount role . . . in policy making." His overstatement emphasizes our present situation: The administrator will and must make decisions which are not simply—and perhaps not always fundamentally—reflective of popular wants or aimed at keeping the way open for social change. He is, in other words, a politician, not only in the sense that he possesses the skill to achieve his assigned organizational goals in a fragmented political system, but also in the sense that he influences the character of those affected by his decisions and partially determines the nature and direction of popular participation in politics. Unless the conditions which make such administrative action necessary are to be drastically changed, the American polity will continue to be not simply democratic, but a "mixed" regime; two qualitatively different principles of rule will operate in it simultaneously. Perhaps what we most need, then, is not further efforts to redefine democratic administrative responsibility, but thought about the proper ends and forms of that mixture.

Editorial Note

The general discussion on this topic at Minnowbrook was very short, and tended to run back to discussions already treated in the La Porte, White, and Biller chapters. A short quotation from one participant's comments may indicate how this transition was made:

We have already talked a lot about confrontation,—and about the possibility that the politics of confrontation would result in a standoff, perhaps accompanied by violence and break-up, and so on. The Harmon paper offers, I think, a very attractive alternative. It says, essentially, that there is a way out of this if you look to the internal tendency of the administrator toward self-actualization or mental health, or whatever. Perhaps the administrator can be made such a man that he can do what the environment demands without having to go through the potentially disruptive engagements of confrontation.

7

Empirical Theory

In his assessment of empirical theory in Public Administration in this chapter, Philip Kronenberg is as critical as the preceding authors were of other aspects of Public Administration. Of course, much of the earlier assessments of inadequacy had rested upon deficiencies in theory, and many of the problems which Kronenberg identifies are integral parts of arguments which were made in earlier chapters. Kronenberg selects two bodies of theoretical literature for special focus: comparative national Public Administration and organizational behavior. An important part of Kronenberg's remarks return to the concern with social relevance which has already appeared as a principal theme of the conference. Bob Zimring, in his comments, agrees with and extends Kronenberg's criticisms of the state of empirical theory.

The Scientific and Moral Authority of Empirical Theory of Public Administration

Philip S. Kronenberg

The emerging phenomenon of a new Public Administration draws our attention to the directions—which we all have some burden for shaping—of its development. My objective is to comment on the question "Where do we go from here?" with respect to systematic empirical theory of Public Administration.

Where we go from here in building the empirical theory of a new Public Administration depends upon where we are at present and where we think we should be. I suggest that we can best make judgments on these latter two points by examining the *scientific* and *moral authority* of that empirical theory.[1]

By the scientific authority of a body of theory I mean the extent to which theoretical work is legitimated as a scientific enterprise. How "scientific" is empirical theory of Public Administration? Four criteria can help in answering this question. First, when we speak of theory (or theories) of Public Administration, is there general agreement on the specifications of the field of inquiry, on the aspects of reality to which "empirical Public Administration theorists" address themselves? (Some might argue that the answer to this first question could bear on the merit of *having* something called theory of Public Administration.) Second, there is the question of systematization: To what extent are events which interest students of Public Administration capable of being linked to one another by reason of their location in a system of explanations?[2] Third, a question is suggested by the word "empirical." The issue is not over empirical referents, "in principle or in fact," in theoretical statements; this can be taken for granted. Instead, the question is one of the empirical *quality* of these statements: How empirically explicit and operational are its concepts, what criteria of evidence are used to determine rejection and level of confidence in propositions, and to what extent have given findings been replicated? Fourth, how theoretically adequate are propositions in the field of inquiry? That is, to what degree has theoretical work been engaged in explanation? To what extent has the question "Why?" been raised amidst the determination of empirical regularities and correlations?[3] The function of theory is explana-

[1] I am indebted to Professors Alfred Diamant, John Dorsey, Gary Wamsley, and York Willbern for reading and criticizing an earlier version of this essay. The remaining flaws are mine.

[2] Ernest Nagel, a philosopher of science, takes the position that it is the "organization and classification of knowledge on the basis of explanatory principles which is the distinctive goal of the sciences." Nagel, *The Structure of Science: Problems in the Logic of Scientific Explanation* (New York and Burlingame: Harcourt, Brace and World, 1961), p. 4.

[3] The "Why?" under consideration in explanation is not a motivational "Why?" and certainly not a metaphysical "Why?" It is "Why?" in the sense of "How did *x* happen?" or "What factors account for *x*?" See Richad S. Rudner,

tion; theoretical adequacy rests on the ability of statements to explain something. During one of the great feuds in American sociology, George C. Homans drove home this integral connection between theory and explanation in the following assertion which had clear reference to the work of Talcott Parsons:

Much modern sociological theory seems to me to possess every virtue except that of explaining anything. Part of the trouble is that much of it consists of systems of categories, or pigeonholes, into which the theorist fits different aspects of social behavior. No science can proceed without its system of categories, or conceptual scheme, but this in itself is not enough to give it explanatory power. A conceptual scheme is not a theory. The science also needs a set of general propositions about the relations between the categories, for without such propositions explanation is impossible. No explanation without propositions! But much modern sociological theory seems quite satisfied with itself when it has set up its conceptual scheme. The theorist shoves different aspects of behavior into his pigeonholes, cries, "ah-ha!" and stops. He has written the dictionary of a language that has no sentences. He would have done better to start with the sentences.[4]

The moral authority of theory means here the degree to which its *priorities* of inquiry are legitimated by reflecting the preferences of the participants in the political system. There are many choices to be made within the vast range of phenomena which Public Administration theorists examine and try to understand. Do our theoretical efforts lead us to raise questions which serve the needs of those who live in our political society and which offer the possibilities for improvement of their lives? How should we answer for Public Administration a question which Kenneth Boulding has raised about economics?

Does economics, as George Stifler has suggested, make people conservative? If so, it is perhaps because it simply points out the difficulties and dangers of heroic action and makes people appreciate the productivity of the commonplace, of exchange and finance, of bankers

---

Philosophy of Social Science (Englewood Cliffs, N.J.: Prentice-Hall, 1966), pp. 59–63. The traditional conception of scientific explanation is based on a deductive paradigm. Treatments of the deductive paradigm can be found in Nagel, *op. cit.*, Chapter 3, and R. B. Braithwaite, *Scientific Explanation: A Study of the Function of Theory, Probability, and Law in Science* (Cambridge, England: Cambridge University Press, 1953). An interesting challenge to this deductive tradition is found in Meehan, *Explanation of Social Science: A System Paradigm* (Homewood, Ill.: The Dorsey Press, 1968).

[4]George C. Homans, *Social Behavior: Its Elementary Forms* (London: Routledge & Kegan Paul, 1961), pp. 10–11.

and businessmen, even of the middle class which our heroic young so earnestly despise. Perhaps this is why so many young radicals today have abandoned economics as a poisoned apple of rationality which corrupts the pure and heroic man of their identities and sympathies. Economics is a reconciler, it brings together the ideologies of East and West, it points up the many common problems which they have, it is corrosive of ideologies and disputes that are not worth their costs. Even as it acts as a reconciler, however, does it not undermine that heroic demand for social mutation which will not be stilled in the voices of our young radicals?[5]

It is the thesis of this chapter that there are some important limitations on the scientific and moral authority of empirical theory of Public Administration and that limitations on moral authority are the more critically problematic for the character of an emerging new Public Administration. This thesis will be defended by considering the levels of scientific authority which can be attributed to the two major areas of theoretical work in Public Administration, assessing the moral authority of this body of theory, and reaching some conclusions about the implications of these for new Public Administration. Last is a remedial proposal aimed at the enhancement of the scientific and moral authority of theory in this field.

Scientific Authority

An evaluation of the scientific authority of a theoretical literature involves an attempt to measure the extent to which the body of theory can be viewed as a *legitimately scientific* endeavor. Four criteria have been suggested above to aid this evaluation: (1) the degree of specification of the field of inquiry (theory of what?); (2) the extent to which the explanatory propositions in this field are linked together in a system of explanations (systematization); (3) the empirical quality of propositions; and (4) the theoretical adequacy of propositions as statements of explanation. The degree of specification of the field and its systematization are discussed in the next two sections below. The empirical quality and theoretical adequacy of the field are assessed together in separate sections which focus on the two substantive areas of greatest contemporary theoretical development

[5]Kenneth E. Boulding, "Economics as a Moral Science," *The American Economic Review* (March, 1969), p. 11.

in Public Administration: comparative Public Administration and organizational behavior.

Theory of What?

Theorists of Public Administration—like many other social scientists—have not delineated the boundaries of the object of their theorizing very well at all. When Dwight Waldo wrote "The Administrative State Revisited" in 1965, he pointed to this boundary issue as one of the most pressing intellectual problems in Public Administration:

> I can think of nothing more germane to contemporary Public Administration . . . than substantial research, exhibiting high scientific standards as these are measured in contemporary social science, devoted to the question, What distinguishes public administration, quantitatively and (or) qualitatively, from other administration?[6]

As of that publication date, Waldo was aware of only two ongoing studies that would satisfy his challenge. What accounts for the lack of attention to this question?

One factor may be that some of us continue to ask the question "Will the *real* Public Administration please stand up?" That is, our theorizing is alleged to be a moot and "academic" exercise until we can come to grips with the real essence of Public Administration in all its complexity and uniqueness. I doubt that we have either the wit or will to maximize in this quest. Even if we had the cognitive prowess and vigorous resolve, there remains the real epistemological question of whether we can ever know any *one* reality of Public Administration. All we can know is what our senses tell us and—through still mysterious extrapolations from this sentient base—what imagination and intuition can lead us to expect. *We construct reality* and the boundaries of those things we wish to understand. In Public Administration, as in other fields of inquiry, there are *many* realities. Events do not cohere naturally and organize themselves. Theorists organize experience and search for patterns of meaning. We do little to advance the richness of de-

---

[6]Dwight Waldo, "The Administrative State Revisited," *Public Administration Review* (March, 1965), p. 26.

scription or the quality of explanation by clinging to monistic assumptions about reality and hoping for the big breakthrough.[7]

Another impediment to consensus over the boundaries and content of what we study stands in testimony to the plural realities of Public Administration. That impediment is the eclectic character of our theoretical efforts. To paraphrase most liberally the words of Winston Churchill: Never in the field of human inquiry were so many typologies, definitions, techniques, conceptual frameworks, models, and analytical schemata offered by so many in the name of heuristic promise. But this overabundance is to be expected. Whatever may be the future verdict on von Bertalanffy's prophecy that there is a "general tendency towards integration in the various sciences, natural and social,"[8] that happy state is not here in Public Administration scholarship. We are in a period of "extraordinary science," to use Kuhn's expression,[9] a period of preparadigmatic or multiparadigmatic activity in which conceptual, methodological, technological novelty and creativity are promoted amidst and virtual babel of competing languages, theoretical postures, analytical boundaries, and research priorities.[10]

The lack of clarity in the specifications of Public Administration as a field of empirical theoretical inquiry is part of a process of paradigmatic change of major intensity. This lack is

[7]For an expanded discussion of this issue, see James Heaphey and Philip Kronenberg, *Toward Theory-Building in Comparative Public Administration: A Functional Approach* (Bloomington: Comparative Administration Group Occasional Papers, 1966). For a more exhaustive and seminal exploration of this issue in the context of political systems, see the first five chapters of David Easton, *A Framework for Political Analysis* (Englewood Cliffs, N.J.: Prentice-Hall, 1965).

[8]Ludwig von Bertalanffy, "General System Theory," *Main Currents of Modern Thought* (1955), reprinted by permission in Nicholas J. Demerath III and Richard A. Peterson, *System, Change and Conflict* (New York: Free Press, 1967), p. 118.

[9]Thomas S. Kuhn, *The Structure of Scientific Revolutions* (Chicago: University of Chicago Press, 1962).

[10]For a stimulating discussion of these issues with respect to organization theory see Martin Landau, "Sociology and the Study of Formal Organization," and Glenn Paige, "The Cycle of Normal Science," in Dwight Waldo, *et. al., The Study of Organizational Behavior: Status, Problems and Trends* (Washington, D.C.: Comparative Administration Group Special Series No. 8, 1966), pp. 37–58.

a fact of life for those who theorize about Public Administration and, presumably, this is the way it must be from time to time if theoretical obsolescence is to be overcome in the development of a field of science. But such processes have costly implications for the scientific authority of empirical theory of Public Administration. The shortcomings in the specifications of the field which were discussed above are only expressions of those costs.

Systematization

Another major cost levied by paradigmatic change is on the systematization of knowledge and ideas about Public Administration. James Heaphey, in a recent assessment of comparative Public Administration, concluded that there are four different "visions" or overarching approaches to study in this field which are not necessarily interdependent. Thus, evidence gathered under the guidance of one approach may contribute little to the data requirements of the other approaches.[11] The goal of systematic theory—that is, the articulation of facts with a system of explanations—is certainly imperiled by such multiple visions. This point leads me to suggest that Dwight Waldo's "elephantine problem" in organization theory[12]—the confusion resulting from theorizing about different parts of the "elephant"—may even involve four different elephants if Heaphey's count is correct. If we are looking at different things through different lenses for different purposes and collecting data that may have no direct relevance for the efforts of one another, the prospect for systematization of our theoretical enterprise is dubious, at least for the near future. This rejection of monistic assumptions and the acknowledgment that there are multiple dimensions of reality are healthy traits for a dynamic and formative science. But these attitudes can be abused; there

[11]James Heaphey, "Comparative Public Administration: Comments on Current Characteristics," *Public Administration Review* (May–June, 1968), pp. 242–249.

[12]This phrase refers to the fable of several blind men attempting to describe an elephant. "In view of the inclusiveness, the diversity, the amorphousness of the materials put under Organization Theory heading nowadays, one must conclude that, if they all concern the same elephant, it is a very large elephant with a generalized elephantiasis." Dwight Waldo, "Organization Theory: An Elephantine Problem," *Public Administration Review* (Autumn, 1961), p. 216.

is much potential here for letting everyone "do his thing," which is a costly process for systematic inquiry. Eclecticism is not a free economic or intellectual good.

Empirical Quality and Theoretical Adequacy

Other costs for theory associated with this state of paradigmatic flux lie in the realms of the empirical quality and theoretical adequacy of our work. These two issues are considered below by examining the two dominant strains of theoretical development in Public Administration in the past twenty-five years: comparative Public Administration and organizational behavior. Competent and exhaustive efforts at sifting and evaluating these two bodies of literature have been made by others.[13] The purpose here is to highlight some growth points

[13]Some useful statements in the comparative national area can be found in the following sources: Lynton K. Caldwell, "Conjecture on Comparative Public Administration," Roscoe C. Martin (ed.), *Public Administration and Democracy: Essays in Honor of Paul H. Appleby* (Syracuse: Syracuse University Press, 1965), pp. 229–244; Alfred Diamant, "The Relevance of Comparative Politics to the Study of Comparative Administration," *Administrative Science Quarterly*, (June, 1960), pp. 87–112; Milton J. Esman, *The CAG and the Study of Public Administration: A Mid-Term Appraisal* (Bloomington, Ind.: Comparative Administration Group Occasional Papers, 1966); Ferrel Heady, "Comparative Public Administration: Concerns and Priorities," Ferrel Heady and Sybil L. Stokes (ed.), *Papers in Comparative Public Administration* (Ann Arbor: Institute of Public Administration, University of Michigan, 1962), pp. 1–18; Ferrel Heady, "Comparison in the Study of Public Administration," Heady (ed.), *Public Administration: A Comparative Perspective* (Englewood Cliffs, N.J.: Prentice-Hall, 1966), pp. 1–13; James Heaphey, "Comparative Public Administration: Comments on Current Characteristics," *op. cit.*; Warren F. Ilchman, "Rising Expectations and the Revolution in Development Administration," *Public Administration Review* (December, 1965), pp. 314–328; Joseph LaPalombara, "An Overview of Bureaucracy and Political Development," LaPalombara (ed.), *Bureaucracy and Political Development* (Princeton: Princeton University Press, 1963), pp. 3–33; Roy C. Macridis, *The Study of Comparative Government* (New York: Random House, 1955, Part I; Nimrod Raphaeli, "Comparative Public Administration: An Overview," Raphaeli (ed.), *Readings in Comparative Public Administration* (Boston: Allyn and Bacon, 1967), pp. 1–25; William J. Siffin, "Toward the Comparative Study of Public Administration," Siffin (ed.), *Toward the Comparative Study of Public Administration* (Bloomington, Ind.: Indiana University Press, 1959), pp. 1–22; Dwight Waldo, *Comparative Public Administration: Prologue, Problems, and Promise* (Washington, D.C.: Comparative Administration Group Special Series No. 2, 1964).

Several overviews of different facets of the organizational-behavior literature are: Warren G. Bennis, "Behavioral Sciences Perspective in Organizational Studies," *Changing Organizations: Essays on the Development and Evolution*

that bear on the empirical quality and theoretical adequacy of these two areas. I will first make some general comments on characteristics common to both Public Administration and

of Human Organization (New York: McGraw-Hill, 1966), pp. 181–211; Warren G. Bennis, "Leadership Theory and Administrative Behavior: The Problem of Authority," *Administrative Science Quarterly* (December, 1959), pp. 259–301; Charles E. Bidwell, "The School as a Formal Organization," James G. March (ed.), *Handbook of Organizations* (Chicago: Rand McNally, 1965), pp. 972–1022; Peter M. Blau and W. Richard Scott, *Formal Organizations* (San Francisco: Chandler Publishing Co., 1962), Chap. 1, 2, and Bibliography; Tom Burns and G. M. Stalker, "Mechanistic and Organic Systems of Management," *The Management of Innovation* (London: Tavistock, 1961), pp. 96–125; Donald R. Cressey, "Prison Organizations," March (ed.), *op. cit.*, pp. 1023–1070; Michel Crozier, *The Bureaucratic Phenomenon* (Chicago: University of Chicago Press, 1964), Parts Three and Four; Richard M. Cyert and James G. March, "Antecedents of the Behavioral Theory of the Firm," *A Behavioral Theory of the Firm* (Englewood Cliffs, N.J.: Prentice-Hall, 1963), pp. 16–19; Alfred Diamant, "The Bureaucratic Model: Max Weber Rejected, Rediscovered, Reformed," Ferrel Heady and Sybil L. Stokes, *Papers in Comparative Administration* (Institute of Public Administration, University of Michigan, 1962), pp. 59–96; Anthony Downs, *Inside Bureaucracy* (Boston: Little, Brown, 1967); Amitai Etzioni, *A Comparative Analysis of Complex Organizations: On Power, Involvement, and Their Correlates* (New York: Free Press, 1961), pp. xi–xx, 3–67; Alvin W. Gouldner, "Organizational Analysis," Robert K. Merton, *et. al.* (eds.), *Sociology Today* (New York: Basic Books, 1959), pp. 400–428; Mason Haire, "Introduction—Recurrent Themes and General Issues in Organization Theory," Haire (ed.), *Modern Organization Theory*, (New York: John Wiley and Sons, 1959), pp. 1–15; Peter B. Hammond *et. al.*, "On the Study of Administration," James D. Thompson *et. al.*, *Comparative Studies in Administration* (Pittsburgh: University of Pittsburgh Press, 1959), pp. 3–25; Herbert Kaufman, "Organization Theory and Political Theory," *The American Political Science Review* (March, 1964), pp. 5–14; Kurt Lane, "Military Organizations," March (ed.), *op. cit.*, pp. 838–878; James G. March and Herbert A. Simon, *Organizations* (New York: John Wiley and Sons, 1958), pp. 12–47 (the author's interpretations of "classical" and bureaucratic organization theory); Robert L. Peabody and Francis E. Rourke, "Public Bureaucracies," March (ed.), *op. cit.*, pp. 802–837; Charles Perrow, "A Framework for the Comparative Analysis of Organizations," *American Sociological Review* (April, 1967), pp. 194–208; Charles Perrow, "Hospitals: Technology, Structure, and Goals," March (ed.), *op. cit.*, pp. 910–971; Joseph A. Schlesinger, "Political Party Organization," March (ed.), *op. cit.* pp. 764–801; Herbert A. Simon, "Some Problems of Administrative Theory," Simon, *Administrative Behavior*, 2nd ed. (New York: Macmillan, 1957), pp. 20–44; Ralph M. Stogdill, "Dimensions of Organization Theory," James D. Thompson (ed.), *Approaches to Organizational Design* (Pittsburgh: University of Pittsburgh Press, 1966), pp. 1–56; James D. Thompson, *Organizations in Action* (New York: McGraw-Hill, 1967), especially pp. 3–13; Stanley H. Udy, Jr., "The Comparative Analysis of Organizations," March (ed.), *op. cit.*, pp. 678–709; Dwight Waldo, "Theory of Organization: Status and Problems," Waldo, *et. al.*, *The Study of Organizational Behavior, op. cit.*

organizational behavior followed by a separate assessment of each.

Studies of both formal organizations and national administrative systems were active fields of research and speculation prior to World War II. But not until after the war did the objectives, mood, and style which characterize the contemporary scene emerge. Global conflict, postwar reconstruction, new nationalisms, the Cold War, and (last but not necessarily less potent) Herbert Simon and Fred Riggs have all been assigned responsibility for the tumult in these and other fields of social inquiry. Little can be added here to what has been said elsewhere regarding causes in this effervescent phase of our scholarship. One effect is clear though: The period of the late forties and early fifties was marked by the beginning of a vigorous drive based on the proposition that the ideology and fundamental methodology of the natural sciences should be adopted and adapted by those in the social sciences. The carrot held out to those who would follow the new wave of science is the theme around which this paper is focused: the development of systematic empirical theory (substitute "knowledge" for "theory"; the latter was to be the means to achieve the former). In practice this development meant different things to different advocates and critics. For many it has tended to mean comparative study, theoretically based empirical research, and methodological rigor.[14]

Comparative study was a key which would liberate the study of Public Administration and government from the old evidential restraints. Roy Macridis virtually equated science with comparative study, calling the latter "the closest approximation to the scientist's laboratory possible for the student of politics."[15] Hammond, Thompson, and their colleagues made much the same point with a different referent in mind:

Significant aspects of administration seldom lend themselves to controlled experimentation . . . The experiment, however, is only one

[14]My remarks in the next three paragraphs were drawn in large measure from five sources: Nagel, *op. cit.*; Chapter 13; Albert Somit and Joseph Tanenhaus, *The Development of American Political Science* (Boston: Ally and Bacon, 1967), Chapter XII; Raphaeli, *op. cit.*; Daniel Lerner (ed.), *Evidence and Inference* (Glencoe: Free Press, 1959), and Heinz Eulau, *The Behavioral Persuasion in Politics* (New York: Random House, 1963).

[15]Macridis, *op. cit.*, p. 4.

of several valid strategies for gaining scientific knowledge. When it is practicable, experimentation is a most economic way of comparing phenomena with and phenomena without a certain treatment; but the absence of opportunities to manipulate phenomena in no way negates the possibility of gaining reliable knowledge through controlled observation of comparable events . . . The *comparison of administrative phenomena* can and should proceed immediately, but as the field develops, the comparison of *alternative theories* will be of utmost importance. [Emphasis added.][16]

Thus, the comparative mood linked rather neatly with the growing interest in empirical theory. This orientation required the selection of an empirical unity of analysis. This choice was behavioral: the actions of individual persons, especially as conceptualized in specified patterned aspects of behavior such as roles, organizations, or decisions. This choice of perspective was accompanied by a commitment to methodological individualism and the rejection of the use of collective terms that were typical of traditional, more institutional scholarship.[17] The emulation of the natural sciences also put a high priority on quantification and the use of various statistical and mathematical techniques for data manipulation.

Closely linked to this inclination toward quantification was an emphasis on "rigor" which now approximates the emotive value of Motherhood. While rigor is never well defined, it generally means some combination of terminological precision, observance of the canons of logic, operationalization of key terms, explication of criteria for testing propositions, efforts to identify data limitations, and stating of criteria for selection of data sources. Another dimension of rigor, which easily could have been placed in the preceding category because of its intimacy with the behavioral mood, is the commitment to positivism. This commitment celebrated empirical facts and held values or moral questions to be outside the province of scientific inquiry, except as elements of data. Linked to the value-neutral profession is the priority given to "basic" research and to the curtailment of emphasis on application. The working tradition which is the prototype of this positivistic stance is exemplified by a remark of Nobel Laureate Dr. Otto Hahn, who, in 1938, discovered how to split

[16]Hammond, *et. al.*, *op. cit.*, p. 8.
[17]Nagel, *op. cit.*, pp. 535–546.

the atom. When Dr. Hahn learned that an atomic bomb had been dropped on Hiroshima, he was reported to have said, "I never thought anything warlike would come of my discovery of nuclear fission. I am a scientist and like all scientists am interested only in discovery and not application."

My characterizations of these comparative-behavioral-methodological orientations are closer to expressions of moods by their advocates than a faithful reporting of what has come to pass. The comment which David Easton made about behavioralism in 1964 seems to fit Public Administration in the case of these three orientations: "It may be . . . that the battle for acceptance has really been won, but if so, it is by no means over as yet and not everyone has been willing to give credence to the good news. There are some who would say that we are mistaking a series of continuous preliminary skirmishes for the main engagement."[18]

Now we can turn to a more detailed assessment of the empirical quality and theoretical adequacy of comparative Public Administration and organizational behavior, respectively.

Comparative Public Administration

Comparative Public Administration (or "comparative national Public Administration," to use its more formal label) has taken vigorous steps to overcome assumptions and models rooted in Western experience. Much of this work has been done within the past decade under the auspices of the Comparative Administration Group through seminars, national conferences, exchanges of occasional papers, and the recent expansion of study committees covering a broad number of subject-matter specialties. In the course of these activities, the orientations and people involved were often interchangeable with those of the new comparative politics. For various reasons—scholarly interests, resources, academic entrepreneurship, public policy requirements —primary attention was directed to the nonindustrialized countries. The journal articles and books oriented to the nonindustrialized countries that occurred in a fairly short span of time might suggest that our empirical knowledge of Public Ad-

[18]David Easton, "The Current Meaning of 'Behavioralism,'" James C. Charlesworth (ed.), *Contemporary Political Analysis* (New York: Free Press, 1967), p. 11.

ministration in the East and West had been more than equalized. Such a suggestion needs to be qualified by at least two considerations.

First, much of the new writing on nonindustrialized countries focused on new ways to conceptualize political and administrative phenomena in these countries and to propose models and theories to accommodate this range of phenomena. The data used in most of these studies tended to exemplify or enhance the plausibility of theoretical construction and arguments rather than test discrete propositions. An example of this tendency was John Dorsey's application of his information-energy scheme to an examination of political development and bureaucracy in Vietnam.[19] The result was a skillful and convincing piece of analysis, but no theory was tested. Instead, relationships that were theoretically "interesting" and meaningful for trying to understand political change were *illustrated* by a systematic examination of some relationships among communication patterns, rates of energy conversion and demands of political elites in Vietnam.

A second characteristic of this comparative literature which belies equality in our understanding of East and West is the matter of "window dressing: the putting of old wine in new bottles." This charge has been made by some about the work of Fred Riggs, Talcott Parsons, Herbert Simon, Karl Deutsch, and other grand theorists, and it may have merit in isolated cases.[20] The more significant problem, however, is the introduction of new concepts without carrying the burden of their implications into analysis. "System," "dynamic," "change," "function," "development," "environment," "process," "cybernetic," *et al.* have become catch words that we all employ on occasion without honoring the special obligations that may be attached to their use. The most objectionable examples of this tendency have been found in textbooks and readers that invoke all of the "in" pieces of jargon in section titles and editorial overviews, while changing little in

[19]John T. Dorsey, Jr., "The Bureaucracy and Political Development in Viet Nam," LaPalombara, *Bureaucracy and Political Development, op. cit.*, pp. 318–359.

[20]For an interesting criticism of the work of Fred W. Riggs, see Martin Landau, "Theoretical Problems of Administrative Reform in Developing States: A Commentary," paper presented at CAG Proseminar, March 27, 1968, Cambridge, Massachusetts.

the substance of the presentation.[21] Less objectionable and more relevant to comparative studies are area specialists and traditionalists who do the social-science "shuffle": introduce their essay with a quotation from a rabid behavioralist, affirm the importance of models, propose a set of analytical categories or suggest a typology, and then ignore all of this paraphernalia and write the same insightful study that they would have written had behavioralism never sullied the good name of scholarship. Prime specimens of this genre are Merle Fainsod's "Bureaucracy and Modernization: The Russian and Soviet Case," and *The Politics of the Developing Areas* edited by Almond and Coleman.[22] Taking Fainsod as an example, the first six pages present a brief discussion of four schemes for classifying public bureaucracies.

[21]The fifth edition of *Public Administration* (New York: Ronald Press, 1967) by John M. Pfiffner and Robert Presthus can be suggested here to exemplify this problem, largely because it is one of the *best* of the textbook lot and has a venerable role in the history of Public Administration.

The chapter on "Comparative Administration" comprises 23 pages of the 550 pages of the text. Eighteen of these 23 pages deal with British or French administration, a surprising bias in view of the widespread scholarly interest in the non-Western developing countries by 1967, the year of publication of the book. This chapter also has a six-page section on "Recent Theory and Research in Comparative Administration." It includes two brief paragraphs which *refer to*—without benefit of bibliographic citation—Max Weber's conception of the evolution over time of authority systems and administrative forms. The authors deal with this very complex set of ideas with the following brief treatment which is devoid of even simple definitions:

"In each stage a *primary* basis of authority exists, although all stages tend to overlap. Patriarchal and patrimonial stages are characterized by *traditional* authority, whereas the contemporary bureaucratic era is dominantly one of *legal-rational* authority. The third ideal type of authority, *charismatic*, based upon magical personal qualities, flourishes in the prebureaucratic stages, but tends to be submerged in the collective, rational, rule-oriented ethos of modern bureaucratic organizations" (p. 79).

There were only nine bibliographic references in this section on recent theory and research in comparative administration. Of the nine references, five were explicitly about British administration, politics or society.

A number of other key ideas are given abrupt treatment in this text; Weber's ideal-type contruct of the bureaucratic model gets less than two pages (pp. 41–42); the notions of cybernetics and feedback are given just a little more than a page (pp. 119–120); and the difficult subject of decision making is wrapped up in 19 pages (pp. 108–126).

[22]Merle Fainsod, "Bureaucracy and Modernization: The Russian and Soviet Case," LaPalombara (ed.), *Bureaucracy and Political Development*, *op. cit.*, pp. 233–267; Gabriel A. Almond and James S. Coleman (eds.), *The Politics of the Developing Areas* (Princeton: Princeton University Press, 1960).

Next, it is indicated that classifications of this kind "have their obvious inadequacies as well as their suggestive applications . . . unless one is prepared to try to come to grips with historical experience in all its complexity and time dimensions, one runs the very real danger that any comparative treatment of the modernizing role of bureaucracies will be shallow, narrow and timebound, and reflective of little more than contemporary melioristic concerns."[23] Fainsod then goes on to write a persuasive historical analysis of the pattern of Russian-Soviet bureaucratic influence on modernization.

In brief, the empirical character of comparative Public Administration is *illustrative* of what might be done in theory-based empirical research that is not rooted in Western countries. It points to approaches, needs, and the potential of empirical theory. Such efforts represent legitimate pretheoretical work, but it is not enough. Although conceptualization has been a central issue (it has been nominal rather than operational), as has the formulation of some general hypotheses, there has been little testing of propositions and almost no replication, and our confidence in what we know ought to be very modest. Modesty is particulary called for in identifying notions we can reject with confidence. Recognizing this need is not to say that nonbehavioral traditionalists and area specialists make no important contributions to theory. They are the pioneers and their contributions have been impressive. Their insights continue to thrust to the heart of understanding. And their data are no less empirical because they are historical. But occasional flashes of insight are not enough to erect a cumulative body of knowledge. And plausible evidence or an interesting case to support an hypothesis is insufficient; repeated tests of hypotheses are necessary in order to insure that there is compelling evidence in support of interpretations in addition to their mere consistency with some initial observations.[24] Good theory can begin with a hunch but its successful elaboration into a systematic body of theory which can be associated with data requires more than brilliant art.

[23]Fainsod, *op. cit.*, p. 239.
[24]See Merton's remarks on *post factum* sociological interpretations in Robert K. Merton, *Social Theory and Social Structure*, revised and enlarged edition (New York: The Free Press, 1957), pp. 93–95.

A final thought on the empirical quality of comparative Public Administration studies: What happened to comparative analysis of the industrialized countries, especially the United States? Part of the rationale behind the comparative administration movement in the United States was that the perspectives gained through analysis of administration in other countries—especially the nonindustrialized states—would liberate us from our traditional modes of conceptualizing and theorizing about Public Administration at home. Little has been done to tap the enormous generation of data and methodologically sophisticated collaborators in the industrialized countries. The Jacob and Fried studies of German and Italian field administration[25] were conceptually interesting and represented important contributions to our knowledge about Public Administration in two countries, but their essentially historical, idiographic approach[26] stands outside efforts to build and test theory by comparison. A most promising piece of research in progress is the Blank-Diamant research of the administration systems of Germany, France, Spain, *and the United States*,[27] but there are few such studies in the works.

The distinction between the empirical quality of our theory as just discussed and its theoretical adequacy is not "neat." My concern in what follows is with the degree to which theoretical work is explanatory work. To what extent do our theoretical activities involve us in explanation and how adequate are these explanations? How well has Public Administration theorizing contributed to what Hempel has called one of the principal purposes of science: "attainment of a simple, systematically unified account of empirical phenonmena."[28] Since I touched earlier on the is-

[25]Herbert Jacob, *German Administration Since Bismark* (New Haven: Yale University Press, 1963); Robert C. Fried, *The Italian Prefects: A Study in Administrative Politics* (New Haven: Yale University Press, 1960).

[26]Fred W. Riggs, "Trends in the Comparative Study of Public Administration," *International Review of Administrative Sciences*, (1962), pp. 9–15.

[27]This project was an outgrowth of a working paper on the statistical measurement of administrative variables. See Blanche Davis Blank, *A Proposal for a Statistical Approach to Comparative Administration: The Measurement of National Bureaucracies* (Bloomington: Comparative Administration Group Occasional Paper, 1965).

[28]Carl G. Hempel, *Philosophy of Natural Science* (Englewood Cliffs, N.J.: Prentice-Hall, 1966), p. 84.

sue of systematization, I will turn now to the level and scope of generalizations in theoretical work.

The emphasis of the theoretical work in comparative Public Administration has tended to be at the level of grand theory in the sociological tradition. Many of the concepts and analytical strategies are derived from the functional approach which has supported much of the theoretical work in sociology. This sociological tradition has oriented us toward questions about the social structure of.the state; the factors influencing the legitimation of state action; and the mutual influences of state bureaucracy and the political, economic, and social patterns of the society.[29] Our intellectual debts to Weber, Merton, Parsons, and Levy, among others, are huge. While this tradition provided us with terminology and methodology and helped us break away from theoretically moribund and ethnocentric views of Public Administration, it did not give us a system of theory. Reinhard Bendix and Semour Martin Lipset have acknowledged that sociology has not generated a theoretical framework for political inquiry. They see agreement on certain priorities for inquiry, such as consensus, legitimacy, and social order, but not a body of theory.[30] I would say further that the functionalist arguments—and their connections with general systems theory—might "more profitably be construed as expressing a directive for research."[31] Functionalism may thus be seen as a heuristic device to stimulate empirical exploration into interdependency, persistence, and change in Public Administration.

The scope of explanations we attempt in our theoretical work is clearly a product of our untidy paradigmatic situation. Some insist that a structural focus on behavior in state bureaucracy is the test strategy for comparative theoretical work: They want to explain behavior in various public bureaucracies in spite of the

[29]These points of emphasis on the anticipated and unanticipated consequences of action in social structure have served as the defining foci of political sociology. See Scott Greer and Peter Orleans, "Political Sociology," Robert E. L. Faris (ed.), Handbook of Modern Sociology (Chicago: Rand McNally, 1964).

[30]Seymour M. Lipset and Reinhard Bendix, "The Field of Political Sociology," Lewis A. Coser (ed.), Political Sociology (New York: Harper and Row, 1966), p. 15.

[31]Carl G. Hempel, "The Logic of Functional Analysis," Llewellyn Gross (ed.), Symposium on Sociological Theory (New York: Harper and Row, 1959), p. 301.

possibility that formally similar structures may have different functions in different societies.[32] Although we often have been urged to reject structure for function, what we try to explain within a tortured structural-functional rhetoric seems structural more often that not.[33] At a common sense level we tend generally to give structures a label based on our expectations of the primary consequences of their operation. But when we seek determinants of events and try to get at causality, functional arguments raise some serious questions. Flanigan and Fogelman[34] and Herbert Spiro[35] have explored many of the problems connected with functional analysis and systems theory.

The most serious of these problems for a theoretical enterprise is the difficulty associated with trying to make explanatory statement of the form *A has the function B for C*. Structural-functionalism is built on the notion that any social system (C) has certain system problems (B) that must be solved if (C) is to persist or adapt to stress.[36] The major difficulties in using this structural-functional formulation are to define the functions $(B_{1,2,...,n})$ which support or maintain the system (C) and to specify the events $(A_{1,2,...,n})$ that will generate the required functions. Flanigan and Fogelman remark that "while these difficulties may not be in principle insurmountable, they bode ill for structural functionalism."[37] These difficulties also bode ill for

[32]See Ferrel Heady, *Public Administration: A Comparative Perspective, op. cit.*

[33]See Fred W. Riggs, "Professionalism, Political Science, and the Scope of Public Administration," *The Annals of the American Academy of Political Science and Social Science,* No. 33, Monograph 8 (October 1968). Also see his "Models in the Comparative Study of Public Administration," Fred W. Riggs and Edward W. Weidner, *Models and Priorities in the Comparative Study of Public Administration* (Chicago: Comparative Administration Group Special Series No. 1, 1963), pp. 14–18.

[34]William Flanigan and Edwin Fogelman, "Functionalism in Political Science," Don Martindale (ed.), *Functionalism in the Social Sciences* (Philadelphia: The American Academy of Political and Social Science, 1965), pp. 111–126.

[35]Herbert J. Spiro, "An Evaluation of Systems Theory," Charlesworth (ed.), *Contemporary Political Analysis, op. cit.,* pp. 164–174.

[36]This formulation of the structural functional position is based on Talcott Parsons, Robert F. Bales, and Edward A. Shils, *Working Papers in the Theory of Action* (New York: Free Press, 1953), pp. 177–181; and Marion Levy, Jr., *The Structure of Society* (Princeton: Princeton University Press, 1952), p. 62.

[37]Flanigan and Fogelman, *op. cit.,* p. 125.

Public Administration theory. We have not been able to specify boundaries or define characteristics of the major systems in which we have an interest. We cannot say much about the ability of a system to cope with its "problems" unless we have some better way to talk about system maintenance or change. If the physical existence of the United States were to end tomorrow, it might be said that the administrative system and the political system and all other social systems in the country failed to "cope" with stress. That is an easy measurement decision. Situations short of Armageddon become more problematic for the functional theorist. We tend to try to resolve such problems by reference to our own norms and preferences. Although we cannot suggest satisfactory concepts of maintenance or change, we find ourselves involved in establishing curricula and research programs in development administration. And these curricula and programs lead to the application of physical and social technologies whose consequences for major social systems are unknown and which, for the present time, escape satisfactory and consistent calculation. About the best we can do is to evaluate effects on very limited measures of performance (gross national product, civil disorder, challenges to governmental legitimacy reported by the media, production of goods and services in specific sections, and the like).[38] Of course, the interpretation given to each measure is subject to challenge.

Even if we could claim useful measures of system maintenance and change, the problems of determining what functions are required to achieve certain system states are great. Beyond that, the determination of predictable connections between events and the satisfaction of functional requisites remains.

Our theoretical work in comparative national administration

[38]The focus of attention in comparative Public Administration that carries the label "development administration" roams over a vast array of concerns ranging from broad issues of political change such as the role of the military as an instrument of political development to relatively pedestrian questions in organization and management. I have made no attempt to speak to this literature in spite of the fact that its concerns have been important to the *raison d'être* supporting comparative administration. Some have characterized comparative administration as the scientific or "pure" dimension and development administration as the operational or "applied" side of the field. I do not find this to be a particularly helpful distinction given the fluid state of the enterprise and the limitations under which it operates.

has provided new direction for inquiry, supplied expectations about findings, and helped to raise important questions. But in terms of accomplishment, we are just beginning to toddle.

Organizational Behavior

The literature on formal complex organizations offers a dramatic contrast to the comparative Public Administration literature. Although contemporary theoretical work in both fields draws its principal approaches from the same sociological origins, organizational research owes a far greater debt to sociology. Most of the important theoretical inquiry about organizations has been by sociologists and social psychologists.

The empirical base of the organizational-behavior (or empirical organization-theory) literature is vastly stronger and more methodologically sophisticated than the comparative Public Administration literature. But our focus on Public Administration introduces important qualifications.

First of all, it is perhaps unfair to contrast the research products of studies of discrete formal organizations with studies of national politico-administrative systems. Problems of data collection and complexity are rather dissimilar. Access to key actors in a large number of formal organizations of a given type is relatively easy. This is not the case when entire political systems are compared. The complexity of goals and social interactions in the two types of systems are also quite different. Although we have tended to move beyond the notion of profit or efficiency as the single goal of formal organizations into an awareness of multiple goals, we are still talking about a rather small number of goals. Only in "total institutions" of the type that Erving Goffman examined—prisons, mental institutions, monasteries—do we see the goal complement of formal organization begin to approach that of a polity, if with far less complexity.[39]

A second caveat regarding the empirical quality of the organizational-behavior literature is that much of it ignores organizations in the public sector. Although some of the most significant studies of organizational behavior have been of public organiza-

[39]Erving Goffman, "The Characteristics of Total Institutions," Walter Reed Institute of Research, *Symposium on Preventive and Social Psychiatry* (Washington, D.C.: U.S. Government Printing Office, 1957).

tions—Selznick's *TVA and the Grass Roots,* for example—the great bulk of this literature focuses on business organizations. We have experienced a trend away from this monopoly of business-oriented research in the last decade or so, thanks to the largess of the National Institutes of Health and the Public Health Service. With the growth in research activities of medical sociology and of graduate institutes in social work has come a widening base of empirical studies in public-health and welfare organizations. However, these recent events do not represent a satisfactory state of affairs for the student of public organizations. Studies of organizational behavior are needed in a variety of situations if we are to widen our knowledge of the public sphere. Our diffuse party organizations, legislative bodies, regulatory agencies, courts, working organizations of chief executives in various jurisdictions, the host of commissions, task forces, and sundry *ad hoc* structures that dot the terrain of modern governance are all apt subjects for modern organizational analysis.

A third qualification on the state of empirical studies of public organizations is the lack of "comparativeness" in the cross-cultural or cross-national sense. When we speak of the "organizational-behavior literature," we are talking essentialy about an American literature. Certainly there have been important contributions by foreign scholars such as Michel Crozier and Nikolas Luhman.[40] But they are in limited numbers and have not facilitated the kinds of comparisons that would augment our efforts to test propositions generated in the context of the United States. We have not yet solved the problems of trying to "control" for the effects of different cultures on social behavior.

Despite these reservations, the empirical quality of organizational research for the purposes of theoretical work in Public Administration is high. Although we may lack data about a wide range of public organizations, the quality of theoretical work on other types of organizations enables us to have a useful range of

[40]Michel Crozier, *The Bureaucratic Phenomenon* (Chicago: University of Chicago Press, 1964) and Nikolas Luhman, *Funktionen und Folgen formaler Organisation* (Berlin: Schriftenreihe der Hochschule Speyer, 1964), XX. For a useful statement on the character of organization theory outside of the United Staes see Hans H. Jecht, "Comments on 'Theory of Organizations: Status and Problems,' " Waldo, *The Study of Organizational Behavior . . ., op. cit.,* pp. 29–36.

discrete articulated expectations about behavior in public organizations. We have done extensive research on organizations similar to many public organizations.

Theorizing about organizational behavior has basked for many years in the warm glow of a stable paradigm: the bureaucratic model as amended (that is, a stable paradigm *relative* to the disorder elsewhere in theoretical Public Administration). This paradigm has served both descriptive and prescriptive functions. I would take a further step and suggest that there is a second paradigm at work, at least in descriptive tasks, which is the alter ego of our bureaucratic model. This idea has been developed with great skill in *The Management of Innovation* by Burns and Stalker. They posit two polar models of organizational behavior which they label mechanistic and organic. The notions of machine model and organic, organismic, or natural systems model or some variation on these labels have been part of our subculture for years. But I think the positions of Burns and Stalker differs in an important way from some of the earlier formulations.

The early dichotomies had reference to approaches to research rather than to systematic differences in patterns of behavior in organizations. The earlier view was reflected in the distinction made by Etzioni between "goal models" and "system models."[41] The goal model would be sensitive to questions of efficiency, organizational rationality, and the like. The system model would be interested in survival and, in true structural-functional style, in the requisites to maintain the organizations as a discrete entity. Official goals would be a benchmark for looking at all of the eufunctional and dysfunctional occurrences in the "life cycle" of an organization. Etzioni and others were saying that if you look at different things and ask different questions, the answers will be different. Burns and Stalker, on the other hand, see the two models as reflecting different clusters of patterned events in organizations. Briefly, they hypothesize that the mechanistic model is found where environmental and technological factors affecting the organization are stable. The behavior which they claim

[41]Amitai Etzioni, *Modern Organizations* (Englewood Cliffs, N.J.: Prentice-Hall, 1964), pp. 16–19; and "Two Approaches to Organizational Analysis: A Critique and a Suggestion," *Administrative Science Quarterly* (1960), pp. 257–278.

will emerge is a fairly good operationalization of the bureaucratic model: functional differentiation, hierarchical authority, and an emphasis on local loyalty. The organic model calls for the fluid *ad hoc* matching of special skills and tasks as conditions change, a network or collegial authority pattern, and a fostering of expertise which is attractive to relevant groups in the environment.

The importance of Burns and Stalker's formulation is a harbinger of a trend toward integration of empirically supported propositions. Students of organizational behavior already have delineated a formidable array of variables in the analysis of organizations. For example, in one book, *Organizations* by March and Simon, a rough count indicated they have specified relationships among 250 variables. Organization theorists have also advanced and tested a large number of empirical propositions. James D. Thompson, in a superb book, *Organizations in Action*, developed an impressively comprehensive scheme of 62 propositions from empirical studies. The value of Burns and Stalker, Thompson, and others is that they are attempting to build explanatory bridges within the growing body of tested propositions.

A kind of natural by-product of this theory-integrating mood has been the breaking down of many of the traditional theoretical bases for distinguishing types of organizations. Organizational theorists used to study business organizations, or voluntary organizations, or military organizations, and so on. The growing activity in organizational research after World War II led many to the conclusion that, though such class labels based on traditional criteria were still relevant, other criteria might be *more* relevant. For example, along certain dimensions some schools might more closely resemble certain factories than certain other schools. This growing concern with a reformed comparative-organizational analysis led some to inquire into the generic characteristics of organizations and their administration. The late Edward H. Litchfield spoke of developing a "general theory" of administration which could supplant such "part theories" as hospital administration, educational administration, business administration, and Public Administration.[42] Due to the importance of new classification systems to this kind of enterprise, a number of different typologies began to appear in the

[42]Edward H. Litchfield, "Notes on a General Theory of Administration," *Administrative Science Quarterly* (June 1956).

late fifties. These were based on a wide range of variables including compliance, decision issues, prime beneficiary of actions, and technology, among others. There was a certain defensive quality connected with pride of authorship for awhile, but this has been replaced with a willingness to exploit the ideas of the typology builders by incorporating their key variable into one's own framework. *Organizations in Action* is a prime example of this integrative thrust. In it Thompson has established relationships among a large number of empirical studies, models, and hypotheses drawn from Simon, Dill, Gulick and Urwick, Selznick, Parsons, Perrow, and others who range across the spectrum of theory of organization (indeed, the only organization theorist of any reputation that he did not include was Etzioni).

Moral Authority

The moral authority of a body of theory is more difficult to appraise than its scientific authority. Moral authority involves the setting of priorities about what events we wish to explain with our theory. Because our resources and energies are limited at any point in time, we must choose among theoretical tasks. By taking moral authority into account, we endeavor to evaluate how these choices square with the needs of those who are part of the political community.

The notion of the moral authority of theory may seem a bit odd. We have accepted science—and its theoretical correlates—so enthusiastically in the United States and elsewhere in the West that we tend to take it for granted. But science and its related theoretical enterprises are increasingly being subjected to skepticism and questioning. Fears that science may be getting "out of control" are especially pronounced where social science is concerned; social science to its critics means social engineering which means, in turn, a potential for social manipulation at the hands of the powerful. Critics of social science—and of Public Administration theory—challenge the priorities and foci of attention. Their challenge may be that we spend too much effort on Chinese administration and not enough on Chicago administration. Or that we should spend more effort on understanding the processes whereby workable political communities can be nurtured in Black ghettoes rather than how police units can be made more effective suppressors of these community-building processes. In either case the legitimacy of theoretical objectives is brought into question. The issue is not how "good" the theory is within a scientific frame of reference; rather it is how "good" the theory and its concomitants are for society. This decision is clearly a matter of political judgment. It is a matter of making choices among society's problems and allocating scarce intellectual resources in specific directions.

One way to assess the moral authority of a body of theory is to ascertain how well supported—an indicator of legitimacy—theoretical work in a given area appears to be in terms of prestige and financial inducements. Another mode of assessment is to take certain value premises and measure the extent to which theoretical endeavors are supportive of such premises. The acquisition and analysis of data in line with the first mode of assessment is a sizable task which is beyond the scope of this paper. The second mode is not much easier but at least a probe can be attempted here.

As an example, consider a value that presumably undergirds a democratic political system. One value premise that is central to most conceptions of democratic politics is what might be called *political resonance*: Officialdom should maintain obligatory responsiveness to the preferences of participants in the political community. Christian Bay alludes to this concept in *The Structure of Freedom:*

The most basic political question, in a sense, is one that the average man can answer with more authority than anyone else; does he like the present state of affairs? Does he want the government and its policies to continue, or does he insist on change? At intervals of few years this questions ought to be put before the voters, and they ought to have a real choice between alternative men and alternative policies, domestic as well as foreign.[43]

Charles Hyneman makes the point more forcefully perhaps in his definition of a principal type of democratic polity:

A regime in which those who compose the government [the officialdom] are under some compulsion to find out what the people want done and to do what they understand the people want done.[44]

[43]Christian Bay, *The Structure of Freedom* (with a new preface; New York: Atheneum, 1965), p. 381.

[44]Charles S. Hyneman with the collaboration of Charles E. Gilbert, *Popular Government in America: Foundations and Principles* (New York: Atherton Press, 1968), p. 3.

How well does comparative Public Administration and organizational behavior stand a test of political resonance? Quite well if political resonance is majoritarian and elite-oriented. Not well, I judge, if our assessment is sensitive to the preferences of minority groups or underprivileged participants in a political system.

Empirical theoretical work in comparative Public Administration shows substantial concern for the political environment in which public organizations must operate. Comparative Public Administration also reveals an emphasis on the problems of the developing nations which has drawn it into a marked concern with the processes of national development. This perspective has led some scholars into the highly prescriptive study of "development administration." Even scholars who have a primary commitment to empirical theory and descriptive-analytical inquiry have gravitated toward a *development bias*. One effect of this bias, which couples a concern for political environment with an interest in development, has been to focus attention of theorists such as Esman on the processes whereby political elites mobilize mass or majoritarian support for their policies and incumbency.[45] Of course, these elite-centered orientations can be at the expense of minority-group interests or involve the restriction of civil liberties. Some, like Huntington, argue that development involves the change or destruction of entrenched traditional institutions and interests which require the concentration of power in the hands of modernizing elites.[46] Others, such as LaPalombara and Riggs, see the concentration of power in the hands of elites who act in the name of modernization as being a clear threat to the development of democratic processes.[47] Be that as it may, there is emerging an interesting shift in the focus of some students of development which enhances rather than diminishes the importance of democratic values. They are taking the concepts and theoretical insights generated in their study of the

[45]Milton J. Esman, "The Politics of Development Administration," in John D. Montgomery and William J. Siffin (eds.), *Approaches to Development: Politics, Administration and Change* (New York: McGraw-Hill, 1966), pp. 59–112.

[46]Samuel P. Huntington, "The Political Modernization of Traditional Monarchies," *Daedalus* (Summer, 1966), p. 768.

[47]Joseph LaPalombara, "An Overview of Bureaucracy and Political Development," in LaPalombara (ed.), *Bureaucracy and Political Development* (Princeton, N.J.: Princeton University Press, 1963), pp. 3–33; Fred W. Riggs, "Bureaucrats and Political Development: A Paradoxical View," LaPalombara, *op. cit.*, pp. 120–167.

developing nations and applying them to inquiry about the problems of American society.[48] It is ironic that a theoretical bias
which enhanced authoritarian norms in developing nations is
now emerging as an instrument to enlarge and make more viable
the participation of American citizens who heretofore were denied equal access to the opportunities of a democratic political
system.

Statements of praise about the moral authority of theoretical
work on organizational behavior must be more restrained in tone
than those about comparative Public Administration. Much of
the character of theoretical inquiry into organizations has been
devoted to illuminating the weaknesses of the bureaucratic model
which impede the preference of organizational elites. The human-relations movement, for example, was a reaction to the rigidities of the bureaucratic model. But the motivation behind
much of human-relations inquiry was to improve the ability of
superordinate personnel to elicit productive work and cooperation from their subordinates with their goals for the organization. Antibureaucratic theorists such as McGregor, Likert, and
Argyris attack the rational structure of bureaucracy and call for
greater employee participation in decisions.[49] Yet it is fairly
clear that they intend that participation be chiefly in decisions
concerning implementation of primary organizational goals
rather than in the evaluation and redefinition of such goals. This
kind of employee participation makes reasonable sense when one
is concerned with private organizations. It makes little sense when

[48]An example of this shift in focus is found in the recent work of William J.
Siffin, Director of the Program in Political and Administrative Development of
Indiana University's Department of Political Science. Siffin, who is an accomplished student of the developing countries, especially in Asia, has devoted
increasing attention to the translation of knowledge acquired in nonindustrialized nations to the analysis of problems of planning, educational development,
and social change in the United States.

For a general discussion of some of the contributions of development
administration and comparative Public Administration to the American political
setting, see Kenneth Jowitt, "Relevance of Comparative Public Administration
to American Political Life," paper read at Annual Conference, American
Society for Public Administration, Miami, Florida, May 20, 1969.

[49]Douglas McGregor, *The Human Side of Enterprise* (New York: McGraw-
Hill, 1960); Rensis Likert, *New Patterns of Management* (New York: McGraw-
Hill, 1961); and Chris Argyris, *Understanding Organizational Behavior* (London:
Tavistock, 1960).

public organizations are the referent. The fact that much of our empirical work on organizational behavior has drawn on business and welfare organizations which rely on the norms of private property of several social welfare professions further skews this orientation.

Theory for What?

Where do we go from here? What directions should empirical theory of Public Administration take as we thrust out toward a new Public Administration?

Comparative Public Administration and organization behavior are the main growth points of empirical theory in the new Public Administration. The gaps in the development of these two facets of empirical theory are substantial. Both facets are "soft" areas of scholarship and there are many points at which conceptual development and field research must be enlarged. Their scientific shortcomings which were probed in the preceding sections are in no sense irreversible. Nor should they be interpreted as the fruits of the uninspired labors of unimaginative scholars. The problems have not been and will not be overcome easily. We cannot afford to throw the baby out with the bath water in the name of building a new Public Administration. The rhetoric of "generation gaps" neither honors the important contributions of those earlier generations of scholars nor gives us perspective on the flaws and weaknesses of their work and our own.

The new Public Administration must cope with these weaknesses in empirical theory and innovate in selected directions. This chaper, by pointing up limitations in the quality of systematic empirical theory, represents an exhortation for greater scientific authority in the pursuit of our tasks. Obvious steps called for in the future are to better delineate and seek agreement on the nature of the things we study, to improve the empirical quality and theoretical adequacy of our work, and to raise the level of systematization of our explanations of Public Administration phenomena. But the new Public Administration requires more than these things. We must add to our emphasis on better science—scientific authority—a critical second criterion: moral authority.

During an interview late in 1968, Mr. Kenneth Washington discussed the programs to improve educational opportunities for Afro-Americans and other minorities which he coordinates for the system of higher education in California. One of his remarks was that the "colleges are just going to have to cease to be ivy-walled islands where one searches for ethereal truths. . . they must now use their expertise to resolve social ills."[50] Kenneth Washington was not the first one to raise this issue about how we should use our scarce scientific and intellectual resources. It was raised in the thirties under the provocation of circumstances which were at least as stressful for scholarship in a compelling book by Robert S. Lynd, *Knowledge for What?* In that book, Lynd charged that it is the responsibility of social science "to keep everlastingly challenging the present with the question: But what is it that we human beings want, and what things would have to be done, in what ways and in what sequence, in order to change the present so as to achieve it?"[51] His was the challenge of moral authority.

In terms of empirical theory, the building of a new Public Administration would seem to require our sensitivity for both scientific and moral authority. Several goals and emphases in future theoretical work toward that building process can be suggested.

First, expand field research on public organizations. It is granted that research on nonpublic organizations provides a basis for theoretical expectations about public organizations. But research on the latter is essential if we are at least to challenge the biases generated by our study of the former. For example, it seems that many of the problems confronting our public colleges and universities in the United States may result from the actions or reactions of scholar-administrators or trustees who premise their behavior on a conceptual framework grounded in notions about nonpublic organizations. Some appear to view students as "consumers" and faculty as "labor" to their "management"

[50]Curtis J. Sitomer, "Black Militants Besiege Colleges," *The Christian Science Monitor* (December 31, 1968), p. 11.

[51]Robert S. Lynd, *Knowledge For What? The Place of Social Science in American Culture* (Princeton: Princeton University Press, 1939), p. 250.

rather than viewing all as having a legitimate role in participation in the many decision-making processes of the university.

The study of universities and other public organizations is, of course, the responsibility of the scholar. Much of the responsibility for the care and imagination with which such research may be conducted rests with the individual scholar. But not all of it. Public organizations *have not been entirely open* in granting access to researchers, especially in the more controversial areas of public policy. And beyond their mere cooperation, such organizations should provide resources to encourage basic theoretical inquiry rather than to promote work along the largely problem-solving lines which have characterized their support in the past.

Second, expand research on organization in hostile environments and crisis situations. Those who support the controlled disruption of certain social institutions in order to reform, radicalize, or replace them, together with those who would protect such institutions, have both demonstrated feet of clay and a heavy-handed ineptitude in their understanding of threat, violence, and counterviolence. The fact that the use of violence and its threat has produced certain changes in society which are welcomed by various segments of the society points to its selective functionality. Violence by and against the state is a reality; its use in defense of "law and order," "justice," "freedom," "change," "human rights," or even because it makes some people "feel good" has made it a part of the political terrain of the United States and other countries. Achieving an understanding of *how* it works and *why* is too important to be ignored. Yet in only one general theoretical study of organizations was the variable of hostile or benign environments even made explicit.[52]

Third, there should be wider efforts to conceptualize and examine interorganizational behavior. Public administration is very much a matter of the interaction of shifting clusters of public organizations. The notion that such organizations are embedded in some form of social, political, cultural, and physical matrix is not a new idea. Plato was sensitive to this point in his *Republic*. Apparently, we have to be reminded. In the past

[52]March and Simon, *Organizations, op. cit.*, p. 50.

twenty years we have been alerted to the "ecology of government,"[53] the "ecology of Public Administration,"[54] the "organization-set,"[55] and most recently, the "causal texture of organizational environments."[56] Despite current trends in organizational literature which focus greater emphasis upon organization-environment interfaces and the structure of relationships among organizations, the state of theory in this area is primitive.[57]

Fourth, enlarge the resources committed to comparative administrative research. The building of more sophisticated empirical theory of Public Administration cannot rely on American data alone. The comparative-administration movement has done much to promote such scholarly commitments, but resources must be made available to encourage wider efforts. The theory-building stage has operated very much at the level of grand theory so it is appropriate that more explicit middle-range thrusts be made. One research strategy that may have merit is to focus research at the micropolitical level defined in terms of specified interorganizational systems. LaPalombara has pointed to the need for comparative politics research at a partial-systems level rather than a whole-systems level.[58] Comparative research focusing on several interorganizational systems would reflect a

[53]John W. Gaus, *Reflections on Public Administration* (University, Ala.: University of Alabama Press, 1947), pp. 1–19.

[54]Fred W. Riggs, *The Ecology of Public Administration* (New Delhi: Asia Publishing House, 1961).

[55]William M. Evan, "The Organization-Set: Toward a Theory of Interorganizational Relations," in James D. Thompson (ed.), *Approaches to Organizational Design* (Pittsburgh, Pa.: University of Pittsburgh Press, 1966), pp. 173–191.

[56]F. E. Emery and E. L. Trist, "The Causal Texture of Organizational Environments," *Human Relations* (February, 1965), pp. 21–32.

[57]As late as 1968, one organizational theorist felt obliged to examine the extent to which organizational change processes are induced by the environment. She made this comment: "Despite Darwin's enduring insight, theorists of change, including biologists, have continued to focus largely on internal aspects of systems." See Shirley Terreberry, "The Evolution of Organizational Environments," *Administrative Science Quarterly* (March, 1968), p. 613.

For a theoretical and empirical study of interorganizational behavior in which the notion of an *interorganization* is developed as an analytical unit, see Philip S. Kronenberg "Micropolitics and Public Planning: A Comparative Exploration of the Interorganizational Politics of Planning" (unpublished doctoral dissertation, University of Pittsburgh, 1969).

[58]Joseph LaPalombara, "Macrotheories and Microapplications in Comparative Politics: A Widening Chasm," *Comparative Politics* (October, 1968), pp. 52–78.

level of administrative behavior which exhibits greater complexity than patterns of elementary social behavior[59] and less complexity than those found in micropolitical systems. Study of the micropolitics of interorganizational systems can provide a more manageable analytical link between the formal organization in its most elementary form and the total political system. These comparative research activities should not be limited to cross-national comparisons alone (although these are the most perplexing because of the constant problem of distinguishing the impact of cultural factors on behavior from other systematic influences which account for the differences and similarities in phenomena). Comparative research into different "types" of organizations and into administrative systems in different subcultural groupings within the same political system should also be pursued.

A *fifth* suggestion which bears on the building of the new Public Administration is to develop a more continuously integrated and operational conception of the nature of politics and administration. These two concepts are far too central to our theoretical aspirations to be used in the casual way that they often are. This conception should be more continuously *integrated* in the sense that the connectiveness of these two ideas are demonstrated as falling along a single—if complex—continuum. It should be made more *operational* by making explicit the specific behavioral acts which consistute the points along the politics-administration continuum. The things we do in our research suggest that this complex continuum is actually composed of a number of continua relating to patterns of authority, control, communications, leadership strategy, technology, and environmental relations, among others. These patterns emerge in organizational or interorganizational contexts and represent—as they manifest themselves—the things we discuss in our inquiry into Public Administrative theory. When these patterns are rapidly changing and nonprogrammed and there is substantial contention over the value premises which undergird them, we can say that the behavior being observed is essentially *political*. On the other hand, we can say that we are dealing with an essentially *administrative* situation when the behavior we are

[59]George C. Homans, *Social Behaviour: Its Elementary Forms* (London: Routledge & Kegan Paul, 1961), p. 2.

observing is characterized by rather programmed and stable communications, authority, leadership, and control patterns, among others, and where a working consensus exists among participants over the important value premises of action. Thus the operation of a congressional committee would be interpreted as an administrative phenomenon subject to analyses and expectations appropriate to administration when committee members reflect essential agreement on objectives and tactics and enjoy stable patterned relationships along several of these selected analytical dimensions. On the other hand, an executive agency, despite its formal bureaucratic structure, would be assessed as a political system if it were ascertained that the main analytical dimensions being studied reflect instability and that there is a large measure of uncertainty about important value commitments of the members. Of course, a variety of mixed situations would lie along this complex "governance" continuum between the poles of maximum politics and maximum administrative behavior.

Each of these suggestions relating to the promise of a new Public Administration should be interpreted with recognition that judgments about what theoretical work we will do involve moral *choice*. The emphases we place in carrying out our theoretical work have effects on human lives; they become the premises for action by those who formulate and execute public policy. This emphasis is not a recommendation for abandoning a concern for greater scientific achievement. We cannot ignore the implications of data because they threaten or contradict our political or ethical preference. But it is terribly important for us to recognize that the standard of choice based on the grounds of scientific authority are not sufficient. The answer to the question "Theory for what?" must clearly be "For man to prevail!"

Public Administration Theoretical Inventory:
A Strategy for Systematization

We are very limited in our ability to judge either the scientific or moral authority of our theoretical work in Public Administration. Our aspirations for the development of systematic empirical theory run into dual problems of cognitive limitations and budgetary limitations. The ability of scholars to adequately process, integrate, and evaluate the multiple streams of empirical theory that fall under the Public Administration rubric is approaching its limit. Furthermore, the intellectual and economic resources which can be applied to these several tracks of theoretical inquiry and the necessarily related field research are in very short supply. Our quest for a new Public Administration cannot ignore these constraints.

Our theoretical work has been challenged for putting "old wine in new bottles." Much of the criticism of new theory is that it is *not* new, but amounts to little more than a rephrasing or "rediscovery" of old or extant notions. No doubt this charge is valid in many cases. On the face of it, distinctions of "oldness" and "newness" are unimportant. How sound and valid on empirical grounds, how useful for explaining and stimulating further explanation are more to the point. But in our preparadigmatic confusion we are often faced with a paradoxical tendency to accept certain old but untested ideas as fundamentally sound and conceptually adequate at the same time that we seize upon many new notions as a basis for theoretical elaboration and empirical testing. The upshot is that we have difficulty in discriminating between conventional wisdom and verified theory (of whatever vintage).

If social science were a no-cost enterprise we could satisfy ourselves with the recognition that the growth of knowledge is a matter of fits and starts in a nonlinear pattern. But social-science research is expensive and there are great opportunity costs involved in support for exploration and testing of various hypotheses. Much of the theory-based empirical work may amount to little more than methodological training (which has value, of course) unless we can *compare* the fruits of these efforts with existing hypotheses. To do this we have to be able to array hypotheses side by side, with their philosophical assumptions and empirical indicators, and with data about the extent and circumstances of their empirical verification. This necessity seems quite basic. Without some means for comparative analysis of ideas we are in poor shape to know where we have been and what courses of theoretical development hold out the greatest promise for the investment of research resources.

Wise men have made this kind of comparative analysis in the past. We are reaching the point where the geometric growth of conceptual and propositional materials is exceeding the capacities—and perhaps resolve—of wise men and the rest of us to filter, strain, and synthesize their implications. I propose that one partial solution is the development of a *Public Administration Theoretical Inventory* (PATI).[60]

A theoretical inventory is simply a collection of empirical propositions, accompanied by definitions of key concepts and some criteria of evaluation. Glenn Paige, in his excellent paper on proposition building, suggested five evaluative criteria: precision of statement, degree of confirmation, empirical scope, theoretical relevancies, and the nature of assumptions.[61]

PATI would be built on punch cards and, eventually, tapes. A number of considerations would have to be worked out, such as the scope of the literature search. But the basic information would include the raw statement of each proposition; nominal and, where possible, operational definitions of key concepts; the philosophical assumptions underlying each proposition; and a description of the sample and population used. Initially, the raw propositions could be retrieved by some keyword indexing system like KWIC or KWOC. The real design problems would come in the attempt to classify and code the other elements of information. Ultimately, some means should be devised to translate propositions into some form of generic language using normal English terms based on common empirical referents. If the resources needed to move to that stage could be obtained, we could have a basis for developing a useful symbolic language that would be a foundation for very elegant and precise modeling without falling into the trap of using scientific-looking notation that provides an artificial mask for little evidence and sloppy conceptualization.

I think theoretical inventories which facilitate rapid manipulation and retrieval of their contents are as important to building social science as data banks (and are less likely to become ob-

[60]I wish to express my thanks to Professors William Glaser, James Heaphey, and Fred Riggs, and to Dr. Satrio Joedono, for their reactions to an earlier statement of this proposal.

[61]Glen D. Paige, *Proposition-Building in the Study of Comparative Administration* (Washington, D.C.: CAG Special Series No. 4), p. 22.

solete). Theoretical inventories that exploit the remote access and storage and high-speed capabilities of modern information-processing technology can have a central role in building empirical social theory. If we are to advance the state of theory and improve conceptualization, we have to develop theoretical inventories that will enable us to compare and refine the language and empirical referents of the ideas we use in our multi-disciplinary, pancultural scholarship.

It is appropriate to view the PATI proposal as one involving an experiment, a pilot project in theory-building for a New Public Administration. Due to the relatively strong empirical grounding of studies of organizational behavior, one initial strategy for building PATI would be to draw upon the organization-theory literature. This could be done with interested scholars from several institutions, perhaps on an interdisciplinary basis. The organization-theory literature has some distinct advantages to offer such an enterprise. First, the literature is a product of scholarship in several disciplines. Second, our basis for comparative theoretical development can be enhanced to the extent that materials can be secured from non-Western countries. Third, the literature is increasingly empirical and quantified. Fourth, the conceptualization is fairly elegant and the behavioral referents are reasonably explicit. Finally, PATI—however verified or testable the entries might be—would constitute an anthology of our empirical administrative thought.

Comment: Empirical Theory
and the New Public
Administration

Bob Zimring

What is the "new Public Administration?" To what extent is the empirical study of Public Administration relevant to the new Public Administration? Can the empirical study of Public Administration in its current stage of development lead to a systematic body of knowledge of the administrative process in public organizations while at the same time making itself relevant to the new Public Administration? These, I think, are the three major questions which have to be answered by those concerned with the relationship between empirical theory in Public Administration and the new Public Administration.

I find myself in basic agreement with Professor Kronenberg's evaluation of the state of the art of empirical Public Administration. The major problem I find with the paper is Kronenberg's conception of what constitutes the new Public Administration and its relationship with empirical Public Administration. I shall first comment on Kronenberg's analysis of empirical Public Administration and his prescription for its improvement. I shall then proceed to his analysis of the relationship between the new Public Administration and empirical Public Administration.

If I read him correctly, Kronenberg's major criticism of the current state of empirical theory in Public Administration is that there is very little sound, systematic, cumulative empirical theory in the field. Of the various subfields within Public Administration, organization theory offers the most hope for developing rigorous empirical theory. By implication then, Kronenberg suggests that the other subfields in Public Administration should follow the lead of those in organization theory if they are to develop a rigorous empirical theory. To facilitate the process of aggregating individual research findings in organization theory into a unified, systematic, and cumulative theory of organizational behavior, Kronenberg proposes the development of a theory bank. This theory bank would provide relatively easy access to findings in the field and would thus enable one to move quickly to the frontiers of knowledge in organization theory and to begin to develop some valid middle-range theory. Presumably the other subfields in Public Administration would follow suit and develop their own theory banks. It would then be possible to tie together these various theory banks into a consolidated theory bank of empirical Public Administration and then to develop empirically reliable broad-gauge theory of Public Administration.

I tend to agree with Kronenberg's analysis of the state of development of empirical theory in Public Administration, with one major addition. I would extend his conclusions to cover the entire field of Public Administration, including organization theory. The basis of this extension is a conviction that the main difficulty encountered in developing a systematic body of empirical theory in Public Administration lies with the research strategy employed by most investigators specializing in organizational theory.

In order to develop empirically based middle-range theory in Public Administration it is necessary that the individual research findings be cumulative. Unfortunately, most of the findings of individual research studies in Public Administration, including those in organization theory, are not cumulative. I recognize that this is a bold statement to make. There are many aspects of research in organization theory which would appear to suggest that it does in fact offer a very sound base upon which to initiate the construction of some good empirical theory. A great amount of the work in organization theory meets a number of the criteria for scientifically defensible theory. The work in this field, especially those items cited in March and Simon, *Organizations*[1] and Blau and Scott, *Formal Organization*,[2] are quantitative and replicable. However, they are not, strictly speaking, cumulative. That is, it is not possible to logically extend the individual research findings which characterize much of the empirical work in organization theory beyond the specific case analyzed by the individual investigator(s).

Why is this so? Or, to put the question somewhat differently, under what conditions is it possible to make inferences from a sample to a larger universe? The answer, of course, is when the sample is representative of the universe. How do we know whether the sample is representative of the universe? How do we know whether the sample is representative of the universe from which it is chosen? Basic sampling theory tells us that every element in the universe should have an equal chance of being selected. If this rule is followed it is then possible to estimate by means of various statistical tests the extent to which the sample is representative of its universe.

[1]James G. March and Herbert A. Simon, *Organizations* (New York: John Wiley and Sons, 1958).
[2]Peter Blau and W. R. Scott, *Formal Organizations* (San Francisco: Chandler, 1961).

When I contend that it is not possible to logically generalize from most of the findings in the field of Public Administration, including organization theory, I am suggesting that most of the findings are drawn from samples which are unrepresentative of the universe they purport to be drawn from, that is, public agencies and their clientele. Most of the work in Public Administration is based upon varying kinds of analyses of behavior in one or more government agencies, industrial and commercial organizations, and small groups of college students. Usually the choice of the specific agency, firm, or group of students for study is dictated by ease of access, low monetary costs, ready availability, and similar factors. Thus, the sample of organizational units studied is biased in favor of those having these characteristics. What of those elements in the universe of Public Administration which do not possess the characteristics of those which have been studied? What can be said of them from the basis of organizations which have been studied? Very little, I am afraid. What I am suggesting here is that no strategy has been developed which would enable students of Public Administration to select public agencies and other units of analysis in such manner as to permit generalizations logically valid for the entire universe of Public Administration. Thus, students of Public Administration are placed in the position of making general statements about their field on the basis of a large number of unrepresentative studies. It is as if students of voting behavior were forced to make generalizations about the electorate in presidential elections on the basis of interviews with the electorate in Ann Arbor, Princeton, and Berkeley.

I imagine that to some this argument might sound somewhat pedantic. Students of Public Administration have to work within the constraints imposed upon them by the size of research budgets, the openness of public organizations, and similar factors. Thus, the funds may often times be lacking for the utilization of more sophisticated sampling procedures which could be used to secure a more representative cross section of the universe of Public Administration for analysis. Perhaps a number of researchers in the field do feel this way. However, very few of them, especially those in the field of organization theory, express such modesty in their published research. I think that it is the rare study which clearly states the specific universe to which the findings can be generalized and the strategy used in selecting the subject of the analysis. No amount of sophisticated statistical analysis or mathematical model building can make the findings in a particular study apply to a broader universe than is justified by the method used in selecting the specific cases for analysis. I think we have entered the stage of statistical overkill. We already have and use much more sophisticated analytical techniques than can be justified to generate findings which have very little general applicability.

As a first step toward the construction of a Public Administration theory bank, I think it would be appropriate to develop a research strategy which could be used to produce the type of findings appropriate to the development of a theory bank. Specifically, the construction of a meaningful theory bank, as opposed to an inventory of noncumulative research findings, cannot begin until students of Public Administration abandon the case-study approach to the field and develop sophisticated techniques which will enable them to produce findings which are applicable to a specified universe of public organizations and not limited to the specific case under investigation. Only when the obvious biases in the selection of the units of analysis now common in too much of Public Administration research are overcome will the creation of a theory bank make any sense.

The solution of the methodological problems involved in the empirical study of Public Administration is primarily of concern to those interested in improving the quality of empirical Public Administration. How is all of this relevant to the new Public Administration? Before answering this question it is necessary to define what the new Public Administration is. Kronenberg identifies it with a concern for pressing social problems and with making the public bureaucracy more responsive to the desires of the people. He suggests that empirical Public Administration and the new Public Administration could be made compatible if the former were to focus its attention more on the substantive concerns of the latter. Thus Kronenberg appears to suggest, if I read him correctly, that the primary difference between the old and the new Public Administration is one of scope and emphasis. The new empirical Public Administration should get involved and look at what is bugging society at the moment. I submit that the difference between the new Public Administration and traditional empirical Public Administration is much more fundamental than Kronenberg suggests, and in fact goes directly to the philosophical underpinnings of contemporary empirical social science and Public Administration.

If the new Public Administration as the phrase is used in the late sixties has any relationship to the movements for a "new sociology" and "new political science," and a new "social science in general," then I think it has to be defined as a break from value-free or value-neutral empirical research and in terms of a desire to make the academic study of the social universe directly concerned with questions of social justice. This new posture implies that social scientists will make value judgments in their professional capacities. This last statement goes directly against the traditional positivist stance which has guided much postwar empirical research in the social sciences and which states that social scientists as social scientists cannot make any value judgments. The "is" and the "ought" are separated by an unbridgeable gulf. The new social science, with which I think the new Public Administration identifies, should seek to bridge this gap.

My argument, then, is that social relevance is not the distinguishing characteristic of the new Public Administration. In fact, it can be shown that throughout most of its academic existence, Public Administration has been concerned with and influenced by the dominant social concerns of the age. After all, some of the early student-practitioners of Public Administration were in the forefront of the drive for municipal reform and similar social concerns of the times. More recently students of Public Administration have eagerly done the bidding of the establishment and have sought to improve the efficiency of public bureaucracies. Thus, concern with contemporary social problems is not new to Public Administration. It should be noted, however, that in the past most of this concern has focused on the problem of how to better secure certain middle-class values from the political system. Thus, the concern with municipal reform centered on cutting down on graft and corruption and making the government more efficient. There has been less concern with structuring public agencies so that they provide access to the politically powerless.

Nor do I think we can differentiate new Public Administration from old on the basis of the concern of the former for responsiveness of the public bureaucracy to the wishes of the people. My impression of the new social science is that it expects its practitioners to take the lead in agitating for social change which will produce social justice and equality and not merely be content with devising structures which will act as sounding boards for the dominant political groups. The new Public Administration should be concerned with making the public bureaucracy an instrument for achieving social justice and equality. This concern is very different from that of simply making the government responsive to the wishes of a majority of the people

The difficulties of relating empirical Public Administration to the search for social justice are both logical and political. I am relatively optimistic about overcoming the logical difficulties. This optimism is based upon the discussion of the logic of empirical inquiry found in Thomas Thorson's *Logic of Democracy*[3] and in Barrington Moore's essay on the limits of tolerance in scientific inquiry.[4] Thorson develops a very convincing and powerful method for logically justifying a democratic political system. I think it would be possible to use the technique employed by Thorson to develop a logical justification for some basic dimensions of social justice. Barrington Moore, using an existential approach, also suggests a potentially fruitful approach to linking empirical and scientific inquiry to a concern for and commitment to social justice. I think that the ideas developed in these two essays offer an appropriate point of departure for the development of a new logic of empirical inquiry which will be relevant to the concerns of the new Public Administration.

Let us assume then that it will be possible to develop a logical justification for linking the empirical-scientific method of Public Administration to the substantive concerns of the new Public Administration as I have defined it in this paper. The next ques-

[3]Thomas Thorson, *Logic of Democracy* (New York: Holt, Rintehart & Winston, 1962).

[4]Barrington Moore, Jr., "Tolerance and the Scientific Outlook," in Robert P. Wolf, Barrington Moore, Jr., and Herbert Marcuse, *A Critique of Pure Tolerance* (Boston: Beacon Press, 1965), pp. 53–80.

tion that has to be asked is whether the existing structure of the academic and governmental communities will support energetic and sophisticated attempts by students of Public Administration to relate themselves professionally to the broad cause of social justice.

I do not know whether the reward structure in universities and government will support a heightened social conscience on the part of students of Public Administration. In determining the likelihood of support for new departures let me try to spell out in a little more detail just what these new departures would consist of. I can think of three broad tasks which social scientists could perform, two of which are particularly relevant to students of Public Administration. The first task, for which Public Administration is probably not particularly well-suited, is the specification and justification of some of the concrete dimensions of social justice. A second task consists of the analysis of existing policies, programs, administrative and political structures, and the like to determine the extent and type of equities present in the existing social and political structures. Given the tremendous role played by nonelective public agencies in the United States today, this task is one which could greatly benefit from the properly guided expertise of students of Public Administration. The third task is that of developing and securing the adoption of specific programs which are designed to remedy existing inequities in the system. Here again, the prominence of public organizations suggests that students of Public Administration are in a position to play an important role.

In short, I am suggesting that students of Public Administration should use their professional resources, expertise, and time to work for social justice in their individual areas of specialization. This effort is what the existing academic and governmental establishments would be asked to support. It would require a basic reorientation for most students of Public Administration. At this point in time I do not know whether such a reorientation on the part of the established leadership in the academic world and government is possible or whether they would lend significant support to those who are interested in opting for this new course of action. In fact, I wonder if there is a sufficient number of academicians who are really interested in moving in the direction suggested here, given the possible risks involved. Thus, it may be necessary for the new Public Administration to develop outside of the existing institutional framework and thinking of the university and government.

Editorial Note

The general discussion following the comments by Kronenberg and Zimring was short and moved quickly away from the criticism and suggestions offered about empirical theory. The reason for this digression may be the one that a participant offered: "There is just nothing to argue about here; Kronenberg has characterized the problems in ways that are immediately acceptable as accurate and insightful." Some slight argument did develop, however, over the question of value neutrality in social science:

A: Why is it necessary to justify doing empirical studies? Must all empirical studies be justified in terms of some sort of normative context before they are conducted?

B: I think they should be. I would argue that the studies themselves should be socially, academically significant.

A: But that suggests something else. For example, a study might be academically and socially justifiable only in an empirical sense.

B: I don't think it could be justifiable in only an empirical sense if you mean by that "without reference to normative significance." I deny that you can divorce normative from empirical study.

C: I would like to suggest that the charge can be made the other way around: he who would impose upon our thinking processes with his normative judgments should also make certain that he has checked out the various empirical questions that must be faced before we can take any normative position seriously.

8

Comparative Public Administration

In his contribution to this chapter, Keith Henderson grapples with the past, present, and alternative futures of comparative Public Administration as a field of study from the standpoint of "noncomparative" "United States Culture" Public Administration.* He attempts to assess the merits of intranational comparative study (that is, the transference of the comparative perspective to the study of Public Administration within the United States) with special attention to current American problems and relevance to practicing public administrators. Kenneth Jowitt responds to Henderson's argument in a critical defense of "The Relevance of Comparative Public Administration."

A New Comparative Public Administration?

Keith M. Henderson

My appointed task is to undertake "a critical evaluation of what's gone right and what's gone wrong in the study of compara-

*The original versions of the essays in this chapter were published (soon after the Minnowbrook Conference) in the *Journal of Comparative Administration*. Subsequent to their presentation at Minnowbrook and publication, Professor Henderson substantially revised his essay and the revised version is presented here. Professor Jowitt's essay is printed here in substantially the same form in which it was presented at the Minnowbrook Conference.

This essay, in a slightly different form, was originally published under the title "Comparative Public Administration: The Identity Crisis" in the *Journal of Comparative Administration*, Volume I, No. 1 (May, 1969) and is reprinted by arrangement with Sage Publications, Inc., publisher of the journal, and the Comparative Administration Group.

tive and perhaps development administration, with a look into the future." Such a formidable assignment—particularly the mandate to be a futurist—is appropriately entered into only with considerable humility and with the saving thought that state-of-the-art literature on comparative Public Administration has been developed to a high level of proficiency.[1]

In the myriad in-house—that is, within the Comparative Administration Group—treatments of comparative Public Administration, only Dwight Waldo has seriously attempted to relate the movement to a broader concern with American Public Administration.[2] Caldwell and others have alluded to possible spillover effects, but these are only incidental comments.

The present discussion seeks to interpret the past, present, and future of comparative Public Administration (and development administration) as a field of study from the standpoint of

[1]For example: Lynton K. Caldwell, "Conjectures on Comparative Public Administration," Roscoe Martin (ed.), *Public Administration and Democracy: Essays in Honor of Paul H. Appleby* (Syracuse: Syracuse University Press, 1965), pp. 229–244; Richard A. Chapman, "Prismatic Theory in Public Administration: A Review of the Theories of Fred W. Riggs," *Public Administration* (London: Winter, 1966), pp. 415–433; Milton Esman, *The CAG and the Study of Public Administration: A Mid-Term Appraisal* (Bloomington: Comparative Administration Group, 1966); Milton Esman, "The Ecological Style in Comparative Administration," *Public Administration Review* (September, 1967), pp. 271–278; Ferrel Heady, *Public Administration: A Comparative Perspective* (Englewood Cliffs, N.J.: Prentice-Hall, 1966), Chap. 1; Ferrel Heady, "Comparative Public Administration: Concerns and Priorities," Ferrel Heady and Sybil L. Stokes (eds.), *Papers in Comparative Public Administration* (Ann Arbor, Mich.: Institute of Public Administration, 1962), pp. 1–18; James Heaphey, "Comparative Public Administration: Comments on Current Characteristics," *Public Administration Review* (May/June, 1968), pp. 242–249; Keith M. Henderson, *Emerging Synthesis in American Public Administration* (London: Taplinger [Asia Pub.], 1966), Chap. 4; Warren F. Ilchman, "Rising Expectations and the Revolution in Development Administration," *Public Administration Review* (December, 1965), pp. 314–328; Robert Jackson, "An Analysis of the Comparative Public Administration Movement," *Canadian Journal of Public Administration* (March, 1966), pp. 108–130; R. S. Milne, "Comparisons and Models in Public Administration," *Political Studies* (1962), pp. 1–14; Nimrod Raphaeli (ed.), *Readings in Comparative Public Administration* (Boston: Allyn & Bacon, 1967), Chap. 1; Edgar L. Shor, "Comparative Administration: Static Study Versus Dynamic Reform," *Public Administration Review* (September, 1962), pp. 158–164; Dwight Waldo, *Comparative Public Administration: Prologue, Problems and Promise* (Chicago: American Society for Public Administration, 1964), also reprinted in Preston P. LeBreton (ed.), *Comparative Administration Theory* (Seattle: University of Washington Press, 1968), pp. 92–138.

[2]Waldo, *op. cit.*

"noncomparative" "United States Culture" Public Administration.

Non-Riggsian Comparative

It is sometimes forgotten that several years elapsed between the first flowerings of American interest in Public Administration in the developing countries after World War II and Fred Riggs' capture of the movement in the late 1950's. When the Public Administration Clearing House sponsored a Conference on Comparative Administration at Princeton in 1952, the outcome was a continuing committee intended to develop "criteria of relevance" and a design for field studies in foreign countries. The conference approached the American Political Science Association which approved the creation of a subcommittee on comparative administration under Wallace Sayre's Committee on Public Administration. Interest was not confined to the American political-science establishment. In 1953, the International Political Science Association sponsored a panel on comparative Public Administration, chaired by Charles S. Ascher. Under auspices of the International Institute of Administrative Sciences in Brussels, additional studies were prepared on comparative experience in various European countries. In a lesson which has probably been lost on us, efforts directly affiliated with political science as a discipline failed to attract sufficient support to survive.

F. W. Riggs and the Ford Foundation

Blessed by the Ford Foundation, the Comparative Administration Group of the American Society for Public Administration (hereafter CAG), under Fred Riggs' leadership, was able to prosper where others had failed. Papers by Riggs in the early 1960's set the intellectual tone for "comparative" study. In a 1962 article, Riggs identified three trends—one fairly clear and the other two emerging—in the "comparative study of public administration."[3] The first was a movement from normative toward

[3]Prepared originally for delivery at the 1961 annual meeting of the American Society for Public Administration and published as "Trends in the Comparative Study of Public Administration," *International Review of Administrative Sciences*, 28 (1962), 9–15.

empirical approaches, the second from idiographic to nomothetic approaches, and the third from nonecological to ecological modes of thought. In Riggs' view both the broad field of Public Administration and the subfield of "comparative studies" had gradually developed an awareness of the difference between empirical and normative work and had begun increasingly to stress empirical description and explanation. Under the rubric "empirical" Riggs distinguished unique historical or contemporary case studies from approaches which seek generalizations, laws, or hypotheses. The case studies, of course, are idiographic; the generalizations are nomothetic. Finally, there was a dimly discernible trend from nonecological studies, in which administrative institutions are abstracted from their environments, to ecological approaches in which politics and administration are dealt with as aspects of a total system. Truly comparative studies, of course, are empirical, nomothetic, and ecological.

Early products issued under the aegis of the CAG were, implicitly if not explicitly, severe in their indictments of traditional Public Administration thinking: The *raison d'être* was to correct the inadequacies of parochial, unsystematic, noncomparative study. American Public Administration eschewed theory; comparative administration wallowed in it. American Public Administration was culture-bound; comparative sought systematic cross-cultural and cross-national insights. American Public Administration was oriented toward the practitioner; comparative pursued understanding for understanding's sake. On most points, comparative Public Administration, as reflected in the CAG, was antithetical to "United States Culture" Public Administration study. This orientation may not have been the Ford Foundation's vision, but it was the fact.

Early CAG Efforts

Writing in 1962, Ferrel Heady—then Director of the Institute of Public Administration and Professor of Political Science, University of Michigan—identified five "motivating concerns" in comparative studies in administration:

(1) The search for theory;
(2) The urge for practical application . . . ;

(3) The incidental contribution to Comparative Administration of advances in the study of comparative politics generally;

(4) The recent interest of scholars trained in the continental administrative law tradition, and

(5) The intensified analysis on a comparative basis of perennial problems of public administration.[4]

These concerns present as good a framework as any for discussing what comparative Public Administration has been.

In the early 1960's, the first of these concerns was clearly dominant in the literature, marking something of a shift away from the case-study approach of Siffin's 1959 volume, *Toward the Comparative Study of Public Administration*,[5] yet realizing the hopes expressed in Fred W. Riggs' essay in that volume.[6]

The CAG described its subject in the following manner: "theory of public administration as applied to diverse cultures and national settings" and "the body of factual data, by which it can be expanded and tested."[7] In addition, some attention was given to "development administration" which was too elusive to define precisely but related to an "action-oriented, goal-oriented administrative system"[8] or "major societal transformation, a change in system states"[9] in the developing areas. "Development administration" seemed, at least in early formulations, to have a heavier normative content that "comparative Public Administration."

The intellectual roots of comparative Public Administration theory lie in American behavioral science, but the foremost mentor—through his translated works—was clearly Max Weber, the German sociologist. Prior to 1946 few American scholars of administration had heard of Max Weber. His influence grew as sociological contributions made impact after the war and the

[4]Heady, Heady and Stokes (eds.), *op. cit.*, p. 3.

[5]William J. Siffin (ed.), *Toward the Comparative Study of Public Administration* (Bloomington: Department of Government, Indiana University, 1959).

[6]Fred W. Riggs, "Agraria and Industria—Toward a Typology of Comparative Administration," Siffin (ed.), *op. cit.*, pp. 23–116.

[7]Heady and Stokes (eds.), *op. cit.*, p. 4.

[8]Edward W. Weidner, "Development Administration: A New Focus for Research," Heady and Stokes (eds.), *op. cit.*, p. 98.

[9]Milton J. Esman, "The Politics of Development Administration," John D. Montgomery and William J. Siffin (eds.), *Approaches to Development: Politics, Administration and Change* (New York: McGraw-Hill, 1966), p. 59.

"ideal-typical" model of bureaucracy was found to express what Public Administration structuralists had been saying all along.

Although the vocabulary of Weber and Riggs became familiar to all, the empirical testing of theory in systematic fashion was never realized. Inadequate statistics, problems of access, language barriers, expenses which foundations seemed reluctant to share, hostile or indifferent governments and study subjects, and other obstacles conspired to frustrate would-be researchers who could not operate from some firmer base than comparative Public Administration. When obstacles were partially overcome, the results were sometimes disastrous nonetheless. Contrasted with empirical field research, the building of grand theoretical models in the tradition of Weber and Parsons could be considerably more intriguing and rewarding.

But theory was often perceived to be at the opposite pole from Heady's second motivating concern: the urge for practical application. However, practical application was a very weak urge in contrast to other urges on the part of leading members of the CAG. Nor did interest in this sphere grow with the passage of time. A questionnaire distributed in October 1966 to the 440 members of CAG and returned by 250 (over 200 of whom were academicians or graduate students) showed a predominant interest in research and teaching.

There was not a consistent, sustained, wide-spread, or strongly stated appeal for linking the theoreticians with the practitioners under the aegis of the CAG nor for an investment of resources in stimulating empirical research nor for pursuing the work of the CAG into such practical realms as training and consulting. In sum, proposals to channel CAG efforts into the sphere of action received very short shrift among respondents.[10]

On the other hand, the Ford Foundation, patron of CAG's endeavors, had expressed a desire to see the application of knowledge. "With all this theorizing and all this study, what are you going to do about it?" asked the Foundation's George Gant. No convincing answer was forthcoming.

Heady's third concern, comparative politics, as represented by the Committee on Comparative Politics of the Social Science Research Council, seems to have presented an abundance of riches

---

[10]*CAG Newsletter* (June, 1967), pp. 12 and 13.

to many CAG members. Here were recognized political scientists, dissatisfied with traditional "comparative" studies, pursuing systematically the same basic scholarly interests held by CAG members, although with considerably less emphasis upon "bureaucracy" or "administration." The search for appropriate typologies for polities or political systems paralleled—and in part inspired—a search for bureaucratic or administrative typologies.

The fourth motivating concern identified by Heady was the mutuality of interests of European scholars trained in the continental administrative law tradition.[11] A wide number of contacts have been forged by CAG's Europe subcommittee, many of which would be expected to last even with the demise of a parent Comparative Administration Group. An ambiguous relationship exists with the International Institute of Administrative Sciences —of which the American Society for Public Administration is a national unit—since the orientation of IIAS has differed sufficiently from CAG's to discourage close liaison.

Heady's fifth point—intensified analysis of perennial problems—relates easily to the fourth. Comparative Public Administration was seen by many, before the dominance of theoretical writings, as the overseas extension of traditional Public Administration concerns such as control and responsibility, personnel, budgeting, and organization and methods studies. A broader perspective would thus be provided on American administrative problems, and the exchange of experiences would be mutually beneficial.

Some of the interest in overseas phenomena by Public Administration teachers was simply a fascination with cultural oddities. However, for many years the European countries had been studied in their formal administrative dimensions. Moreover, it was understandable that Public Administration would be willing to pursue academically what had already become established practice in numerous missions to developing countries. A strong case has been made by people such as Emil Sady for the transfer of administrative techniques enlightened by understandings of application in various countries, and for the impor-

---

[11]Heady mentioned Paul Meyer, Fritz Morstein Marx, Brian Chapman, André Molitor, and Roman Schnur.

tance of cross-national exploration of administrative procedures involving personnel, financial controls, and organization and methods devices.[12] Comparative Public Administration did not assume this role and it has been generally conceded that little has been contributed to the expert in the field whose orientation typically remains what it was and whose task is specified by his sponsoring agency.

Current Foci

If the motivating concerns listed by Ferrel Heady in 1962 provide convenient categories for discussing the diverse activities in comparative Public Administration through the mid-sixties, the accelerating pace of academic change—which often reduces trends to a matter of months—makes it difficult to neatly classify the panoply of interests represented in the CAG.

In an incisive article appearing in the May/June 1968 *Public Administration Review*, James Heaphey takes comparative Public Administration to task for the severe myopia of its "prevailing visions," particularly the vision "academic analysis." Heaphey clearly states the identity problem:

> What is the subject of this field? Is it comparison, per se? If so, does comparison imply similarities or differences, or both? What is the purpose of the field—to increase rationality in American technical assistance programs; to understand why administrators behave as they do in different cultural settings; to describe the variety of administrative laws, rules, and regulations around the world; to find a language about administration that enables one to talk in the language used by modern American social science, or what? If the field has more than one purpose, has the relationship between the purposes been adequately articulated?
>
> Is this a scholarly or a professional field—and is such a distinction valid? Is it both?[13]

Heaphey raises many of the most critical questions in his brief article. Yet, in spite of its tone, one could hardly call the author

[12]See, for example, Emil Sady, *The Need for Comparative Studies of Practical Problems of Urban Administration* (Bloomington: Comparative Administration Group, 1966); "Classification as a Basis for Comparative Analysis of Practical Problems in Public Administration," Keith M. Henderson (ed.), *Comparative Public Administration: Theory and Relevance* (New York: Graduate School of Public Administration, New York University, 1967), pp. 11–26.

[13]Heaphey, *op. cit.*, p. 248.

unsympathetic to the movement. He has written significant Occasional Papers[14] and is a member of CAG's Executive Committee.

An even more searching series of questions than suggested by Heaphey concerns the very existence of the "field." Might not Martin Landau's analysis of broader Public Administration study be applied with equal force to comparative Public Administration?

The postwar definitions have given rise to a set of problems which challenge the integrity of the "field." These, designed to counteract the rigidities of the politics-administration dichotomy, are so extensive as to provide little meaning. They make it virtually impossible to specify an area of activity that cannot be considered within the scope of administration.[15]

What, it can be asked, is *not* within the scope of comparative Public Administration?[16] While there are certain dominant themes—the developing countries, the political system, and the like—it is hard to know what the central thrust might be and equally hard to find anything distinctly "administrative" in that thrust. The full range of political-science, economic, sociological, historical and other concerns seems relevant. This diffuseness may not be a serious obstacle if it gives way—again in Landau's terms —to an agreed upon paradigm.[17]

[14]James Heaphey, *Spatial Aspects of Development Administration: A Review and Proposal* (June, 1965); (with Philip Kronenberg), *Toward Theory-Building in Comparative Public Administration: A Functional Approach* (Bloomington: Comparative Administration Group, 1965).

[15]Martin Landau, "The Concept of Decision-Making in the 'Field' of Public Administration," Sidney Mailick and Edward H. Van Ness (eds.), *Concepts and Issues in Administrative Behavior* (Englewood Cliffs, N.J.: Prentice-Hall, 1962), p. 9.

[16]Picking Occasional Papers at random off the shelf, we find the following titles: *Politics and Processes of Africanization; Planned Control of the Bio-Physical Environment; Education, Administration and Development; The Colonial Stage of Political Development: The American Case; The Temporal Dimensions in Models of Administration and Organization; Polity, Bureaucracy and Interest Groups in the Near East and North Africa; The Social Context of National Planning Decisions: A Comparative Approach; The Comparison of Whole Political Systems; Ecology of Development; Leadership and Time; The Problem of the Public Enterprise.*

[17]Martin Landau, "Sociology and the Study of Formal Organization," Dwight Waldo and Martin Landau, *The Study of Organizational Behavior: Status, Problems and Trends* (Washington, D.C.: Comparative Public Administration Group Special Series No. 8, 1966).

Following Thomas S. Kuhn, Landau has indicated that the study of formal organization, as with other "normal sciences," passes through various stages before arriving at that condition which a community of scholars accept on a more or less continuing basis as a discipline or field. Prior to the cumulative or "paradigmatic" stage, there exist a plethora of competing views, languages, and logics. "There is neither a common research tradition nor the necessary consensus for a common field of inquiry. Each of the competing schools questions the others, adventurism is rampant, and commonly accepted standards of control do not exist. This stage can be preliminary to a science, or it can appear as a temporary condition which follows upon the rejection of a common paradigm."[18] In the Landau interpretation, it is Max Weber who provided the paradigm for the study of bureaucratic (or formal) organization. Other paradigms— behavioral rather than structural—are also plausible for comparative Public Administration. But can a single paradigm arise from the diverse thinking of CAG?[19]

Probable Futures

The best brand of futurism is probably that which projects present trends which assume no major "surprises." If comparative Public Administration attempts this, two states appear probable. One is decline into relative obscurity; the other is subordination under comparative politics.

Decline is possible for a number of reasons. Just as interest in overseas institutions and practices of administration arose coincidentally with the United States commitment to aid European and developing countries following World War II, interest may decline as major attention and funding shift to problems of the American cities and away from unpopular overseas involvements. The decline in financial support for comparative study, the disenchantment of students with cross-national study, and the continued rejection of CAG thinking by the Public Administration

[18]*Ibid.*, p. 39.
[19]Regard the subcommittees: Africa, Asia, Comparative Urban Administration and Politics, Educational Administration, Europe, Latin American Development Administration, Legislative Studies, Organization Theory, Planning, Systems Theory.

"establishment" may conspire together to relegate comparative Public Administration to insignificance. Since the lack of relevance of CAG-type enterprises renders them uninteresting from the practitioner's point of view, those practitioners may by their indifference influence the Public Administration establishment to completely reject comparative Public Administration.

A more probable—and from many points of view more desirable—future state places comparative Public Administration squarely within the confines of comparative politics. This trend already seems predominant. Within the last several years, a shift seems to have occurred from the highly abstract systems models —structural-functional, input-output, and so on—to developmental models concerned not only with the uses of history and with the European experience generally, but also with the broadly "political." This shift is found in Fred W. Riggs' own work, often set forth initially as CAG Occasional Papers.[20] Public administration (in the institutional or functional sense) becomes, for Riggs, a by-product[21] of the primary category, the polity, and of significance not by itself but in relation to its role in political development. In this interpretation Riggs has moved considerably closer to the prevailing vision of the Committee on Comparative Politics and even further away from "applied" research. Methodologically distinct but also derived from political-science premises is the recent empirical field work of Alfred Diamant and Blanche Blank on European bureaucracies[22] and of Ralph Braibanti—based largely on secondary research with documents —on Southeast Asia.[23] A forthcoming book by Warren Ilchman

[20]For example: Modernization and Development Administration (January, 1966); Ambivalence of Feudalism and Bureaucracy in Traditional Societies (September, 1966); The Idea of Development Administration: A Theoretical Essay (December, 1966); The Political Structures of Administrative Development (April, 1967); The Comparison of Whole Political Systems (1967).

[21]Sometimes a by-product of primary importance, however, as in Fred W. Riggs' monumental study, Thailand: The Modernization of a Bureaucratic Polity (Honolulu: East-West Center Press, 1966).

[22]Originally, Blanche D. Blank, A Proposal for a Statistical Approach to Comparative Administration: The Measurement of National Bureaucracies (Bloomington: Comparative Administration Group, 1965).

[23]For example: Ralph J. Braibanti, Research on the Bureaucracy of Pakistan (Durham: Duke University Press, 1966); Ralph J. Braibanti (ed.), Asian Bureaucratic Systems Emergent from the British Imperial Tradition (Durham: Duke University Press, 1966).

and Todd La Porte, two younger political scientists, may turn out to be among the most definitive statements of the field.[24] On balance, the surmise is that comparative Public Administration will establish a place for itself *within* the discipline of political science.

Desirable Futures

An alternative to the above may be summarized as follows:

1. Public Administration as an academic field is undergoing a serious identity crisis of its own.[25]

2. Comparative Public Administration reflects an intellectual rigor lacking in the broader field and has attracted a large number of younger Public Administration academicians.

3. Methodological and theoretical sophistication in comparative Public Administration can be utilized to discipline inquiries and applications in the broader field of Public Administration which is now faced with a perplexing number of academic problems within the United States culture context.

To appreciate this argument, Public Administration must be thought of as something more than a subfield of political science. Public Administration is in a position to claim for itself the role of understanding and improving the management of public (or government) executive organizations, while relinquishing to political science the metatask of critically examining bureaucracy as a problem involving power and control. Public Administration would become the study of the real and proper structure and functioning of government executive organizations (one level of analysis) and the behavior of the organizational participants, in various environments. Comparative Public Administration would assume intellectual leadership of the field, extending its concerns into "United States Culture" Public Administration.

[24]Warren Ilchman and Todd La Porte, *Comparative Public Organization: Analysis and Synthesis* (Boston: Little, Brown, forthcoming).

[25]If in doubt, see John C. Honey, "A Report: Higher Education for Public Service" and the commentaries thereon in the *Public Administration Review* (November, 1967), and "Theory and Practice of Public Administration: Scope, Objectives, and Methods," Monograph 8, American Academy of Political and Social Science (October, 1968). The Minnowbrook Conference and this volume may perhaps also serve as evidence of Public Administration's identity crisis.

Intranational Study

When one assesses the factors making this new role for comparative Public Administration appear feasible, one is guided—perhaps overmuch—by the temper of the times. A drastically limited foreign-aid budget, disaffection with commitments such as the Vietnam war (known to almost every literate schoolchild in the world through the mass media), and a handful of Camelots[26] have limited the opportunities for unhindered scholarly field work by Americans in developing countries. On the other hand, American cities and developing regions—for example, Appalachia, New England, the Ozarks, and the Upper Great Lakes[27]—provide attractive options for scholarly comparative analysis. The Comparative Urban Administration and Politics Committee of CAG, from its inception, defined its scope to include the United States, and an obvious link to the strong emphasis upon urban problems in public affairs and Public Administration programs exists here. Other elements of comparative Public Administration might follow the same pattern, seeking linkages to the more "parochial" domains of academic Public Administration.

It is apparent that Public Administration specialists will be called upon to assist in various ways in studying and prescribing "solutions" to compelling contemporary American problems. The applied character of much Public Administration work may facilitate the acceptance as expertise of ideas on such matters as housing, traffic, law enforcement, health and welfare, and provision of other government services. Recognition of the administrative complexities of new federal, state, and local programs will open the door to expanded training opportunities for officials (note Title IX, "Education for the Public Service"),

[26]The Camelot project involved the measuring and forecasting of revolutionary and insurgency movements in developing areas. Publicity concerning it gave rise to severe outcries against United States Government policy, especially in Chile in 1965, and led to its cancellation. See Irving L. Horowitz (ed.), *The Rise and Fall of Project Camelot* (Cambridge: M.I.T. Press, 1967).

[27]These four regions are discussed in: United States Department of Commerce, Economic Development Administration, *Regional Economic Development in the U.S.: Part I and Part II*, A Series of Papers Prepared for Working Party No. 6 of the Industry Committee, "Policies for Regional Development," OECD, October, 1967 (Washington, D.C.: Department of Commerce, 1967).

evaluating and restructuring of government agencies, establishing of new relationships with clients, and application of knowledge concerning management practices. Computer utilization, PPB, and quantitative techniques from the private sector such as PERT and CPM will be accorded increased significance in government. Public Administrationists, including comparative Public Administration specialists, will probably have numerous prospects of relating themselves to tasks defined by the priorities of the political process.

The advantage of comparative Public Administration over other segments of academic Public Administration in addressing these tasks is that it is already organized as a coherent focus with a considerable coterie of adherents. Primarily but not exclusively trained in political science, members of the Comparative Administration Group represent a reservoir of talent (as of late 1968 there were over 500 members) and a record for scholarly publication unrivaled in other Public Administration subfields.

Also, since the pursuit of theoretical and methodological elegance has not been confined to concrete cross-cultural or cross-national referents, model-building exercises have heuristic value for intranational study. Yet another, but more self-interested, reason to argue for the redirection of comparative Public Administration toward urban and regional problems—perhaps by radically expanding the existing work of CAG's Comparative Urban Administration and Politics subgroup—is that this might help to correct one of CAG's prominent weaknesses (as seen by many), a disdain for dealing with "practical" problems.

More important, it might well be argued that the United States has its own developing areas which stand in need of the same kind of attention given to developing areas in the third world.

While comparative Public Administration's self-critical (as well as critical) posture may limit its effectiveness, somewhere along the line it would seem necessary for CAG or its successors to make a declaration of intent to be useful. Strictly esoteric concerns or political analyses of political units will never justify a "comparative approach" to the practicing decision maker. Although Emil Sady and Milton Esman have made cogent statements on this point,[28] they seem to have persuaded few academicians. Perhaps the case is overstated to say that most academicians associated with CAG are not interested in the practitioner. What, on the other hand, is the evidence to the contrary? The young academician in comparative Public Administration is at an even greater disadvantage in this respect than his senior colleagues who gained practical experience during the Second World War. The new breed is a pure scholar, untainted by the world of government, and because of his age and lack of government experience it is hard for him to relate to the government executive.

Here is a dilemma. The attraction of the CAG for distinguished American and foreign scholars draws talent into the Public Administration orbit which would not otherwise be available. In addition, scholars who would have abandoned the field for more stimulating areas have kept their affiliation with administrative study, and younger academicians have been drawn to the fold. These circumstances favor comparative Public Administration to a greater degree than other subfields, suggesting that intellectual capacity is available here if it only could be marshaled for the invigorating of Public Administration. However, the very nature of the intellectual attraction discourages dialogue with the practicing official. The official needs assistance in assessing the demands of his environment, developing appropriate strategies and tactics, understanding his own role in the larger scheme of things, knowing what new technologies are available and how they might be used, and otherwise acquiring specific intelligence on a given topic. He is a problem solver with a job to be done. The academician's orientation, however, tends to be toward pure rather than applied research.

In the final analysis, it would seem that Public Administration cannot survive unless it becomes relevant to current American problems, and cannot become relevant until its major academic strengths are brought into contact with the practitioner, especially the urban administrator. The gap between academic and practical interests can be bridged, however, with studies that enlighten and those that answer specific, administratively defined problems. After all, administrators deal every day with decision

[28]Sady, *op. cit.*; Esman, "The CAG and the Study of Public Administration," *op. cit.*

problems amenable to comparative analysis. Beyond the statistical, sample survey, and cost-benefit studies which are always comparative, a variety of narrative cases can be treated on a paired or multiple basis through point-to-point comparisons. Analyses performed by administrative assistants and other officials use comparative or quasi-comparative methods.

Rational decision making, modified as required by political exigencies, or political decision making, modified as required by rational considerations, is presumably a commonplace which varies in quality in accordance—among other factors—with the quality of information available. One of the many styles of decision making involves a point-by-point comparison of like experiences, each experience acting as a "control group" for the others. At their most sophisticated, simulation models manipulated by computer can replicate real-life situations and project consequences of administrative action. Thus, decisions for routing a Bay Area Rapid Transit system, to cite an example, are properly not solely "intrasystem" but recognize the experience in other centers of high mobility, high density, and rapid economic advance. Comparative analysis may preserve one from egregious miscalculations.

If some agreement can be reached on the proper frameworks for comparison, then in the middle ground between idiographic exposition and the building of grand theoretical models comparative Public Administration may ultimately prove to be useful to administrators. But the basic argument is not that comparative Public Administrationists must carve out their own niche in intranational study by immediately agreeing on units (nonpolitical or otherwise) to be compared and ways of comparing them; rather, it is that the inquiring and critical spirit of comparative Public Administration, as shown in the CAG, be carried over into United States Public Administration. The protest implicit in CAG activities has provided lessons in conceptualization, in proposition building, in method, in logic, and in semantics that might well be transplanted back to the American soil. Without abandoning cross-cultural or cross-national study—rather by enriching American study with nonparochial perspectives—intranational comparative analysis could be pursued with the tools and skills of CAG members thus reemphasizing the importance of comparison (as well as other modes of analysis), publicness (an antidote to the generic concerns of most organization theorists), and administration (as opposed to entirely political interests). Such is the challenge of a "new" comparative Public Administration.

There is no escape, no alternative: if we are to rise to our responsibilities and opportunities, if we are to remain (I use it again) *relevant* and not become obsolete, we must become "urbanists," "metropolitanists" or whatever the proper term may prove to be.

Relations with other disciplines and professions is close to the heart of the matter. Many of the problems . . . will relate to traditional interests of the mother-discipline, Political Science. If Political Science supplies the necessary help and guidance, well and good, but if not we must "go it alone" or seek assistance elsewhere.[29]

Comment: The Relevance of Comparative Public Administration

Kenneth Jowitt

I should like to address myself to the statement that the field of comparative Public Administration "remains ill defined and estranged" from what Keith Henderson has called "United States Culture" Administration; and to the statement that the lack of relevance of CAG-type enterprises renders them uninteresting from the practitioner's point of view. Henderson's conclusion is that "in the final analysis, it would seem that Public Administration cannot survive unless it becomes relevant to current American problems, and cannot become relevant until its major academic strengths are brought into contact with the practitioner . . . ."

The question of relevance being a contextual one, any discussion of the relevance of comparative Public Administration to

[29]Dwight Waldo, "The Administrative State Revisited," *Public Administration Review* (March, 1965), p. 20.

This essay was originally published under the title "The Relevance of Comparative Public Administration to American Political Life" in the *Journal of Comparative Administration*, Volume I, No. 1 (May, 1969) and is reprinted by arrangement with Sage Publications, Inc., publisher of the journal, and the Comparative Administration Group.

American Public Administration must specify the major characteristics of the American context. One current major characteristic—that the United States in many ways is experiencing a
revolutionary domestic situation—has received increasing though
hardly unopposed recognition.[1] And yet even this recognition is
often a seriously incomplete one.

It has always seemed to me that American culture and administration were highly congruent in one respect. In their ideal
expression both of them emphasize the routine and in some way
avoid the critical. For those of us who accept the main orientation of Weber's work and who think they understand what is
meant by an ideal type, the relation between administration and
routine appears quite clear. However, I feel there is an almost
complete lack of appreciation for the relationship which exists
between American culture, the "American experience," and the
emphasis within the United States on the routine over the critical.
Routine and critical refer here to the types of problems that are
perceived, and even more to the way in which they are conceived
or formulated by individuals concerned in some way with public
policy.

More than anyone else, Louis Hartz has seen and defined the
distinctive element within the "American experience." In his
work on *The Liberal Tradition in America*, Hartz notes that
while "we have . . . been told that it is we . . . who are the most
'revolutionary' nation on earth . . . Nothing is farther from the
truth . . . ." In fact, Hartz states, "it is the absence of the experience of social revolution which is at the heart of the whole
American dilemma."[2] For Hartz, and for me, the major consequence of the "American experience" is the tendency to perceive, conceive, and react to problems in terms of technique (incidentally, it is to this propensity of ours that the Chinese refer
when they speak of us as "paper tigers").

The relation of all this to comparative administration is actually quite direct. Hartz saw in America's international involvement after the World War the source of "forces working toward

[1]See Dwight Waldo's "Public Administration in a Time of Revolutions,"
Public Administration Review (July/August, 1968), pp. 362–368.
[2]Louis Hartz, *The Liberal Tradition in America* (New York: Harcourt,
Brace, 1955), pp. 305–306.

a shattering of American provincialism abroad as well as at home."[3] Yet, both at the level of foreign policy and within the discipline of administration, the shattering Hartz talked about has been more formal than real. With respect to foreign policy, evidence of shattering exists not only in our Vietnam policy but also in our involvement in the Dominican Republic and Bolivia. In the field of comparative Public Administration, the formal nature of the "shattering process" finds expression in the large incidence of "state-of-the-discipline" literature.

However, it is not solely the fault of either policy makers or students of administration that this has been the case thus far. That to date we have been greatly limited to a formal appreciation of the changes in the world has mainly been a consequence of the fact that these changes had not until very recently begun to make their appearance within the United States itself. Such changes, the indirect consequences of our involvement in the world, have begun to manifest themselves, and these manifestations are the primary data with which we must deal. The major significance of the appearance of these changes is that currently the United States is in a critical situation, a situation which threatens the definition of our political life, and simultaneously offers us the opportunity to substantially improve upon that definition. Within the political sphere, the 1968 presidential elections raise serious questions in my mind about whether or not the opportunities presented by this critical situation have been taken advantage of. Whether or not such opportunities will be utilized within the sphere of Public Administration is still an open question; this analysis and statement are an attempt to increase such a possibility.

The major problem currently facing American administration theorists and practitioners is *conceptualization*: how problems are defined. In another work, Hartz has stated that the "American cannot grasp the relativity of the form in which his historical substance has been cast."[4] The domestic events of the last five years, however, have created a situation within which the American can do just that. Currently, America is experiencing a

[3]*Ibid.*, p. 308.
[4]Louis Hartz (ed.), *The Founding of New Societies* (New York: Harcourt, Brace & World, 1964), p. 118.

situation that—at least potentially and objectively—allows and in a sense demands an "inward enrichment of culture and perspective." In Hartz's words, "what is at stake is nothing less than a new level of consciousness . . . in which an understanding of oneself and an understanding of others go hand in hand."[5]

Supposedly, statements such as these are precisely the type that have led to the "estrangement" of administrative theorists and students from practitioners, to the lack of relevance of the former group to the latter. Let us then approach the question of relevance in a more explicit manner and in the process evaluate the extent to which comparative Public Administration has to date contributed in any way to the "practical" handling of current domestic problems.

In one sense the "isolation" or nonrelevance of comparative Public Administration to date has been a very positive fact, especially to the extent that this isolation has been characterized by attempts to appreciate the "relativity" of the forms and substance which characterize administration. At one point in his paper, Henderson talks about "Fred Riggs' capture of the movement in the late 1950's." If one looks at things in terms of developmental stages—that is, in terms of those problems which are of major importance for an individual or organization at a specific point in time—this "capture" was a very good thing. In a formal sense it allowed for the autonomy of a theoretical endeavor and in a substantive sense for the creation of a body of theoretical statements which are recognized as important relevant contributions even by those most concerned with making administrative theory operational.[6] However, my major argument is that the work accomplished by Riggs and others is at this point in time of great practical relevance to the conditions of American political-administrative life.

Presently, Public Administration is indeed a part of and a witness to a "time of revolutions." However, one outstanding feature of revolutions is the extent to which the participants and

---

[5] Hartz, *Liberal Tradition in America, op. cit.*, p. 308.

[6] For instance, see the number of favorable statements about Riggs' work contained in Warren F. Ilchman's "Rising Expectations and the Revolution in Development Administration," *Public Administration Review* (December, 1965), pp. 314–328.

witnesses to such phenomena resist or miss either their character or implications. An example of this kind of resistance is the statement in the Honey report which argues that the "negative factors" domestically and with reference to our foreign policy, while tragic, are transitory.[7] The recent and worthwhile attempts to increase the relevance of comparative Public Administration to the current situation in the United States and to the problem of governmental performance in other areas of the world exemplify the second phenomenon, that of misinterpretation. Most of these revisions are concerned with relating more effectively to the practitioner, and, in the words of one of the "revisionists," with helping eventually "to improve the statesman's choices." My argument is not at all with the aim, but with the thrust of the revisionist argument.

To increase the relevance of comparative Public Administration to the "real world" requires at least two things: (a) an appreciation of the lesson involved in recent developments within the United States, and (b) an acceptance of the notion of complementarity.[8] The existence of a major domestic crisis within the United States today has made a good deal of the existing body of comparative-administration analysis highly relevant. As a consequence of this crisis, we are in the position of being able to clearly see a number of political and ideological dimensions connected with the "American experience" that are usually hard to perceive and difficult to assess in terms of significance. Suddenly America has lost a good deal of its presumed uniqueness. Troops occupying cities, black revolts, political dissension, superimposition of issues—many of the phenomena which supposedly characterize underdeveloped or backward states are currently visible in "postindustrial," "end of ideology" America. In short, the relativity of our political and administrative form and substance is being demonstrated by what the Marxists would term "life itself," and with this demonstration the relevance of analyses heretofore limited to "developing" countries for our own situation

---

[7]John C. Honey, "A Report: Higher Education for Public Service," *Public Administration Review* (November, 1967), p. 295.

[8]For a discussion of this concept, see James Heaphey, "Comparative Public Administration: Comments on Current Characteristics," *Public Administration Review* (May/June, 1968), pp. 242–249.

should become increasingly apparent. If what is demanded from administrative theorists and students is indeed what Peter Savage has termed "socially useful knowledge," and if relevance demands that we should offer better information enabling statesmen to make better choices, the work of individuals like Riggs is highly relevant in a very immediate sense. Such work is not a panacea, but it is relevant precisely because events in our national life have demonstrated quite concretely that while America is distinctive, it is by no means unique.

The above argument is intended not so much as a defense of Fred Riggs, but as a defense of theory and of its relevance, especially in the *form* which it has taken under individuals like Riggs. One might remember that Lenin was something of a practitioner, and yet as a theorist he was concerned with more than concrete programs, common-sense understanding, and empirical indicators. Given the developments within the United States over the last decade, foci such as those stressed by Riggs, Eisenstadt, Heaphey, and others should be seen as highly relevant for students and practitioners in "United States Culture" Public Administration. In fact, I consider an appreciation of the relevance of such theory to the current situation within the United States as basic to any successful attempts to increase the relevance of Public Administration. Because of this belief, I admit to a "Leninist position" of often worrying more about the "Social-Democratic" revisions of the development-administration school(s) than about the less viable though persistent traditional POSDCORB and Honey-report syndrome. I worry to the extent that the various exponents of "development administration" feel it personally, professionally, and theoretically necessary to substitute their concern with concrete programs for an adequate understanding of the problems which create the need for programs.

The "opportunity" presented to students and practitioners of administration as a consequence of the critical events in our environment consists mainly of raising our conceptual self-consciousness. This undertaking, however, involves more than having political scientists and administrative theorists focus on the aforementioned concrete programs, empirical indicators, or organizations. Above all, it demands an appreciation of the critical, political, and character-defining nature of the problems which currently confront us, and of working with a perspective which will facilitate such an appreciation. Such a perspective exists in the body of comparative political and administrative work which is currently available, work of a "broadly theoretical nature." Without such a perspective, "development administration" in its various forms will offer no more than a minimal amount of relevance to political-administrative personnel who attempt not only to deal with problems but to define them as well. Comparative Public Administration which deals with theory of a broad type directly related to political concerns and political science allows for consideration of a greater range of program-solutions than theory with a more limited focus. Moreover, general comparative theory relates more completely to the type of situation which currently characterizes the United States, and helps prevent a return to POSDCORB under the rubric of development administration. The latter may appear under the guise of being more relevant or of working within what is given. However, the given in any situation may not be the necessary or possible.

These points can be elaborated more concretely by reference to two areas which Dwight Waldo has mentioned in his paper, "Public Administration in a Time of Revolutions."[9] The first area is that of the relation between agricultural policy and urban migration in the United States. The second concerns the confrontation of rational bureaucratic organizations and certain types of clientele. To date, the problem of urban migration has been dealt with and conceived of largely as a technical problem concerning relief, welfare, and employment. Yet, in specifying types of programs which could perhaps most adequately deal with the problem, a conceptualization of the problem of agriculture policy and urban migration in terms of mobilization and the need for political and expressive as well as administrative and instrumental assimilation might provide the necessary base for a (new) type of analysis which would be narrower in scope. The second example is very similar. Waldo refers to a number of analyses which focus on the rational organization confronting the childlike clientele. In an environment such as ours, where con-

[9]Waldo, *op. cit.*

sciousness of conflict is low and experience with critical forms of conflict has been limited and denied, the heavy stress on psychological and social-psychological modes of explanation is not surprising. A different conception of the relationship between organization and clientele is possible, one that should be meaningful to increasing numbers of students as a consequence of their familiarity with comparative literature and their supposed ability to understand the types of demands and grievances being expressed by the clientele of governmental agencies. One may see in the relationship of governmental organization and clientele an instrumental organization attempting to deal with a problem that has a largely expressive rather than childlike component. "Clients" may resent the perspective and orientation of the bureaucratic administrative organization and may desire to deal with it not simply in terms of a role such as welfare recipient, but as a whole personality, as a citizen. Conceived in this fashion, the problem and related programs become broader; the problem itself assumes a relativity since it is by no means unique in nations characterized by change. The experience of the Mapai party in Israel, the Communist Party in China, and the political machines in the early decades of the twentieth century in this country assume a rather direct practical relevance when the problem is thus conceived, and the study of such experiences may perhaps be seen as having a payoff other than intellectual self-gratification.

Let me now turn to the notion of complementarity in order to complete my argument. Even if one accepts the notion that currently the major requirement for increasing the relevance of comparative Public Administration to the problems within the United States today is a reconceptualization of those problems in terms which recognize their critical nature, define them in political rather than technique terms, and see them as distinctive but not unique; and even if one accepts the argument that the conditions which exist today allow for such a reconceptualization, this alone is not adequate for sufficiently increasing the relevance of comparative Public Administration. As Henderson and others have stated, the student must relate more effectively to the practitioner. This relationship should be greatly facilitated if the practitioner—despite his role-biased position and the bias of socialization in American culture—begins to conceptualize existing problems in a "relative" framework which allows him to conceive of problems as comparable to those which exist in other national settings and which enables him to arrive at a more complex appreciation of the various dimensions of the problems confronting him. However, one point should be clear: Theorists as well as practitioners must to varying degrees engage in a little raising of consciousness. Furthermore, what is required for a more effective definition of both theory and practice as well as for a more relevant integration of the two is not that the practitioner become a theorist or that in his "developmental" enthusiasm the theorist attempt to become the statesman's alter ego (shadow would be the more likely outcome). Rather, both a more effective division of labor and a greater degree of consciousness are needed. It is to such a division of labor that I refer with the term complementarity. The idea and the acceptance of its relevance to our concerns involve certain consequences for the necessities of the near future.

To begin with, one must accept the fact that separate and professional schools of public affairs will not in their isolation allow us to "take care of business." The distinction to be made here is between autonomy and isolation. Autonomous schools of public affairs are valuable and even necessary insofar as they allow for and defend the existence of values, perspectives, and training relevant to the conception and implementation of public policy. However, in order to insure their value I would argue that it is necessary to prevent their isolation from the disciplines of political science and sociology, even at the cost of irritation and frustration. There must be a structural relationship between such endeavors and not one based on the mere intention of maintaining some links. Without such a relationship, the needed increase in self-consciousness and ability to conceptualize will be subject to even greater obstacles than it currently encounters, and practice will continue to be routine-technique oriented with advice of a similar quality coming from the student of public affairs. There must be a relation between what Henderson has termed the "new breed" of administration scholars "untainted by the world of government," and the inhabitants and adherents of schools of public affairs, practitioners, and students. Such relations need not be direct in each case. The critical responsibility falls on those at the

mediating level of schools of public affairs. Moreover, such relations need not be entirely harmonious. "One-best ways" and
Mary Parker Follett-like solutions do not, and should not be expected to, exist in situations of change and uncertainty.

One point might be added here about this new "untainted-by-
government breed" noted by Henderson. Aside from the fact that
I am one of them, I would argue that they are very relevant to the
practitioner for the significant reason that a lack of governmental
experience is not to be equated with a lack of political involvement, concern, or insight. In fact, their lack of previous government experience, their youth, and political concern should permit this group of individuals to be receptive to what is currently
occurring within the United States and to be able to conceptualize and formulate such developments in a more adequate manner
than has been the case so far.

Conclusion

The situation within the discipline of Public Administration
and within the United States today is a mixed one. There is no
guarantee that a "new realism" will appear within either setting.
For Public Administration to increase its relevance both in terms
of theory and practice, a conceptual breakthrough is a necessary
and first step, a breakthrough which is possible given both the
critical conditions which exist within the United States and the
existence of a body of work in comparative politics and administration which would facilitate such a conceptual reorientation.
Along with these existing circumstances there is a need for more
theoretically specific formulations designed to relate more effectively to the practitioner. Such formulations should, however,
recognize that no theory is going to provide a book of answers
for practitioners or statesmen operating in situations which demand choices. In a real sense, theoretical statements which highlight the political, cultural, and ideological variables and dimensions of a given setting are those best designed to aid the
statesman in making choices. Finally, a complementary, though
not frictionless, relationship among those with varying interests
in Public Administration is necessary. The development of such
a relationship depends on the recognition and acceptance of the

need for it by all interested parties. There is no assurance of a positive outcome in attempts to increase the relevance of comparative Public Administration to "United States Culture" Public Administration. In any case the outcome will be less than optimal. However, the opportunity for a positive outcome and the responsibility for attempting to secure one do exist. The fulfillment of the opportunity depends mainly upon fulfillment of the responsibility.

9

Policy Making

The following discussion by Ira Sharkansky—"Constraints on Innovations in Policy Making: Economic Development and Political Routines"—marks another shift in emphasis and style in this volume. This chapter is the first of two which deal with practical problems of administration in the areas of budgeting, program planning, and implementation which have been predominant in Public Administration literature. They will thus strike some readers as considerably less "theoretical" than the previous chapters in the sense that they could be said to represent a narrowing of focus from the general and global to the narrow and specific. To others, it will appear otherwise; and for some tastes, no doubt, these chapters will also appear *too* theoretical, for while they focus upon specific questions which are related to administrators' problems and to isolated concerns of researchers, they do so in a theoretical manner. The literature and themes which concern Sharkansky represent an active and growing research debate and tradition in the field of political science which he believes has "profound importance for the policy makers." His effort is to seek, through an examination of the relevant research literature, "an understanding of which limitations may come to the policy maker from economics and which from his own decision routines, and under what conditions these limitations are likely to inhibit innovation." Herman Mertins, Jr. comments upon Sharkansky's argument.

Constraints on Innovation in Policy Making: Economic Development and Political Routines

Ira Sharkansky

Two factors have been identified as constraints on policy making in the recent literature of political science.[1] The first is the level of economic development within a jurisdiction. Presumably, this level limits the magnitude and quality of the "policy outputs" that the jurisdiction may produce. The second is the set of routine decision processes that government officials find useful. These processes threaten to screen out "foreign" messages that might demand a change in basic policies. In one sense, the discussion in the current literature of these two constraints reflects the historic controversy between economic determinists and those who see behavior as motivated by personal forces independent of economics. In another sense, however, these two factors have a common message that has profound importance for the policy maker. Both economic constraints and the constraints of routine decision processes limit the administrator's capacity for innovation. This common implication from different social-scientific traditions presents the focus of this chapter. There is a burgeoning literature in political science that permits us to address these topics with the confidence that comes from reliable information. In an assessment of the current literature, we shall seek an understanding of which limitations may come to the policy maker from economics and which from his own decision routines, and under what conditions these limitations are likely to inhibit innovation.

Constraints on the Policy Maker from the Level of Economic Development

Thomas R. Dye provides the clearest statement of the argument that the level of economic development within a jurisdiction imposes severe limits on the nature of policy outputs that

[1]My thanks to Professor Michael Cohen of the University of Georgia for his helpful comments on an earlier draft.

may be produced.[2] He and several others examine the economic-policy relationship in American state and local governments by means of simple, partial, and multiple correlation and regression techniques using both individual variables and factor analyses of large sets of variables. High levels of economic development—measured by such variables as percent urban, per capita personal income, median education level, and industrial employment—are generally associated with high levels of expenditure and service outputs in the fields of education, welfare, and health. Service outputs in these fields are measured by teacher salaries, the rates of pupil attendance in schools and success on a national examination, average welfare benefits, and the incidence of medical facilities. Economic development may provide the wherewithal to purchase these services, or increase the service demands of clientele groups. In contrast to these findings, however, are results in the areas of highways and natural resources. In these areas, economic development is inversely associated with levels of spending and services (as measured by highway expenditure and mileage, and the magnitude of state wildlife and park activities). Explanations are tentative, and in some cases conflicting. Highway and natural-resource programs may draw their impetus from long distances between population centers and wide-open spaces. The politics of rural states may facilitate the use of "pork barrel" or "log-rolling" techniques to authorize a dense network of roads between scattered settlements. In contrast, congestion produced by industrialization and urbanization may render highway construction prohibitively expensive and politically controversial.[3] Or because urban highways transport many vehicles more efficiently than rural highways, industrialization and urbaniza-

[2]Thomas R. Dye, *Economics, Politics and the Public: Policy Outcomes in the American States* (Chicago: Rand McNally, 1966). See also Richard E. Dawson and James A. Robinson, "Inter-party Competition, Economic Variables, and Welfare Policies in the American States," *Journal of Politics* (May, 1963), pp. 265–289; Richard I. Hofferbert, "The Relation between Public Policy and Some Structural and Environmental Variables in the American States," *American Political Science Review* (March, 1966), pp. 73–82; and Ira Sharkansky, "Regionalism, Economic Status and the Public Policies of American States," *Southwestern Social Science Quarterly* (June, 1968).

[3]Dye, *op. cit.,* p. 161.

tion may actually reduce the cost of roads that are adequate for demands.

Dye emphasizes the importance of economic development for the policy maker by comparing the economic impact on policy with the impact from characteristics of the state political system. He finds that political characteristics long thought to affect policy—voter participation, the strength of each major party, the degree of interparty competition, and the equity of legislative apportionment—have little influence which is independent of economic development. A well-developed economy affects both a high-participatory, high-competition political system and a certain pattern of policy outputs. In conclusion, Dye warns his reader to be cautious in expecting policy changes to result from alterations in the political system. Although he does not talk directly to the question of the latitude which is available for innovation, he does not encourage optimism in the face of economic constraints.[4]

Analysis of Economic Development as a Constraint on Policy

Several problems of the economic-policy research caution against a simplistic acceptance of its findings. These should not lead us to discount the impact of economic development on policy outputs. However, looking closely at the literature, we can acquire a more refined understanding of where—and how much—the level of economic development is likely to restrain the policy maker.

The first problem in the economic-policy linkage lies in the temptation to exaggerate its strength. It is true that economic development and policies generally stand in the relationships to one another that are outlined above. Yet the relationships are not so strong as to preclude noneconomic factors from having a crucial impact on the nature of public policy. Dye reports 356 coefficients of simple correlations between policy measures and his four economic measures of income, urbanism, industrialization, and education, but only 16 of them (4 percent) are strong enough to indicate that an economic measure explains at least one half the interstate variation in a policy measure. He also

<hr>

[4]*Ibid.*, p. 301.

reports 54 coefficients of determination that show the combined strength of his four economic measures with policy measures. Only 19 of these (35 percent) indicate that all economic measures together explain one half of the interstate variation in policy. Governments in many states either surpass or fail to reach the policy norms that generally are associated with their levels of economic development.

A second problem with the economic-policy proposition is that its proponents have not presented a fair opportunity for noneconomic factors to show their influence on policy outputs. In several publications, measures of party strength and competition, voter turnout, and the equity of legislative apportionment have had to carry the burden of representing "political factors that might influence policy independent of economic conditions."[5] Several pieces of new research demonstrate influences on policy that are independent of economic development. Lineberry and Fowler show that the structure of local governments can moderate the impact that social-economic characteristics are likely to have on levels of taxation and expenditure.[6] Using the state governments as my laboratory, I find that the elements of federal aid, the state share of state and local government expenditures, tax effort, and the routines of incremental budget making have strong relationships with expenditures that are independent of economic conditions.[7]

A third limitation in the economic-policy argument is the tendency to overlook the likelihood that the economy varies in its influence over policy makers. This variatior can occur between different levels of government, different eriods of time, different kinds of public service, or at different levels of affluence. Without knowing the conditions that permit economic conditions to limit the discretion of policy makers, we cannot move beyond the citation of the economy as an "important" determinant of policy.

One of the practices that limits the specificity of the eco-

[5]*Ibid.;* Dawson and Robinson, *op. cit.;* and Hofferbert, *op. cit.*

[6]Robert L. Lineberry and Edmund P. Fowler, "Reformism and Public Policies in American Cities," *American Political Science Review* (September, 1967), 701–716.

[7]Ira Sharkansky, *Spending in the American States* (Chicago: Rand McNally, 1968), Chaps. 3–4.

nomic-policy linkage in some recent research is the tendency to examine the combined policies of state and local governments within each state. This practice has a firm basis in research traditions. State and local activities are combined in order to "control" for interstate variations in the responsibilities assigned to each level of government: "In State A the government may perform functions that in State B are left to localities."[8] Although the state-plus-local convention is useful for some purposes, in this case it covers over significant differences between the economic-policy linkage as it operates at each level of government. Economic-policy linkages appear to be strongest in the arenas of local governments. Data for 1962 show that the coefficient of simple correlation for *per capita personal income* with the *per capita expenditures of state governments* is .14, that with the total of *local government spending* within each state is .82, and that with the total of *state and local government spending* within each state is .62. A variety of research techniques show similar findings. It is the officials of localities, and not state agencies, who feel the greatest pressure from their economic surroundings.[9]

Differences in economic resources and fiscal opportunities help to explain the greater dependence of local governments—as opposed to state governments—on the economic resources within their jurisdiction. Most local governments must draw upon a limited geographical area for resources, and they are confined to only one major revenue source (the property tax), which generates a great deal of political controversy. State governments draw upon their larger jurisdiction and can transfer resources from "have" to "have-not" communities. State officials also have wider revenue options that include taxes on income and retail sales. The state income and sales taxes appear to be less upsetting politically than the local property tax, and the state taxes appear to be less vulnerable to an economic down

[8]James A. Maxwell, *Financing State and Local Governments* (Washington, D.C.: Brookings Institution, 1965), p. 2.

[9]Compare the findings reported in Harvey E. Brazer, *City Expenditures in the United States* (New York: National Bureau of Economic Research, 1959) with those in Ira Sharkansky, *Spending in the American States, op. cit.,* chap. 4.

turn.[10] As a result, state officials can escape many of the constraints on policy that seem to originate in the economic sector and limit the policy discretion of local government officials. Federal officials can also escape economic constraints, partly because of their ability to tax resources of the weathy areas throughout the country, and partly because of their power to borrow in the face of current deficits in the taxing-spending balance. Indeed, the federal government operates numerous programs to control levels of employment, interest, and wages, and may be as much the master as the subordinate of the economy.

As research has progressed, we have been able to identify other variations in the influence of economic conditions over public policy. A cross-sectional study of economic and political conditions in 115 nations shows much stronger relationships than those which appear in cross-sectional studies of American state and local governments. Where the spread in wealth is so great—as it is among the nations of the world—the impact of wealth on policy may appear stronger than where most jurisdictions cluster around their average level of wealth.[11] One study of policy making in the American states tends to confirm this: It concludes that economic-policy relationships are *least confining* in the middle range of states whose economic conditions are most alike. Under these conditions, peculiarities in state politics may have a great deal to do with the kinds of policies that are enacted.[12]

Within the United States, the influence of economic conditions on state and local government policies appears to be

[10]As suggested by the following coefficients of simple correlation between the per capita receipts by state and local governments from various taxes and per capita personal income, 1962. Note that it is the property tax whose receipts vary most directly with economic conditions.

Property tax	.55
Personal income tax	.25
General sales tax	-.01

See also Ira Sharkansky, *Spending in the American States, op. cit.,* pp. 86–89.

[11]Marvin E. Olsen, "Multivariate Analysis of National Political Development," *American Sociological Review* (October, 1968), pp. 699–711.

[12]John G. Grumm, "Structural Determinants of Legislative Output," a paper presented at the Conference on the Measurement of Policies in the American States, Inter-University Consortium for Political Research, Ann Arbor, Michigan, 1968.

diminishing. Table 1 shows a continuing decline in the economic-policy relationship since 1903. Policy makers now have
more opportunities to spend at levels above the "norm" for their
economic conditions. Some of this increased flexibility may
reflect the growth in federal aid. By transferring resources from
"have" to "have-not" jurisdictions, grants-in-aid make up for
some of the differentials between states. Also, state and local
governments now have a more flexible tax structure. With state
taxes on personal incomes and/or retail sales now used by over
40 of the states (whereas no state used either tax at the beginning of the century), and numerous local governments now turning to these forms of taxation, policy makers can tap an increasing proportion of the resources within their own
jurisdictions. Even the poorest states (such as Mississippi,
South Carolina, Arkansas, Vermont) have some pockets of
wealth that can help support services in their poorest counties.

TABLE 1. RELATIONSHIPS BETWEEN STATE AND LOCAL GOVERNMENT
EXPENDITURES PER CAPITA AND PERSONAL INCOME PER CAPITA:
COEFFICIENTS OF SIMPLE CORRELATION

Year	Coefficient
1903	.920
1932	.839
1942	.821
1957	.658
1962	.645
1964–65	.558

Source: Alan K. Campbell and Seymour Sacks, *Metropolitan America: Fiscal
Patterns and Governmental Systems* (New York: The Free Press, 1967), p. 57.

It is also apparent that economic conditions exercise less
constraint on some kinds of policy than others. The political
saliency of a policy is one of the factors that can lessen the influence of economics. To the extent that programs are made the
subject of prominent disputes among individual candidates and
political parties, they can provoke the use of substantially more
resources than is normally associated with the jurisdiction's level

of wealth. Officials "try harder" under the impetus of public demand. Under other conditions—when public demand runs counter to a program—there is less performance than expected on the basis of economic conditions.[13] Another line of research has examined different conceptions of economic resources (*total economic resources* and the *distribution* of those resources among income groups) as they affect different conceptions of public policy (the *total service output* of a jurisdiction, and the *distribution* of benefits among different income groups). The magnitude of resources in jurisdiction has shown more influence over services than does the nature of income distribution in a jurisdiction.[14] Also, magnitude of resources seems to affect the total volume of benefits produced, more than their distribution to residents of different income groups.[15] We can speculate that policy makers are sensitive to the total resources available when facing such issues as the number of teachers, the number of schoolrooms, the miles of highway, the acres to be purchased for state parks, or the amount of money to be spent on public welfare. Policy makers may be more sensitive to political constraints when they consider questions of distribution: where to assign the teachers or build the schoolrooms, which sites to select for the highways or the parks, or how much to pay different classes of welfare recipients.

Constraints on the Policy Maker from His Own Routines

Political routines are another kind of restriction which may—like economic resources—limit the policy discretion of certain officials. Political routines are decision processes that win the favor of policy makers because they simplify a complex set of considerations. A routine either prescribes the decision that will be made with respect to certain types of problems, or it

[13]Charles F. Cnudde and Donald J. McCrone, "Party Competition and Welfare Policies in the American States," *American Political Science Review* (September, 1969), pp. 858–866; and Ira Sharkansky and Richard I. Hofferbert, "Dimensions of State Politics, Economics and Public Policy," *American Political Science Review* (September, 1969).

[14]Thomas R. Dye, "Income Inequality and American State Politics," *American Political Science Review* (March, 1969), pp. 157–162.

[15]Bryan Frye and Richard Winter, "The Politics of Redistribution," Stanford University, 1969, mimeographed.

identifies those criteria which should receive priority consideration in decision making. In another publication, I describe several routines which are used by policy makers in the United States.[16] They include incremental budgeting, legislators' acceptance of the executive's budget recommendations, regional patterns of consultation among the policy makers of different states and localities, and the assumption that improvements in public services will result from increases in government expenditures. The archetype of the policy routine is incremental budgeting. Because it is so characteristic and because it has received the greatest attention in the literature, it serves as the focus for this consideration of routines.

Charles Lindblom provides the clearest explanation for the attractiveness of political routines among policy makers. In a number of publications he documents the limitations inherent in the often prescribed "rational comprehensive" method of decision making.[17] A rational comprehensive technique requires an official to recognize the whole range of alternatives that face him, identify his goals, rank his preferences for each alternative, define the resources necessary for each alternative, and make the final selection on the basis of all relevant information. Lindblom writes that this approach to decision making fails to take into account the limitations of intelligence, time, organization, and policy discretion that are available to public officials. Limitations of time and intelligence restrict the capacity to identify the full range of alternatives and resources that are available at the moment of decision. Limitations of organization and politics restrict the clear announcement of long-range goals and the preference ranking of alternatives. The announcement of basic goals may generate conflict among actors who might have agreed—each with different goal expectations—on specific proposals. Another set of problems for rational comprehensive decision making comes from the strong legal and political traditions that rest upon the constitutional separation of powers and checks and balances. Our governments

[16]Ira Sharkansky, *The Routines of Politics* (Princeton: Van Nostrand, 1969).

[17]Charles E. Lindblom, "The Science of 'Muddling Through,'" *Public Administration Review* (Spring, 1959), pp. 257–264; "Decision Making In Taxation and Expenditure," in *Public Finances: Needs, Sources and Utilization* (Princeton: National Bureau of Economic Research, 1961), pp. 295–336.

were designed to hinder agreements on centrally designed policies. Conflict and accommodation (Lindblom's "partisan mutual adjustment") are more characteristic of policy making in the United States than are concerted efforts to identify and serve the public interest.

Incremental budgeting and other routines are popular among officials who find themselves incapable of practicing rational comprehensive decision making. Routines limit the number and type of criteria that policy makers feel obliged to consider before they reach a decision. Incrementalists do not consider the full range of an agency's budget. Rather than risking an opening of old controversies, they accept the legitimacy of established programs and agree to continue the previous level of expenditure that has ·provided for these programs. They limit their task by focusing on the increments of change proposed for the new budget, and by considering the narrow range of goals represented in these departures from established activities.

Analysis of the Incremental Routine

The power of incremental budgeting is apparent in the statistical relationships between current and previous levels of government expenditures. Table 2 shows coefficients of simple correlation between total per capita state expenditures in 1965, and those in eleven previous periods back to 1903. When past and present spending are only three years apart (representing in most cases the expenditures of two consecutive budget periods), the correspondence is virtually perfect. Although state governments increased their spending during 1963–65, they remained in essentially their same positions relative to one another. Undoubtedly, there are reallocations from one year to the next within budgets which remain relatively fixed in their total sums. However, the power of previous expenditures remains strong in budget considerations, and inhibits policy makers from accepting major innovations.

As the span between current and previous expenditures increases, the correspondence between spending positions lessens. There is an increasing opportunity for factors to enter the budget process that are remote from the situation in that

TABLE 2. COEFFICIENTS OF SIMPLE CORRELATION (PRODUCT-MOMENT)
BETWEEN TOTAL STATE GOVERNMENT EXPENDITURES PER CAPITA
IN 1965 AND 1903–1962

Year	Coefficient
1962	.94
1957	.85
1952	.85
1947	.63
1942	.72
1939	.61
1929	.61
1924	.53
1918	.49
1913	.52
1903	.44

Source: Ira Sharkansky, *Spending in the American States* (Chicago: Rand McNally, 1968), p. 40.

past year. Yet even with increasing time between a current year and a past year, the expenditures of the past continue to be the nucleus around which later expenditures have grown. Even expenditures of sixty-two years earlier show a relationship with current expenditures! Despite several major wars, population shifts, transformations in the economy, and manifold increases in the expenditures of each state, there remains some resemblance in the spending positions of most state governments now and then.

The behavior which is central to incremental budgeting is the reluctance of budget reviewers to permit major increases in the expenditures of individual agencies. At the federal level, one study of the 1947–62 period found that the House and Senate Appropriations Committees permitted a 6 percent (or more) increase to fewer than 24 percent of the agencies that appeared before them. The Committees permitted a 12 percent (or more) increase only 10 percent of the time.[18] At the state level, Table 3 shows that both the governor and the legislature in most of nineteen states react negatively to the acquisitiveness of agency

[18]Richard F. Fenno, Jr., *The Power of the Purse: Appropriation Politics in Congress* (Boston: Little, Brown, 1964), p. 578.

requests.[19] Both the governor and the legislature imposed the largest budget cuts on the agencies that requested the greatest increase in funds. The size of the agency request appears to be unimportant in the decisions of the governor and the legislature. Budget reviewers respond primarily to the size of *increments*.

There is some indication that incremental budgeting is most

TABLE 3. COEFFICIENTS OF SIMPLE CORRELATION BETWEEN PERCENTAGE OF AGENCY REQUESTS APPROVED BY THE GOVERNOR AND THE LEGISLATURE, AND MEASURES OF THE AGENCY REQUEST

| | Coefficients Between: | | | |
| | Governor's approval and: | | Legislature's approval and: | |
	Agency budget size	Percent increase requested	Agency budget size	Percent increase requested
Florida	.04	−.80	.03	−.63
Georgia	.08	−.86	.02	−.82
Idaho	.45	−.70	.04	−.80
Illinois	.07	−.52	.03	−.51
Indiana	.10	.13	.04	−.27
Kentucky	.18	−.94	.06	−.77
Louisiana	.12	−.82	.00	−.48
Maine	.08	.22	.24	.18
Nebraska	−.23	−.59	−.09	.51
North Carolina	−.05	−.20	−.04	−.20
North Dakota	−.01	−.84	.17	−.80
South Carolina	.06	−.30	.00	−.17
South Dakota	.02	−.75	.00	−.70
Texas	−.10	−.63	−.25	−.06
Vermont	−.16	−.67	−.12	−.61
Virginia	.12	−.56	.07	−.27
West Virginia	.16	−.57	.01	−.65
Wisconsin	−.03	−.61	−.08	−.28
Wyoming	−.15	−.82	−.18	−.70

Source: Ira Sharkansky "Agency Requests, Gubernatorial Support and Budget Success in State Legislatures," *American Political Science Review* (December, 1968).

[19]See Ira Sharkansky, "Agency Requests, Gubernatorial Support and Budget Success in State Legislatures," *American Political Science Review* (December, 1968).

confining in those arenas which feel the greatest pinch from their level of economic development (that is, in state and local, rather than federal governments). At the federal level, incrementalists seem willing to examine the *changes in expenditure and service outputs* that are requested for each agency.[20] In the state and local governments that have been examined closely, however, there is a more narrow concentration on the *increments of dollars* that are requested. In his study of budgeting in Illinois, Thomas J. Anton finds decision makers relying on a simplistic set of rules that reveals little concern for program-related values.[21] Decisions rely almost entirely on the dollar value of agency requests as they compare with previous budgets, and the reviewers' estimates of the tax revenue to be available in the coming biennium. Because reviewers tend to cut new requests without regard to their effect on programs, administrators in Illinois often expand services by shifting funds within budgets that reveal minimal change. Thus, the state-budget process stands as a deterrent to innovation that policy makers must circumvent, rather than as a device for the executive or the legislature to inspect and adjust proposed innovations.

John P. Crecine's findings about budgeting in Detroit, Cleveland, and Pittsburgh document how incremental budget makers in the mayor's office can parcel out annual increases in revenues without concern for program values.[22] When budget makers expect a revenue surplus they distribute it among most agencies on the basis of fixed priorities that have no relation to programs. Salaries are given first preference, equipment gets second rewards, and maintenance gets the remainder. A contrary priority is used when the forecast indicates a need to reduce budgets below present levels. Cuts are made first in maintenance, then in equipment, and last in salaries. Those items which promise the greatest political appeal—regardless of program—receive the best treatment.

[20]Aaron Wildavsky, *The Politics of the Budgetary Process* (Boston: Little, Brown, 1964), Chap. 3.

[21]Thomas J. Anton, *The Politics of State Expenditure in Illinois* (Urbana: University of Illinois Press, 1966).

[22]John P. Crecine, "A Computer Simulation Model of Municipal Resource Allocation," a paper delivered at the Meeting of the Midwest Conference of Political Science, April, 1966.

Several factors may explain the federal-state-local differences in the tendency of incremental budget makers to consider increments in programs, as well as increments in dollars. Federal budgeting proceeds with more and better-trained staff assistance within both the executive and legislative branches. Moreover, the federal government has more productive revenue devices, particularly its ability to borrow easily in the face of an expected budget deficit. In contrast, many state and local authorities must balance expenditures with revenues, or can borrow only by using the revenue bond for a limited type (revenue-producing) of service. The product of better staff and more resources at the federal level may be a greater awareness of program opportunities on the part of budget analysts, and a greater likelihood that program values will be built into their consideration of budget increments.

Implications for the Policy Maker in Economic Determinism and Political Routines

Both the economic dependence of public policy and the routinization of decision making may inhibit the innovative potential of government agencies. The level of economic development which exists in a jurisdiction may restrict innovation, especially among local officials. The restrictions on policy from routine decision rules (like incremental budgeting) may be even more universal than those coming from the economy. Because routines lead officials to rely on a fixed set of criteria, they make it difficult for new or unusual circumstances to provoke a major deviation from the normal pattern of decisions. Officials are reluctant to break with their routines. Routines are flexible in the face of changes in the environment, but it may take something approaching a national trauma to permit a high incidence of nonroutine decisions. One study found that events of the depression, World War II, the Korean conflict, and postwar economic reconversions produced only limited and temporary departures from incremental budgeting.[23]

[23]See Ira Sharkansky, *The Routines of Politics, op. cit.,* Chap. IX.

Opportunities to Escape the Constraints of Economic
Determinism and Political Routines

Innovative policy makers have not rested in the face of limitations that may be imposed by economic dependence or political routines. Two factors that promise some escape from these restrictions are intergovernmental aid and reformed budgeting (especially PPB). The first device provides "foreign" money to low-income jurisdictions that are hard pressed to support their service needs with locally available resources, and provides an alternative revenue device for those jurisdictions whose capacity to collect taxes or borrow money is confined by limited revenue powers. Grants also provide a club which officials may use to break the routine of incremental budgeting. The availability of outside money can justify unusual increments in state or local budgets because of the added funds that the expenditure will bring into the jurisdiction. Some federal-aid programs are especially useful to those who wish to escape the incremental routine because they require the establishment of distinct agencies to administer the new programs. These agencies—for example, housing authorities, urban renewal authorities, or anti-poverty units—enter the budget process with a previous expenditure of zero, and necessarily escape incremental constraints during their first budget period.

Planning-programming-budgeting (PPB) represents an effort at budgetary reform whose practitioners hope to substitute rational comprehensive decision making for the routines of incrementalism. In one sense, PPB offers an alternative routine that may be more hospitable to innovation. Its features include:

1. Identification of principal outputs for each service agency;
2. A systems analysis that identifies the inputs which are most significant in the production of each service output;
3. The identification of costs for alternative combinations of inputs, and the values of the outputs likely to be produced by each combination;
4. The calculation of a cost-benefit ratio for each combination of inputs and outputs.

The experience with PPB is too current to permit anything like a thorough assessment of its possibilities and limitations. A number of agencies at federal, state, and local levels are using forms of PPB, and a literature is developing out of their experience.[24] Some observations in the literature suggest that this new routine may not succeed in replacing the more well established incrementalism.

A major criticism of PPB focuses on its inability to provide budgeters with an evaluation of "political" costs and benefits associated with their support of certain programs. Aaron Wildavsky is an outspoken critic of PPB who cites it for failing to provide information about three types of political costs:

1. *Exchange costs*—the costs of calling in favors owed, and the costs of making threats in order to get others to support a policy;

2. *Reputational costs*—the loss of popularity with the electorate, the loss of esteem and effectiveness with other officials, and the subsequent loss of one's ability to secure programs other than those currently under consideration;

3. *The costs of undesirable redistribution of power*—those disadvantages that accrue from the increase in the power of individuals, organizations, or social groups who may become antagonistic to oneself.[25]

An advantage to incrementalism is that it sharply limits the political costs which have to be calculated. When incrementalists accept the base of previous expenditures as legitimate, they excuse themselves from reviewing the whole range of tradition, habits, and prior commitments that are subsumed within existing programs. PPB threatens to perpetuate controversy (and discomfort for budget makers) with its rationalist analysis of alternative approaches to each major program.

[24]David Novick (ed.), *Program Budgeting: Program Analysis and the Federal Budget* (Washington, D.C.: U.S. Government Printing Office, 1965); "Planning-Programming-Budgeting Symposium," *Public Administration Review* (December, 1966), pp. 243–310; "Planning-Programming-Budgeting System Reexamined: Development, Analysis, and Criticism Symposium," *Public Administration Review* (March/April, 1969), pp. 111–202; Robert Dorfman, *Measuring Benefits of Government Investments* (Washington, D. C.: Brookings Institution, 1965).

[25]Aaron Wildavsky, "The Political Economy of Efficiency: Cost-Benefit Analysis, Systems Analysis, and Program Budgeting," *Public Administration Review* (December, 1966), pp. 292–310.

Another accusation directed at PPB is that systems analyses focus on the ingredients of program inputs and outputs that are easy to investigate. Many of the systems analyses and cost-benefit analyses that have been published introduce their subject matter with an impressive list of potential service determinants and likely products of the service. But the analysis itself typically deals with a few of the inputs and outputs, seemingly selected on no more substantial basis than analytic convenience. Thus, practitioners of PPB may base their recommendations on a routine that is no more *comprehensive* in its rationality than incremental budgeting.

The usefulness of PPB may be greatest in the military, where the major goals—deterrence of war, defense of country, and victory in war—are clear and widely accepted among the officials who make budget decisions. Elsewhere, goals are subject to intense controversy. In many cases, different legislators and interest groups agree to support specific activities, but would conflict bitterly if they had to agree about the long-range accomplishments of the programs. Even in the case of agencies with relatively noncontroversial goals, the value of PPB is limited by the extent to which the costs and benefits of programs can be measured. The value of an American soldier's life, the value of the life of a peasant in a foreign country, or the payoffs of a research and development project must be considered in many phases of military planning; but they hardly lend themselves to simple or indisputable pricing. Some factors are worth more than their market price indicates. PPB also encourages centralized decision making (by officials who assess information relevant to goals, resources, and prospective performance). Yet a prominent characteristic of American government is decentralized decision making, with spokesmen of different government units or interest groups bargaining with one another. A participant's definition of a policy's feasibility is "a seat-of-the-pants judgment." The relevant "cost" questions are: "Will it 'go' on the Hill?" "Will the public buy it?" "Does it have political appeal?"[26]

[26]Ralph Huitt, "Political Feasibility," Austin Ranney (ed.), *Political Science and Public Policy* (Chicago: Markham, 1968), pp. 163–167.

Summary and Conclusions

In many government agencies, the innovator must work within the confines set by the level of economic development and cope with set routines of decision making that discourage drastic change in policy. Yet these constraints do not appear to operate with equal force in all contexts. There is a growing volume of research that defines the importance of these constraints with respect to their influence over certain types of governments, certain kinds of policies, at certain periods of time, and at certain levels of affluence. Even where these constraints are most prominent, there are devices that might permit an imaginative policy maker to escape them. Federal grants-in-aid offer outside resources plus billyclubs over state and local incrementalism. PPB with its system analysis and cost-benefit analysis may bring some of the elusive advantages of rational comprehensive decision making to budgeting. However, those who wish to keep government programs within the limits viewed as "economically feasible," and those who are attracted to established political routines are unlikely to welcome PPB as a replacement for their own habits, or to help PPB facilitate innovation.

At this juncture, it seems appropriate to recommend more research. Political scientists have just begun to measure the impact of economic conditions and decision-making routines on policy making, and to specify the conditions under which each constraint is more or less powerful. This work represents a departure from past scholarship in its reliance on the operational definition of its concepts, the measurement of independent and dependent variables, and the use of sophisticated statistical procedures. By learning where the constraints of economic conditions and decision routines press most severely, we can adjust our reformist inclinations to focus on those situations which are most in need of—and perhaps most amenable to—change.

Comment: The Problems of Change
in Policy-Making Behavior

Herman Mertins, Jr.

Ira Sharkansky's discussion provides a useful analysis of certain aspects of the constraints faced in policy making. Nevertheless, it fails to arrive at conclusions that are new or surprising for either the practitioner or the academic. The tremendous impact of economic development and economic constraints on the development of a budget can hardly be questioned. Similarly, anyone who has prepared a budget or studied budgetary analysis is all too familiar with the problems that the constraints of political routine present for the budget maker. Of course, we still have to learn a good deal about the constraints that rational comprehensive budgeting imposes on decision makers.

Concealed Program Changes: A Note of Caution

Perhaps the more important question to be considered is the manner in which the author reaches his conclusions. I am referring to the risky and often misleading technique of conducting analysis and drawing major conclusions on budgetary trends using *bottom line* economic figures alone. Most of Sharkansky's conclusions are based on *per capita* expenditures and program *totals*. Very often this approach fails to recognize the impact of shifts of emphases and direction within programs. Such changes may take place slowly but their cumulative effects can be extremely important.

In some respects, not recognizing this fact—that a program operating under the same label over a five- or ten-year period cannot be assumed to be the same program at the end of the period that it was in the beginning—might lead us to be more critical of incremental budgeting than we might otherwise be. Internal budgetary innovation is often masked by external labels imposed by law, regulations, habit, or the needs of convenience. New programs often wear the clothes of the established. If change or innovation is to be identified, this surface must be probed. The overview may produce data indicating areas for further exploration but one cannot assume it to be an adequate substitute for in-depth analysis.

Sharkansky's comparison of budgetary constraints among levels of government deserves a special note. That changes in the relationships between recent and past expenditures at the state and local levels have, by and large, not been comparable to those at the federal level can hardly be questioned. The data are convincing enough. But the possible explanation for this tendency could well be expanded. Certainly one factor to be considered as contributing to this result is the *human distance* between legislator and affected citizen. On the local scene, citizen redress can be rather immediate through a number of communications channels. Results are often immediate and devastating. Not so at the national level—at least in most cases. The channels of reaction often are clogged or inoperative. The level of federal expenditures dwarfs all other governments. The pressure for control may assume some importance in generalized terms but seldom are specific programs intelligently criticized. In sharp contrast, the local legislator faces person-to-person "heat" on many specifics. Many citizens consider federal taxation oppressive but to a large extent subject to minimal control on their part. But their local taxes are something else.

More Reasons for Incrementalism

As far as incrementalism in budgeting is concerned, Sharkansky has done an excellent job of outlining the rationale for its use. But this analysis could be extended to cover some very important additional factors as well.

The budgetary systems of most agencies of government invite an incremental approach. After all, traditional practice calls for an annual budget. Most programs have to be reduced to a series of one-year segments, except for those aspects of programs that involve longer term capital commitments.

We also have to recognize that in the budgetary process—no matter what "type"—most program changes are slow to evolve. Most budgets represent programs that mix tradition and reorientation. Of course, some innovative administrators have been able to bring about a far-reaching revamping of the programs of their agencies. But it should not be assumed that the appearance of new governmental programs signals the overhaul of the "budgetary base." If we look at the budget of New York City over the past several years, for example, we note there have been some new programs instituted. However, this should not obscure the fact that, for the most part, these changes have been *additive*— built on top of the existing program superstructure—as supplements to the traditional.

The responsible budgetary administrator has another very severe constraint: No matter how sophisticated the administrator is, he still must submit his recommendations for program funds to legislative "reviewers" whose motivations and knowledge sharply diverge from his own. For the most part, legislative committees cannot be expected to have the detailed knowledge of programs possessed by program administrators. Their reactions to the budget may, more than any other factor, reflect concern for personal political survival. In turn, this consideration may lead to overconcern for bottom-line totals and underconcern for the specifics of individual programs. So this set of circumstances represents a notable constraint for the typical administrator as "defender of the budget."

Another constraint springs from the fact that the initial purpose of developing a budget was to meet the needs of accountability. Historically, interest in program purpose took second place to the focus on honesty. The primary goal was to assure that public funds were not absconded with or squandered. The long tradition of assuring honesty and a secondary concern for program effectiveness in accomplishing purpose favors incrementalism. It thus appears "safer" to many legislators to assume last year's level of expenditures and concentrate on the additions. In contrast, comprehensive budgeting often appears much less secure to legislators.

Personnel management and personnel commitments also favor the incremental approach. In a practical sense, large numbers of personnel cannot be shifted among the elements of a rather complex program structure on a more or less continuing basis. If a "zero-base" budget is employed, the assumption is that no one has a position until specific programs are approved and funded This approach has merits but poses substantial difficulties for organizational recruitment and career-planning activities. Complete fluidity and flexibility do not represent organizational realities and this helps to explain the continuing appeal and utilization of incremental budgeting.

Another factor strongly supporting the continuation of incrementalism relates to the quality of program analysis that can be performed for traditional programs versus new programs. Over a period of time, staff engaged in analyzing programs are able to develop a "toolhouse" of measures that can assist in determining how well programs are administered and whether they are accomplishing their purposes. Certain measures of efficiency—standard costs and the like—can be developed for traditional programs.

New programs and innovative approaches usually cannot be subjected—at least immediately—to the kind of searching analysis accorded traditional programs. This fact, in part, probably explains some of the difficulties that have been encountered in the administration of the various poverty programs. The absence of precedent, the lack of previous experience, the questions of which standards constitute efficient performance—all illustrate the problems that new programs face. In many cases, there simply are all too few people who know very much about them.

PPB: Claims and Reality

The numerous claims that have been made for PPB should also be mentioned. In spite of claims to the contrary, the primary approach of the "new budgeting" remains microeconomic. We find very few applications of macroeconomics to the PPB process to date. If PPB continues to follow the course that has been set thus far, it may be that its primary thrust will remain extremely narrow. The people who become most influential in the administration of the system may possess outstanding capabilities in the fields of microeconomics and mathematics, but lack the broader conceptions of realistic cross-program comparisons and the political savvy that lie at the heart of political survival. The danger involved here is that "budgetary technology" may substitute, quite inadequately, for the exercise of acute political judgment.

On the other hand, there is the hope that more broadly based systems analysis will be employed to augment the political process and serve to sharpen the bases of decision making. If this trend develops, the way might be provided for bringing people into the budgeting process who possess nontechnical but nevertheless highly pertinent backgrounds. In the meantime, we should not assume that macroorientation represents the "state of the art." Obviously it does not.

The Challenges of Constraints

Finally, it should be noted that Sharkansky has raised several serious and important questions. My response to these is in itself a series of questions: How are we to react to the challenges of constraints? Can practical strategies be developed to lessen the impact of these constraints? Are the solutions suggested in past decades—solutions which were rarely applied—to be suggested again? When faced with the kinds of constraints which the author outlined in the field of economic development, do we reach back into the past and resurrect once again the proposal to revamp our total tax structure in terms of creating a single income tax, abolishing property taxes, and encouraging progressive taxes exclusively, and the like?

The responses to such questions will prove crucial to the solution of a number of problems, particularly urban problems. If we look at our past national record—and here I include the problems of budget as well as those of many other areas—we observe the tendency to allow serious concerns to drift to the stage of severe crisis before the inertia that stands as a block to most problem solving is overcome. Do we have contributions to make which are particularly suited to the "here and now"? Do we have anything better to suggest than PPB? Are there practical ways to overcome the constraints which Sharkansky has outlined?

It would appear that those who would advise the policy maker must themselves demonstrate the capacity to innovate and to develop approaches that satisfy the constraints of both high-level administrative performance and political feasibility.

10

Administrative Rationality

The parts of the last chapter which dealt with PPB and incremental budgeting are most germane to the present chapter. Herman Mertins' comments, which served as a conclusion to the former chapter, might as easily be a prologue to the present one. Ira Sharkansky's comments about PPB, although faithfully reproducing criticisms, was by and large optimistic as to PPB's promise. Mertins, in his turn, suggested optimism about PPB ought to be softened a bit by an accurate appreciation of its present quite narrow manifestation. In this chapter, S. Kenneth Howard takes a quite critical look at PPB—in a manner which recalls La Porte's advice to inquire into the presuppositions of a model's authors—and asks what kind of rationality it is that those who would "'rationalize' public-expenditure decisions" have in mind. And in a manner which adds weight to and draws strength from some earlier chapters (notably Harmon's discussion of normative theory), he discusses the complex world of the administrator. David Parker's comment is a criticism of traditional theories in Public Administration and a stout defense of PPB.

Analysis, Rationality, and Administrative Decision Making

S. Kenneth Howard

From earliest times, public administrators have been urged to be rational in their actions. The latest importuning for rationality comes under the label of planning-programming-budgeting. At the heart of PPB lies an ill-defined process called analysis. Administrators can justifiably contend that they analyzed alternative courses of action prior to making decisions long before PPB arrived on the scene.

But somehow this new analysis is different. For one thing, it emphasizes a high degree of quantification so that a variety of mathematical techniques can be applied to a problem. Linear programming, game theory, computerized simulation models, and a host of other sophisticated techniques can be employed once a sufficient level of quantification has been obtained. Although the jargon in the field is very imprecise, all of these techniques might come under the heading of cost-utility analysis. In fact, it is the emphasis upon this kind of analysis that is supposed to separate the new program budgeting from the many activities—particularly at state and local levels—previously engaged in under this same name.[1]

Analysis and Rationality

Analysis is urged because it will bring rationality into public problem solving and decision making. The literature in this field is replete with references to "improving" decision making and to "rationalizing" the decision-making process. Despite all these modern trappings, are the underlying ideas of analysis really new?

The crux of a PPB system is program analysis. The term "program analysis" as used in a PPB system essentially consists of the process of determining the relevant objectives, synthesizing alternative means toward these objectives, and identifying the costs and effectiveness (i.e., the "benefits" or "returns") of each alternative. Estimation of the costs for alternatives and the estimation of how the costs are likely to vary with changes in significant program characteristics are major parts of the analysis.[2]

Bereft of its verbiage, this statement says this: Define the goal, find alternative ways to achieve that goal, evaluate those alternatives, and select the most appropriate one. These ideas are

[1]David Novick (ed.), *Program Budgeting: Program Analysis and the Federal Budget* (Cambridge: Harvard University Press, 1965).

[2]State-Local Finances Project, "The Role and Nature of Cost Analysis in a PPB System," *PPB Note 6* (Washington, D.C.: George Washington University, April, 1967), p. 1.

scarcely new; they are the major components in the long-standing model of "rational" or "economic" man. Thus, rather than any unique underlying ideas, what is probably different about analysis in the PPB context is its level of sophistication and its emphasis upon quantification. Notions of rationality are as important in the newer formulations as in the older, but how is rationality to be determined?

Determining Rationality

As a concept, rationality has something to do with thinking, reason, and reasoning processes. An action seems rational if it is agreeable to reason—if it is not absurd, preposterous, extravagant, or foolish, but rather intelligent, sensible, self-conscious, deliberate, and calculated. All of these terms beg a very important question: *who* will judge; from whose viewpoint is an action to be deemed rational? The soldier who throws himself on a live grenade, thereby saving other men, may act rationally from the viewpoint of his commanding officer, who would rather lose one man than several; irrationally from the viewpoint of his wife, who wanted a live husband back home; and rationally or irrationally from his own viewpoint, depending on whether he wanted to return to his wife and family or preferred to commit suicide rather than see that crew again and found a way to accomplish this and look like a hero at the same time.

Simon makes the same point in his groundbreaking work, suggesting that there are various types of rationality, including objective, subjective, conscious, deliberate, organizational, and personal.[3] To this list administrative rationality—which is of prime concern here—could well be added. In Simon's terms, administrative rationality lies between personal and organizational, if we recognize that administrators are individuals located in organizations. In this situation they must try to keep their personal goals and organizational objectives in sufficient harmony that they can retain their personal sanity as well as their administrative position, and perhaps even advance in the hierarchy. This balancing appears to take place between the poles of personal and organizational rationality and to be a distinct type for

[3]Herbert A. Simon, *Administrative Behavior* (New York: Macmillan, 1958), pp. 75–78.

which the term administrative rationality seems appropriate. This distinction is not meant to suggest that personal and organizational goals must be or always are in conflict. This is obviously not so, or men would rarely enter into organized activities; but it is also obvious that tensions between these goals and values do arise, particularly for administrators.

Rationality in Analysis

If rationality can only be evaluated from some viewpoint, it is proper to ask what perspective is being taken by those proponents of program analysis who seek to "improve" and "rationalize" public-expenditure decisions. The theory, concepts, and jargon associated with these proposals come predominantly from the discipline of economics, and it is economic rationality that lies at their heart. The techniques employed indicate which alternative will accomplish a given objective for the least cost, or which alternative will accomplish the most for a given cost. If goals were defined with sufficient precision, and if "costs" were defined broadly enough, these techniques would constitute nirvana for decision makers. Not surprisingly, most of the "cost" estimates are related to items that have a market value or can be estimated in market terms. Other types of costs must be handled very crudely, if at all. In addition, the more precisely goals are defined, the narrower they tend to be, so that the tougher and more complex the problems become from the administrator's viewpoint, the less and less useful he finds these analyses. Nonetheless, this kind of analysis can sharpen understanding of the kinds of trade-offs (what is *not* being done so that something else can be) that are being made, and can, in general, be of great assistance to the decision maker. At the very least, these techniques should help avoid selection of the worst alternatives, and this is no mean accomplishment. With experimentation and experience in using these approaches, most economists hope to get better at defining goals and at quantifying more adequately most aspects of a decision problem. There is every reason to expect continued improvement along these lines with commensurate additional help for administrators.

However, economic rationality has its own Achilles heel, particularly when the resource-allocation decisions entail considerations well beyond those of simple or pure economic efficiency. It has long been recognized that a dollar is probably more valuable to a man who has few of them than to a man who has millions of them, even though the monetary value of each dollar is the same. This assumption has led to the idea of utility: that there are differences in the personal pleasure or pain (utility or disutility) that individuals derive from the same event, usually one in which some kind of cost is incurred or benefits are received. To decide which course of action is preferable in such a situation, the decision maker needs to sum the utilities and disutilities of all the persons affected (that is, to make interpersonal utility comparisons). This kind of comparison is a good theoretical guide, but thus far welfare economists and other social scientists have been unable to make this concept operational in any generally valid and meaningful manner. Welfare economic theory provides much of the theoretical underpinning for the current PPB discussions, but it does not provide useful criteria to the operating administrator.

In summary, rationality can be determined only from a particular viewpoint, goal, or value system. The rationality being urged in PPB is that of economics, and for its complete realization it requires a degree of precision in goal definition and quantification of relevant costs which are presently beyond our capabilities. Its ultimate yardstick for evaluating alternative actions— utility—is not now capable of practical application in the operating world.

Administrative Decision Making

It is appropriate to turn next to the decision-making process into which these new analytical techniques and their types of rationality are to be inserted.[4] Since World War II, administra-

---

[4]The literature relevant to the balance of this paper is extensive. Specific references and notes will be limited for the sake of simplicity, and also to avoid any attempt to determine who deserves credit for being the originator of a given idea. Indeed, many of these ideas handily predate any of the authors cited here. The most useful writings other than Simon, *op. cit.*, have been the following: David Braybrooke and Charles E. Lindblom, *A Strategy of Decision* (Glencoe, Ill.: Free Press, 1963); "Governmental Decision-Making, A Symposium," *Public Administration Review* (September, 1964), pp. 153–165; Carl J. Friedrich (ed.), *Nomos VII: Rational Decision* (New York: Atherton Press, 1964); Charles

tive writings and research have probably given no topic as much attention as decision making. In the face of this vast array, it is necessary to stake out the small part of the field to be treated here. No effort will be made to define a "decision" or to determine when, in effect, a decision has been made. Attention will be limited to decision making as a process and to describing certain characteristics of that process rather than to the decisions or results that flow from it. Moreover, although the next section will deal in part with the administrator as a decision maker, no effort will be made to get deeply into the psychological aspects of individual choice, perception, or other relevant ideas concerning choice patterns and processes of individuals. Finally, attention will be focused on the decision-making environment faced by the individual administrator, not upon social or aggregated decision making. On this score, the literature jumps from one perspective to another with wonderful facility, but perhaps there is a lesson to be learned from economics. The rules and ideas that make sense in dealing with a single individual or household budget or economy are often wrong, inapplicable, or socially harmful if pursued by a national economy as a whole. It may be that our present concepts describe the decision-making process in particular administrative situations well, but we have failed to discern those factors that render these same ideas and concepts inapplicable when applied to the social level.

Some Characteristics of Administrative Decision Making

The following characterizations of the decision-making process seem appropriate from the viewpoint of the individual administrator:

1. It is often difficult to determine precisely what the problem is. One of the great benefits ascribed to systems analysis is that it

E. Lindblom, "The Science of 'Muddling Through,'" *Public Administration Review* (Spring, 1959), pp. 79–88; James G. March and Herbert A. Simon, *Organizations* (New York: John Wiley & Sons, 1958), esp. Chap. 6; David W. Miller and Martin K. Starr, *The Structure of Human Decisions* (Englewood Cliffs, N.J.: Prentice-Hall, 1967); Herbert A. Simon, *Models of Man* (New York: John Wiley & Sons, 1957), esp. Chap. 15; Herbert A. Simon, *The New Science of Management Decision* (New York: Harper and Row, 1960); "Special Issue on Decision Making," *Administrative Science Quarterly* (December, 1958).

often helps to expose what the problem really is, rather than what it was thought to be before more careful exploration, and to define more accurately what information is needed to solve it.

2. Goals that might be used to establish criteria for distinguishing a good decision from a poorer one are often ill defined and unclear. In addition, goals may change over time and the importance attached to any particular goal may vary from one situation to another.

3. Means and ends can become intertwined so that the desirability of a goal may depend upon how it is to be accomplished and at what cost.

4. The lack of clearly defined goals and the ambiguity of means and ends may make the criteria of a good decision very unclear. Is the decision maker seeking to optimize in some sense (in *what* sense?), or will he settle for less?

5. There is a need for creativity in proposing alternatives, in gathering data, and in analyzing alternatives: A possible course of action cannot be selected if it is never even thought of.

6. A varying amount of uncertainty is always present.

7. Available information is more or less limited. The amount of information available often affects the degree of uncertainty felt by the administrator. At the same time the administrator must be aware of the uncertainty absorption[5] that takes place in the communications network during the transmission of the information he does have. Information can be power—especially if it is exclusively possessed—because it can be transformed to suit the desires of the possessor.

8. Timing is often important, and time can be crucial in two other respects: The amount of it available in which to analyze the situation may be limited, and the administrator is always confronted with the cumulative effect of past decisions.

9. Decision making tends to be a group process. For most purposes the day of the great individual decision maker has passed. The group nature of the process tends to reduce the chance of overlooking some alternatives, and it may have a favorable effect on morale by allowing participation in policy formulation. On the other hand, the greater the number of participants, the more likely that disagreements over goals and other matters will occur.

[5]See March and Simon, *op. cit.*, pp. 164–166.

10. Decision making tends to be sequential. A variety of models depicting the various steps in this process have been proposed.[6]

The Administrator and His World

The decision-making process having been characterized, an attempt can now be made to analyze the environment the administrator sees. A proper beginning for understanding the environment in which the administrator is supposed to utilize this process is the administrator himself.

The administrator has his own value system, his own capacities, his own biases and prejudices, and his own perceptions of the world: in short, the set of characteristics that make him who he is. He is not the totally rational creature postulated in economic theory. His goals are not clear, he cannot manage the tremendous number of calculations required in evaluating comprehensively every consequence of every alternative before him, and as a processor of information and data he can scarcely rival machines in speed and accuracy. Clearly he has an irrational as well as a rational side. His rationality is bounded on all sides—"he is limited by his unconscious skills, habits and reflexes; he is limited by his values and conceptions of purpose, which may diverge from the organization goals; he is limited by the extent of his knowledge and information."[7] Over time, all of these limitations can be altered, more or less, but at any given time they provide the personal environment within which the administrator must make a decision. The best we can say for administrative man, assuming his psychological makeup is normal, is that he intends to be rational or he is intendedly rational.[8] Ordinarily he does not make wrong decisions. When he does, his rationality is probably administrative—in that murky area where organizational and

[6]There are, of course, also nonsequential models. For example, Pfiffner suggested that decision making is not linear but more nearly circular, and can better be viewed as a process of fermentation, or as a galaxy network. See John M. Pfiffner, "Administrative Rationality," *Public Administration Review* (Summer, 1960), p. 129.

[7]Simon, *Administrative Behavior, op. cit.*, p. 241.

[8]At this point we ask only that the actions he takes seem likely to accomplish the goals he is pursuing. We are avoiding the issue of whether those goals are *worth* pursuing.

personal goals are brought into workable juxtaposition—or objective, where some outside observer evaluates whether the actions taken seem reasonably related to the objective sought.

Other people are a part of the environment in which the administrator must carry on his decision-making processes. He knows that these individuals are subject to the same limitations upon their rationality as he is. It comes as no real surprise to him, then, that others viewing a given problem may not perceive it exactly as he does. From the multitudinous objective facts that might relate to a certain situation, the administrator must decide which "facts" are to be recognized in defining both the problem and the decision required. Others with different value systems and perceptions may not accept that these are indeed the facts, or that they are relevant. Even if men can agree on the facts, they may not agree on the meaning or weight that ought to be assigned to those facts. For example, economists may agree as to what has happened during a period of time to wholesale prices and to the value of unfilled orders in durable-goods industries, but they may disagree about the importance to be assigned to these facts and about the relation these factors have to changes in the entire gross national product.

This discussion leads to another characteristic of the administrator's environment: It is one of tension and conflict more than of peace and tranquility. The amount of potential conflict an administrator faces or has to evaluate will vary in part with his level in the organizational hierarchy. The higher he is, the broader a perspective—the wider the variety of interests and the greater potential sources of disagreement—he will need to consider.[9] A number of other factors—age of the organization, its size, its prestige, the nature of its program—will also affect the amount of conflict perceived in the environment. In public life, however, control and influence over general social policy are highly sought

[9]Interestingly, the narrower the range of interests the administrator needs to consider, and the less complex his calculations need to be, the more helpful analytical techniques may become. The differences among the alternatives from which he must select will become less and less great with this narrowing, and the noneconomic factors will become more and more nearly equal, thus allowing the economic aspects of the alternatives to become increasingly important in indicating the "best" choice.

commodities, and conflict situations are daily fare for many administrators.

Conflicts are sometimes rooted in basic value differences among the participants. As a result, it is often difficult to get agreement on the goals that are being pursued in any particular situation. In fact, in public life an explicit definition of goals can often be the most divisive course of action an administrator could adopt; it could lead to the demise of his organization. Community-action agencies provide an interesting example of conflict environments for administrators who are not too high in the hierarchy[10] and of the danger in being explicit about goals if the purpose is to survive so that something (however ill defined) is done about an emotion-laden and socially divisive problem in the local community.

Administrators have another objection to the explicit definition of goals: Such statements tend to reduce their flexibility. This tendency is heightened if the goals are made public. Despite the frustrations that a lack of goal clarity may entail, most administrators appear to prefer broad and ambiguous objectives so that they can adapt their actions and decisions to the specific situations they face. We may prefer a system of laws rather than of men, but the ability to be flexible will remain jealously guarded among public administrators.

Action Orientation

Another important characteristic of the administrator is his action orientation. He wants to get things done.

Disciplined, orderly thought is the characterization given to analysis, but disciplined orderly thought suggests certain traits: reflectiveness, self-criticism, and the willingness to reconsider past commitments without self-justification. However rarely or frequently encountered in the general human population, these are not traits characteristic of the action-oriented, incisive individuals who reach policy-making positions. Questioning and self-doubt lead to Hamlet-like decisionmakers.[11]

[10]Ironically, most community-action agencies are private nonprofit corporations rather than public agencies.

[11]James R. Schlesinger, "Uses and Abuses of Analysis," memorandum prepared at the request of the Subcommittee on National Security and International Operations of the Committee on Government Operations, U.S. Senate, 90th Congress, 2d Session (1968), p. 5.

In order to get action, the administrator is more likely to "muddle through" than to proceed in accordance with the model of rationality. He will not seek to know all consequences of alternatives, but only those derived from the alternatives presently before him. He will concentrate on those marginal values and marginal differences that separate present from proposed policies. He will seek agreement on policies rather than on values or goals, recognizing that men can support the same policy because each foresees its fulfilling his goal, which may be quite different from and sometimes incompatible with the goals of the other policy supporters. The administrator's idea of a good decision or policy tends to be one that achieves sufficient agreement among the concerned individuals or organizations that continued progress (as he defines it) is possible. He will perhaps seek a decision that maximizes, but he will settle for—and is far more likely to get—one that satisfices. In general, he will proceed by making incremental changes rather than sweeping, comprehensive ones.[12] He is less uncertain about the consequences that will flow from incremental changes since past experience with similar policy provides some guidance. In addition, sweeping changes, particularly in public life, may generate a level of conflict that is intolerable to the survival of the organization. Undoubtedly there may be organizations that should be swept aside, but the administrator can surely be forgiven if he considers the survival of his own organization rather vital and if, over his career, he has developed a capacity for equating the work of his organization with the public interest.

A high order of judgment is required as the administrator tries to estimate how others will respond to certain actions on his part. There is some hope that computers will help reduce uncertainty by making information more readily available, but the ability of a computer to apply that information to a specific complex, interdependent decision choice seems far off, if ever to

[12]It has been suggested that incremental changes or decisions assume fundamental decisions at various points. The type of evaluation of alternatives or scanning that the administrator needs to do may vary with the type of decision or exploration of the situation that he wants to make. There is the constant problem in this approach of separating the big potatoes from the small ones, but the idea is suggestive. See Amitai Etzioni, "Mixed-Scanning: A 'Third' Approach to Decision-Making," *Public Administration Review* (December, 1967), pp. 385–392.

be reached at all. It is not enough to know the pattern of responses given in certain situations by middle-aged, white, Anglo-Saxon, Protestant males with college educations from Ivy League schools. The administrator must evaluate how a specific individual who fits into these categories will respond in this particular environment. Undoubtedly, things now considered unquantifiable will become capable of quantified analysis in the future, but the role of judgment is not likely to diminish appreciably in decision making.

As the administrator tries to deal with the complexity and uncertainty he faces, he seeks ways of simplifying his problem. Such simplifications are imperative because there is an enormous discrepancy between his cognitive abilities—even if they are abetted by electronic computers and other devices—and the complexity of the problems he is attempting to solve. Often more information will help, but it takes time and money to get more information, and these two resources are not often abundant in public agencies.[13] In reducing the burden of his calculations, the administrator may break a problem into smaller parts, may deliberately ignore parts of it in the hope that others will look after what he ignores, may develop decision criteria (such as satisfice) that will accelerate his way through the maze despite the fact that increased speed contains obvious risks, and may develop practices (such as proceeding incrementally rather than sweepingly, except under the most dire circumstances) that enable him to comprehend more readily the business he is about.

This description of the administrator's world is not totally satisfying, nor totally accurate or comprehensive. But, it is probably a more nearly accurate picture than the rational model, or any other that we have, of the administrative world that surrounds public budgeting, the environment into which the economic rationality of program analysis is being pushed.[14]

[13]This point is well appreciated by some proponents of PPB: "in practice, comprehensiveness may be too costly in time, effort, uncertainty and confusion." Arthur Smithies, "Conceptual Framework for the Program Budget," in Novick (ed.), *op. cit.*, p. 45.

[14]This point is the major thrust of Aaron Wildavsky, *The Politics of the Budgetary Process* (Boston: Little, Brown, 1964). A similar conclusion has been reached about budgeting in Illinois. See Thomas J. Anton, *The Politics of State Expenditure in Illinois* (Urbana: University of Illinois Press, 1966), pp. 248–255.

Administrative Rationality

The major thesis of this analysis thus far is well summarized by the following:

. . . administrative rationality differs from orthodox conceptions of rationality because it takes into account an additional spectrum of facts. These are the facts relative to emotions, politics, power, group dynamics, personality and mental health. In other words, the data of social science are facts just as much as the carbon content of steel or the dollars and cents in the salary fund. The administrator is forced by environment to take social science data into account in making his decisions. Thus it may seem economically irrational to get rid of a troublesome school principal by "kicking her upstairs" to an assistant superintendency, but it [may prove] quite rational from an administrative standpoint.[15]

The suggestion that practicing administrators have a kind of rationality peculiarly their own can be illustrated in other ways. In a high-quality, academically dominated discussion of decision making, it was a renowned veteran federal official who pointed out that the first step in decision making is deciding whether there is indeed a problem requiring a decision.[16] In his own model of decision making, he showed an interesting departure in a list of steps that was otherwise fairly conventional and in keeping with the rational decision-making model.[17] After the alternatives have been analyzed and the course of action chosen, he suggests that the choice be promptly rejudged. At first this might appear to be typical bureaucratic procrastination and delay, but it is actually a much more sophisticated proposal and reflects the understanding of a man who has been bloodied on the field of combat. In effect, he proposes an effectiveness study of the alternative selected by evaluating that choice in light of four questions:

1. Will it achieve the purpose?

See also Aaron Wildavsky, "The Political Economy of Efficiency: Cost-Benefit Analysis, Systems Analysis, and Program Budgeting," *Public Administration Review* (December, 1966), pp. 292–310.

[15]Pfiffner, *op. cit.*, p. 126.

[16]Roger W. Jones, "The Model as a Decision-Maker's Dilemma," *Public Administration Review* (September, 1964), p. 160. In this short article, Jones delightfully humbles academics on all sides.

[17]*Ibid.*

2. Will it solve the problem?
3. Is it feasible?
4. Are there undesirable results to offset the advantages?

Obviously, an acceptable decision must satisfy these standards, but in the process of analysis and evaluation, a decision may appear desirable because that with which it is being compared— the other alternative—is so bad. With this step, the decision maker is brought back to his central problem—not that of selecting the alternative that is best among those he thought of, but that of finding one that will achieve its purpose, solve the problem, not have too many offsetting disadvantages, and is feasible.

Administrative rationality also would require that systems analysis be undertaken on a problem only if the following questions can be answered affirmatively:

1. Does the problem require a decision?
2. Can the analysis be finished before the decision must be made?
3. Would more information make a difference to whoever will make the decision?[18]

In determining the criteria of a good decision, administrative rationality would suggest the following practical guides to the administrator, although the decision that satisfies them all would be rare indeed.

1. The decision must have some degree of conformance with the personal interests, values, and benefits of the decision maker.
2. The decision must meet the value yardstick of superiors.
3. The decision should be acceptable to those affected as well as to those charged with its implementation.
4. The decision should possess "face validity"; it should appear reasonable in its context.
5. The decision should contain built-in justifications that will furnish an excuse and possible avenue of retreat if results are not as anticipated.[19]

[18]Gloria Grizzle, "Systems Analysis in Dade County," unpublished paper presented at the Operations Research Society of America/Institute for Management Science Joint Meeting, San Francisco, California, May 1–3, 1968, p. 9.
[19]Pfiffner, *op. cit.*, p. 129.

Administrative rationality provides the standards that should be employed in determining whether the actions of an administrator make sense. It has a biting edge and a taste of reality so often lacking in academic discussions of decision making. The administrator strives to operate in accordance with the traditional model of rationality, but he must consider factors not readily suited or much too complex for comprehensive appraisal. In understanding his situation, he must consider not only the economics of the problem, but, in addition, its normative aspects as represented by his own value system and those of others directly involved, and the likely behavior or reactions of others in response to his decisions. At the same time he must strive—so long as his personal values permit—to aid the organization in its continued survival and in the accomplishment of its objectives. Many of the most important variables an administrator must consider are not particularly amenable to mathematical manipulation. Economic rationality and analysis have an important role to play, but administrative rationality requires much, much more.

Conclusion

This paper has not intended to denigrate the contribution economic analysis can make to the process of allocating scarce public resources. Proponents of these techniques have made their use central to the implementation of a planning-programming-budgeting system.[20] The new system appears to have enormous potentialities, and it should not be cast aside lightly simply because it does not readily conform to present practices.

The purpose of the paper has been to suggest that economic rationality can make a definite contribution to public decision making, but the public administrator must practice a kind of rationality that encompasses a great deal more than economics.

Anyone in government knows that most decisions on spending emerge from a political process and are most heavily influenced by value judg-

[20]From an administrative point of view, it is very doubtful that the most significant payoffs in PPB will come from these analyses. The greatest benefits may be derived from the new way information is presented and organized and from the kinds of questions these presentations, without fancy analyses, generate among decision makers. Although interesting, debate about this point lies well outside the scope of this paper.

ments and the pressures brought to bear by a wide range of interested parties.[21]

Every theory must simplify if the calculations and analyses it employs are to be useful at all. But there is the inherent danger in such simplification that the resultant theory will not be applicable to the real-world phenomena it is trying to explain. Current theories of rational decision making are for the most part quantitative, and this characteristic seems to enhance the dangers in simplification. The tendency is to select for most careful consideration those factors capable of exact treatment, essentially those that are quantifiable. The remaining considerations are too often deemed outside the scope of the theory that undergirds the model. The danger in this approach was pointed out long ago:

We either ought not to pretend to scientific forms, or we ought to study all the determining agencies equally, and endeavor, so far as it can be done, to include all of them within the pale of the science; else we shall infallibly bestow a disproportionate attention upon those which our theory takes into account, while we misestimate the rest, and probably underrate their importance.[22]

The public administrator is and must be concerned about a range of variables that cannot be handled readily by any of the more or less mechanical means presently at his disposal. He must maintain a balance and use his own judgment, employ his own administrative rationality, in determining how much weight to assign these latter factors as against those more capable of quantified manipulation.

Few would deny the following:

We base our decisions on predictions which fall short of even our limited capacity for estimating probabilities, compute our utilities on the basis of isolated goals rather than of total outcomes, and cling to incompatible goals. The area in which we may profitably be guided by criteria of rationality is large indeed.[23]

---

[21]William Gorham, "Notes of a Practitioner," *Public Interest* (Summer, 1967), p. 4.

[22]John Stuart Mill, *A System of Logic* (New York: Longmans, Green, 1936), p. 583.

[23]Felix E. Oppenheim, "Rational Decisions and Intrinsic Valuations," Friedrich (ed.), *op. cit.*, p. 220.

But the key to this discussion lies here:

What I have been getting at is something beyond Aristotle's caution that it is the mark of an educated man not to demand more exactness in the treatment of a subject than the subject allows. It is that a preoccupation with even the exactness that is possible does an injustice to less glamorous but nonetheless important components of the problem of rational decision-making.[24]

Comment: The Inadequacy of Traditional Theories and the Promise of PPB as a Systems Approach

David F. Parker

Kenneth Howard argues that the skeptical reaction to planning-programming-budgeting displayed by practicing administrators is not based solely upon bureaucratic inertia and fear of change, but has its roots in valid theoretical and practical considerations. He proposes that the demands for economic rationality be tempered by the realities of "administrative rationality."

I would like to take issue with the two major themes underlying this argument:

1. That "administrative rationality" constitutes a logical decision-making framework for resolving public problems and current government operational difficulties;

2. That planning-programming-budgeting is simply another attempt to introduce economic analysis techniques into government decision making.

Administrative Rationality

Howard points out that "rationality can be determined only from a particular viewpoint, goal, or value system." I submit that the administrative rationality he would have us support is determined from a viewpoint and value system which is rooted in

[24]Abraham Kaplan, "Some Limitations on Rationality," Friedrich (ed.), *op. cit.*, pp. 61–62.

traditional theories no longer adequate for resolving current government problems.

The recurring outbreaks of civil disturbances over the past few years are only one example of the failure of governments at all levels to satisfactorily fulfill the increasing responsibilities delegated to them. As pointed out by the Kerner Commission, "No democratic society can long endure the existence within its major urban centers of a substantial number of citizens who feel deeply aggrieved as a group, yet lack confidence in the government to rectify perceived injustice and in their ability to bring about needed change."[1] In addition to the critical problems affecting the urban poor, governments are beset with a myriad of unresolved major problems—such as highway and airport traffic congestion, air and water pollution, increasing criminal activity and drug addiction, and shortage of education, health, rehabilitation and recreational facilities—which affect all citizens.

At the same time governments are beset by a large and increasing array of unresolved organization needs. The following examples demonstrate:

Better definition of government responsibilities in tackling major social problems;

Improving the effectiveness of present government programs in meeting societal requirements;

More rapid and more meaningful responses to emerging state and local problems;

Stimulation of innovation with state and local government organizations to resolve public problems;

Acquisition and retention of a large percentage of highly qualified professionals in all fields;

More efficient and effective use of scarce resources (men, money facilities);

More efficient and effective intergovernmental and public-private relationships in tackling major public problems;

Improved means of coordinating development planning, program planning, and fiscal planning.

These organization needs have become more apparent to gov-

---

[1] *Report of the National Advisory Commission on Civil Disorders* (New York: Dutton, 1968), p. 288.

ernment leaders as public awareness of unresolved social problems has increased. But changes in the present complex systems of governments to meet these needs have thus far been largely unsuccessful. It seems that these critical organization needs—and closely related major social problems—will not be resolved until government leaders become fully aware of the shortcomings of traditional management and organization theories and implement corrective measures throughout government organizations.

The shortcomings of traditional theories of government management and organization in resolving current organization needs and social problems might be synopsized in terms of three major areas of inadequacy:

The formulation and evaluation of objectives was initially regarded as the exclusive responsibility of elected officials. It has, of course, long since been recognized that administrators are constantly and deeply involved in this process, but the myth of administrative subservience to objectives set solely in the political forum is perpetrated by administrators as a convenient means by which they can avoid difficult basic policy issues and concentrate upon more comprehensible internal management issues. Over the past forty years, needs and demands for new and enlarged public goods and services have increased at an accelerating rate, and governmental organizations have become correspondingly large and custodial orientation to a service orientation which is much harder to define. More and more professionals of all kinds, with their separate group principles and objectives, have been enlisted in government service. These factors—increased size and complexity of public needs and government organizations, the pronounced change in government's role from a custodial to a service orientation, and increased professionalization— have compounded the task of formulating and evaluating ends to the extent that this function can no longer be avoided or reduced to vague references to the "public interest." Traditional theories are simply no longer adequate with respect to the formulation and evaluation of the ends of government action.

Traditional theories of government organization concentrated upon means. A formal hierarchy of authority was deemed essential. As stated by Luther Gulick over thirty years ago, organization is interrelating subdivisions of work "by allotting them to men who are placed in a structure of authority, so that the work may be coordinated by orders of superiors to subordinates, reaching from the top to the bottom of the entire enterprise."[2] Such theories viewed the government as an impersonal technical mechanism which could be continually improved through the improvement of methods and procedures. But, as pointed out by Philip Selznick, "The tendency to emphasize methods rather than goals . . . has the value of stimulating full development of these methods, but it risks loss of adaptability and sometimes results in a radical substitution of means for ends."[3]

Of perhaps greatest importance in assessing the current inadequacy of traditional theories is the basic concept of a centralized structure of authority. According to Herbert Simon, "Man does not generally work well with his fellow man in relations saturated with authority and dependence, with control and subordination, even though these have been the predominant human relations in the past."[4] Efficiency in the means of government actions and effectiveness in achieving the ends of government actions may well rely more on personal leadership qualities throughout the government organization than on technological advances within a depersonalized authority structure as advocated by traditional theories of organization and management.

In sum, I find it impossible to condone Howard's plea for support of "administrative rationality," for I firmly believe that it is precisely this kind of rationality, based on values rooted in outmoded traditional theories of organization and management, which is suppressing innovation and effective action in our so-called modern governments.

Planning-Programming-Budgeting

Definitions of planning-programming-budgeting (PPB), or planning-programming-budgeting system (PPBS), seem to vary

[2]Luther Gulick, "Notes on the Theory of Organizations," Luther Gulick and L. Urwick (eds.), *Papers on the Science of Administration* (New York: Institute of Public Administration, 1937), pp. 3–50.

[3]Philip Selznick, *Leadership in Administration* (New York: Harper and Row, 1957), p. 12.

[4]Herbert A. Simon, *The New Science of Management Decision* (New York: Harper and Brothers, 1960), p. 49.

according to the background of the definer. It has been defined as cost-benefit analysis, marginal-utility analysis, systems analysis, operations research, program budgeting, policy planning, and a great variety of combinations of each.

With the exception of Mayor Lindsay of New York City and possibly a few others, government leaders seem to have little understanding of the scope and potential impact of planning-programming-budgeting. Many appear to view this concept as a resurgence of the efficiency techniques promoted by the Hoover Commission;[5] many others evidently view it as a computerized data-processing device;[6] and those who have done a little reading on the subject often describe it solely in terms of economic analysis.[7] Very few political leaders, administrators, or even academics seem to grasp the fact that the planning-programming-budgeting concept introduces a fresh way of thinking about government activities. PPB introduces the business orientation of concentrating upon product as the basis for all major decisions. In so doing, it paves the way for a new era of rationalization in government management based upon an output-oriented value system.

Herbert Simon maintains that this country is now in the midst of a major revolution in the art or science of management and organization. He states that the growth of operations research over the past twenty years has introduced the "systems approach" into

[5]The Hoover Commission referred to the systematic use of workload cost comparisons as both performance budgeting and program budgeting. Some understandable confusion has arisen over the output-oriented concepts being promulgated through planning-programming-budgeting due to the fact that the first major book on the subject was entitled "Program Budgeting": David Novick (ed.), *Program Budgeting: Program Analysis and the Federal Budget* (Cambridge: Harvard University Press, 1965).

[6]Systems analysis is a problem-solving methodology applicable to a wide range of complex problem situations. However, for some years systems analysts have been recognized as a superior brand of computer programmer highly trained and experienced in the use of computers for problem solving. It is not surprising, then, that many who hear of planning-programming-budgeting as an application of systems analysis immediately relate this concept to computers and data processing because of their familiarity with the term systems analyst.

[7]This is probably due to the fact that planning-programming-budgeting does include economic analysis as an integral segment. But it is a mistake to equate planning-programming-budgeting with economic analysis, for this new concept is far broader in scope than economic analysis. It is not simply a package of tools and techniques, but rather a fresh way of perceiving government activities which includes many useful analytic techniques from the past.

management: "[I]t means designing the components of a system and making individual decisions within it in the light of the implication of these decisions for the system as a whole."[8] This approach, according to Simon, is leading to revolutionary changes in the decision-making techniques of the past. But the effects of the systems approach have not seemed to penetrate into tradition-bound government organizations except for the resolution of specific technical problems.

I would define planning-programming-budgeting as an attempt to introduce the systems approach (as defined by Simon) into government organizations. Howard correctly states that "the jargon in the field is very imprecise," but I cannot agree with him that PPB is simply a label for a bundle of cost-utility analysis techniques. To pigeonhole PPB in this manner is to reduce it to the status of another attempt to improve the means of government actions. But, when conceived in its entirety as a systems approach to government decision making, PPB offers a means for the restructuring of traditional organization and management theories into a framework for a new "administrative rationality" wherein management decisions at all levels of the organization are made and evaluated with respect to planned and produced goods and services to specific clientele groups.

According to Howard, "most administrators appear to prefer broad and ambiguous objectives so that they can adapt their actions and decisions to the specific situations they face . . . [T]he ability to be flexible will remain jealously guarded among public administrators." It seems to me that this very ambiguity in the aims of government is a serious deterrent to the resolution of public problems and organization difficulties. Inability to delineate ends leads to a focus on means as the criteria for decision making, a situation which constrains government administration to the traditional response function. But, Howard states, the administrator "has developed a capacity for equating the work of his organization with the public interest." This statement must be subject to serious question in these days of rising civil unrest and obviously unresolved major public problems.

Planning-programming-budgeting now offers a means whereby

[8]Simon, *op. cit.,* p. 15.

inputs and outputs can be considered together at all levels of the organization, thus making it possible for central leaders to decentralize many input decisions and still maintain responsibility through management by objectives and output-effectiveness information. Such a system relies for its success on a major change in the practices, procedures, and attitudes of administrators to facilitate meaningful policy participation by program professionals and clientele groups in order that truly effective approaches can be developed for the resolution of public problems and organizational difficulties.

Despite the apparent logic and necessity of such major change, efforts toward its achievement have been frustrated by the lack of understanding of the present system and its inadequacies and by the tremendous complexity of the current system even in relatively small state and local governments. Unless planning-programming-budgeting is recognized as a major innovation toward the larger goal of increased decentralization and rationalization of decision making, it appears doomed to a role of instigating continual but relatively meaningless minor improvements in the information flows of centralized decision-making systems.

Conclusion

It is Kenneth Howard's view that "sweeping changes . . . may generate a level of conflict that is intolerable to the survival of the organization." But the survival of the organization may be equally threatened by the failure to implement basic changes. As pointed out by Kahn and Wiener in *The Year 2000,*

If we are as intellectually unprepared for events at the beginning of the twenty-first century, and lack as much understanding of the issues as we did in 1929, 1941, and 1947, we are not only likely to be subjected to some very unpleasant surprises, but unnecessarily to exacerbate and prolong their negative consequences—perhaps to the extent that desirable institutions and values will be irrevocably overwhelmed.[9]

These authors may well be optimistic in allowing thirty years for such preparation. A lesser time period may be more realistic if government leaders continue the slow-response trends of past

[9]Herman Kahn and Anthony J. Wiener, *The Year 2000* (New York: Macmillan, 1967), p. 357.

years and public problems continue to accelerate in scope and number.

As Dwight Waldo makes clear in "Public Administration in a Time of Revolutions,"[10] we are living in an era of great and rapid change. Where courageous and far-sighted political leaders are not forthcoming to redirect the course of governments, the challenge for change in government organizations must be taken up by concerned administrative professionals—not to give the practicing administrator support and assurance in adhering to antiquated theories and practices, but to help him move forward to a new era of government management specifically designed for rapid and effective action on mounting public problems.

Editorial Note

Although the discussion of the essays of this chapter was extremely brief because of time constraints, it indicated that the essays were seen as related to earlier discussions, as the following short quotation indicates:

> There is the possibility that the practitioner is hearing on all sides "For God's sake, be creative! Take these opportunities and do something with them!" And he doesn't know how to do it, partly because no one has given him—to take a line from Orion White's essay—"the technology of adaptation." No one has shown him, for example, how to use confrontation as an opportunity to be creative. Now if we know the answer to that we ought to be communicating it to him a lot better than we are. And if it's asked, "Is PPB a possible lever for change?" the answer, I think, must be "Yes." I think it has some enormous implications. They are *not* in economics, though, they are in Public Administration.

[10]Dwight Waldo, "Public Administration in a Time of Revolutions," *Public Administration Review* (July/August, 1968), pp. 362–368.

11

Toward
a New Public
Administration

H. George Frederickson

In full recognition of the risks, this is an essay on new Public Administration. Its first purpose is to present my interpretation and synthesis of new Public Administration as it emerged at the Minnowbrook Conference on New Public Administration. Its second purpose is to describe how this interpretation and synthesis of new Public Administration relates to the wider world of administrative thought and practice. And its third purpose is to interpret what new Public Administration means for organization theory and *vice versa*.

To affix the label "new" to anything is risky business. The risk is doubled when newness is attributed to ideas, thoughts, concepts, paradigms, theories. Those who claim new thinking tend to regard previous thought as old or jejune or both. In response, the authors of previous thought are defensive and inclined to suggest that, "aside from having packaged earlier thinking in a new vocabulary there is little that is really new in so-called new thinking." Accept, therefore, this caveat: Parts of new Public Administration would be recognized by Plato, Hobbes, Machiavelli, Hamilton, and Jefferson as well as many modern behavioral theorists. The newness is in the way the fabric is woven, not necessarily in the threads that are used, and in arguments as to the proper use of the fabric—however threadbare.

The threads of the Public Administration fabric are well known. Herbert Kaufman describes them simply as the pursuit of these basic values: representativeness, politically neutral competence, and executive leadership.[1] In different times, one or the other of these values receives the greatest emphasis. Representativeness was preeminent in the Jacksonian era. The eventual reaction was the reform movement emphasizing neutral competence and executive leadership. Now we are witnessing a revolt against these values accompanied by a search for new modes of representativeness.

Others have argued that changes in Public Administration resemble a zero-sum game between administrative efficiency and political responsiveness. Any increase in efficiency results *a priori* in a decrease in responsiveness. We are simply entering a period during which political responsiveness is to be purchased at a cost in administrative efficiency.

Both the dichotomous and trichotomous value models of Public Administration just described are correct as gross generalizations. But they suffer the weakness of gross generalizations: They fail to account for the wide, often rich, and sometimes subtle variation that rests within. Moreover, the generalization does not explain those parts of Public Administration that are beyond its sweep. Describing what new Public Administration means for organization theory is a process by which these generalizations can be given substance. But first it is necessary to briefly sketch what this student means by new Public Administration.

What Is New Public Administration?

Educators have as their basic objective, and most convenient rationale, expanding and transmitting knowledge. The police are enforcing the law. Public-health agencies lengthen life by fighting disease. Then there are firemen, sanitation men, welfare workers, diplomats, the military, and so forth. All are employed by public agencies and each specialization or profession has its own substantive set of objectives and therefore its rationale.

What, then, is Public Administration?[2] What are its objectives and its rationale?

[1]Herbert Kaufman, "Administrative Decentralization and Political Power," *Public Administration Review* (January-February, 1969), pp. 3–15.

[2]Frederick Mosher and John C. Honey wrestle with the question of the relative role of professional specialists as against the generalist administrator in public organizations. See Frederick Mosher, *Democracy and the Public Service* (New York: Oxford University Press, 1968), pp. 99–133. See also John C. Honey, "A Report: Higher Education for the Public Service," *Public Administration Review* (November, 1967).

The classic answer has always been the efficient, economical, and coordinated management of the services listed above. The focus has been on top-level management (city management as an example) or the basic auxiliary staff services (budgeting, organization and management, systems analysis, planning, personnel, purchasing). The rationale for Public Administration is almost always better (more efficient or economical) management. New Public Administration adds *social equity* to the classic objectives and rationale. Conventional or classic Public Administration seeks to answer either of these questions: (1) How can we offer more or better services with available resources (efficiency)? or (2) How can we maintain our level of services while spending less money (economy)? New Public Administration adds this question: Does this service enhance social equity?

The phrase social equity is used here to summarize the following set of value premises. Pluralistic government systematically discriminates in favor of established stable bureaucracies and their specialized minority clientele (the Department of Agriculture and large farmers as an example) and against those minorities (farm laborers, both migrant and permanent, as an example) who lack political and economic resources. The continuation of widespread unemployment, poverty, disease, ignorance, and hopelessness in an era of unprecedented economic growth is the result. This condition is morally reprehensible and if left unchanged constitutes a fundamental, if long-range, threat to the viability of this or any political system. Continued deprivation amid plenty breeds widespread militancy. Militancy is followed by repression, which is followed by greater militancy, and so forth. A Public Administration which fails to work for changes which try to redress the deprivation of minorities will likely be eventually used to repress those minorities.

For a variety of reasons—probably the most important being committee legislatures, seniority legislatures, entrenched bureaucracies, nondemocratized political-party procedures, inequitable revenue-raising capacity in the lesser governments of the federal system—the procedures of representative democracy presently operate in a way that either fails or only very gradually attempts to reverse systematic discrimination against disadvantaged minorities. Social equity, then, includes activities designed to enhance the political power and economic well-being of these minorities.

A fundamental commitment to social equity means that new Public Administration attempts to come to grips with Dwight Waldo's contention that the field has never satisfactorily accommodated the theoretical implications of involvement in "politics" and policy making.[3] The policy-administration dichotomy lacks an empirical warrant, for it is abundantly clear that administrators both execute and make policy. The policy-administration continuum is more accurate empirically but simply begs the theoretical question. New Public Administration attempts to answer it in this way: *Administrators are not neutral. They should be committed to both good management and social equity as values, things to be achieved, or rationales.*

A fundamental commitment to social equity means that new Public Administration is anxiously engaged in change. *Simply put, new Public Administration seeks to change those policies and structures that systematically inhibit social equity.* This is not seeking change for change's sake nor is it advocating alterations in the relative roles of administrators, executives, legislators, or the courts in our basic constitutional forms. Educators, agriculturists, police, and the like can work for changes which enhance their objectives and resist those that threaten those objectives, all within the framework of our governmental system. New Public Administration works in the same way to seek the changes which would enhance its objectives—good management, efficiency, economy, and social equity.

A commitment to social equity not only involves the pursuit of change but attempts to find organizational and political forms which exhibit a capacity for continued flexibility or routinized change. Traditional bureaucracy has a demonstrated capacity for stability, indeed, ultrastability.[4] New Public Administration, in its search for changeable structures, tends therefore to experiment with or advocate modified bureaucratic-organizational forms. Decentralization, devolution, projects, contracts, sensitivity training, organization development, responsibility expansion, confrontation, and client involvement are all essentially

---

[3]Dwight Waldo, "Scope of the Theory of Public Administration," James C. Charlesworth (ed.), *Theory and Practice of Public Administration: Scope, Objectives and Methods* (Philadelphia: The American Academy of Political and Social Sciences, October, 1968), pp. 1–26.

[4]Anthony Downs, *Inside Bureaucracy* (Boston: Little, Brown, 1967).

counterbureaucratic notions that characterize new Public Administration.[5] These concepts are designed to enhance both bureaucratic and policy change and thus to increase possibilities for social equity. Indeed, an important faculty member in one of the best-known and largest Master in Public Administration programs in the country described that degree program as "designed to produce change agents or specialists in organizational development."

Other organizational notions such as programming-planning-budgeting systems, executive inventories, and social indicators can be seen as enhancing change in the direction of social equity. They are almost always presented in terms of good management (witness McNamara and PPB) as a basic strategy, because it is unwise to frontally advocate change.[6] In point of fact, however, PPB can be used as a basic device for change (in McNamara's case to attempt to wrest control from the uniformed services, but in the name of efficiency and economy). The executive inventory can be used to alter the character of the top levels of a particular bureaucracy, thereby enhancing change possibilities. Social indicators are designed to show variation in socioeconomic circumstances in the hope that attempts will be made to improve the conditions of those who are shown to be disadvantaged.[7] All three of these notions have only a surface neutrality or good-management character. Under the surface they are devices by which administrators and executives try to bring about change. It is no wonder they are so widely favored in Public Administration circles. And it should not be surprising that economists and political scientists in the "pluralist" camp regard devices such as PPB as fundamentally threatening to their conception of democratic government.[8] Although they are more subtle in terms of change, PPB, executive inventories, and social indicators are of

[5]In a very general way most of these are characteristics of what Larry Kirkhart (see Chap. 5 above) calls the consociated model.

[6]See especially Charles L. Schultze, *The Politics and Economics of Public Spending* (Washington, D.C.: The Brookings Institution, 1969).

[7]The general "social equity" concern expressed in the essays in Raymond A. Bauer, *Social Indicators* (Cambridge, Mass.: MIT Press, 1967) is clearly indicative of this.

[8]Aaron Wildavsky, *The Politics of the Budgetary Process* (Boston: Little, Brown, 1964) and Charles Lindblom, *The Intelligence of Democracy* (New York: Glencoe Free Press, 1966).

the same genre as more frontal change techniques such as sensitivity training, projects, contracts, decentralization, and the like. All enhance change, and *change is basic to new Public Administration.*

New Public Administration's commitment to social equity implies a strong administrative or executive government—what Hamilton called "energy in the executive." The policy-making powers of the administrative parts of government are increasingly recognized. In addition, a fundamentally new form of political access and representativeness is now occurring in the administration of government and it may be that this access and representativeness is as critical to major policy decisions as is legislative access or representativeness. *New Public Administration seeks not only to carry out legislative mandates as efficiently and economically as possible, but to both influence and execute policies which more generally improve the quality of life for all.* Forthright policy advocacy on the part of the public servant is essential if administrative agencies are basic policy battlefields. New Public Administrationists are likely to be forthright advocates for social equity and will doubtless seek a supporting clientele.

Classic Public Administration emphasizes developing and strengthening institutions which have been designed to deal with social problems. The Public Administration focus, however, has tended to drift from the problem to the institution.[9] New Public Administration attempts to refocus on the problem and to consider alternative possible institutional approaches to confronting problems. The intractable character of many public problems such as urban poverty, widespread narcotics use, high crime rates, and the like lead Public Administrators to seriously question the investment of ever more money and manpower in institutions which seem only to worsen the problems. They seek, therefore, either to modify these institutions or develop new and more easily changed ones designed to achieve more proximate solutions. *New Public Administration is concerned less with the Defense Department than with defense, less with civil-service commissions than with the manpower needs of administrative agencies on the one hand and the employment needs of the society on the other, less with building institutions and more with design-*

---

[9]See especially Orion White's essay in this volume (Chap. 3) on this point.

ing alternate means of solving public problems. These alternatives will no doubt have some recognizable organizational characteristics and they will need to built and maintained, but will seek to avoid becoming entrenched, nonresponsible bureaucracies that become greater public problems than the social situations they were originally designed to improve.

The movement from an emphasis on institution building and maintenance to an emphasis on social anomalies has an important analogue in the study of Public Administration. The last generation of students of Public Administration generally accept both Simon's logical positivism and his call for an empirically based organization theory. They focus on generic concepts such as decision, role, and group theory to develop a generalizable body of organization theory. The search is for commonalities of behavior in all organizational settings.[10] The organization and the people within it are the empirical referent. The product is usually description, not prescription, and if it is prescription it prescribes how to better manage the organization internally. The subject matter is first *organization* and second the type of organization—private, public, voluntary.[11] The two main bodies of theory emerging from this generation of work are decision theory and human-relation theory. Both are regarded as behavioral and positivist. Both are at least as heavily influenced by sociology, social psychology, and economics as they are by political science.

New Public Administration advocates what could be best described as "second-generation behavioralism." Unlike his progenitor, the second-generation behavioralist emphasizes the *public* part of Public Administration. He accepts the importance of understanding as scientifically as possible how and why organizations behave as they do but he tends to be rather more interested in the impact of that organization on its clientele and *vice versa.* He is not antipositivist nor antiscientific although he is probably less than sanguine about the applicability of the natural-science model to social phenomena. He is not likely to use his behavior-

[10]See especially James March and Herbert Simon, *Organizations* (New York: John Wiley and Sons, 1963).

[11]See especially Amitai Etzioni, *A Comparative Analysis of Complex Organizations* (New York: Glencoe Free Press, 1961).

alism as a rationale for simply trying to describe how public organizations behave.[12] Nor is he inclined to use his behavioralism as a facade for so-called neutrality, being more than a little skeptical of the objectivity of those who claim to be doing science. He attempts to use his scientific skills to aid his analysis, experimentation, and evaluation of alternative policies and administrative modes. *In sum, then, the second-generation behavioralist is less "generic" and more "public" than his forebear, less "descriptive" and more "prescriptive," less "institution oriented" and more "client-impact oriented," less "neutral" and more "normative," and, it is hoped, no less scientific.*

This has been a brief and admittedly surface description of new Public Administration from the perspective of one analyst. If the description is even partially accurate it is patently clear that there are fundamental changes occurring in Public Administration which have salient implications for both its study and practice as well as for the general conduct of government. The final purpose of this chapter is a consideration of the likely impact of new Public Administration on organization theory particularly and the study of administration generally. (The term "theory" is used here in its loose sense, as abstract thought.)

Organization Theory and New Public Administration

Understanding of any phenomenon requires separating that phenomenon into parts and examining each part in detail. In understanding government this separation can reflect institutions such as the traditional "fields" in political science—Public Administration, legislative behavior, public law, and so forth. Or

[12]An exchange occurring at an informal rump session of the Minnowbrook Conference is especially illustrative of this. Several conferees were discussing errors in strategy and policy in the operations of the United States Office of Economic Opportunity. They were generalizing in an attempt to determine how organizations like O.E.O. could be made more effective. Several plausible causal assertions were advanced and vigorously supported. Then a young but well-established political scientist commented that causal assertions could not be supported by only one case. True correlations of statistical significance required an "N" or "number of cases" of at least thirty. The reply was, "Has Public Administration nothing to suggest until we have had thirty O.E.O.'s? Can we afford thirty O.E.O.'s before we learn what went wrong with the first one? By ducking into our analytical and quantitative shelters aren't we abdicating our responsibilities to suggest ways to make the second O.E.O. or its equivalent an improvement on the first?"

this separation can be primarily conceptual or theoretical such as systems theory, decision theory, role theory, group theory—all of which cut across institutions.

Public Administration has never had either an agreed upon or a satisfactory set of subfields. The "budgeting," "personnel administration," "organization and management" categories are too limiting, too "inside-organization" oriented, and too theoretically vacant. The middle-range theories—decisions, roles, groups, and the like—are stronger theoretically and have yielded more empirically, but still tend to focus almost exclusively on the internal dynamics of public organizations. The new Public Administration calls for a different way of subdividing the phenomenon so as to better understand it. This analyst suggests that there are four basic processes at work in public organizations and further suggests that these processes are suitable for both understanding and improving Public Administration. The four suggested processes are: the distributive process; the integrative process; the boundary-exchange process; and the socioemotional process.

The Distributive Process

New Public Administration is vitally concerned with patterns of distribution. This concern has to do first with the *external* distribution of goods and services to particular categories of persons, in terms of the benefits that result from the operation of publicly administered programs.

Cost-utility, or cost-benefit, analysis is the chief technique for attempting to understand the results of the distributive process. This form of analysis presumes to measure the utility to individuals of particular public programs. Because it attempts to project the likely costs and benefits of alternative programs it is a very central part of new Public Administration. It is central primarily because it provides a scientific or quasi-scientific means for attempting to "get at" the question of equity. It also provides a convenient or classic Public Administration rationale for redistribution. Take, for example, McNamara's justifications for decisions based on cost-utility analysis in the Department of Defense. These justifications were generally urged on the basis of substantive military criteria.

Because of the emergence of "program-planning-budgeting

systems" we are beginning to see, in the policy advocacy of the various bureaus and departments of government, their attempts to demonstrate their impact on society in terms of utility. Wildavsky and Lindblom have argued that rational or cost-utility analysis is difficult if not impossible to do. Further, they contend, rational decision making fundamentally alters or changes our political system by dealing with basic political questions within the arena of the administrator. To date they are essentially correct, empirically. Normatively they are apologists for pluralism. Cost-benefit analysis can be an effective means by which inequities can be demonstrated. It is a tool by which legislatures and entrenched bureaucracies can be caused to defend publicly their distributive decisions. The inference is that a public informed of glaring inequities will demand change.

Like the executive budget, rational or cost-benefit decision systems (PPB) enhance the power of executives and administrators and are, again, a part of new Public Administration. Because PPB is being widely adopted in cities and states, as well as in the national government, it seems clear that new Public Administration will be highly visible simply by a look at the distributive processes of government over the next decade or two. The extent to which PPB will result in a redistribution which enhances social equity remains to be seen.

Benefit or utility analysis in its less prescriptive and more descriptive form, known in political science as "policy-outcomes analysis," attempts to determine the basic factors that influence or determine policy variation.[13] For example, "outcomes analysts" sketch the relationship between variations in public spending (quantity) and the quality of nonspending policy outcomes. The policy-outcomes analyst attempts to determine the relationship between the levels of spending in education and the IQ's, employability, college admissibility, and the like of the products of the educational process. This analysis is essentially after the fact, and indeed is commonly based on relatively out-of-date census data. It is, therefore, useful to new Public Administration, but only as a foundation or background.

[13]For a good bibliographic essay on this subject see John H. Fenton and Donald W. Chamberlayne, "The Literature Dealing with the Relationships Between Political Process, Socioeconomic Conditions and Public Policies in the American States: A Bibliographic Essay," *Polity* (Spring, 1969), pp. 388–404. See also Chap. 9 above.

A newer form of distributive analysis is emerging. This approach focuses on equity in the distribution of government services within a jurisdiction and asks questions such as: Does a school board distribute its funds equitably to schools and to the school children in its jurisdiction, and if not is inequity in the direction of the advantaged or disadvantaged? Are sanitation services distributed equitably to all neighborhoods in the city, and if not in what direction does inequity move and how is it justified? Is state and federal aid distributed equitably, and if not how are inequities justified?[14]

Patterns of internal-organization distribution are a traditional part of organization theory. The internal competition for money, manpower, status, space, and priorities is a staple in organization theory as any reading of the *Administrative Science Quarterly* indicates. We learn from this literature the extent to which many of the functions of government are in essence controlled by particular bodies of professionals—educators, physicians, attorneys, social workers, and the like. We learn how agencies age and become rigid and devote much of their energies to competing for survival purposes. We learn the extent to which distribution becomes what Wildavsky calls a triangulation between bureaus, legislatures (particularly legislative committees), and elected executives and their auxiliary staffs.[15] Finally, we have whole volumes of aggregated and disaggregated hypotheses which account for or attempt to explain the decision patterns involved in the internal distributive process.[16]

In new Public Administration the internal distributive process is likely to involve somewhat less readiness to make incremental compromises or "bargain" and somewhat more "administrative confrontation." If new Public Administrators are located in the staff agencies of the executive, which is highly likely, they will doubtless be considerably more tenacious than their prede-

[14]Equity is now a major question in the courts. Citizens are bringing suit against governments at all levels under the "equal protection of the laws" clause claiming inequities in distribution. Thus far the courts have taken a moderate equity stance in education and welfare. See John E. Coons, William H. Clune, and Stephen D. Sugerman, "Educational Opportunity: A Workable Constitutional Test for State Structures," *California Law Review* (April, 1969), pp. 305–421.

[15]Aaron Wildavsky, *op. cit.*

[16]March and Simon, *op. cit.;* Downs, *op. cit.;* and James L. Price, *Organizational Effectiveness* (Homewood, Ill.: Irwin, 1968).

cessors. The spokesman for an established agency might have learned to pad his budget, to overstaff, to control public access to records, and to expand his space in preparation for the compromises he has learned to expect. He might now encounter a zealot armed with data which describe in detail padding, overstaffing, and suppressed records. Therefore an organization theory based primarily on the traditional administrative bargaining process is likely to be woefully inadequate. There is a need to develop a theory which accounts for the presence of public administrators considerably less willing to bargain and more willing to take political and administrative risks.

It is difficult to predict the possible consequences of having generalist public administrators who are prepared to rationalize their positions and decisions on the basis of social equity. Administrative theory explains relatively well the results of the use of efficiency, economy, or good management as rationale. We know, for instance, that these arguments are especially persuasive in years in which legislatures and elected executives do not wish to raise taxes. But we also know that virtually anything can be justified under the rubric "good management." When public administrators leave the safe harbor of this rhetoric, what might occur? The best guess is a more open conflict on basic issues of goals or purposes. Some administrators will triumph, but the majority will not; for the system tends to work against the man seeking change and willing to take risks for it. The result is likely to be a highly mobile and relatively unstable middle-level civil service. Still, actual withdrawal or removal from the system after a major setback is likely to be preferred by new public administrators to the psychic withdrawal which is now common among administrators.

One can imagine, for instance, a city personnel director prepared to confront the chief of police and the police bureaucracy on the question of eligibility standards for new patrolmen. He might argue, backed with considerable data, that patrolman height and weight regulations are unrealistic and systematically discriminate against deprived minorities. He might also argue that misdemeanor convictions by minors should not prohibit adults from becoming patrolmen. If this were an open conflict, it would likely array deprived minorities against the majority of the city council, possibly against the mayor, and certainly against the chief and his men (and no doubt the Police Benevolent Association). While the new public administrator might be perfectly willing to take the risks involved in such a confrontation, present theory does not accommodate well what this means for the political system generally.

The Integrative Process

Authority hierarchies are the primary means by which the work of persons in publicly administrated organizations is coordinated. The formal hierarchy is the most obvious and easiest-to-identify part of the permanent and on-going organization. Administrators are seen as persons taking roles in the hierarchy and performing tasks that are integrated through the hierarchies to constitute a cohesive goal-seeking whole. The public administrator has customarily been regarded as the one who builds and maintains the organization through the hierarchy. He attempts to understand formal-informal relationships, status, politics, and power in authority hierarchies. The hierarchy is at once an ideal design and a hospitable environment for the person who wishes to manage, control, or direct the work of large numbers of people.

The counterproductive characteristics of hierarchies are well known.[17] New Public Administration is probably best understood as advocating modified hierarchic systems. Several means both in theory and practice are utilized to modify traditional hierarchies. The first and perhaps the best known is the project or matrix technique.[18] The project is, by definition, temporary. The project manager and his staff are a team which attempts to utilize the services of regularly established hierarchies in an on-going organization. For the duration of the project, the manager must get his technical services from the technical hierarchy of the organization, his personnel services from the personnel agency, his budgeting services from the budget department, and so forth. Obviously the project technique would not be effective were it not

[17]See Victor Thompson, *Modern Organization* (New York: Knopf, 1961); Robert V. Presthus, *The Organizational Society* (New York: Knopf, 1962); and Downs, *op. cit.*

[18]David I. Cleland and William R. King, *Systems Analysis and Project Management* (New York: McGraw-Hill, 1968); David I. Cleland and William R. King, *Systems, Organizations, Analysis, Management: A Book of Readings* (New York: McGraw-Hill, 1969); George A. Steiner and William G. Ryan, *Industrial Project Management* (New York: Macmillan, 1968); John Stanley Baumgartner, *Project Management* (Homewood, Ill.: Irwin, 1963).

for considerable top-level support for the project. When there are conflicts between the needs of the project and the survival needs of established hierarchies, top management must consistently decide in favor of the projects. The chief advantage of projects are of course their collapsible nature. While bureaucracies do not disestablish or self-destruct, projects do. The project concept is especially useful when associated with "one time" hardware or research and development, or capital improvement efforts. The concept is highly sophisticated in engineering circles and theoretically could be applied to a large number of less technical and more social problems.[19] The project technique is also useful as a device by which government contracts with industry can be monitored and coordinated.

Other procedures for modifying hierarchies are well known and include the group-decision-making model, the link-pin function, and the so-called dialectical organization.[20] And, of course, true decentralization is a fundamental modification hierarchy.[21]

Exploration and experimentation with these various techniques is a basic part of new Public Administration. The search for less structured, less formal, and less authoritative integrative techniques in publicly administered organizations is only beginning. The preference for these types of organizational modes implies first a relatively high tolerance for variation. This includes variations in administrative performance and variations in procedures and applications based upon differences in clients or client groups. It also implies great tolerance for the possibilities of inefficiency and diseconomy. In a very general sense this preference constitutes a willingness to trade increases in involvement and commitment to the organization for possible decreases in efficiency and economy, particularly in the short run. In the long run, less formal and less authoritative integrative techniques may prove to be more efficient and economical.

There are two serious problems with the advocacy by new

[19]H. George Frederickson and Henry J. Anna, "Bureaucracy and the Urban Poor," mimeographed.

[20]See Rensis Likert, *New Patterns of Management* (New York: McGraw-Hill, 1961); and Orion White, "The Dialectical Organization: An Alternative to Bureaucracy," *Public Administration Review* (January-February, 1969), pp. 32-42.

[21]Kaufman, *op. cit.*

Public Administration of less formal integrative processes. First, there may develop a lack of Public Administration specialists who are essentially program builders. The new Public Administration man who is trained as a change agent and an advocate of informal, decentralized, integrative processes may not be capable of building and maintaining large, permanent organizations. This problem may not be serious, however, because administrators in the several professions (education, law enforcement, welfare, and the like) are often capable organization builders, or at least protectors, so a Public Administration specialist can concentrate on the change or modification of hierarchies built by others.

The second problem is the inherent conflict between higher- and lower-level administrators in less formal, integrative systems. While describing the distributive process in Public Administration it was quite clear that top-level public administrators were to be strong and assertive. In this description of the integrative process there is a marked preference for large degrees of autonomy at the base of the organization. The only way to theoretically accommodate this contradiction is through an organizational design in which top-level public administrators are regarded as policy advocates and general-policy reviewers. If they have a rather high tolerance for the variations in policy application then it can be presumed that intermediate and lower levels in the organization can apply wide interpretive license in program application. This accommodation is a feeble one, to be sure, but higher-lower-level administrative relations are a continuing problem in Public Administration, and the resolution of these problems in the past has tended to be in the direction of the interests of upper levels of the hierarchy in combination with subdivisions of the legislative body and potent interest groups. New Public Administration searches for a means by which lower levels of the organization and less potent minorities can be favored.

The Boundary-Exchange Process

The boundary-exchange process describes the general relationship between the publicly administered organization and its reference groups and clients. These include legislatures, elected executives, auxiliary staff organizations, clients (both organized and individual), and organized interest groups. The boundary-exchange process also accounts for the relationship between levels of government in a federal system. Because publicly administered organizations find themselves in a competitive political, social, and economic environment, they tend to seek support. This is done by first finding a clientele which can play a strong advocacy role with the legislature, then by developing a symbiotic relationship between the agency and key committees or members of the legislature, followed by building and maintaining as permanent an organization as is possible.

The distributive and integrative processes which have just been described call for vastly altered concepts of how to conduct boundary exchange in new Public Administration.[22] Future organization theory will have to accommodate the following pattern of boundary exchange. First, a considerably higher client involvement is necessary on the part of those minorities who have not heretofore been involved. (It is unfair to assume that minorities are not already involved as clients; farmers, bankers, and heavy industries are minorities and they are highly involved clients. In this sense all public organizations are "client" oriented.) This change probably spells a different kind of involvement. A version of this kind of involvement is now being seen in some of our cities as a result of militancy and community-action programs, and on the campuses of some universities. A preferred form of deprived-minority-client involvement would be routinized patterns of communication with decentralized organizations capable of making distributive decisions that support the interests of deprived minorities, even if these decisions are difficult to justify in terms of either efficiency or economy.

In a very general way, this kind of decision making occurs in time of war with respect to military decision making. It also characterizes decision patterns in the Apollo program of the National Aeronautics and Space Administration. These two examples characterize crash programs designed to solve problems that are viewed as immediate and pressing. They involve a kind of backward budgeting in which large blocks of funds are made available for the project and wide latitude in expenditures is tolerated.

[22]James Thompson, *Organizations in Action* (New York: McGraw-Hill, 1967).

The detailed accounting occurs after the spending, not before, hence backward budgeting. Under these conditions what to do and what materials are needed are decided at low levels of the organization. These decisions are made on the presumption that they will be supported and the necessary resources will be made available and accounted for by upper levels of the organization. This same logic could clearly be applied to the ghetto. A temporary project could be established in which the project manager and his staff work with the permanently established bureaucracies in a city in a crash program designed to solve the employment, housing, health, education, and transportation needs of the residents of that ghetto. The decisions and procedures of one project would likely vary widely from those of another, based on the differences in the circumstances of the clientele involved and the political-administrative environments encountered. The central project director would tolerate the variations both in decisions and patterns of expenditures in the same way that the Department of Defense and NASA cover their expenditures in times of crisis.

The danger will be in the tendency of decentralized projects to be taken over by local pluralist elites. The United States Selective Service is an example of this kind of take-over. High levels of disadvantaged-minority-client involvement are necessary to offset this tendency. Still, it will be difficult to prevent the new controlling minorities from systematic discrimination against the old controlling minorities.

From this description of a boundary-exchange relationship, it is probably safe to predict that administrative agencies, particularly those that are decentralized, will increasingly become the primary means by which particular minorities find their basic form of political representation. This situation exists now in the case of the highly advantaged minorities and may very well become the case with the disadvantaged.

The means by which high client involvement is to be secured is problematic. The maximum-feasible-participation notion, although given a very bad press, was probably more successful than most analysts are prepared to admit. Maximum feasible participation certainly did not enhance the efficiency or economy of OEO activities, but, and perhaps most important, it gave the residents of the ghetto at least the impression that they had the capacity to influence publicly made decisions that affected their well-being. High client involvement probably means, first, the employment of the disadvantaged where feasible; second, the use of client review boards or review agencies; and third, decentralized legislatures such as the kind sought by the Brownhill School District in the New York City Board of Education decentralization controversy.

The development of this pattern of boundary exchange spells the probable development of new forms of intergovernmental relations, particularly fiscal relations. Federal grants-in-aid to states and cities, and state grants-in-aid to cities will no doubt be expanded, and probably better equalized.[23] In addition, some form of tax sharing is probably called for. The fundamental weakness of the local governments' revenue capacity must be alleviated.

The use of the distributive and integrative processes described above probably also means the development of new means by which administrators relate to their legislatures. The elected official will probably always hold continuance in office as his number-one objective. This means that a Public Administration using less formal integrative processes must find means by which it can enhance the reelection probabilities of supporting incumbents. Established centralized bureaucracies do this in a variety of ways, the best known being building and maintaining of roads or other capital facilities in the legislators' district, establishing high-employment facilities, such as federal office buildings, county courthouses, police precincts, and the like, and distributing public-relations materials favorable to the incumbent legislator. The decentralized organization seems especially suited for the provision of this kind of service for legislators. As a consequence it is entirely possible to imagine legislators becoming strong spokesmen for less hierarchic and less authoritative bureaucracies.

The Socioemotional Process

The Public Administration described herein will require both individual and group characteristics that differ from those presently seen. The widespread use of sensitivity training, T tech-

---

[23]Deil S. Wright, *Federal Grants-In-Aid: Perspectives and Alternatives* (Washington, D.C.: American Enterprise Institute for Public Policy Research, 1968).

niques, or "organizational development" is compatible with new Public Administration.[24] These techniques include lowering an individual's reliance on hierarchy, enabling him to tolerate conflict and emotions, and indeed under certain circumstances to welcome them, and to prepare him to take greater risks. From the preceding discussion it is clear that sensitizing techniques are parallel to the distributive, integrative, and boundary-exchange processes just described.

Socioemotional-training techniques are fundamental devices for administrative change. These techniques have thus far been used primarily to strengthen or redirect on-going and established bureaucracies. In the future it is expected that the same techniques will be utilized to aid in the development of decentralized and possibly project-oriented organizational modes.

A recent assessment of the United States Department of State by Chris Argyris is highly illustrative of the possible impact of new Public Administration on organizational socioemotional processes.[25] Argyris concluded that "State" is a social system characterized by individual withdrawal from interpersonal difficulties and conflict; minimum interpersonal openness, leveling, and trust; a withdrawal from aggressiveness and fighting; the view that being emotional is being ineffective or irrational; leaders' domination of subordinates; an unawareness of leaders' personal impact on others; and very high levels of conformity coupled with low levels of risk taking or responsibility taking. To correct these organizational "pathologies" Argyris recommended that:

1. A long-range change program should be defined with the target being to change the living system of the State Department.

2. The first stage of the change program should focus on the behavior and leadership style of the most senior participants within the Department of State.

3. Simultaneously with the involvement of the top, similar

[24]See especially the essays of Larry Kirkhart (Chap. 5) and Orion White (Chap. 3) above.

[25]Chris Argyris, "Some Causes of Organizational Ineffectiveness Within the Department of State" (Washington, D.C.; U.S. Government Printing Office [Center for International Systems Research, Occasional Paper No. 2], November, 1966).

change activities should be initiated in any subpart which shows signs of being ready for change.

4. The processes of organizational change and development that are created should require the same behavior and attitudes as those we wish to inculcate into the system (take more initiative, enlarge responsibilities, take risks).

5. As the organizational development activities produce a higher level of leadership skills and begin to reduce the system's defenses in the area of interpersonal relations, the participants should be helped to begin to reexamine some of the formal policies and activities of the State Department that presently may act as inhibitors to organizational effectiveness (employee evaluations and ratings, promotion process, inspections). The reexamination should be conducted under the direction of line executives with the help of inside or outside consultants.

6. The similarities and interdependencies between administration and substance need to be made more explicit and more widely accepted.

7. The State Department's internal capacity in the new areas of behavioral-science-based knowledge should be increased immediately.

8. Long-range research programs should be developed, exploring the possible value of the behavioral disciplines to the conduct of diplomacy.

The characteristics of the State Department are, sad to say, common in publicly administered organizations. While Argyris' recommendations are particular to "State," they are relevant to all highly authoritative hierarchy-based organizations.

While new Public Administration is committed to wider social equity, the foregoing should make it clear that a more nearly equitable internal organization is also an objective.

Conclusions

The search for social equity provides Public Administration with a real normative base. Like many value premises, social equity has the ring of flag, country, mother, and apple pie. But surely the pursuit of social equity in Public Administration is no more a holy grail than the objectives of educators, medical doctors, and so forth. Still, it appears that new Public Administration is an alignment with good, or possibly God.

What are the likely results for a *practicing* public administration working from such a normative base? *First*, classic public administration on the basis of its expressed objectives commonly had the support of businessmen and the articulate and educated upper and upper-middle classes. The phenomenal success of the municipal-reform movement is testament to this. If new Public Administration attempts to justify or rationalize its stance on the basis of social equity, it might have to trade support from its traditional sources for support from the disadvantaged minorities. It might be possible for new Public Administration to continue to receive support from the educated and articulate if we assume that this social class is becoming increasingly committed to those public programs that are equity enhancing and less committed to those that are not. Nevertheless, it appears that new Public Administration should be prepared to take the risks involved in such a trade, if it is necessary to do so.

Second, new Public Administration, in its quest for social equity, might encounter the kinds of opposition that the Supreme Court has experienced in the last decade. That is to say, substantial opposition from elected officials for its fundamental involvement in shaping social policy. The Court, because of its independence, is less vulnerable than administration. We might expect, therefore, greater legislative controls over administrative agencies and particularly the distributive patterns of such agencies.

Third, new Public Administration might well foster a political system in which elected officials speak basically for the majority and for the privileged minorities while courts and the administrators are spokesmen for disadvantaged minorities. As administrators work in behalf of the equitable distribution of public and private goods, courts are increasingly interpreting the Constitution in the same direction. Legislative hostility to this activity might be directed at administration simply because it is most vulnerable.

What of new Public Administration and academia? First let us consider the theory, then the academy.

Organization theory will be influenced by new Public Administration in a variety of ways. The uniqueness of *public* organization will be stressed. Internal administrative behavior—the forte of the generic administration school and the foundation of much of what is now known as organization theory—will be a part of scholarly Public Administration, but will be less central. Its center position in Public Administration will be taken by a strong emphasis on the distributive and boundary-exchange processes described above.

Quantitatively inclined public-organization theorists are likely to drift toward or at least read widely in welfare economics. Indeed it is possible to imagine these theorists executing a model or paradigm of social equity fully as robust as the economist's market model. With social equity elevated to the supreme objective, in much the way profit is treated in economics, model building is relatively simple. We might, for example, develop theories of equity maximization, long- and short-range equity, equity elasticity, and so on. The theory and research being reported in the journal *Public Choice* provides a glimpse of this probable development. This work is presently being done primarily by economists who are, in the main, attempting to develop variations on the market model or notions of individual-utility maximization. Public organization theorists with social-equity commitments could contribute greatly by the creation of models less fixed on market environments or individual-utility maximization and more on the equitable distribution of and access to both public and private goods by different groups or categories of people. If a full-blown equity model were developed it might be possible to assess rather precisely the likely outcomes of alternative policies in terms of whether the alternative does or does not enhance equity. Schemes for guaranteed annual income, negative income tax, Head Start, Job Corps, and the like could be evaluated in terms of their potential for equity maximization.

The less quantitatively but still behaviorally inclined public-organization theorists are likely to move in the direction of Kirkhart's "consociated model." They would move in the direction of sociology, anthropology, and psychology, particularly in their existential versions, while the quantitatively inclined will likely move toward economics, as described above. And, of course, many public-organization theorists will stay with the middle-range theories—role, group, communications, decisions, and the like—and not step under the roof of the grand theories such as the consociated model, the social-equity model, or the so-called systems model.

What does new Public Administration mean for the academy? One thing is starkly clear: We now know the gigantic difference between "public administration" and "the public service." The former is made up of public-management generalists and some auxiliary staff people (systems analysis, budgeting, personnel, and so on) while the latter is made up of the professionals who man the schools, the police, the courts, the military, welfare agencies, and so forth. Progressive Public Administration programs in the academy will build firm and permanent bridges to the professional schools where most public servants are trained. In some schools the notion of Public Administration as the "second profession" for publicly employed attorneys, teachers, welfare workers will become a reality.

Some Public Administration programs will likely get considerably more philosophic and normative while others will move more to quantitative management techniques. Both are needed and both will contribute.

The return of policy analysis is certain in both kinds of schools. Good management for its own sake is less and less important to today's student. Policy analysis, both logically and analytically "hard-nosed," will be the order of the day.

Academic Public Administration programs have not commonly been regarded as especially exciting. New public administration has an opportunity to change that. Programs that openly seek to attract and produce "change agents" or "short-haired radicals" are light years away from the POSDCORB image. And many of us are grateful for that.

12

The Minnowbrook Perspective and the Future of Public Affairs: Public Administration *Is* Public-Policy Making

W. Henry Lambright

Unless I completely misunderstood the drift of the discussion that took place at Minnowbrook, the overwhelming feeling on the part of those present was this: Public administrators are increasingly unable to manage change and universities are seemingly unable to prepare them so they can. The Minnowbrook meeting was quite unstructured so I may well be reading my own view into what happened. If so, I apologize to my colleagues, for this *is* my impression of the general state of Public Administration. At the root of the dilemma is the fact that few people in government or in the universities have a grasp of what Public Administration is. I believe it is something much more significant and creative than most seem to realize.

Public Administration is public-policy making. As such, it involves both politics and management, utilizes a multitude of disciplinary and professional perspectives, and constitutes a professional calling beyond the immediate specialty a man performs. Public Administration, as a concept, unites those who practice and those who teach and write about public-policy making. Paul Appleby called Public Administration "public leadership of public affairs directly responsible for executive action." He believed Public Administration and public-policy making were one, and declared, "If admission that this is true seems to exalt administration, it must be seen that the emphasis on politics subordinates the administrator, exalts the politicians, and thereby exalts the citizen."[1]

The politics-administration dichotomy is dead, but the ghost continues to haunt us, to narrow the vision of even those who take Public Administration seriously. Virtually everyone now admits that Public Administration exists in a political environment and that the administrator must interact with forces in that environment. The administrator is a participant in the political process, a politician in that he must engage in conflict resolution, exercise discretion, and make decisions affecting competing claims. At the same time, most will admit that Public Administration is not entirely politics; there are basic managerial functions relating to the utilization of men, money, and other resources to accomplish organizational purposes. But research has not developed a model that accounts for *both* these roles.[2] Those who emphasize the politics of Public Administration have gone one way and those who are interested in the managerial aspects have gone another. There is little communication between the two schools, and the consequences for Public Administration as practice and discipline have been unfortunate. Our scholarship and all too often our practice are bifurcated.

A public administrator who is not both manager and politician will fail as public-policy maker. He cannot spend all his time on the politics of a program or he will neglect to manage it effectively. He cannot devote himself only to its management, however, or he will soon find he has no program to administer. The failure of an executive to understand the necessity and virtue of his being both administrator and politician at once in order to be an effective public officer is at the heart of many of the critical problems facing bureaucracies (universities as well as governments) today.

[1]Paul H. Appleby, "Public Administration and Democracy," in Roscoe C. Martin (ed.), *Public Administration and Democracy: Essays in Honor of Paul H. Appleby* (Syracuse: Syracuse University Press, 1965), pp. 336–337, 339.

[2]See Dwight Waldo, "Scope of the Theory of Public Administration," in *Theory and Practice of Public Administration: Scope, Objectives, and Methods,* Monograph 8 in the series of the *Annals* of the American Academy of Political and Social Science, October 1968, pp. 1–26.

Policy Making without Administration

In no case is it more important for the public-policy maker to be a good administrator than in that of the President. Even at his level administration may seem unglamorous, but the capacity of the President to manage the federal government determines the fate of the nation. As Stephen K. Bailey has written:

The seriousness of this issue can hardly be overstated. In question is the capacity of an eighteenth century constitutional arrangement of widely diffused and shared powers and a nineteenth century system of political pluralism to deal effectively with twentieth century problems of technological, social, and economic interdependencies—at home and abroad.

Unless the President devotes substantial attention to making the system work—an effort involving persistence and the employment of high political skills—the consequences for the future of the American polity could be serious in the extreme.[3]

All too often this fusion of "managing" and "high political skills" is not understood or taken sufficiently seriously by the President. At his position the political dimensions of leadership tend to predominate. Indeed, the typical President is usually so busy initiating programs or putting out the latest foreign or domestic fire that he seldom has time to ask such managerial questions as those raised by Bailey:

How can the federal government identify, mobilize, train, and release the energy of the most impressive talent in the nation for developing and carrying out federal policy?

How can staff and line arrangements in the executive branch contribute to more rational and imaginative policy inputs to political decision making, and how can they contribute to more effective and coordinated policy implementation?[4]

The President as Chief Executive

Recent advances in budgeting techniques and various federal reorganizations may give the impression the President is up on his job. This is an illusion. The President is sadly deficient in his resources for deciding what to do, and in then carrying through

---

[3]Stephen K. Bailey, "Managing the Federal Government," in Kermit Gordon (ed.), *Agenda for the Nation* (Washington: Brookings, 1968), p. 301.
[4]*Ibid.,* p. 303.

on his decisions. With respect to policy analysis the President is highly dependent upon the departments and agencies theoretically responsive to him. Policy tends to seep upward, the consequence of a multitude of bureaucratic overtures and compromises. What may be good policy in terms of specialized interests of the agencies may not be good from the President's vantage point.

To be sure, it is possible that what an agency wants is what the President ought to want. But this is not necessarily so. More often than not, the presidential perspective is different since it takes into consideration a broader range of factors. Hopefully, it more closely approximates the needs of the nation. If it does not, the country is in trouble. The Office of President must, in our system, perform the role of countering special interests of agencies and their congressional and pressure-group allies by representing the general interests of the people as a whole. To the extent the President fails to do this, everyone—sooner or later—loses.

More assistance to the President, in terms of staff and outside advice, may lead to better policy decisions. But decisions need implementation. With respect to the operational side of government, academics have generally been indifferent, associating this most directly with that academic black sheep, "Public Administration." Presidents have had to be interested but they have been continually frustrated in their attempts to improve their policy-implementation capabilities.

William Carey, for many years a high-ranking Bureau of the Budget official, has commented that a President's "reach" and authority extend "no further than his Cabinet officers and a limited group of presidential appointees." Carey argues that it is extremely difficult for the President to transmit his perspectives and preferences to the men of upper and middle management, particularly in the field offices. Public-policy decisions thus fall apart as they move down the line of administration. A better presidential hold on policy execution is essential. Carey sees merit in the Chief of Staff function as performed for Eisenhower by Sherman Adams. "With all its exaggerated formalities," he declares, "the White House in the Eisenhower years came

closer to organizing for the scale of the presidential job than anything before or since."[5]

While the President must supply over-all direction to Public Administration, he cannot give it vitality and energy if the
resources are not available. Not just financial resources are involved. Most important in improving the work of government
are people, a fact often ignored—by Presidents and by those
who write about them.

What was true at the time of the President's Committee on
Administrative Management (Brownlow Committee) report in
1937 is true today: The President needs help. And nowhere is
this more the case than in the public-manpower field. In 1968,
during hearings on "Modernizing the Federal Government,"
Senator Abraham Ribicoff exclaimed:

> What worries me is that throughout many of these programs we are
> very shortsighted. We do not go for training programs; we do not de-
> velop the great skills that we need. We pass programs and say, "Go
> ahead and get 600 new trained people in this field."
>
> I think I recall Secretary Wirtz being before us in our cities' hear-
> ings and he said: If it was a question of a hundred million dollars for
> manpower programs and 20 competent skilled men, he would take the
> 20 competent skilled men and not the $100 million.
>
> So, one of the things we have—one of the difficulties of all our pro-
> grams—is that when the executive asks, the Congress votes substantial
> sums of money. When you cannot make them effective or administer
> them properly, this causes deep disillusion, because, while money is
> needed, you will never solve any problem by money alone. The answer
> lies in how that money is administered, how it is spent and how it is
> used.
>
> Now, to me, I think it is self-defeating for us to vote substantial
> sums of money if we cannot translate that money into action. Many
> people feel that once you get money you solve a problem. That is a very,
> very small percent.[6]

It is ironic but fitting that Ribicoff should cite Wirtz's comment. Here was Wirtz, who, as Secretary of Labor, was charged
with society's manpower-development programs. Yet he was
complaining about his *own* manpower problem. It points up the

[5]William D. Carey, "Presidential Staffing in the Sixties and Seventies,"
Public Administration Review (September-October 1969), pp. 450–458.

[6]United States Senate, Committee on Government Operations, Subcommittee on Executive Reorganization, *Hearings, Modernizing the Federal Government,* 91st Congress, 2nd Session, 1968, pp. 185–186.

idiocy of talking about rebuilding the nation's cities without strenuous efforts at the same time to find and train the personnel who will be charged with the rebuilding task. It is evidence of the bifurcation in public-policy making—of policy making without providing means to carry out the policy.

The President cannot afford to deal only with the politics of a problem. He must follow through concretely with its management. Undoubtedly his most intractable but important management need—the one that, more than money, is likely to bring many of his programs to grief in the future—is the shortage of skilled manpower. Leonard Lecht of the National Planning Association has calculated the number of workers needed to achieve a variety of national goals by 1975.[7] The publisher of *Science* has written that if Lecht is right "we can devote large sums to urban renewal, pollution abatement, improved education, better health, space, defense, and other goals, but there will not be enough workers to do everything desirable."[8] Unless and until the President gives this dilemma his time and energy his policy pronouncements will represent the symbols, not the realities, of action.

More than the nitty-gritty of personnel management is involved. Government's manpower needs reflect and influence those of the larger society. Manpower decisions involve jobs. Jobs are not just a policy means. In a nation where unemployment exists they are a policy goal. To make intelligent choices combining policy goals and manpower requirements, the President will need assistance of the highest quality. The existing machinery for advising the President is inadequate. It is time to look again at some of the proposals of the Brownlow Committee.

That Committee wished to enable the President to manage the government's manpower. The route it chose to achieve that objective was controversial, but probably the best one if real progress is to be made. The Brownlow Committee suggested abolishing the Civil Service Commission and transferring the responsibility for personnel management to a Personnel Director who—like the Director of the Bureau of the Budget—would be "the

---

[7]Leonard Lecht, *Manpower Needs for National Goals in the 1970's* (New York: Praeger, 1969).

[8]Dael Wolfle, "What Goals to Emphasize," *Science* (April 18, 1969), p. 249.

President's man." The idea was to transfer the safeguarding of the merit system to a Board with only advisory and investigatory powers. As Herbert Kaufman has noted, the Brownlow proposals aimed at returning

to the Chief Executive the personnel powers that were his in form, but in substance were actually wielded by a Civil Service Commission functioning, like other specialized agencies, with remarkable independence. A single officer, close to the President and the problems of the line agencies, would be more apt to interpret his mission in terms of program accomplishments, it was contended, than in terms of technical compliance with detailed regulations regardless of the effect on the program.[9]

The personnel recommendations got nowhere when first introduced, and would face tough sledding if resurrected today. All the "advances" in public-personnel management would be displayed by those opposed to change. Whatever the advances—and there has been progress—they have been far outdistanced by the growth and complexity of the public-manpower network.

The problems of managing regular public employees are heightened by the uncounted contract employees in corporations and universities across the country who are now dependent for their livelihood on government funds. This situation is not a minor matter. A considerable portion of very scarce scientific, engineering, and technical manpower has been employed directly or indirectly in military and space efforts for several years. When we make policy decisions, those decisions seldom stop at an agency's edge. In getting to the moon, for example, NASA spent 90 per cent of its funds outside government, coordinating the work of 20,000 industrial enterprises, 200 universities, 400,000 highly skilled men and women, and hundreds of leading scientists, engineers, and managers. As the NASA budget goes down, what happens to the extraordinary human capability that has been built up? Does it atrophy? Scatter? Can various specialized teams that are phased out by NASA be redeployed to other areas of public concern? Can any given *agency's* laboratory become more truly a *government* laboratory?

[9]Herbert Kaufman, "The Growth of the Federal Personnel System," in Wallace Sayre (ed.), *The Federal Government Service* (Englewood Cliffs, N.J.: Prentice-Hall, 1965), p. 64.

And what about all the problems caused by the multitude of intergovernmental programs? Each one presents a new manpower worry for the President multiplied by three levels of government. In short, any Personnel Director's responsibilities would have to be considerably broader than the Brownlow Committee might have imagined to even begin to approach the requirements of contemporary administrative management.

The President must consider ways to mobilize, train, and manage the manpower he needs to carry out public policy. Otherwise he will be doing far less than he should as the nation's Chief Executive. He must understand that government's role as an employer now extends beyond formal government to encompass the indirectly employed contractors and grantees. It reaches across agencies and through federal, state, and local jurisdictions. It entails cognizance of the young, the old, the black, and others (including women), whose talents could better be utilized in the public service. It looks to the future and thereby embraces manpower planning and educational policy.

"Some day," John Gardner has stated, "it will be recognized that skilled attention to the supply, quality, and development of the men and women who make up an organization is the most critically important factor in the effectiveness of the organization."[10] The federal government is the President's organization. And how he manages manpower in and through that organization affects the whole society. Attention to public human-resources needs in this broad sense must come from the White House. Elevating Personnel to the status now enjoyed by the Bureau of the Budget—giving it the necessary tools and authority—is the first step in giving *people* the managerial attention money now has.

Can State Manage Foreign Policy?

Next to the President's lack of attention to the human-resource dimensions of his job, possibly the most glaring and serious example of attempting to make policy without managing it is found in the State Department. The State Department stands first among the departments of the federal government but only in

[10]John Gardner, "The Luckiest People," *Good Government* (Fall 1967), p. 4.

theory and protocol. There is no area of public policy as important as foreign policy, but in the view of many close observers, none is so badly administered. One fundamental reason for this is simply that State Department personnel—particularly foreign-service officers—think they are "above" administration. In 1962 the Herter Report put it succinctly:

> The Department of State has concentrated primarily on formulating and coordinating foreign policy. It has not developed adequately either the attitudes or the machinery needed to relate policies to the operations required to carry them out. This is true both with respect to the Department's role in the Executive Branch as a whole, and with respect to its own internal activities. The traditional concept of the Foreign Service diplomat has not fostered what might be called a "programming sense." There has been some disposition, reflected in organizational shifts in the not too distant past, to divorce the Department from "operations" so that it could engage exclusively in policy matters. Such a divorce, never consistently sought or fully effected, is clearly not feasible in today's context.
>
> The Committee is convinced that the Department's capacity to assist the President in coordinating the programs and operations of the entire Federal Government in the field of foreign affairs must be strengthened. *Likewise, the tendency within the Department to view what is called "administration" as separate, subordinate and of little relevance to the foreign policy function, must be corrected.* [Emphasis added.][11]

It is well known that President Kennedy was greatly disappointed in the capacity of the State Department to manage itself, much less guide the foreign policies of other agencies. He called it a "bowl of jelly." If the State Department has, as many believe, become less and less central to the foreign-policy machinery of the United States, at least part of the reason may lie in the incapacity of its most powerful unit—the Foreign Service—to view its generalist role *broadly* enough to include that of administration.

Policy Making without Politics

If the President and State Department invariably, but for different reasons, tend to give too little time to the administrative side of public-policy making, there are numerous other places in

---

[11]*Personnel for the New Diplomacy: Report of the Committee on Foreign Affairs Personnel* [The Herter Report] (Washington: Carnegie Endowment for International Peace, 1962), p. 10.

government—federal, state, and local—where the reverse seems more the norm. In such cases administrators appear to be rigid, unable to innovate, more interested in the techniques of their work than the needs of their clients. This may be quite a serious problem at the local level where government often presents its worst image in the form of seemingly insensitive bureaucrats. The capacity of public executives in urban areas to adapt policies to changing needs is particularly critical at this point in history. There were times at Minnowbrook when some participants, discussing this problem, came as close to being "antiadministration" as some New Left students. Politicizing administration through the device of client participation or confrontation techniques might make public organizations more responsive to change. It might also destroy them if carried too far. Somehow the basic work of the organization still has to get done. The service, whether providing social-welfare checks or educating children, has to be performed. Administration in a democracy need not be "efficient," but it should be effective. Needed is balance between the managerial and political roles of the public administrator at all levels of government. But even more than managerial-political techniques are essential if good policy making by public executives is our goal.

Politics and Administration—and Values

What is needed is a sense of the public interest. An administrator's values are crucial. Public Administration in a democracy, Appleby emphasized, should be guided by a sense of purpose. Public Administration should "respect and contribute to the dignity, the worth, and the potentialities of the citizen."[12] There was great stress on values at Minnowbrook. Some asked, "What if a society became repressive? What then? Should the administrator down the line obey orders? Should he be guided by his own values?" This question came up again and again during the discussions. Most of the time the answer was that the administrator should follow his own conscience. Much less dramatic, though difficult, ethical questions were raised. It was recognized that a public administrator's values inevitably entered into his

[12]Appleby, *op. cit.*, p. 337.

decisions. Given the political nature of his role, how could they not? Some practitioners wanted to know if those in universities could suggest ethical criteria or standards to help them make decisions. The academics had little to say on this point, but there obviously must be a better response than "Do your own thing." Professors of Public Administration will have to try harder.

Divisions of the university other than Public Administration programs or public-affairs schools are apparently already going a long way toward shaping criteria by which administrators decide the public interest. Frederick Mosher has documented the degree to which we are becoming an increasingly specialized, professionalized society. Our governments directly employ over one-third of all the professionals working in the United States. This is three times as many as private organizations employ, and the government hires a good many more via grant and contract. Many of these directly and indirectly employed professionals are in high positions and exert considerable influence over significant areas of public policy. Most of them have graduated from professional schools other than those of public affairs. Many have never taken a course called Public Administration and some probably do not even admit to being public administrators. Like foreign-service officers, they see themselves as oriented toward substantive rather than managerial concerns. In eschewing their roles as public administrators they fail as public servants. In proclaiming professional values as guides to executive action they are unsuccessful even in what they regard as substantive decision making.

Professional training that is deep but narrow inevitably prejudices the way such specialists approach public-policy questions. To be truly effective public executives, professionals must come to understand their own biases. They must come to see public-policy making in all its complexity. They must come to understand that to be a public administrator is to be *more* than a doctor, or lawyer, or scientist who happens to work for government. How? Mosher looks to the universities for help. He says:

Almost all of our future public administrators will be college graduates, and within two or three decades a majority of them will have graduate degrees. Rising proportions of public administrators are returning to graduate schools for refresher courses, mid-career training, and higher degrees. These trends suggest that university faculties will have growing responsibility for preparing and for developing public servants both in their technical specialties and in the broader social fields with which their professions interact.

He concludes his book by remarking, "The universities offer the best hope for making the professions safe for democracy."[13] As I indicated at the beginning of this essay, however, there were many at Minnowbrook—myself included—who were dissatisfied with the capacity of universities to "educate for the public service." Of course, it is easy to be dissatisfied. It is more difficult to do better. The educational challenge is worth the effort, however.

Education for Public-Policy Making

We can teach a man some rudimentary management techniques; we can give him an understanding of the political process and how the public executive fits in; we can, through case studies and various simulation exercises, give him vicarious experience with some of the ethical dilemmas public administrators face in interpreting the public interest. We can do all that and do very little in terms of educating for public service. We know that those formally educated in Master of Public Administration programs constitute but a small fraction of public executives. Education for the public service presently amounts to education for the staff functions; education for the professions produces public executives as intellectual "fallout" from education for other purposes. Such executives, as Mosher has suggested, leave much to be desired.

From the point of view of preparing public-policy makers, neither kind of education is good enough as it stands. The "Honey Report" has supplied some ideas on where to go from here.[14] I agree with most of what Honey says, but feel he should have said more. His document is too conservative. If Public Administration is public-policy making, then we in the universities ought

[13]Frederick C. Mosher, *Democracy and the Public Service* (New York: Oxford, 1968), p. 219.

[14]John C. Honey, "A Report: Higher Education for Public Service," *Public Administration Review* (November 1967).

to give it the attention it deserves. The significance of the task demands university-wide attention, because neither schools of Public Administration nor other professional schools by themselves have the resources needed for the task. A university is organized by discipline and professional specialty. Public policy is a blend of many disciplines and professional perspectives. An education that produces a good political scientist, for example, may not suffice for a practicing public administrator. What public administrators need is an educational program that unites knowledge for action rather than subdividing it for research. One can envision a master's or doctoral program in Health and Public Policy, for example. A student in such a program might take courses in the School of Public Health or in a medical school, intern as an administrator at the National Institutes of Health, and write a master's thesis or dissertation dealing with specific policy issues and policy alternatives rather than a discipline-based subject. He would be encouraged to think realistically but futuristically. He would have to learn early to anticipate the next crisis. Our aim would be to produce a man who can manage change.

This suggestion is not meant to cast aspersions on the research doctorate. I am completely in favor of the disciplines becoming more and more rigorous, even if that rigor frequently makes them more isolated from what many will consider relevant social issues. I am opposed to politicizing the university and organizing it for social action. The more scientific the social sciences become, for example, the more potentially *useful* they become—*if* there is someone to *translate* them into the language of action. The university can be true to its own historic and unique functions as well as to its broader and very real social responsibilities only if it can do a better job of educating such translators. The public administrator of the future must be able to understand social science (and some natural science and technology), to be able to *use* the knowledge that is available, and, above all, know enough to ask the right questions.[15]

[15]James Carroll, "Science and the City: The Question of Authority," *Science* (February 28, 1969), pp. 907–908, suggests that dealing with the problems of the city will require the development of a social technology—"a method of organizing fiscal, legal, architectural, planning, managerial and technological expertise."

To do its job the university must give as much thought to producing public administrators as it does to producing professors, doctors, lawyers, or other professionals. There is room in the university for a number of career "tracks": for the research scholar, for the "regular" professional, and for the kind of public administrator I have proposed. The latter will be the most difficult to train because he must, by definition, be able to think in policy-relevant terms, and that means synthesizing knowledge, pulling together the basic research ideas from different parts of the academic setting and applying them to his policy area. Such a man, once in government, could serve as the link society so badly needs between the world of knowledge and that of power.

The Government against Itself

Would it make any difference if the university as an institution took education for the public service seriously? Would public employers know how to use talent thus produced? As my earlier argument with respect to public policy and personnel indicates, I suspect the answer is "No." Government at all levels has done precious little to find better ways to identify, train, develop, and use talent. There are exceptions in the case of some federal agencies. But generally the lack of a presidential perspective on government manpower requirements has so limited the status and vision of the personnel function as to render such attempts few and far between. All the university's efforts to produce better public executives may well be neutralized by the government's own "antileadership vaccine."[16]

It is essential that government rethink, redefine, and ultimately restructure existing public-personnel systems. It is equally imperative that the university reform its education for the public service. Government and the university must work more closely to bring about the necessary reforms. They have a common interest at stake. Never before has it been so true that the fate of us all depends on the quality of our public-policy making. And public-policy making *is* Public Administration.

[16]For a broad view of how society generally immunizes young people against tendencies to leadership, see Chapter XXII, "Leadership," in Helen Rowen, *John W. Gardner: No Easy Victories* (New York: Harper, 1968).

13

The Minnowbrook Perspective and the Future of Public Administration Education

Frank Marini

To attempt to finely define what we have called "the Minnowbrook perspective" or even to describe the rough configurations of that perspective is, as the reader realizes by now, not an easy task.[1] Yet the themes and concerns which were uncovered and discussed in the earlier chapters of this volume constitute, to a certain extent, a mutually supportive complex and in some sense one can see a coherence emergent if not established. The clearest way to catch sight of the distinguishing marks of the Minnowbrook perspective is probably to juxtapose it with conventional Public Administration as reflected in our traditional and educational literature and institutions. This comparison is probably what leads to the appellation "new Public Administration." A minute example of such juxtaposition may help: From the perspective of Minnowbrook, it is unlikely that Gulick's question —"What is [read also "should be"] the work of the chief executive? What does he [read also "should he"] do?"—would be answered as it was by Gulick. Whatever the answer may be from the Minnowbrook perspective—and this, I believe, is less than finally evolved—it is much more than POSDCORB.[2]

[1]Portions of this chapter are drawn from remarks I made in the Maxwell Forum Series at Syracuse University in October, 1969 (printed in *The Maxwell Review*, Spring, 1970) and at a NASA/OUA meeting December 11, 1969 in Washington, D.C. I wish to thank the NASA/Syracuse Project and the National Aeronautics and Space Administration for encouragement and sustenance while I tried to think about new directions in Public Administration by discussing the subject with colleagues around the country. Personal thanks are due to Dwight Waldo, George Frederickson, and Frank McGee, who function always as my colleagues and teachers.

[2]POSDCORB, of course, refers to Planning, Organizing, Staffing, Directing,

I anticipate that some readers of this volume respond to the question implied in the first chapter with one or another form of "No": They will feel that the concerns and themes of this volume are not new; that they are as a matter of fact those of "old Public Administration." With reference once more to the example above, they will think that probably Gulick—and certainly they—knew that there was much more than POSDCORB involved, and that as a matter of fact they saw Public Administration pretty much as Minnowbrook participants seem to have seen it.[3] Whatever the attitude of others may be, I am not against cross-generational cooperation, and so I say "Well and good; glad to hear it!" But I cannot forebear pointing out that our educational literature, institutions, and socialization do not indicate this happy state of affairs.

It is about one aspect of this unhappy and unprofitable incongruence between what some call "new Public Administration" and the typical educational presence of Public Administration that I wish to speak.[4] My main topic is the professional and educational consequences of trends and directions in Public Administration. Many of these trends are new or have new aspects; thus in a sense there is a "new Public Administration brewing," and the chapters in this volume are but a part and a glimpse of it. But that "brewing" will never culminate in full richness unless Public Administration education is based upon a recognition of it. I will speak then about "beyond Minnowbrook," but first I will attempt to identify some aspects of the

---

Coordinating, Reporting, Budgeting. Gulick's questions and answer [from p. 13 of Luther Gulick and L. Urwick (eds.), *Papers on the Science of Administration* (New York: Institute of Public Administration, 1937)] was: "'What is the work of the chief executive? What does he do?' The answer is POSDCORB."

[3]There is some evidence (however "impure" and inconclusive) that the opinions of Minnowbrook participants on many presumed "generational" questions were not greatly dissimilar from those of a random sample of the membership of the American Society for Public Administration, and that age was in most cases not a key variable. See H. George Frederickson and Frank Marini, "Is the 'Minnowbrook Perspective' Representative?" (unpublished paper presented at the Annual Conference of the American Society for Public Administration in Miami, Florida, May 19–21, 1969).

[4]"Typical" does not, of course, mean "universal." I realize that there are enlightened institutions—both educational and "practicing"—about. (Indeed, I work in one.)

Minnowbrook perspective which seem to me to have critical import for the future of Public Administration education.

The Minnowbrook Perspective

Views may appropriately differ as to the essence of the Minnowbrook Conference. Some will feel that certain of the chapters in this volume, for example, are more important or more central to "new Public Administration" than others. I will concentrate here on those aspects of the Minnowbrook papers and Minnowbrook discussions which seem to me most directly related to the future of Public Administration education.

Toward a "Relevant" Public Administration

Several of the subthemes which developed under the general demand for a more relevant Public Administration could have been anticipated.

"Relevance to our 'Turbulent Times,'" for example—though it means different things in different discussions—can today surprise only by its absence. Thus, that discussions focused upon decentralization, organizational devolution, participatory concepts, and so on was not surprising in terms of the world in which we live (though some would hold that it was surprising in view of our literature, professional conferences, training, and usual professional concerns).

Similarly, the demand for "relevance to *our* problems" which appeared in suggestions that comparative Public Administration devote more of its attention to comparison of Public Administration *within* the United States is not surprising. Several pleas were made for comparative urban administration, for regional comparison of administration, for comparison of similar and dissimilar organizational units, and so on. Some will read this as "neoisolationism," others as a newfound desire to be relevant to problems of our society, and still others as a function of fluctuations in funding proclivities of the government and foundations. It should be noted that not every Minnowbrook participant was anxious to abandon past directions in comparative Public Administration, but even the defense of past theoretical and cross-national comparisons was usually cast in terms of their relevance to the problems and possibilities of *our* society.

Relevance to "the practitioner" was another prominent subtheme. Although there was a widespread sentiment that scholars and practitioners alike should resist defining their work in traditional "organizational-loyalty" terms and "nuts-and-bolts" terms, there was also great desire to relate to the real problems of the real administrative world. Developments such as PPB were defended as facilitating decentralized and participatory management and as significant levers for change, but they were also castigated for being simplifications that were not of much help to public administrators.

The insistence that Public Administration should recover relevance was embedded in arguments quite critical of the contemporary state of the academic literature of Public Administration, quite firm in insistence upon normative introspection, and openly wed to the consideration of fundamental values as well as factual or analytical premises. Even when the topic was empirical theory, there was a return to a concern with social relevance: The answer to the question "Knowledge for what?" Kronenberg concluded, "would seem to be that we *must* use our science and apply our talents for the improvement of the human conditions." This conclusion is, of course, quite similar to those reached in other Minnowbrook discussions, and is expressed in practically the same language as La Porte's.

Postpositivism

"A break from the recent emphasis on value-free or value-neutral empirical research," which for Bob Zimring is a principal definitional element of "new Public Administration," can be read as a declaration of independence from, if not antipathy toward, positivistic philosophical orientations. The integral relationship between this attitude and the "social-relevance" theme (or what Frederickson, in his essay, calls "social equity") is clear; indeed the sentence from which the above statement was quoted continues: "and a desire to make the academic study of the social universe directly concerned with questions of social justice." Zimring's belief that new Public Administration "implies that social scientists will make value judgments in their professional capacities"—although it did not meet with unanimous support at Minnowbrook—is related in obvious ways to the arguments of La Porte, Kronenberg, and Frederickson as well as to the agenda which Peter Savage recommended for the small-group discussions. And one of the ways Zimring suggests the necessary "new logic of inquiry" could be developed—by utilizing techniques such as Thomas Thorson's—is also suggested and attempted to a degree by Harmon.

As Larry Kirkhart traces out recent developments in the social sciences and their relationship to Public Administration, some of the characteristics which lead some to speak of postpositivism become clear. The impact of humanistic psychology, existentialism, phenomenology, and so on—when joined with the feeling that recent social-science orientations have not been "relevant" and other methodological developments such as the interest in unobtrusive measures—may bring about a major reorientation of epistemology and research and education philosophy.

Adapting to Turbulence in the Environment

Several of the Minnowbrook papers and much of the discussion centered upon the rapidly changing environment of Public Administration and the capacity of the discipline, public organizations, and public administrators to adapt to environmental turbulence. Several of the papers had called attention to what Biller called "bizarre and unexpected anomalies," and found, with him, that our knowledge is called into question by the growing complexity and interdependency of our society. Biller's warning—"By simply doing what we know how to do in a period where that makes increasingly less sense, we continue to pave the way for either languishment in irrelevance or greater contribution to the compounding rather than the solving of problems"—reinforces the plea for relevance. Much of the discussion at Minnowbrook and in this volume assumes that Public Administration must abandon its hold upon procedures and theories derived from earlier essentially stable periods and must concentrate upon creating theories and public units appropriate for turbulent environments.

In his discussion, Orion White suggested that confrontation is a possible adaptive process. Confrontation and participatory procedures were discussed as possible techniques of adaptation both in terms of internal organizational processes (that is, self-actualizing, open, honest behavior within the organization) and in terms of client-organizational interaction (openness and honesty toward clients and widespread client participation). Both optimism and caution were manifest in discussions of confrontation; the discussion touched upon the sorts of dangers which Friedland and Crenson had suggested, and attention was called to the danger that confrontation could result in catastrophic collapse or some massive repression used to simplify the situation. The positive side of the argument tended to stress cautious confrontation, the educative effects of participation (what Crenson referred to as the character-building quality of participation), and the development of a tolerance for turbulence.

New Organizational Forms

Confrontational administration and client-focused bureaucracies—both concepts grew out of discussions of relevance, confrontation, and turbulence—assume and urge significant changes in organizational forms. So too does the idea of the self-actualizing and proactive administrator discussed in Harmon's paper on normative theory. In his attempt to make his way toward a theory of Public Administration by concentrating upon the reform of our essentially Weberian organization theories, Larry Kirkhart offered a "consociated model" of organization. Kirkhart's consociated model of organization fits so closely with the ideas of La Porte, White, and Biller on relevance, participation, confrontation, and value involvement on the one hand, and Michael Harmon's notions of the function and role of the individual administrator on the other, that the sense of unity of perspective seems uncanny.

Although there was a widespread antihierarchical sentiment at Minnowbrook—and this is reflected in several of the chapters in this volume—not all participants were convinced a consociated model would work. Indeed, in a report of his small group's discussion, one participant asserted in obvious frustration, "I thought it was an excellent example of why the consociated model doesn't work." Some participants took a different tack, however, and asserted a faith that the consociated model could be found in "the real world," while others thought "the real world" at best an unaccommodating host. Kirkhart put the consociated model forward not as *the* alternative to bureaucracy but as perhaps *one* alternative, and there was probably greater agreement at Minnowbrook that alternatives to bureaucratic organizational forms were needed than that the consociated model was the best practicable alternative. It should also be noted, however, that the consociated model seems a quite appropriate concept for gathering together and organizing many of the chief analyses and recommendations of other Minnowbrook papers.

Related to the support for new organizational forms is the espousal of a different mode of behavior for administrators. Some ways in which the behavior of administrators is assumed to need change are implied in the call for confrontational administration, consociated organizations, and client-focused organizations. But there was also a variety of arguments which urged a more proactive posture for public administrators generally. A considerable concern for personal morality and organizational integrity in public organizations was a thread which wove its way through many Minnowbrook discussions.

Client-Focused Organizations

A topic of considerable interest to Minnowbrook participants was client-organization interaction. Orion White introduced the question of the relationship of bureaucracies to their clients as an important theme, as did Robert Biller. Various subthemes of this concern were pursued in the Minnowbrook discussions. Some held that a sort of goal displacement was typical of public organizations, with the perpetuation of the organization assuming a more important position than performing the client-oriented functions for which many public organizations had been created. A variation on this notion was that structures and typical behavioral patterns were established for the implementation of policy without sufficient recognition that the structure and typical behavior are themselves an aspect of policy. There was considerable support for the argument that there must be a greater emphasis upon client loyalty and program loyalty than there has been in the past.

Summary

The themes and concerns which were developed at the Minnowbrook conference have come to be commonly referred to in

Public Administration circles as "the Minnowbrook perspective," "the young Public Administration movement," "new Public Administration," and similar terms. The chapters in this volume constitute a rich complex of ideas and concerns, and for the time being some people will choose to emphasize certain of them while other people choose others. The result is that the existence or configurations of new Public Administration will mean different things to different people. I have emphasized the aspects of the Minnowbrook perspective which seem to me most important for the future of Public Administration education under the following headings: Toward a "Relevant" Public Administration, Postpositivism, Adapting to Turbulence in the Environment, New Organizational Forms, and Client-Focused Organizations. I turn now to the implications of such a perspective for present and future education in and for Public Administration.

Educational Implications of "New Public Administration"

"New Public Administration" obviously calls for a close linkage of research, teaching, and the practice of government with the troubles and changes of our society. This statement seems to describe an obvious and old approach. Yet, it is somewhat harder to build this close linkage in many of our present schools than might at first be apparent. I will speak briefly about three types of evolving schools before I turn my attention to the optimal school and to the Public Administration of the future.

The Main Types of Public Administration Schools

The important new schools can conveniently be classified under three main headings: schools of administrative science, schools of public-policy analysis, and a blend of the two. *Schools of administrative science* are frequently generic schools by label and business schools with a management-science bias in reality. They are usually heavily oriented toward quantification, computer technology, modeling, and systems designs. In this sense, they are a blend of computerized Taylorism and simulation of rational processes for planning and problem solving. They get support with relative ease. When oriented toward the business firm, their technology and even their results are immediately

applicable to the problems of firms and hence they are supported in the way that business schools are always supported.
Moreover, they create—almost as a "spin-off"—a steady flow
of students who, for many reasons, quickly acquire influence in
large firms and who in turn support the movement toward management science and their old schools. Finally, such schools are
easy for government agencies to support: first, because their
endeavors and products look useful to the movement's members
on the line in the agencies; second, because they look new and
"sciency"; and third, because their products and activities are
sufficiently esoteric to be relatively politically "safe."

These schools and the endeavors here associated with them
are creating a management technology of considerable utility
for certain kinds of problems. But management science, ironi-
cally enough, is limited in the same way that scientific management was. Its utility increases as the programmed nature of its
problems and the predictability of its environment increases.
Its utility increases as efficiency (especially as expressed in
units of economy) increasingly becomes the dominant goal. Its
utility is increased as the problem is moved toward the "attainment of consensual goals" and away from the "deciding between
conflictual goals" or the "inventing-of-goals" end of the continuum. In short, as the problem becomes one of implementation (especially very complex implementation) and economy
(of some sort), this kind of school begins to shine. But if the view
presented in this volume of our society and the demands upon
Public Administration in these times is anywhere near accurate,
these limitations are critical. Still, many of the tasks which public and private administrators face can be eased by the technology of management science. The balanced position of Public
Administration with regard to such technology and perspectives
will be the same as its sensible reactions to budgeting techniques, organization and management, or PPB: It is a helpful
thing for administrators to have, but it is nowhere near the
entirety of Public Administration.

The schools of public-policy analysis which are springing up
will probably be social-science oriented, economics dominated.
The movement in support of these schools is a reaction to public problems. Such schools will reintroduce norms and values
in terms of open prescriptive advice hinged to careful measure-

ment, futurism, sophisticated cost-benefit analyses; they will emphasize the estimation of effects, side-effects, and the like throughout the system. They will give implementation consultation, midpath assessment, and so on. They will not train administrators except insofar as training others to do the same kind of analysis is appropriate training. That is, they will train "public policy analysts" (for which there is a substantial need).

A blend of these two types of schools will most likely occur when quantifiers predominate at a public policy analysis school. The combination will *pretend* to exist in cases where management science schools see support or some other incentive for studying "a public agency" or "a public problem." In this case, however, the management science school's treatment of the agency or problem can make significant contributions chiefly when the agency or problem is in important respects like a business firm or business problem. It will not be very helpful where the agency or problem is, in important respects, "public" or "turbulent" because the perspective and methodology will "privatize" it as a convenience to analysis.

The Optimal Future State of Public Administration

The optimal school of the future will, in some ways, also be a blend of management science and public-policy analysis. Let me suggest some dimensions of my conception of such a school by discussing the optimal future state of Public Administration, the type of school this calls for, and the curricula of the future.

For healthy survival, Public Administration will need to accept more and more an action orientation to public problems. It must become increasingly involved in the policy-formulation and policy-analysis sides of the enterprise. Public Administration must become more developmental and "change-agent" oriented; it will become more critical of existing circumstances (but funding arrangements, "kinship" ties, and other factors will militate against *much* more criticism). Because Public Administration will be more problem oriented, it will become more interdisciplinary or multidisciplinary. It will co-opt clients and extraorganizational concerns into its realm. Public Administration will more frankly, more enthusiastically, and with more fanfare emphasize its education for the public-service aspect (but will argue that research and teaching are related to this—which will not hurt the research if education is broadly defined, as it must be). Public Administration will be a research, training, problem-solving focus which attracts people from a diversity of backgrounds whose corporate identity will rest less in what sort of department gave them their working papers than in what kinds of things they are interested in doing and can do.

Consequences will also be in the realm of value orientation; not that the new Public Administrators will necessarily have new or "better" values than their predecessors (although they may), but they will see the questions of their values as more directly connected to their expertise, talents, and jobs than their predecessors did. Like many things, this new consciousness is a mixed bag. Much good and much evil can come from such a situation. And it has the potential for arrogant fanaticism if the values and circumstances are not continually scrutinized.

Other changes are implied for "organizational loyalty": Frequently this will take second or lesser place to "program loyalty," "client loyalty," and the like. Changes are also implied for merit systems, for political actions of administrators, and so on. Here, too, there are substantial dangers.

Public Administration will develop a prescriptive-critical-therapeutic relationship in its analysis which will be something like the best rhetoric (and maybe the best reality) of development administration. However, it will recognize development as a continuing enterprise rather than as a matter of economic modernization and will recognize the United States as a developing country. Public Administration will become more comparative (especially intraculturally) and more empirical (in the sense in which "empirical" connotes "understanding observable reality," not in the sense which seems to mean "methodologically sophisticated," "model oriented," "quantifiable," or "grand theoretical"). As my colleague George Frederickson has noted, social equity will become an essential concern. That is, Public Administration will devote more time to contemplating the question of legitimacy and legitimation.

Important changes are implied with reference to the relationship between the social sciences and Public Administration. Public Administration, in important respects, has been, at its best, the applied arm of the social sciences and will become even more so. The kind of thing I get to pretty quickly when I try to figure out what Public Administration is and ought to be is this: "Public Administration is the application of knowledge to problem solving in the public sector." The nature of the case is that much of the knowledge and the process of knowledge seeking that is relevant is encompassed in common definitions of social science.

The Optimal Future School of Public Administration

In the future, Public Administration will more likely be a department, program, or school rather than a part of political science or other traditional disciplines. Public Administration will of necessity develop mechanisms and institutional arrangements to become interdisciplinary or multidisciplinary while selecting relevant interests. Public Administration will be broadly "educational" rather than narrowly "training" because of the complexities of the aspects of value criticism, purpose formulation, and action orientation alluded to earlier. Public Administration will integrate research more closely with education and consulting/practicing. It will devote more attention to midcareer and on-the-job-training types of education, but will find mechanisms to prevent them from being the mockery they frequently are. Public Administration will more broadly define its interests at the same time that it becomes less hung up about its disciplinary identity and will thus relate more closely with the administration of social work, education, police, the military, public health, and so on. Public Administration will deal with its relationships to its old foes—law and business administration—more intelligently while it is dealing with its old disciplinary base—political science—more intelligently. In the process, it will neither capitulate to business administration in the form of a generic school where Public Administration is under the foot of the table (even if the falling crumbs are large), nor insist that there are no similarities or possibilities for fruitful cooperation between business and Public Administration. As a consequence of many of the things I have said above— but also because of (1) the increased government interest in the funding of education for the public service, (2) increased consciousness of the importance of public service to the public and students, (3) increased funding from private sources, and (4) great demands for teachers in the departments and schools of Public Administration which will develop—Public Administration will offer research, course work, and practical experience at every level of higher education from the B.A. to the Ph.D. and into continuing and "nonschool" education processes.

The Public Administration school of the future will either have its own department with its own faculty and thus hire Ph.D.'s in Public Administration, and in other respects become a "discipline," or it will be more like an important interest-group aggregation to which people come with diverse but valuable backgrounds and abilities. Most likely, its research and training faculty will consist mostly of individuals who hold joint appointments with traditional departments, such as is sometimes the case with research and teaching-interest aggregates such as survey-research centers, law schools, and hospitals. In this case, the school or department of Public Administration will need to have some people who hold appointments solely in the unit. Because of the practice connection, the necessity for interdisciplinarity, and the necessary research component, I think the most evocative model is that offered by Dwight Waldo in his suggestion that Public Administration be modeled on medical educational and research institutions.[5] Thus, you would have a school whose social purpose and linkage to activities in the real world were obvious. You would be able to hire and utilize a diversity of research, practical, and educational people and arrangements. You would be better able to think about the internship dimension. There are some problems. The transitional problems of financing and prestige will be substantial in the beginning, especially at schools without strong reputations in Public Affairs and Public Administration. If government funding develops as I anticipate, the transition will be eased somewhat.

The Optimal Future Curricula of Public Administration

The optimal future school of Public Administration will have to link itself in appropriate ways to a variety of other units and

---

[5]Dwight Waldo, "Administrative State Revisited," *Public Administration Review* (March, 1965), pp. 5–30.

foci in the university without losing the consciousness of what Public Administration means. I would like to discuss this inter-relationship under the few headings which seem to me to define the main elements of the curricula of the future.

Core Offering

On the matter of a "Public Administration core," I think the "old" Public Administration was not wrong—though it was somewhat limited (for many reasons, some of which are quite understandable)—when it thought of education for Public Administration in terms of administrative structures, institutions, processes, and POSDCORB. There *is* such a thing as Public Administration. It has as much identity and coherence as many disciplines whose identity is unquestioned in the university setting. We must not, in the search for relevance and innovation, abandon or forget the fact that we have a core of interests, knowledge, and literature which constitutes something not significantly more amorphous than most "disciplines." We must not set up generic schools or public policy schools if it means denying that Public Administration in its past concerns has been talking about important things in important ways. The optimal school of the future will have a core offering which gives it identity. All students will be thoroughly and well introduced to what we know about the enterprise and study called Public Administration. This core, however, if it is to be built sensibly, must be built eclectically. We need psychology, sociology, his-tory, statistics, mathematics, economics, philosophy, political science, and many other components. We must not be so en-slaved by jealousy (and its mother, insecurity) to insist that only people whose degrees or majors were in Public Administration have something to contribute. On the other hand, we must not be easy marks for every huckster who has fancy equipment and fashionable patter: we must allow the best of contributions (whatever the source) to be brought to Public Administration, but we must insist that they be related to Public Administration.

The distinction I am trying to draw here is one that I try to draw frequently with regard to the question of "methodology" in political science. Methods and tools of intellectual endeavors seem to me to be most intelligently treated as just that: methods and tools. Think analogically about tools for a moment. I consider that there are great advantages in having, say, a brandnew power saw. And I can understand an inclination of the possessor of such a new tool to wander about the house "looking for things to saw." But if the kitchen sink began leaking, the person who says, "I'd better see what tools I have that will help me fix this," or "I'd better check with my neighbors to see who knows something about sinks or who has the tools to help with this sink," is in much better shape than the person who is wandering around with his power saw and who doesn't see the sink since he can't saw it. We need, for example, systems analysts, those skilled in quantitative techniques of analysis, model builders, philosophers, psychologists, and a variety of other skilled scholars, teachers, and craftsmen; but regardless of the impressive sophistication of their particular skills we must insist that they be interested in the problems and opportunities of Public Administration. We need to be eclectic, we need to be up to date, but not less than we need to be relevant to the problems of our polity and to the individuals, public entities, and processes which must grapple with these problems.

What this attitude toward the field will mean for the traditional courses and subfields of Public Administration is not as clear; nevertheless these implications are obviously important. Some of them are already apparent. Public Administration must not only give attention to all of its traditional concerns, it must also take account of a much broader range than is frequently encompassed in such courses and subfield definitions. It must take account not only of the public policy implications of public employment and public-employment processes with regard to minority-group employment, collective bargaining, political rights of public employees, and the like. It must also pay as much attention to the personal and organizational development of public employees. Organizational development, personal fulfillment on the job, the necessary prerequisites and facilitations for creativity, "morale" perceived as something more important than a good investment in terms of increased output, and so on must be as important considerations as job classifications and pay scales. Organization and management courses must concentrate as much on new organizational forms, matrix management, nonhierarchical cooperative structures, and other nonbureaucratic forms and procedures, as upon PERT and other techniques. In the area of public budgeting, much work can be done which is more in keeping with the promises usually extended by proponents of PPB than by the gimmicks usually delivered in practice. Many more things could be said about the core of Public Administration, but the chief point I want to make is already clear: We must have a core, we must have an identifiable "Public Administration" in our Public Administration curricula, but that core must be up to date, alive, problem oriented (and especially oriented to "larger" and "longer-range" problems), and relevant; we cannot settle any longer for traditional folklore enclosed in a veneer of new gadgetry.

Elective Emphases

In addition to a core of typical processes, typical institutional arrangements, and so on, Public Administration has other interests. The obvious importance of these other interests and our typically inadequate emphasis upon them is what has led to the public policy analysis movement. The curriculum of the future must have ample flexibility for the student of Public Administration to add to his core knowledge an understanding of one or more of the so-called "substantive" areas of Public Administration. In other words, the student must be not only thoroughly educated in those things administrative, but also introduced at least to those areas of "action and things administered" in which he is actually or potentially interested. I think here of the M.P.A. student being able to build a few courses over and above his core courses in an area such as metropolitan problems, public health, the administration of education, the administration of social welfare, or police administration. Similarly, there should be opportunities for the typical Ph.D. candidate in Public Administration to build a deep and wide knowledge of one or more of these public policy areas. Let me hasten to add that since the future Public Administration schools will see one of their responsibilities as training faculty members for the growing departments and schools of Public Administration as well as the training of analysts and administrators, it may be that some Ph.D.-level students would rather emphasize a subfield of Public Administration (for example, personnel administration, finance administration, and the like) rather than a public-policy area. As long as the school has the facilities to provide such in-depth subfield training, I see no reason why it should not be encouraged.

At first glance, the necessity to provide substantial public policy problem electives and substantial multidisciplinary emphases in the curriculum might seem to be quite a burden and responsibility. It is a considerable responsibility, but less of a burden if one sees the Public Administration school as appropriately utilizing the diverse facilities of the larger university. The healthy Public Administration school of the future, I believe, will forge strong links of cooperation with the other professional schools and units of the university. Thus the school of Public Administration, in dealing with a student who has a considerable interest in the administration of social welfare, ought certainly to encourage that student to make a *systematic* use of the courses offered in a school of social work and in schools of public health as well as other units at the university, and to *integrate* those courses and learning experiences with his central effort in Public Administration. The leadership and diplomatic talent that this integration will require of those in all the units involved cannot be underestimated, but it is necessary. I believe that schools of higher education, schools of social work, and many other divisions of the university will be eager to cooperate with schools of Public Administration in such efforts because professions such as social work and higher education seem to me to be increasingly aware of the administrative dimensions of their problems and opportunities. There are other, perhaps more innovative, cooperative links that ought to be forged. For example, the administration of large research-and-development laboratories and specific scientific-technological projects will require a special kind of administrator; schools of business, schools of engineering, and schools of Public Administration ought to explore the dimensions of their mutual interests in such areas.

Midcareer and On-the-Job Training

The future school of Public Administration will be acutely conscious of the importance of midcareer and on-the-job training experiences and the school's responsibility for relating to and providing such experiences. A number of methods are already in practice or being experimented with and others have been discussed. Continuing education, midcareer, professional sabbaticals (perhaps linked to sabbaticals for academics to get out into a "practitioner" environment), and a variety of other techniques and experiments must be tried. If schools of Public Administration have anything to offer, ways must be devised of delivering it to public administrators who have not been in Public Administration degree programs prior to their employment. I am not convinced that current midcareer and continuing-education curricula and approaches are satisfactory. Much of what I said above when discussing the probable changes in the core courses is relevant here also: These educational experiences can use considerable reform. The new midcareer training will probably more closely approximate the Federal Executive Institute's program than the usual emphases like "What's new in budgeting?" "What's new in personnel?" (followed by a quick run-through of things that are not new to the participants) too often characteristic of present programs. The distinction I am drawing by referring to the FEI—as compared to the usual program—is a greater awareness of the potential of developments such as organizational development, new organizational forms and processes, and a greater awareness of the peculiarities of adult learning.

Research Component

Much of what I have said above has implications for the research component of the new schools of Public Administration. That there will be a research component is implied by my earlier emphasis on the problem orientation of Public Administration and the integration of the learning and action dimensions of the administrative aspect of public problems. The new schools will attempt to integrate research and teaching as closely as they attempt to integrate the "real world" administrative and policy problems with both teaching and research. Much of what I have said about the new methodological, philosophical, problem-oriented, and interdisciplinary aspects of Public Administration will have implications for research philosophy.

The days of a positivistic philosophy of research are numbered, I believe. One can hope that they are numbered throughout the social sciences, and indeed there are some signs that all the social sciences are giving second thoughts to the costs of their "scientific" sophistication. Because Public Administration never accepted as massive a dose of the positivistic perspective and has public problems pressing upon it more immediately, it will probably recover more rapidly than some of its sister specialties. I do not believe that postpositivism implies the rejection of science. I believe what will be rejected is a mythology which bears a closer relationship to the indoctrination received in high-school general-science courses than to the realities of "doing science."

Where the new epistemological and methodological orientations will come from is not yet clear. The current interest in phenomenology and existentialism is, I think, less a sign that these points of view are capable of offering a substitute approach than that the need for a substitute is deeply felt and that the appeal of a more humanistic and action-oriented substitute is substantial. Public Administration here too must accept the best of any contributions that can be made by new research or philosophical refinements while eschewing the irrelevant. Thus, Public Administration research in the future cannot afford to turn its back on whatever contributions phenomenology, existentialism, humanistic psychology, and other endeavors (including systems analysis, techniques of quantification, statistical modeling, mathematical modeling, survey and other research techniques) have to offer to the search for knowledge related to the solution of problems within its purview. It can no more afford to ignore these possible contributions than it can to ignore the society's pressing problems and the involvement of both the study and practice of Public Administration in those problems.

In conclusion I wish to draw attention to dangers or problems which deserve attention and vigilance.

On Study and Practice in Public Administration

I marvel at the contexts in which I encounter the distinction between "academics" and "practitioners" of Public Administration. Whenever I address myself to the practitioner/academic dichotomy, I get confused. That there are schools and bureaus,

I know, but the distinction between academics and practitioners usually goes beyond this division and often incorporates hostility and antagonism at the border of distinction. And a strange aspect of the distinction is that the armies mustered to defend "practitioners" enlist many teachers, and many of the most "academic" of people work in the bureaus. The distinction is more nonsense than sense as it is usually used.

Now, I do not find nonsensical distinctions particularly offensive unless they are harmful in addition to being nonsense. This particular distinction is harmful because it is frequently an obstacle to the development of a healthy, innovative Public Administration. A view that is wider or longer than a particular problem at a particular desk in our culture is easily dismissed as "academic." Critical or innovative notions, the thought that the usual way may not be the inevitable way, and almost any demand for change that is not trivial are also frequently tarred with the "academic" brush. Indeed, stultifying rhetoric exists which suggests that anything that is not training in yesterday's gimmicks "is not really Public Administration." And those who defend the past or the typical in the belief that they are defending the essential, who equate change with erosion or treachery, are to be found in academies, bureaus, and professional organizations alike. And they are dangerous wherever they are found.

Equally dangerous are those who find that any problem, technique, program, plan—in short, anything connected with "doing," "preventing," or "creating" as opposed to "explaining," or "predicting"—is beneath them and their professional corps. The authors of the essays in this volume, it is clear, are at least as disinclined to praise the recent literature in Public Administration *in toto* as they are to praise the whole of the public bureaucracy.

An instructive parallel can perhaps be found in criminology or the study of police science and police work. There is no question that policemen are much beleaguered and that they, least of all, want intractable enemies in their schools and in other areas "making a living off them." But a school of criminology or police science which abandoned a critical perspective on the theory that it must defend and support policemen's activities against all critics would not be worth its salt. A school of police science must be interested in its subject matter and in training and assisting practitioners in their subject area. However, such schools would be defunct the minute they began teaching only that which all policemen already know and want reinforced.

It may be an unchangeable fact of life that good professional schools and their graduates will sometimes be resented most by those people and institutions which they are most interested in understanding, helping, and developing. "You are either for us or agin us" is a common attitude, and it always makes constructive and innovative "being for" difficult. But Public Administration's past problems and present opportunities go beyond this difficulty. Narrow, unimaginative, and "safe" professional drudgery has taken place in academy and bureau. And creative, daring, problem-oriented work has taken place in academy and bureau. The distinction between academic and practitioner as it is usually used is nonsense: Real studying has everything to do with real doing and *vice versa*. The distinction that really matters is a qualitative one, and we have too long allowed phony arguments to cloud our ability to distinguish good from bad.

In the school of the future, problems such as these will hopefully be minimal. If schools and curricula are more relevent to real social and administrative problems, and if administrators in public organizations can more easily encounter truly educational experiences at various stages of their careers, the bad will be easier to weed out from the good and the essential unity of concern between scholars and administrators will be more obvious. Therefore, the very curious and critical problem of an antagonistic relationship among best friends will be seriously ameliorated, if not removed.

On Conscientious Objection to Religious Crusades and the Necessity to Crusade

There is a temptation to write about the future as one foresees it as though it were inevitable. As a matter of fact, to a certain extent I believe the future that this volume suggests for Public Administration is inevitable, but not for all schools, not for all practitioners, and not for all researchers or teachers. At one and the same time, I would like to exhort the reader toward bold concern with the future of Public Administration and caution him against self-righteously indulging in self-congratulation.

We must guard against the assumption that there is presently *a* coherent new Public Administration which it behooves us all to join and defend against the outside. The parallel with the events and rhetoric of the so-called "behavioral revolution" in political science is a close and cautionary one, it seems to me. The feeling that there is *a* behavioral political science (even if there was no compelling definition of it), the closing of ranks around it and building of barriers between it and the "old," "institutional," or "traditional" political science, I think, led to great stupidities, ridiculous claims, bad education—and, most important, has made it very difficult for political scientists to cooperate across the religious barriers set by actions and re-actions in the "revolution." As a consequence, political science has not been able to sort out the good from the bad, the new from the old, or to keep the standards that a serious intellectual effort must have to remain relevant and to resist the detours and trivialities of fads. We must not let this happen with the new trends in Public Administration; indeed, it is partly because it happened elsewhere that there will be, in some sense, a new Public Administration.

We must also guard against complacency with our current efforts and the state of the enterprise. No one should under-estimate the amount of energy and daring it will take to steal a march on this history. Much in the past and the present of Public Administration may be mistaken. The future, though, belongs to those who create it and those who create it bear the responsibility for its fruits.

Index